Histories of the Present

Norman E. Whitten Jr. &
Dorothea Scott Whitten

HISTORIES OF
THE PRESENT

People and Power
in Ecuador

University of Illinois Press
URBANA, CHICAGO, AND SPRINGFIELD

© 2011 by the Board of Trustees
of the University of Illinois
All rights reserved
Manufactured in the United States of America
1 2 3 4 5 C P 5 4 3 2 1
∞ This book is printed on acid-free paper.

Library of Congress Cataloging-in-Publication Data
Whitten, Norman E.
Histories of the present : people and power in Ecuador /
Norman E. Whitten Jr. and Dorothea Scott Whitten.
p.   cm.
Includes bibliographical references and index.
ISBN 978-0-252-03603-3 (cloth)
ISBN 978-0-252-07797-5 (pbk.)
1. Indians of South America—Ecuador—Ethnic identity.
2. Indians of South America—Ecuador—Cultural assimilation.
3. Indians of South America—Government relations.
4. Ethnicity—Ecuador. 5. Acculturation—Ecuador.
6. Ecuador—Race relations. 7. Ecuador—Social policy.
I. Whitten, Dorothea S., 1930– II. Title.
F3721.3.E84W55   2011
305.8009866—dc22   2011008426

Contents

Preface   vii

Acknowledgments   ix

Introduction: To Remake the World   1

Prelude   23
1. Colonial Mentality in Making the World   25

Prelude   43
2. Indigenous Constructions of "Blackness"   45
   Norman E. Whitten Jr. and Rachel Corr

Prelude   65
3. The Topology of *El Mestizaje*   67

Prelude   91
4. The Ecuadorian Indigenous Uprising of 1990   93

Prelude   115
5. Ecuador in the New Millennium   117

Prelude   141
6. Indigenous Ethnographers Portray Their World   143
   Dorothea Scott Whitten

Prelude   163
7. Indigenous Modernity   165

Conclusion: Ethnography and Theory in Cultural Life   187

Notes   203

References   211

Index   243

Preface

In 1987, soon after we had completed a full year of ethnographic research with the Canelos Quichua and Achuar Jivaroan peoples of Amazonian Ecuador, N. Whitten began work on a book entitled *Critical Anthropology*. He wanted to present facets of Afro–Latin American and indigenous cultural systems at the confluence of ethnography and history. During 1986–1987 in Ecuador we had both focused especially on mythohistory and ethnoaesthetics, seeking ways to present the complexities of indigenous thought and imagery in Spanish and English prose to communicate to broad audiences. Together we curated two major exhibitions entitled "Causáunchimi! (We Are Living!)" shown in the Art Gallery of the Museum of the Banco Central in Quito, and the Municipal Building in Puyo, Ecuador (1987).

"Critical Anthropology" did not materialize as a book, but the imagery and ethnoaesthetics project resulted in two books in English, a major exhibition at the Krannert Art Museum at the University of Illinois in Urbana (1988), other gallery exhibitions, and an educational tour of south-central Illinois by two Amazonian potters (1992), Estela Dagua and Mirian Vargas. We later designed and curated a permanent exhibition also entitled "Causáunchimi! We Are Living!" at the Spurlock Museum of the University of Illinois and a temporary exhibit there, "Rain Forest Visions" (2006). The ethnoaesthetic work, which continues, reflects sustained, intensive ethnography, fortified by ongoing interactive interpretation of indigenous mythohistory. Its integration in regional history and ethnography is manifest in our recent book *Puyo Runa: Imagery and Power in Modern Amazonia* (2008).

N. Whitten began Ecuadorian ethnographic research in the northwest rain-forest lowlands with Afro–Latin American people in 1961; by 1968, after spending a year working together in Colombia (1964–1965) and two summers in Nova Scotia (1966, 1967), we began joint ethnography with indigenous Canelos Quichua people of the Upper Amazonian–Andean piedmont rainforest–riverine region in Ecuador. Bit by bit, as we undertook research with diverse people and reflected on culture and life in Ecuador, viewing human activities through varied lenses of local-level knowledge, meaning, and purpose, strong perspectives on a number of subjects, including ethnicity, cultural ecology, aesthetics, cosmology, and especially cultural transformation, emerged and crystallized.

Then, in 1990, a major indigenous uprising occurred in Ecuador; it was followed by a march by indigenous people from Puyo to Quito two years later, and by a series of dramatic indigenous-sponsored disruptive and transformative events that changed the nation in significant ways. In the early 1990s, our engagement with long-range ethnography and history veered from some projects to encompass the forces at work as people we had known for many years set out "to remake the world." The research N. Whitten had undertaken for "Critical Anthropology" came into play again. Not only were transformative events taking place, but we began to see more clearly the transformative dimensions of imagery in indigenous art, performance, and expressions of their lives. We expanded our efforts to forge a conjuncture between wide-ranging anthropological and historical literature and the ways by which indigenous Andean and Upper Amazonian artists perceived a poorly made world in which they were forced to live. We explored and are exploring dimensions of cultural creativity and tenacity within such a world.

By 2008 the goals established over twenty years ago for "Critical Anthropology" had been reached in a series of articles, book chapters, and encyclopedia entries, of which seven are reproduced here in reworked versions. The concept of "critical anthropology," though, so useful in the late 1970s and mid-1980s (e.g., as used in *Cultural Transformations and Ethnicity in Modern Ecuador* [1981] and "Toward a Critical Anthropology" [1988]) changed in some circles into postmodernist solipsisms, so we dropped it from our lexicon. We realized that what we had been dealing with for some time might well be called "transformative dynamics" revealed in the conjunctures of ethnography, history, and literary analysis applied to the harsh realities of ongoing life.

Acknowledgments

Our debts to people are legion. Here we thank a significant aggregate of those who have helped us over the past quarter century. We begin with Kathleen Fine-Dare and Michelle Wibbelsman, who organized two panels in our honor for the 2008 American Anthropological Association meetings in San Francisco. The title of this extended three-part session was "Symbolic Affinities, Pragmatic Engagements: Shaping Latin American Ethnology through the Collaborative Work of Norman and Dorothea Scott Whitten." In order of presentation in the sessions, we are grateful to Linda Seligmann, Michelle Wibbelsman, Jennifer Hardin, Kathy Fine-Dare, Julie Williams, Rudi Colloredo-Mansfeld, Mary Weismantel, Jean Muteba Rahier, Arlene Torres, Diego Quiroga, Rachel Corr, Jonathan Hill, Liz Reeve, Mike Uzendoski, Eduardo Kohn, Mike Cepek, Bill Vickers, and Mike Brown for the sustained reflexivity and insightful and creative commentary that fortified our idea of putting this book together.

In the area of African American and Afro–Latin American studies, work through the years at the University of Illinois at Urbana-Champaign with John Stewart, Marvin Lewis, Dan Littlefield, Dianne Pinderhuges, and Arlene Torres has been most rewarding, as has our continuing association with Michel Laguerre, Doug Midgett, Jean Muteba Rahier, and Richard and Sally Price. Inspirations and collegiality in Andean and Amazonian studies are especially apparent with Rachel Corr, Kathy Fine-Dare, Mary Weismantel, and Michelle Wibbelsman in Andean Ecuador, and Mike Brown, the late Irving Goldman, Jonathan Hill, Liz Reeve, Bill Vickers, Mike Uzendoski, and Neil Whitehead in Amazonia. For ways of thinking about culture creatively through the transformative dynamics of ethnography and history, we are indebted to the late Clifford Geertz, Marshall Sahlins, Mick Taussig, the late Victor Turner, and Peter Worsley. Kris Lane has often provided the glue to bind colonial history to contemporary ethnography and one region of greater Ecuador to another.

Indispensable institutional support from the University of Illinois at Urbana-Champaign has come from the College of Liberal Arts and Sciences, the Graduate College, the Research Board, the Beckman Institute, the Honors Council, and the Center for Latin American and Caribbean Studies. Since 2001, in our roles as curators of the Spurlock Museum, we have had the opportunity to work repeatedly with ethnoaesthetic design of South American materials. Collaboration with Douglas Brewer, Christa Deacy-Quinn, Josh Gorman, Amy Heggemeyer, John Holton, Carol Kussman, Melissa Otero, Stephanie Stout, Jack Thomas, and Beth Watkins has been very rewarding. Dee Robbins, business manager and assistant to the director of Spurlock, has managed our affairs during innumerable trips to Ecuador, and maintained some very complicated systems of communication, for which we are grateful.

Outside funding includes a John Simon Guggenheim Fellowship, a Fulbright-Hays Research Fellowship, grants from the National Science Foundation, the Wenner-Gren Foundation, the Social Science Research Council, Illinois Humanities Council, and the National Endowment for the Humanities. Sustained and extended research in Ecuador since 1990 has been made possible by the efforts of María del Carmen Molestina, Diego Quiroga, Santiago Gangotena, Carlos Montúfar, and Nancy Orellana through the auspices of the Universidad San Francisco de Quito.

Central to our processing of cultural information has been a core of indigenous people of Upper Amazonian Ecuador, descended from the powerful shaman Virgilio Santi. We thank especially his son Marcelo Santi Simbaña; Marcelo's wife, Faviola Vargas Aranda; Virgilio's daughter, Clara Santi Simbaña; and her husband, Abraham Chango. These *compadres* and *comadres* have treated us to a kaleidoscope of knowledge retrieval through travel (with constant commentary), song, shamanic séances, and memorable and retrievable imagery. In the next generation, we are grateful to Alfonso Chango and Luzmila Salazar, both directly connected to powerful, now deceased, shamans, for the intellectualization of the parental cultural knowledge through art and narrative, and for dramatic insights into new dimensions of cultural and spiritual imagery. In other sectors, master potter Jacinta Estela Dagua Malaber has plumbed significant depths of culture and memory with us, as has one of her daughters, Marta Jobita Vargas Dagua. Delicia Dagua has contributed some of the most enduring insights we have experienced.

Back to the older generation, the late Venancio Vargas (son of a powerful Zápara shaman, the late Eliseo Vargas) and his wife, the late Pastora Guatatuca; and the late Soledad Vargas and her brother, the late Gonzalo Vargas (whose father was the great shaman-warrior Nayapi); and Severo Vargas (son of the renowned guide, the late Severo [Acevedo] Vargas) tried in more ways than we once realized to get us to "see" (*ricuna*) through the misleading labels and stereotypes to come to grips with humanity and spirituality and to remain there in a face-to-face relationship. We owe whatever ethnographic insight we may have developed through the years to this minimal set of people and to their ramifying networks of relatives, co-parents, and friends throughout a large sector of Upper Amazonia who have helped us through the years.

Joan Catapano, associate director and editor-in-chief of the University of Illinois Press, facilitated work on this book from its conception to its completion, for which we are most grateful. Kathy Cummins, our indefatigable copy editor, worked with us to straighten out the final manuscript, and then prepared the index; working with her again has been a great pleasure.

Sources

Chapter 1. Condensed and revised version of "The *Longue Durée* of Racial Fixity and the Transformative Conjunctures of Racial Blending." *The Journal of Latin American and Caribbean Anthropology,* 2007. Published by permission of the American Anthropological Association.

Chapter 2. Expanded and revised version of "Imagery of 'Blackness' in Indigenous Myth, Discourse, and Ritual." In *Representations of Blackness and the Performance of Identities.* Jean Muteba Rahier, ed. Greenwood Publishing Co., 1999. Published by permission of Jean Muteba Rahier and Greenwood Publishing Company.

Chapter 3. Revised version of "Symbolic Inversion, the Topology of *El Mestizaje* and the Spaces of *Las Razas* in Ecuador." *The Journal of Latin American Anthropology,* 2003. Published by permission of the American Anthropological Association.

Chapter 4. Revised version of "The Ecuadorian Levantamiento Indígena of 1990 and the Epitomizing Symbol of 1992: Reflections on Nationalism, Ethnic-Bloc Formation, and Racialist Ideologies." In *History, Power, and Identity: Ethnogenesis in the Americas, 1492–1992.* Jonathan D. Hill, ed. Iowa City: University of Iowa Press, 1996. Published by permission of the University of Iowa Press.

Chapter 5. Revised and expanded version of "Ecuador in the New Millennium: Twenty-five Years of Democracy." *The Journal of Latin American Anthropology,* 2004. Published by permission of the American Anthropological Association.

Chapter 6. Significantly revised version of "Actors and Artists from Amazonia and the Andes." In *Millennial Ecuador: Critical Essays on Cultural Transformations and Social Dynamics.* Norman E. Whitten Jr., ed. Iowa City: University of Iowa Press, 2003. Published by permission of the University of Iowa Press.

Chapter 7. Condensed and revised version of "Interculturality and the Indigenization of Modernity: A View from Amazonian Ecuador." *Tipití: Journal of the Society for the Anthropology of Lowland South America* (SALSA), 2008. Published by permission of the Society for the Anthropology of Lowland South America.

Histories of the Present

Introduction
To Remake the World

One of the principal themes of *Histories of the Present: People and Power in Ecuador* is "to remake the world." The phrase is coined as a trope of resistance abstracted from a section in the chapter 4 essay where, in the early 1990s, N. Whitten wrote about "the idea of people remaking the world and being in a world refashioned from the conquered one that the European 'discovery' . . . of 1492 began." In 1990, as we shall see, indigenous and Afro-Ecuadorian people rose up as one not just to protest and to assert themselves, but to announce publicly that an intolerable tension born of long-standing injustices must be openly addressed. They—indigenous Ecuadorian people and Afro-Ecuadorian people—enacted their affirmation that they are fully human; that they deserve rights denied for centuries; and that the European conquest and subsequent colonization of the Americas was nothing to be celebrated in 1992. Mourning was not enough either. People asserted their capacity and intent to remake a social world that had been badly crafted. The reference was to the enduring colonial and hegemonic structures of oppression that originated in southern Europe, moved to northern Europe, were sustained in Latin America, and by the nineteenth century—after the revolutions that promised liberation for all—had come to radiate southward from the United States (chapter 1).

Ethnography, Theory, and Intercultural Experience

Listening to and recording indigenous and Afro-Ecuadorian voices during a sustained period of creative and transformative action imparted a plethora of new and expanded meanings and intensities to systems of local knowledge, social relations, structures of signification, and cosmic orientations that we had been gathering, analyzing, and publishing for professional and public scrutiny and criticism. Ethnography—the description of lifeways of living peoples through intensive interaction often called "participant observation"—became our base for understanding ongoing cultural recrafting across multiple borders. Ethnography also became the source of information for the construction of first- and second-level generalizations and the selection and deployment of appropriate abstractions.

Modern and millennial Ecuador (the two are inextricably intertwined; see Whitten 2003a:8, 2003b:357–358), as a unity of tension promoting transformative change, constitutes the national boundaries of a land that lies athwart the equator in northwestern South America. This region, dramatically scrunched up in its topographical and climatic diversity (e.g., De la Torre and Striffler, eds. 2008; Lane 2002), has been long known as a "cultural mosaic" (e.g., Blomberg 1952) or a "country of contrasts" (e.g., Linke 1960). It might seem improbable that a united people could emerge there. But they can; diverse in orientation, histories, historicities, ethnicities, ecologies, languages, and cosmovisions, they often come together in their deep heritage as intercultural *ecuatorianos*. But when they do not come together during times of crisis, the diversity leads to conflict-ridden distancing and hence the enduring tension between being Ecuadorian and being one of its diverse peoples (Whitten 1996b; N. Whitten and D. Whitten 2008; Whitten et al. 1997).

Serious and extended ethnography should lead to what anthropologists often call theory construction, as opposed to "theorizing" in the sense of "speculating." Ethnography seeks explication while theory is oriented toward explanation, but the two are inextricably linked processually. Anthropologists are constantly challenging one another as to the steps involved in such linkages, and there is no one way to proceed. In our case we have lived with and followed the lives of many Ecuadorian peoples over an extended period of time, visiting at least annually with specific groupings and staying with them from a few months to a year.

The result of such interaction, shared thinking, and intersubjectivity through the reflexivity of ethnographic processes within a framework of sustained academic engagement in anthropology and Latin American and Caribbean area studies has been the compilation of seven chapters for this book. Salient themes arising in ethnography led to the abstraction and deployment of three key concepts: *ethnogenesis, alternative modernities,* and *interculturality.* Together these concepts constitute a theoretical perspective called *transformative dynamics,* which falls into the realm of "action theory" (e.g., Biersack 1999; Geertz 1973; Gerth and Mills 1958[1946]; Greenblatt 1989, 2006; Ortner 1999, 2006).

People express their lives in ways that are often difficult to understand, and theory is supposed to help in the understanding (e.g., Dolgin et al. 1977; Geertz 1973; Turner 1974). Hermeneutics enters here. Imagine a circle with salient theories and methods on the left side and the cultural phenomena we seek to understand on the right side. As we move from our disciplinary tools to the ethnographic realities of ongoing lifeways, we must, as Clifford Geertz once said, "descend into detail, past the misleading tags, past the metaphysical types, past the empty similarities to grasp firmly the essential character of not only the various cultures but the various sorts of individuals within each culture, if we wish to encounter humanity face to face" (Geertz 1973:53).

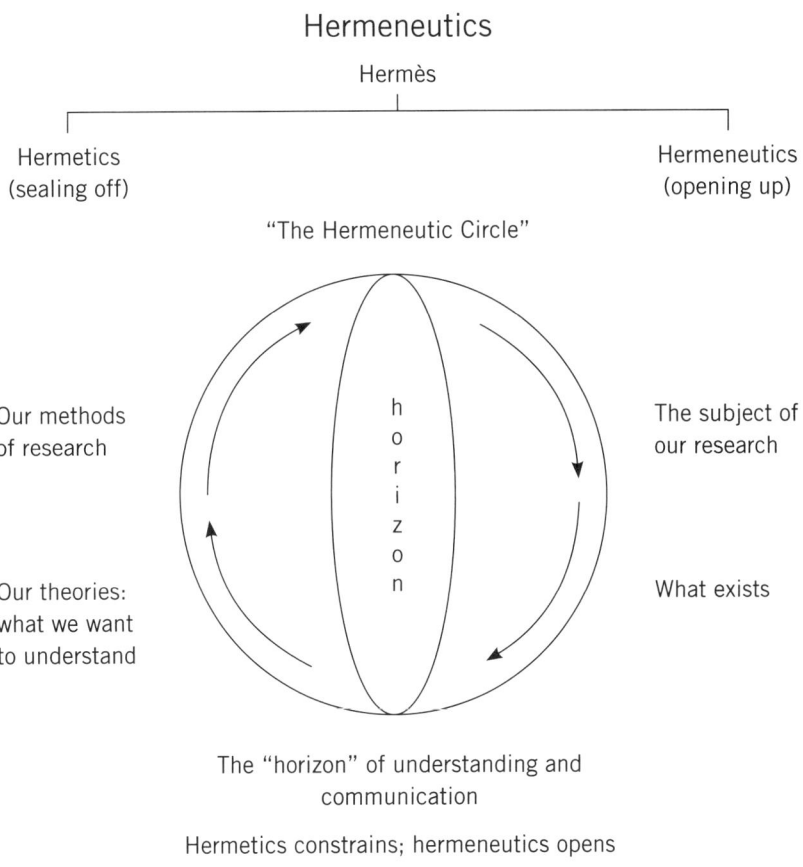

Hermeneutics and hermetics

About a decade after he wrote this, some anthropologists began to claim that Geertz projected an "essentialist" imagery that constituted a "crisis of representation" in our discipline and beyond (contra this perspective see, e.g., Keesing 1994; Gay y Blasco and Wardle 2007:188–195; Geertz 2000, 2002:11–12; Sahlins 2000). Returning to the hermeneutic circle, once we have undergone our encounter and turned back toward our discipline, we may alter, transform, or even discard our theoretical perspectives and refine our methodologies. As we learn more about what we seek, the imaginary vertical zone in the middle of the circle that extends from the top to the bottom—often called the horizon of cultural knowledge—expands. This is the hermeneutic core, the potential increase in understanding that comes from explications encountered on the right side of the circle to inform the left side of the interpretive endeavor. Explicative processes occur as one moves from left to right and then back from right to left, culminating in an expanding cultural horizon, where ethnography contributes to theory—becomes a theory-constructive endeavor—through enhanced processes of interpretation of symbols, metaphors, and tropes extant in ongoing life and in disciplinary canon and criticism. Another way of saying this is that we learn through intersubjective experience with people whose actions and explications in their world offer alternative and often more productive means by which to "sort structures of signification," a process that Geertz (1973:7, 9, 27) argued is fundamental to all cultural analysis. Such alternatives exist in a creative interface between ethnography and theory construction.

If, however, we fortify our theories to "explain away" the phenomena we have encountered, we constrict the horizon and re-create a disciplinary hermetics. These terms, *hermeneutics* and *hermetics,* come from the Greek god Hermès. Hermès was a messenger between divinities and humans, a great orator, and one who helped travelers cross boundaries, but also a trickster and a thief. The hermeneutic–hermetic metaphor of processual contrast mediates between ethnography and theory, explication and explanation. Obviously, care must be taken as we enter this process (e.g., Crapanzano 1992:43–69; Helms 1988:111–116; Ricoeur 1974), but with such care it is very dynamic and productive.

Critical to the process of hermeneutics is the opening up of processes of signification. Theoretical constructions and common sense bestow and imprint on our minds relationships between signifier and signified that ethnography and intersubjectivity break down and reassemble, trickster style (e.g., Gates 1988; Hill 2009). Roger Keesing (1987:161–162) called attention to this cultural phenomenon as being constituted of "webs of mystification." As the multiple relationships among a few signifiers and a plethora of signifieds reconfigure into new webs of signification, ethnography contributes directly to theory construction. This is another reason why we treat ethnography as a method through which to understand and interpret transformative dynamics.

During the national Indigenous Uprising of 1990 (chapter 4), some observers—including to some extent the president of the Republic of Ecuador, Rodrigo Borja Cevallos, and his close associates—tried hard to understand what was unfolding and to explicate what "500 years of oppression" meant to the oppressed. This constituted an expansion of the horizon of intercultural understanding—a cultural and political resignification—within the nation-state that continued two years later during an indigenous march from Puyo in the Upper Amazon to Quito (N. Whitten and D. Whitten 2008; Whitten et al. 1997), the capital of the nation. In both cases, explication of the Spanish verb *levantar* as "to rise up" and "to enlighten" in the national media and in publications intensified the hermeneutic circle's efficacy.

But another side of the discussion over what was happening tried to close down the horizon, to seal off or enshroud enlightenment. Many spokespeople and authors of tracts spoke and wrote about "indians and blacks out of place" (*fuera de su lugar*) and *indios y negros alzados* (unruly indians and blacks; indians and blacks gone wild). Instead of furthering a perception of enlightened people claiming their rights and human dignity, this view depicted or theorized the movement as a horde of "out of place," animal-like beings led by ignorant and intrusive ideologues. Since *lugar* (Spanish, place) can mean "time" in some dialects of vernacular Spanish and in Quichua, there were implications that those in the uprising were "out of time"; relics from the past; savages and barbarians invading civilization; excluded "races" contaminating colonial-crafted hybridity (*mestizaje*). The ethnographer's job is to sort out the levels and nodes of signification in such contrasts to come to grips with the unfolding of insights proclaimed in the dialogical "heat of battle" when submerged social and ethnic sensitivities become public, explicit, and salient.

People in the contemporary world are well aware of anthropology's progress and dilemmas, and many are wary of ethnographers who, some say, come to "steal our culture." Culture—a corpus and flow of symbols and meanings enacted in social life at a given time in a given place—itself has become a concept of self-recognition and self-promotion. Moreover, peoples who are or have been anthropological and historical subjects challenge received histories that marginalize them or relegate their actions as trivial in the flow of the world's significant events. Here anthropologists encounter more than the "descent into detail" revelations can teach; they also learn that one can "see" and eventually document novel ways of constructing a set of cultural images in academic and popular worlds of letters to express perceived realities gleaned through ethnography. When dramatic, transformative events such as the national Indigenous Uprising of 1990 occur, a horizon of insightful cultural interpretation may be produced that leads us deeper into historical imagination and re-imagined theoretical constructions and significations. It is within these expanding interpretive parameters that the seven chapters in this work are presented.

Ecuador: Contrasts and Coherence

In 2008 a constitutional convention was completed in "Ciudad Alfaro," Montecristi, Manabí Province. The city was chosen and named by the president of the republic, Rafael Vicente Correa Delgado, to honor and commemorate the late-nineteenth-century site of a political and cultural revolution led by Eloy Alfaro Delgado, the president's maternal grandfather. In the constitution's final published form, these words open the 212-page document: "Recognizing our millennial roots, forged by women and men in distinct populations [*pueblos*] . . . Ecuador is a constitutional state of rights and social justice, democratic, sovereign, independent, unitary, intercultural, plurinational, and secular" (N. Whitten translation).

To understand the drift and coherence of the ensuing chapters, we need a bit of information on Ecuador set not only in the geography and political topography of South America, for which there is an ample literature, but also set, perhaps especially, in the broad cosmological system that ranges from antiquity through conquest to modernity intertwined with millenniarity (Whitten 2003a:8, 2003b:357–358). The conquest and extended colonial rule in Latin America established a system in need of remaking, and the reference points for this transformation were taken from preexisting culture and from the colonial reworkings themselves (e.g., Newson 1995). We begin with some pre-European history and reconstructed cosmography.

Whatever the time-depth of people living in coastal, Andean, and Amazonian biomes of this complex area, by six thousand or so years ago expanding populations of highly diverse people had developed emerging agricultural systems in which people traded and visited with one another across contrasting physical topographies (Lathrap et al. 1975; Marcos 1986; Porras Garcés 1987). By four thousand, five hundred years ago, and continuing for a thousand years or more, similar stylistic systems—as revealed especially in ceramics and probably cosmic systems—emerged that ranged back and forth across the eastern Pacific rim regions, the northern Andes, and western Amazonas. Archaeologists call this a "horizon" of "co-traditions."

Squash had existed since about six thousand years ago in western Ecuador; maize had arrived from the moist tropics of Central America and from semiarid zones to the north; manioc with accompanying pottery was well established in Amazonia right up into the Andean piedmont; coastal people had settled into pottery-producing village life based on varied agricultural and sea products and had begun a trade in spondylus shell (*Spondylus princeps;* thorny or spiny oysters). The shells are native to the Pacific waters off the coast of Ecuador, but the trade system initiated in that area by five thousand years ago ranged north to what is now Mexico and south to southern Peru. Cultural activities in what is now coastal, Andean, and Amazonian Ecuador assumed and sustained a donor role in the dissemination of innovation northward and southward (e.g., Bray 2008; Marcos 1996).

This system of long-distance exchange articulated with varied trade routes and movements of people up through and over the Andes to the Amazonian region, where systems of exchange were also flowing from east to west. From the Amazonian forested lands and great fluvial systems, long-distance movements were also eastward to central Amazonas, north to the Río Negro region and south to the headwaters of mighty feeder rivers to the Amazon itself. Through it all, in spite of claims to the contrary, early indigenous Ecuadorians constituted multiple founts of innovation and knowledge that predated well-known developments to the north (Mexico) and south (Peru). As some scholars put it, diverse Ecuadorians in their interculturality constituted a highly innovative, donor people.

Indigenous Globality before the European Conquest

Let us begin our focus on culture with that which seems to be sacral in South America generally—an overall cosmovision, or broad numinous orientation—to understand the clashes of times in spaces and places in Ecuador and its vast environs. One view of why we focus on cosmology and cosmogony is given by David Guss in his new foreword to the Yekuana (a Carib-speaking people of Venezuela) Watunna tales in which evil brother Odosha constantly subverts and reverses the good brought into the world by good brother Wanadi: "The implacable question of how an all-powerful and perfect deity could create a world filled with death, evil, and suffering is relevant not only to the people of the Amazon but to all humans everywhere" (Guss 1997:xii; see also Guss 1989).

We would cast this focus somewhat differently, leaving out the "all-powerful and perfect deity" (in this case the Yekuana deity Wanadi), and instead emphasize the ubiquity of evil, terror, suffering, and death as they have come into culture and nature and have endured through time and across spaces (e.g., Whitehead 2003; Whitehead and Wright 2004). There are a number of treatises on South American people that document the stories and images of transformations of spiritual ontologies in the contemporary world as they emerged from chaos and became manifest in ancient powers (e.g., Civrieux 1976; D. Whitten and N. Whitten 1988 and Hill 2009 for other Amazonian people; N. Whitten 1974 and R. Price 1983, 2008 for Afro–South Americans). Contemporary endurance of evil promoting suffering may result in modern protest, defined here as a solemn (and often sacred) affirmation of inner spiritual and corporeal power to confront felt injustice and inhumanity. However we may cast our insights into contemporary life, the enveloping cosmos and the generative cosmogonies emerge to become part of the story.

The cherished Western dichotomy of space (as in geography) and time (as in history), perhaps arising in thirteenth-century Europe, must be set aside in any understanding of native South American cosmology. Reorientation toward a relativistic conceptualization of space-times (chronotopes) is essential to achieve initial understandings and insights. Chronotopes are ancient, historical, modern, futuristic, local, regional, diasporic, and global. They may exist simultaneously, as when beginning times-places encompass the present time and people seek a transformation from one to the other through ritual activity, song, dance, performative drama, fighting, or political protest (Hill 2009; Sullivan 1988; Whitten 1985; N. Whitten and D. Whitten 2008).

Mythic space-time may provide cultural templates upon which people draw to make sense of their known and, especially, unknown universe. Looking overall at mythic dimensions of native peoples of South America, Lawrence Sullivan (1988) finds many phases that are more or less consistent across the diverse region. These include an initial transformation from inchoate actions of sentient entities bringing into being the earth worlds, sky worlds, and underworlds to initiate beginning times-places. The beginnings are punctuated with catastrophic fire or flood, out of which all things transform radically. Culture heroes emerge and undergo violent deaths, only to reappear to structure more events until finally the beginnings of ancestral times-places emerge in different locations.

According to Sullivan (1988), all space-times are framed between the *Primordium,* which includes the prebeginnings and beginnings of everything, and the *Eschaton,* wherein lies the end of the world, the collapse of the cosmos, and the formation of a new universe of existence. Principal emergent figures that have contemporary corporeal representations include the anaconda of the water domain, the jaguar (or puma) of the earth domain, and the harpy eagle (or condor in the Andes) of the sky domain. Metaphoric predications on these beings are legion. Cosmic, Manichean battles in different space-times and in different planes of existence take the world and its inhabitants to the brink of ending everything, to the edge of the *Eschaton*. Such a cosmic brink is often portrayed by people in periodic ritual performances. Space is salient, with the *Primordium* unfolding in the center of the universe and the *Eschaton* existing at its edge.

In the cosmic *Primordium* separations occur, one after another: the separation of earth and sky and then night and day, where night and the moon come to signal disorder as opposed to day and the sun's east–west order. Then comes the differentiation of all species, including humans, then the differentiation of sex, the functions of blood and semen in fertility, fecundity, and danger therein, which leads to a transformation from primordial incest to regulations of sexual relationships and rules of endogamy and exogamy. Eventually one people becomes differentiated from another people, specificity of territories emerges with centers and peripheries. Cultural coherence emerges in the origins of war, origins of marriage, origins of trade, and systems of marriage-war-trade wherein individual bodies and collective bodies both abuse and venerate one another (e.g., Civrieux 1976, 1997[1980]; Guss 1997; Hill 2009; Price 1983).

The catastrophes that beset the American continent with the age of "European discovery" or "encounter" fit into the cosmic mythic domain of the *Eschaton*, and the subsequent (re)-emergence of culture and humanity belongs to the *Primordium* (Sullivan 1988). The end of everything as we know it, in other words, precedes the beginnings of everything that constitutes our cultural being. The relevance of this introductory material will become apparent as the chapters unfold.

Ethnography and Theory Construction

By the end of a very intensive period of ethnography with Canelos Quichua and Achuar indigenous people in 1973 we had grasped something of these matters, and we tried to piece together a coherent picture of indigenous life and the history of Quichua-speaking people of Amazonian Ecuador in the book *Sacha Runa*, published in 1976. Later, after working on a small part of the huge project that resulted in the *Encyclopedia of Religion* (Eliade 1987), Lawrence Sullivan (1988) undertook a synthesis from which our ideas expanded and crystallized. Sullivan used significant portions of *Sacha Runa* to support his generalizations about all of South America, most of which we find convincing or at least provocative of deeper thought and the need for more ethnography. In this way ethnography clearly contributed to theory construction of history and contemporary culture within a vast regional system.

A key dimension of ethnography is sustained and prolonged residence with the people studied; out of such residence travel takes place, and information gathered in one site contributes to understanding what one learns in another location. We learned, as have so many others before us and since, that historicity—what people take to be salient in their pasts—is intricately and inextricably bound to the *landscape* (e.g., Bunker 2006; Corr 2010:59–66, 141–164; Kohn 2008; Trouillot 1995, 2003; Whitehead 2003). Landscape (*tintillu* in Amazonian Quichua), as a holistic sense of environment, constitutes not only a set of sites for a livelihood but also a sacred, cosmic phenomenon embodying everything by which people identify as us and other (e.g., Corr 2010; Reichel-Dolmatoff 1976; Whitten 1978; N. Whitten and D. Whitten 2008). Eduardo Kohn (2008) defines the Ecuadorian tropical forest environment–ecological system of indigenous (and here we would include Afro-Ecuadorian) landscapes in this way: "The tropical forest ... is ... the coevolutionary product of proliferating multispecies networks of signification." With this definition indigenous mythohistory takes its place alongside anthropological theory and becomes a critical link between ethnography and theory as we show in chapters 2, 5, 6, and 7.

When landscape is threatened people react not only politically and economically; their actions are also framed by cosmic structures and dynamics. In such reactions political action and ritual enactment draw from many of the same sources of knowledge and evocation. When one comes to understand the mythopoetic processing of action within a political economy over time, one works in a framework that Marshall Sahlins (e.g., 1976, 1981, 2000), building on the great contributions of historian Fernand Braudel (1980[1958]), calls a "structure of conjuncture." We work with this concept in several chapters and explore it at length in chapter 7 and in the conclusions.

Inca and Spanish Invasions

A cataclysmic event in the formation of what became Ecuador occurred in the late fifteenth century with the Inca invasion of the north, focused particularly on the Andean sector of what is sometimes known as the "Kingdom of Quito" (Lane 2002; Newson 1995; Oberem 1988; Phelan 1967). This extraordinarily complex topographical region, partly mythical in its cultural dimensions, clearly sacral in its historicity, ranged from the southern Pacific Lowlands of what is now southern Colombia and Ecuador east across the Andes and down the Putumayo, Napo, Marañon, and Solimões rivers to what became Iquitos, Peru. The imperial indigenous conquest of Ecuador probably did not seriously affect its ecology or cosmology except by facilitating south–north movement, restricting east–west trade, and imposing an expanded hierarchical system on the Andean portion of Incaic dominion.

What disrupted the known indigenous world enormously was the Spanish conquest, in 1534, which came at a time of a severe fissioning in the Inca polity. Most history focuses especially on the Cajamarca to Cuzco Spanish campaigns, but the Quito conquest was more complex and utterly brutal as competing conquerors forged their domination. The Spanish conquest of Ecuador came to the Kingdom of Quito in three intersecting pathways and constituted one of the most devastating conflagrations known. At times, in the short period of a year, Inca fought Inca; Inca fought Spanish; indigenous Cañari from southern Ecuador fought Inca from south and north; and Spanish fought Spanish, some with Inca troops, some with Cañari troops; other indigenous peoples of Coast and Sierra were caught up in the conflagration (see especially Hemming 1970:151–168; Salomon 2008). The image of the Ecuadorian Andes as a region bathed in indigenous blood lingers to this day in some Amazonian areas.

For indigenous people of the Ecuadorian Andes and parts of the coast this was a veritable *Eschaton* and, soon after, for Africans and Euro-Africans removed from their homeland, it was the same. Out of death came vibrant systems of culture that endured through three hundred years of colonial rule and emerged into modernity to confound power wielders in many ways.

The European Conquest and Colonial Regime

Europeans restructured humanity in the Americas by placing themselves at the apex of a pyramid, with African Americans and indigenous Americans on the bottom. The former were called *negro*, the latter *indio*. Two republics were established under colonial rule, one of the Spanish, the other of the "indians," but blackness (*lo negro*) was left out of the colonial structuring, even though the institution of African and Afro-Hispanic slavery was met everywhere by movements of black self-liberation that established pernicious anomalies to European hierarchy (chapters 1–4). Between the three racialized nodes there arose a system of "breeds," called *castas*, that eventually morphed into the phenomenon called *el mestizaje*, which Ronald Stutzman (1981:45–94) appropriately called "an all-inclusive ideology of exclusion." We explore these dimensions of ethnicity in one way or another in most of the chapters in this work, and especially in chapters 1–3.

The European conquest and subsequent colonial era violently introduced hegemonic Roman Catholic Christianity, first to West Africa in the 1450s and from 1492 on to the Americas with highly variable effects on indigenous and

Afro–Latin American sacrality. It began in the Greater Antilles of the Caribbean in 1492, under the epitomizing banner of Roman Catholic Christianity and Western wealth production through the forced and violent acquisition, sale, and exploitation of indigenous and African labor to acquire gold, pearls, and spices. African, Afro-European, and indigenous American people not only were confronted with unrelenting demands on their bodies and their souls but also were subject to the sustained indignities of an Inquisitorial system that placed their sacred concepts and objects in league with the Christian devil (Silverblatt 2004; Taussig 1997; Whitten and Torres, eds. 1998). By the late twentieth century, the "globalization of monopoly finance capitalist culture" (Hopkins 2001:8) ushered in an era of sustained indigenous rejection of neoliberalism, privatization, and deregulation, which continues in the twenty-first century.

John and Jean Comaroff (2009) go so far as to characterize the hegemony of the corporate transnational Catholic enterprise in late modernity as "the commodification of the numinous essence of faith" (Comaroff and Comaroff 2009:136). In the face of conquest, inquisition, terror, slavery, oppression, relocation, reduction, population collapse, and a myriad of violent indignities, indigenous and Afro-descended religious change from the sixteenth century through the present times-places is characterized by the fusing of ultimate cosmogonic contexts of the *Primordium* and the *Eschaton* with the proximate contexts of political, economic, and cultural transformations.

New people emerge (*ethnogenesis*), new ways of appropriating the accoutrements of contemporary life (*alternative modernities*) come into being, and novel ways of transcending and transacting differences among people (*interculturality*) proliferate. These processes are articulated as cultural structures of conjuncture (e.g., Sahlins 1994, 1999, 2000), in what Hopkins (2001:4, 10) calls a system of "hyperglobalization" subsumed by the Western god Mammon (see also Steigenga and Cleary 2007). The date 1492 sets these processes in motion (chapters 1–3). Two regions exemplify these processes. Long known as the "forest of Canelos" and the "forest of emeralds," they have been the dynamic sites of our ethnographies for many years. We sketch here the known early history of these two regions as they form an emergent conjuncture in the early Spanish-colonial chronotope.

The Forest of Canelos in the Amazonian Territory of Quito

A pattern of colonial violence flowing from the Spanish conquest was forged in 1540–1541 when Gonzalo Pizarro and a relatively small band separated from the huge expedition made up of Spaniards, *indios,* dogs, horses, and pigs that left Quito to find the Land of La Canela and the Land of El Dorado. Pizarro's group and/or his splinter group seems to have spiraled eastward north of the Napo River (see conjectural map in Carvajal 1934[ca. 1541]:48; also Renner 1993), where they finally encountered people where canela trees (called *ishpingu* here, as in the Canelos area) grew. Frustrated by the low quality and sparseness of the canela trees and by the fact that the people he tortured could tell nothing of fabled El Dorado to the east, Pizarro executed some of the natives in two brutal ways: he burned them alive on a barbecue frame, throwing the cooked pieces to the war dogs, and he sicced ("dogged," *aperrear*) the dogs on the living people to kill, dismember, and eat them raw (e.g., Carvajal 1934[ca. 1541]:51; Hemming 2008:22; Varner and Varner 1983:119–124). He did all this in the Land of La Canela somewhere east of Quijos before arriving in the region where the Coca and Payamino rivers flow into the Napo River. There he reunited with Francisco de Orellana, then again split the now decimated expedition crews, with Orellana's group beginning the well-known downriver journey of Spanish "discovery of the Amazon" (e.g., Carvajal 1934[ca. 1541]; Hemming 2008).

Documentation of the actual area of Canelos comes from the Dominicans, who claimed the area as their religious realm some forty years after the Pizarro expedition. In 1887 the Dominican Abbot François Pierre (1983[1889]) traveled from Quito to Quijos to Archidona and Tena, then cut south across the Napo taking a known route southward across the headwaters of the Curaray and Villano river valleys to arrive in Canelos on the banks of the Bobonaza River. His description of his voyage is highly accurate. Places and peoples are depicted such that we easily recognize his route and stopping places a hundred and twenty years later. He takes care to note where Zaparoans were living and makes reference to the Waorani. He notes that Zaparoan-speaking, Jivaroan-speaking, and Quichua-speaking people have long been part of the Canelos system and he writes about other people who fall outside of that system.

He also notes that much attention was given to the northern, Quijos–Omagua regions, where, in 1578–1579, a bloody uprising led by Quijos shamans (called *pendes*) was followed by escalating and pervasive violence and terror that lasted for years (e.g., Oberem 1971; Uzendoski 2004). Pierre, who had access to Dominican archives of the sixteenth century, notes that four curates and their entourages out of Quito were exploring riverine systems and encountering many people in the region radiating out of what is now Puyo (e.g., Naranjo 1977:131–133; Pierre 1983[1889]:96–97).

These Dominicans established the first (and ephemeral) mission of their order at "Canelos" in 1581, moving it from near Puyo to Indillama, to Chontoa, and then to or near the present site of Canelos on the banks of the Bobonaza River where the territory radiated northward toward Villano and eastward toward Pacayacu and Sarayacu (Stirling 1938:24; Whitten 1976a:206–210). Four priests—one of whom was the "Venerable Padre Sebastián Rosero," who was later sainted—and their retinues came from the Andes to Amazonia to reconnoiter the area and to "found" Canelos as a Dominican realm of Catholic Christianity in Amazonia and as an early and ephemeral nucleation. The route they traveled, though, is obscure. It is unlikely that they traveled at that time through Quijos–Archidona–Río Villano. Most likely, the indigenous trade from Canelos to Baños to Pelileo to Ambato, and from Canelos to Riobamba through the region of the Huamboyas, attracted the attention of the expanding Dominican Church. At this point we only know that the Dominicans moved into the land of the Canelos at a very early time, though they spent relatively little time there (e.g., Reeve 2008).

They claimed Roman Catholic ecclesiastical primacy to an area where Quichua was spoken, and where the Inca had never penetrated. It is an area where indigenous people of the Montaña and Upper Amazon traveled from east to west to exchange with Andeans (e.g., Corr 2010). It is also an area with a clear regional cultural system (e.g., Reeve 2008), where Zaparoan and Jivaroan were spoken and people of the two cultural-ethnic systems waged interminable raids on one another. For the next century and a half, Andean Dominicans manifested a sporadic presence in the area from Puyo to Canelos, and we know relatively little about any dynamics in the Canelos area except that the region was known to Andean people through an east-to-west flow of goods, particularly *ishpingu* but also broom fiber, cotton, dyes, capsicum, tobacco, calabashes, bottle gourds, and bird feathers.

The Forest of Emeralds in the Coastal Territory of Quito

In 1545 the first self-liberated Africans and Euro-Africans (*ladinos*) arrived on the northwest coast of the colonial territory of Quito. This arrival, which was followed by more and more African and Afro-Hispanic maroons, took place a mere eight years after the Spanish conquest of the Kingdom of Quito and the founding of what was then "San Francisco de Quito" (now the city of Quito). Later, in 1563, the Spanish Crown established an *audiencia* (a central court system of colonial power; De la Torre and Striffler 2008) in Quito. This founding occurred only four years after the ill-fated expedition of Gonzalo Pizarro to find the Lands of La Canela and El Dorado. Within a half century the northwest sector of the *audiencia* became known both as "Esmeraldas" and "*la república de zambos.*" To the consternation of the Spanish and growing *castas* of *mestizos* in the Andes, whose lives were determined by birth as ruler, subordinant, servant, or slave, Esmeraldas became known for its unbridled freedom of both Afro-Indigenous (Zambo) and indigenous people who remained unconquered and unsubdued by Andean domination (Cabello Balboa 1945[ca. 1583]; Lane 2002; Phelan 1967).

Esmeraldas, so named for its three-tiered canopied verdant rain forest in northwest Ecuador, became home to self-liberated African and Afro-Hispanic people in the mid-1500s. After fortuitous shipwrecks, different groupings seized their freedom in the north and south of the province, intermarried with indigenous people, became the dominant force in the Emerald Province, and resisted all attempts by the Spanish military and the Roman Catholic Church to subdue and subvert them (Cabello Balboa 1945[ca. 1583]). In 1599 direct descendants of one grouping of the original maroons, 56-year-old don Francisco de Arobe and his two sons, don Pedro and don Domingo (ages 22 and 18, respectively), journeyed to Quito to pay homage to the Spanish Court (Lane 2002). Their portraits were painted by an indigenous artist, Andrés Sánchez Gallque, in a magnificent work entitled "Esmeraldas Ambassadors." Today, a restored version of this painting hangs in the Museo de Américas, Madrid. Historian Kris Lane (2002:xi) captures the elegance of these Zambo lords in this manner:

> The men's noses, ears, and lips are studded with strange crescents and balls and tubes of gold. Beneath starched white ruffs flow finely bordered ponchos and capes of brocaded silk, their drape lovingly rendered by the painter: here a foil-like blue, there bronze, now bright orange against velvety black. Only don Francisco's poncho appears to be woolen, perhaps fashioned from imported Spanish broadcloth. The three are further adorned with matching shell necklaces, and don Francisco holds a supple, black felt hat with a copper trim. Don Domingo holds a more pedestrian sombrero . . . and all three appear to be wearing fitted doublets of contemporary, late-Renaissance European style. These are all but hidden, nestled beneath flowing Chinese overgarments, which are, in turn, cut in a distinctly Andean fashion.

Over four hundred and sixty years have passed since the first moments of *cimarronaje* (*marronage,* self-liberation) in Esmeraldas, and over four centuries have gone by since the aesthetic moment of magnificent representation of three of the elite of the earliest Afro-Indigenous American republic. Through three hundred years of colonial rule that featured European-dominated gold lust, slavery of indigenous and African peoples, and a shift from a Renaissance to Baroque ethos, Afro-Hispanic Esmeraldans endured (Lane 2002). They fought in the wars of liberation and later in the Ecuadorian Liberal Revolution. In the twenty-first century, as in previous centuries, they regard themselves proudly as the true Christians of Ecuador (Quiroga 1994; N. Whitten 2005). They manifest some of the most Iberian Spanish and the most African music and storytelling in the Americas, and they are among the poorest people in contemporary Latin America.

Perspectives from the Margins

N. Whitten had been reflecting on his ethnographic and culture-historical studies of Afro-Hispanic peoples of the northwest rain-forest coastal region of Ecuador since well before the 1980s, and we were both involved with ethnography and the culture history of the Canelos Quichua and their Achuar Jivaroan neighbors of the Upper Amazon region of the same country. Afro-Esmeraldan Ecuadorians and Amazonian indigenous Ecuadorians were subject to very similar pressures, lived in very similar environments, and constituted latent forces to reshape the Andean hegemonic structures, which both found oppressive. For a long time now we have been viewing Ecuador from the dual lenses of the dynamic margins, through which we have looked out from Ecuador northward, eastward, and southward to enhance our horizon of cultural knowledge. The essays in this work stem from such reflections and date from experiences epitomized by the 1990 Indigenous Uprising, in which Afro-Ecuadorians of the emerald forest, and indigenous peoples of the forest of Canelos and elsewhere, participated.

Locality, Knowledge, and Ethnography

Ethnography as a theory-constructive endeavor has been a core feature of modern cultural anthropology since Franz Boas (e.g., 1940a) wrote his paradigm-breaking letters on Baffinland (Baffin Island) Eskimo perceptions of nature in 1882 and 1883 (Stocking 1968:136–139). The native Inuit, according to George Stocking, taught "America's foremost cultural anthropologist for the first time 'to realize the significance of culture'" (Stocking 1968:136). In *The Ghost-Dance Religion and the Sioux Outbreak of 1890*, James Mooney (1896) demonstrated convincingly that the concept that we now call "interculturality" was not only complementary to but also a necessary part of the expanding Native American sense of culture that rapidly became a keystone for all anthropological theory.

Mooney's studies of the Ghost Dance acknowledged the context of military conquest in ways that honored and did not make vulnerable those he studied. The care he took shows the development of an anthropology that is conscious of its responsibility to those studied. Mooney studied the Ghost Dance as a legitimate religious formation, describing it with the same honor and respect other scholars used in treatises discussing the historical developments of sacraments of Christianity. (D. Price 2008:xi)[1]

In 1922 Bronislaw Malinowski, in *The Argonauts of the Western Pacific*, gave the profession its first full-scale ethnography of a diverse people in regional perspective, stressing the ethnographer's task to present the natives' points of view. Although his *Scientific Theory of Culture* (1944), published twenty-two years later, inexplicably and radically deviated from the richness of ethnography to create a sterile reductionist "theory," Malinowski's legacy of construction of first-level generalizations from "field data" collected by careful deployment of indigenous symbols in an indigenous language carried anthropology from one contentious theoretical moment to the next.

Western ethnography actually emerges in the period of early modernity (late 1400s) when mercantilism transformed to capitalism in the Americas. We offer here three examples of works that have recently been made available in inexpensive paperback editions. Christopher Columbus, also known as the Admiral of the Ocean Sea, the Bearer of Christ, and the "Discoverer," understood from the imperialist's position the value of description in understanding the difference between "indians" as enemies to be exterminated and other "indians" whose labor could be harnessed for Spanish and personal profit as their souls became the property of the Roman Catholic Church (Wey Gómez 2008; chapter 1, this volume). As administrator of the Indies, he initiated the first Western ethnography of native people in the Americas.

In 1495 he sent the humble friar of the Order of Saint Jerome, Ramón Pané (1999[ca. 1486–1488]), to study and report on a branch of the Arawak-speaking Taíno people in the territory of the cacique Guarionex in "La Española" (now Hispaniola), which includes Haiti and the Dominican Republic. Pané had come to Hispaniola with Columbus in 1493, on the second voyage, and had learned one dialect of Taíno; but Columbus wanted him to study a people of another dialect, and so he did, remaining for some years there and presenting his manuscript to the admiral in 1498 (Pané 1999[ca. 1486–1488]:xiii–xv).

Another early ethnography, this one in German, was produced in 1557 by Hans Staden (2008[1557]), a German Lutheran born in Lisbon who served as a gunner with the Portuguese navy. He was captured by the indigenous Tupi-speaking Tupinambá people on the coast of Brazil, near Río de Janeiro. At this time the Tupinambá were allied with the French, enemies of the Portuguese, who, in turn, were allied with the Tupi-speaking Tupiniguin. Staden was prepared ritually and socially to be eventually eaten. His description, along with that of the priest of the colony of Villegagnon, Franciscan André Thevet, and that of the French Calvinist pastor Jean de Léry (1990[1574]), gives us insightful glimpses of indigenous life in the crucible of Euro-Indigenous transculturation on the Brazilian shores and near interior. Because of the custom of Tupi-speaking peoples of consuming the flesh of "enemies" (many of whom became affines; Viveiros de Castro 1992), Tupi studies are often termed "cannibal cosmography" (e.g., Whitehead 2008:xxxiv). As Whitehead (2008:xxxii) writes, "[T]he religious tensions and conflicts of Europe were transposed to Brazil where the native practice of ritual cannibalism became the colonial mirror of theological dispute over the meaning of the Christian Eucharist."

In 1613, high in the Central Andes, to the south of Ecuador, don Felipe Guaman Poma de Ayala finished writing and illustrating his 1,300-page book-length "letter" to His Majesty King Philip III of Spain to explain how the Inca empire and its people were organized, how they lived prior to conquest and colonization, and how Spanish oppression operated on a day-to-day basis. Guaman Poma's landscape, thirty years in the making, is global, including the beginnings of Christianity in the Garden of Eden and the act of conquest itself, but his specific foci are local-level and regional-level cultural systems of his lived chronotope, projected back to Inca rule. Far more complex in literary structure than the previous two, this treatise uses authorial interculturality to heighten the tensions between colonial rule and indigenous and black subjugation. Fiction is blended with description in Guaman Poma's writing to expose indigenous subjugation in the crucible of Spanish rule. In the twenty-first century, ethnographer and ethnohistorian Billie Jean Isbell (2009) also blends fiction and description to expose class-based exploitation and the grass-roots origins of the Sendero Luminoso movement. With this third ethnography we have a glimpse of early American studies in three major languages: Arawak, Tupi, and Quechua.

These ethnographies—Greater Antillean, coastal Brazilian, and Central Andean—were early-modern attempts to describe peoples alien to Europeans who quickly became part and parcel of the European dominions of the Americas. Of these works only Staden's received attention during the lifetime of the author. Pané's original work in Spanish, presented to Columbus in 1498, has never been found. It was first published as a translation in poor Italian (the author spoke Catalan as a first language and wrote in Catalan-inflected Spanish using Portuguese-like graphemes). This work, now so important to the interpretation of Caribbean and South American history, was not published again until 1974. The monumental work of Guaman Poma—a truly intercultural individual writing forty years after the demise of the Inca empire, and one steeped in the ethnogenesis of his people—was "discovered" by a Peruvian in the Danish Royal Archives in Copenhagen in 1908.

Staden's work became a veritable handbook of detail on cannibalism in the Americas, prompting not only debates on the degrees of savagery in Brazil but also intense reflections on the Eucharist in Roman Catholic Christianity and the European proclivities of anthropophagism between Protestants and Catholics in the St. Bartholomew's Day Massacre during the French Wars of Religion in 1572 (e.g., Staden 2008[1557]:159, 161; Whitehead 2008:xxxii, xxxvi). Issues such as these have fueled a modern or postmodern movement of literature and cinema in contemporary Brazil (Whitehead 2008).

In the late twentieth and early twenty-first centuries, ethnogenesis in the Andes canonizes the work of Guaman Poma, just as new Taíno nationalism in Puerto Rico reveres the ethnography of humble friar Ramón Pané. "Being Puerto Rican," for many, now means descending culturally from Taíno ancestry (e.g., Haslip-Viera 2001); "being Andean" means descending from Inca culture (e.g., Salomon 2008); and "being Brazilian" includes understanding the cultural nature of cannibalism in modernity. In all cases the bridge between shared pasts and contemporary identity is found in one way or another in the confluence of ethnography and indigenous mythohistory.

These early cultural explications of indigenous life in the Americas exist at the conjuncture of ethnography, which is fundamentally synchronic, and history, which is diachronic (e.g., Geertz 2005; Ohnuki-Tierney 1990; Sahlins 2000; Sewell 1999). It is in this conjuncture that scholars such as Clifford Geertz, Peter Worsley (1957), Victor Turner, and Marshall Sahlins stimulated interpretive studies of synchronic texts within a framework of shallow and deep diachrony. Matti Bunzl (2004:439; also Comaroff and Comaroff 2009:46), quoting George Stocking (1992), describes ethnography in this vein as "a history of the present."

Historian William H. Sewell Jr., who turns to Geertz and Sahlins for his inspiration and intellectual guidance, looks to ethnography for the stimulus to interpretive history: "A proper appreciation of synchrony is the secret ingredient of effective diachronic history. . . . no account of a historical transformation can be cogent unless it performs a dialectical oscillation between synchronic and diachronic thinking" (Sewell 1999:42). We stress again the proposition that dynamic transformative synchrony—or, perhaps more accurately, an unfolding history of the present—constitutes the core of ethnography.

(Re)publication in the twentieth century of the three early works discussed above came about as new forms of interpretation (sometimes called the "new historicism," e.g., Hunt 1989; Veeser 1989; Williams and Lewis 1993) entered Western scholarship at the interface of ethnography, history, and literary criticism where the confrontation of established (colonial, racist, neocolonial, neoliberal) and persistent theories of humanity stemming from early modernity and the Age of Enlightenment are severely challenged. Findings, often from a confluence of ethnography, literary analysis, and interpretive history, are that each of these early works and the myriad of publications that came after them constitute a critical discourse on processes of colonialism, racism, and the West, as well as expand significantly anthropological theory in the Americas. It is here that indigenous "mythohistory" articulates to Western professional "reading." As Michael Uzendoski put it in a report on the prospectus for this book, "'culture' transforms our perceptions of the world." Although history and literary criticism contextualize "culture" for readers, it is through ethnography that the significata of culture are revealed and inscribed. As we shall see, during the Ecuadorian national Indigenous Uprising of 1990 (chapter 4), the expressions of conjuncture of people-in-motion and modes of resignification through hermeneutic interpretation parallel in many ways the currents emerging in contemporary scholarship of transformative dynamics.

Drawing on these early ethnographies, Brazilian ethnographer Eduardo Viveiros de Castro (e.g., 1992) can combine the insights from his synchronic ethnography of the Tupi-speaking Araweté with the contextualizations of the German gunner Hans Staden to introduce into late-twentieth-century anthropology the concept of "perspectivism." From Tupi and many other Amazonian points of view, there exist a plethora of perspectives of humanity, spirituality, animality, us and other: where humans see, for example, peccary as prey; peccary (as people) may see humans as predatory jaguars. In this view, humans can take various perspectives on life including relationships among selves and others.

Puerto Rican historian José Juan Arrom (1999) turns to the humble friar Ramón Pané to demonstrate the ways by which interculturality and its Caribbean dynamics unfolded in the crucible of Spanish domination and fairly rapid extinction of the Taíno people of Hispaniola (see also Rodríguez Álvarez 2008). Here the Taíno are not seen as "acculturating" to Spanish lifeways but participating variously through their cosmovision in a transforming human universe that included gods, spirits, Caribs, Spaniards, long voyages, and perspectives of great cultural and symbolic depth (see, e.g., Hill and Santos-Granero 2002).

In the case of Peruvian Guaman Poma (1987[1613]), many authors (e.g., Adorno 1986; Williams and Lewis 1993) demonstrate the literary and imageric power of indigenous Andean interculturality as a native Quechua-speaking, Inca-descended person within a system of Spanish domination strives to present the depth of globalized Andean cultural life to the King of Spain. Guaman Poma writes through tropes of resistance to the pinnacle of Western power to underscore the very power of persistent Andean indigenization of colonial rule, what we will later call contrapower, or forces of resistance.

Contemporary Perspectives on Ethnography and Theory Construction

Each of the essays in this volume tacks back and forth between perceptions by people of their position in society and information from history and socioeconomic analyses encoded in Western writings about human culture in real situations. In the first chapter we examine origins and the persistence of modern racist categories that separate "whiteness" from "blackness" and "indianness" and the ways by which classifications made by Latin American power wielders have espoused ideologies of blending. The impetus for such research and critical commentary of false explanations canonized into theory comes from people with whom we have worked and lived over a very long time. People from many walks of life have explicated models of power and domination that deny them the status of "fully human" vis-à-vis paradigm builders of the powerful and influential. By so doing their tropes and modalities of resistance expose domination and refract hegemony. Through ethnography we were and are drawn constantly to a review of literatures that are normally the exclusive purview of historians but drew the critical attention of specialists in comparative literature in the 1970s, often following the lead of Geertz (1973; e.g., Greenblatt 1999:14).

In chapter 2, N. Whitten and Rachel Corr take an unusual step of seeing how "blackness" is perceived through indigenous models of "race," "history," and "culture." They find that there are multiple ways in culture itself to "sort structures of signification" (Geertz 1973:7, 9, 10, 28) and to confront the dominant and static white-centered Western paradigm with dynamic indigenous ones. Then, in chapter 3, N. Whitten deconstructs the ideology of *el mestizaje* in Ecuador with implications for this prominent ideology of exclusion throughout Latin America. Chapter 4 brings the reader to the great Indigenous Uprising in Ecuador in 1990, after which, in chapter 5, late-twentieth–early twenty-first-century Ecuador receives critical comment from a standpoint of historical and anthropological explanation and indigenous explication. The depth of indigenous intercultural explication in Andean imagery is addressed in chapter 6 by D. Whitten, who treats indigenous artists as native ethnographers. This is followed by N. Whitten's combination of indigenous explication through mythohistory and anthropological understanding of modernity through theory construction of transformative dynamics. In the conclusion we return to issues raised in this introduction and examine them in light of developments in Ecuador and elsewhere in South America.

Prelude

On my (N. Whitten) first trip to Ecuador in 1961, people with whom I spoke in Quito explained to me that "*blancos*" and "*indios*" lived entirely different ways of life. What was stressed was the civilized world of the *blancos,* as typified by the culture of Quito, and the rural, isolated, backward ways of the *indios.* I wanted to study the social system of "*negros,*" and people insisted that there were no black people in the Andes, just in a corner of the northwest coast, a "primitive" region fraught with danger. Some North Americans and Ecuadorians would reluctantly admit, after I asked about this, that there were also *negros* in the Chota-Mira Valley north of the indigenous market region of Otavalo.

About a week after arrival in Quito I took the grueling one-day train trip to the port town of San Lorenzo, my destination from the beginning of this project. Leaving Quito at 4:30 A.M., we arrived in this coastal, rain-forest setting about 8:30 P.M. Saturday night. There I immediately encountered activities of a vibrant Afro-Ecuadorian culture, which was to captivate my interest and research through a very long period of time, even as, in 1968, Sibby and I began ethnography together in Amazonian Ecuador, on the other side of the Andes.

In this Afro-Ecuadorian region, those identifying as *blanco* would sometimes talk to me about their own complexion, often pointing to their arms and saying, quietly, "I am very dark." "Whiteness," however, was their inevitable self-designation, their "racial and cultural identity." The only times I heard the term *mestizo* in these years, which included twelve months' residence in Cali, Colombia, and much travel in the Cauca Valley, the Pacific rain-forest lowlands, and elsewhere, were in the context of the "darkening" of the white, sometimes called *negreando*. This was the taint or stain, the *mancha del indio*, on the white world of culture; *mestizaje*, far from a positive image of national culture, was looked upon in disparagingly negative terms.

By the mid-1970s, in Ecuador, the ideology of *el mestizaje*, the blending, had become a prominent designation by elite people (who continued to identify as *blanco*) for aspiring, upwardly mobile, middle-class Ecuadorians. The world-renowned Ecuadorian painter Osvaldo Viteri, for example, writes that *mestizaje* refers to "Latin American Syncretism," the essence of which is the fusion of "the culture of the sun and the culture of Christ" (Blanco 2010:44). Although many ideologues proclaimed their nation to "be" *mestizo*, some tied such blending to "whitening," called *blanqueamiento*. As the ideology of whitening of blacks and indigenous people to "become" civilized, or partake of "national culture," grew, rejection of *mestizaje* ideology by indigenous and Afro-Ecuadorian people increased. By the 1990s, "*mestizo*," or more pejorative terms connoting "hybridity," were used with increased frequency by those previously stigmatized by the *indio* or *negro* epithets.

Reflecting on these early experiences kept me reading history and working through various literatures on Latin American peoples and cultures. In the first essay in this volume I attempt to paint a broad swath of history across the limited but highly charged vocabulary of race and culture. Although my mind is forever on experiences in Ecuadorian contexts, the forces at work take this piece to Africa, the Caribbean, the Spanish Main, Amazonia, and the Andes.

Chapter 1
Colonial Mentality in Making the World

> The new human beings of the modern world—*español, indio, negro, mestizo, mulato, sambo*—were born out of the same upheaval that made "nations," "bureaucrats," "slavers," "global merchants," and "colonies." It was the modern world's signature to etch economic dominance and political supremacy into a radical cultural design. It was also its signature to hide the social relations that were brewing supremacy and conflict behind a semblance of "race things."
> —Irene Silverblatt[1]

> As tends to happen with martyrs and saints, any undercurrent of doubt is usually excised from the biographies of key figures associated with the defense of Latin America's unique mesticity.
> —Marilyn Grace Miller[2]

Two phenomena of the fifteenth century established the hypostasis of racial fixity that came to constitute a *longue durée* in Western thought: the transformation of diverse African peoples to the category "*negro*," beginning in the 1300s but consolidating by 1440, and the naming of all of the diverse peoples of the Americas as "*indio*" in 1492–1493. As these fixities were established, and as they endured, various cultural conjunctures were also at work to produce social constructions of racial fluidity, hybridity, blending, transformation, and transculturation. Both processes—one of fixity, one of fluidity—characterize contemporary cultural racialization and resistance to such racialization in modern Latin America, just as they did during the colonial and republican eras. We explore some of the facets of these dual processes in this lead chapter to underscore processes sketched in the introduction and to indicate where subsequent chapters fit into the overall transformative processes that have long characterized and continue to characterize Latin American nations and peoples.

The *Longue Durée* of Racial Fixity

Blackness (*lo negro*), as a replacement for other names for African peoples or African-descended peoples, emerged in Andalusia, part of the Kingdom of Castile, in the fourteenth century (Moreno 1999:4). The racialized ethnic category *negro*, black in Spanish, became ascendant as a quality of human chattel between 1450 and 1480 as the Portuguese entrepreneur known as Prince Henry the Navigator sent more and more ships down the coast of West Africa to return with enslaved peoples to be sold in Lisbon and throughout Europe. Ironically, perhaps, as the concept of blackness expanded in Portugal and Spain to include African peoples such as Wolof, Mandingo, Ibo, and Bifara (Rout 1976; Whitten and Torres, eds. 1998), concepts of racial mixture (European-African) together with African conversion to Christianity (Kiddy 2005) became important in the west-coast African slave markets, established and exploited by Europeans (e.g., Berlin 1996; Brooks 2003; Hall 2005; Shaw 2002).

On October 12, 1492, Christopher Columbus (1451–1506) made landfall on one of the islands of the Bahamas, which he named San Salvador, in what was to be called the Caribbean Sea. The very next day he described the natives as a *generación* (generation, connoting ancestry and descent; roughly, lineage) who, he wrote, "are of the color of the Canarians, neither black nor white" (Columbus 1989:66–67). He carefully noted that they should be good and intelligent servants (Columbus 1989:66–68; Wey Gómez 2008). On the way back to Spain with his indigenous captives, the name *indios* (feminine, *indias*) emerged, because Cristóbal Colón, the Admiral of the Ocean Sea and the Bearer of Christ, insisted that he had reached India, gateway to Asia, wherein dwelled the Great Khan and his kingdom of riches.

On February 15, 1493, after his twenty-eight-day journey back to Europe, Columbus, writing from his caravel off the coast of the Canary Islands, penned his famous letter to Luis de Santángel, "Keeper of the Privy Purse to the King of Aragón," which compilers Parry and Keith (1984:58–59) call a "breathlessly exaggerated summary of the outcome of the voyage" (see also Wey Gómez 2008:315–316, 516 nn. 86, 91). Within weeks, soon after Columbus himself reached Iberia, the "Letter to a Prince" was printed in Latin in Barcelona and before long made its way by national print languages throughout major cities of Europe, becoming, by 1494, what Parry and Keith (1984:59) call one of the "ephemeral best sellers of their day" (see also Hulme and Whitehead 1992:9–16). In this letter, not only does the category *indio* become canonized but also the structure of oppression of "Indians" for Spanish profit, which has come down through the centuries (Wey Gómez 2008).

On his second voyage in 1493, Columbus carried enslaved Africans—called *negros*—as well as sugar cane and cattle to the territory he named La Española (now Hispaniola, which includes Haiti and the Dominican Republic), and though he and his fellow explorers, conquerors, and administrators named islands and territories everywhere, creating a new natural geography (and ignoring the native Taíno names; see Hulme and Whitehead 1992:11), he and others routinely used *indio* as a designation for the diverse populations that could be "profitable" for the Europeans (*provechosa* is the word used by Columbus [1989:134–135]). As the geographical constructions became diversified, the cultural constructions of profitable labor became condensed to *indio* and *negro,* glossed in English as Indian and black. Through the Spanish Inquisition (e.g., Silverblatt 2004) and colonial policies and practices, the separation of *negro* and *indio* became concretized and the early-modern perspective of hybridization prevailed. In spite of this concretization, however, salient phenotypic mixtures such as those characterized as *zambo* peoples (e.g., Forbes 1993; Lane 2002; Silverblatt 2004; Whitten and Torres, eds. 1998) emerged and proliferated. Such people had no Spanish, civilized, or Christian admixture. They were "mixed" but not "hybridized" by the criteria of early-modern breeding conceptualizations. We return to these phenomena repeatedly below.

The Spanish Crown soon created two unequal republics: the Republic of Spaniards and the Republic of Indians (e.g., Silverblatt 2004:45). No space other than slavery was reserved for the African and African-descended people whose populations grew and diversified throughout Latin America. In spite of the cultural construction of *español* (which, through evolving colonial history became *blanco,* white) at the top of an economic pyramid with African American and Indigenous American on the bottom, the flow of genes among those of European, African, and Native American descent created phenotypic diversity and a system of multiculture, known in colonial times as *las castas,* "the breeds." It is with the emergence of the *castas* that the modern *día de la raza* became canonized on October 12 as what we know in English as Columbus Day. The *día de la raza* celebrates the blend of cultures and peoples, the ideological resolution to the racialized polarities through the embodiment of *mestizaje,* which, according to many nationalist ideologies, began on the day that Columbus landed in the Bahamas.

Racial Fluidity, the *Castas,* and *El Mestizaje*

In the mid to late 1400s African-Portuguese genotypic, phenotypic, and cultural mixing emerged under many rubrics in various locations on the coast of West Africa (e.g., Berlin 1996; Brooks 2003; Hall 2005; Shaw 2002:27–28). The concept of *mestizaje,* discussed immediately below and intermittently throughout this chapter, begins in the European conquest and colonization of the Americas. Concepts of *mulataje,* which receive less attention in this essay (see Forbes 1993; Shaw 2002; Whitten and Torres, eds. 1998), have Old World referents spanning Europe, the Middle East, and North Africa, expanding to West Africa in the mid-fifteenth century.

In the Spanish colonies, by 1500, the concept of *raza* (race) replaced that of *generación* in the Americas (e.g., England 2006:11) and the phenomenon of *el mestizaje* emerged in the early-modern crucible of European hybridity that stressed the blending of civilization with savagery (Forbes 1993; Whitten and Corr 2001; Whitten and Torres, eds. 1998; chapter 2, this volume). *El mestizaje* means "the blending" or "the mixing" of "races" and the mixing of "cultures" (e.g., de la Cadena 2000; Fuentes 1992; Gillin 1949; Martínez-Echazábal 1998; Mörner 1967, 1985; Torres-Saillant 1998).

Significantly, *el mestizaje,* as it descends from early modernity, means "hybridization" (or hybridizing), the breeding of domesticated with wild to improve the stock, or the breed, or the "blood," or the "race." Hybridity, and hence colonial New World *mestizaje,* exists where civilized is mixed with savage or barbarian. Synonyms given in Spanish-English dictionaries for this phenomenon of culturally constructed miscegenation are half-breed, crossbreed, and half caste. *Mestizo,* the term for the result of the hybrid mixing of Spanish or other Europeans with Africans and Native Americans (sometimes in some places only between Spanish and indigenous people of the Americas), may derive from the medieval Spanish word *mesta,* which referred to an association of cattle breeders.[3]

People in the *castas* were subdivided again and again into imputed "blood mixtures" according to how they appeared to others (Forbes 1993; Mörner 1967; Restall 2005; Silverblatt 2004). Examples included dark people who were only one part white or light people who were three parts white. Other categories proliferated, given names such as "wolf" (*lobo*), "throwback" (*torna atrás, salta pa' atrás*), and even "there you are" (*hay te estás*) or "where are you?" (*'aònde te ej'tás*). The culturally constructed racialized "types" (the phenotypes) were so far from genetic makeup that each of a couple's six children might be categorized as being in a different *casta*. Silverblatt (2004:126) calls this a "typology of looks." It was the label of *mestizo* that encompassed the *castas,* set them off from elite Spanish or whites, and from those classed as black and Indian.

As the socially constructed "race" of diverse people categorized as *mestizo* grew, it remained separate from whites on the top of the economic, social,

Colonial Mentality

and political pyramid and from those classed as *indios* and *negros* on the bottom. To use the words of the late Ronald Stutzman (1981), writing about the twentieth-century education system in Ecuador, *el mestizaje* became an "all-inclusive ideology of exclusion." Two subdivisions of *el mestizaje* endured and a third emerged to confound the entire notion of the tripartite asymmetrical fixities of white, black, and Indian. One of these was the cultural construction of "hybridity" between white and Indian to produce *mestizo*. This is the prototype of *el mestizaje* in many Spanish-speaking nations, especially Mexico. In Guatemala, southeast of Mexico, such people are known as and called *ladinos*. On the other side of the triangle (see diagram below) is the cultural construction of "hybridity" between white and black to produce the *mulato*. This word is more complex and more explicitly racist than *mestizo* (e.g., Forbes 1993:131–220). It comes directly from horse and donkey breeding, wherein the cross between the two produces a sterile mule, from whence derives *mula-ta*, "muled."

What confounded the early-modern Euro-American model of racial hybridity is that indigenous people and people of African descent also interbred, shared cultural systems, and produced "mixed" progeny. Beginning about 1502, the very first African runaways on the Caribbean island of Hispaniola escaped to the forested hills of the interior, occupied by Arawak-speaking Taíno indigenous people, who called these refuge zones *haití*, from which derives the name of the contemporary nation of Haiti (Price 1979[1973]). Indigenous people also fled oppression to areas secured by runaway Africans or to those secured by black people from Spain (known as *ladinos*) who were

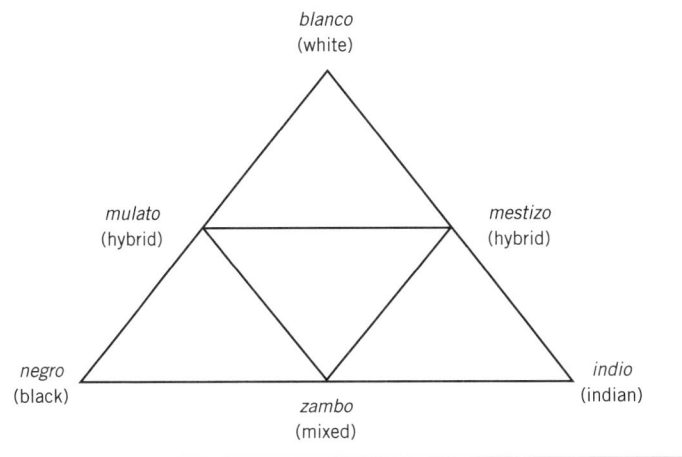

Mestizaje triangles

also enslaved in the Americas as the cultural concept *negro* (black) fused with *esclavo* (slave). The mixture without hybridity of indigenous people and African-descended people became known in many places as *zambo* or *zambaigo* (and in some areas *chino*). They came rapidly to constitute a confrontation with the European-American notions of hybridity because their socially constructed appearances and cultures owed nothing to the conquerors or colonials. The Spanish Crown rejected this category and sought to convert it to *mulato*.[4]

The First Bolivarian Revolution, Racial Fluidity, and *La Raza Cósmica*

The liberator of northern South America from colonial rule, Venezuelan Simón Bolívar, drew explicitly on this inverted triangle within a pyramidal triangle to create an ideology of continental unity against Spain (but not against whiteness) throughout South America. Together with the call for a liberation of enslaved peoples to serve the cause of a revolution in the Americas against colonial rule, he also championed a racial unity bound to common hybridity of the people of the continent. This ideology of hybridity, perhaps ironically, contributed directly to the commemoration of Columbus Day as the *día de la raza* and the nationalist and continent-wide concept of *el mestizaje*. But following the revolutions the idea of oneness shattered in the face of the exclusions of indigenous people, on the one side, and the African-descended people, on the other. Another ideological force was necessary to forge unity in the diversity created by the conquest and three-hundred-year-old colonial regimes.

Marilyn Grace Miller (2004) introduces the hubris of the Mexican educator, philosopher, and politician José Vasconcelos (e.g., 1997[1979]), who coined the figure of speech *la raza cósmica*, "the cosmic race," to refer to the hybridized and whitening peoples of Latin America (see also Torres-Saillant 1998). Although celebrated figures such as Simón Bolívar and José Martí had already posited equations between mixed race and Latin American identity, the 1925 publication of Vasconcelos's *La raza cósmica: Misión de la raza iberoamericana* (*The Cosmic Race: Mission of the Ibero-American Race*) marked the inception of a fully developed ideology of *mestizaje* that tied political and aesthetic self-definition and assertion to a racial discourse at both the national and the regional levels (Miller 2004:27).

Vasconcelos specifically contrasted ideologies of Latin America, as epitomized by the homogenizing vision of Simón Bolívar, with those of North America (the United States), characterized by James Monroe. The former saw beauty and spiritual redemption in the concept of *mestizaje,* in its power of lightening or improving races, while the latter saw the darkening menace of miscegenation and sought to conquer those of darker skin living in Latin America and the Caribbean through what is, to Latin Americans, the infamous Monroe Doctrine (1823). Vasconcelos spelled this out in his book entitled *Bolivarismo y Monroismo: Temas iberoamericanos* (*Bolivarism and Monroism: Ibero-American Themes*) in 1937.

According to Miller (2004), the slogan *Por mi raza hablará el espíritu* (the spirit will speak through my race) was to replace fractured unities drawn together in revolution by warlords, heroes, and political bosses to restore the Mexican people to a new homogeneity. Along the way, a united continent of Latin Americans opposed to the missions of the imperial north was to emerge. The tragic flaw in this cosmic race notion as hubris for national identity or for a continent-wide movement of self-identity was the issue of *blanqueamiento* and its corollary concept *mejorar la raza* (to improve the race). The writings of Vasconcelos (e.g., 1997[1979], 1989) are full of explicit and implicit allusions to *blanqueamiento.* Those classed as *mestizo* were stigmatized for their hybridity with Indian "blood" or (less frequently in most countries) with African-descended phenotypes, both often referred to as *la mancha,* "the stain [of race]" (e.g., Silverblatt 2004). This takes us back to the *longue durée* of racial fixity, with which this chapter began.

Enduring Racism:
Mestizaje as a Polarizing Symbol

The Puerto Rican poet and social critic Fortunato Vizcarrondo (e.g., 1942), in his satirical and ironical writings, summarized this stigmatizing effect of ancestry with the poem "y tu abuela, a'onde ejtá?" ("and where is your grandmother from?" or, figuratively, "where are you hiding your ancestors?"), meaning "you may be lightening but we know you descend from blackness." In some parts of Latin America the concept of *mestizo* refers to the darkening of racial features, not lightening. This is the colonial notion of "throwback." Hybridity, in other words, cuts both ways: in some contexts people who are lightening may be said to be upwardly mobile toward desired phenotypic and cultural features or, in other contexts, they may be said to be backsliding into their darker indigenous- or African-descended roots.

In the Andes of Ecuador and Peru, where the indigenous people far outnumber those of African descent, we encounter the phrase *lo que no tiene del inga tiene de mandinga* (what you don't have of the Inca you have of the Mandinga; e.g., Cornejo 1974). To move from the "racial" to the "cultural" stigmata, one may say or write, "*quien no toca la flauta, toca el tambor*" (who doesn't play the flute [*indio*] plays the drum [*negro*]). These ditties stigmatize those classed as *mestizo* as either indigenous- or African-descended, or a mixture of both. A very prominent liberal intellectual, Osvaldo Hurtado Larrea, one-time president of Ecuador and one-time head of the Christian Democratic political party in Ecuador, also favors the phrase about the Inca and Mandinga in his often-reprinted and updated book *Political Power in Ecuador* (Hurtado 1980[1977]:325, 1997[1977]). He explicates the blending trope by stating that *mestizaje* refers to that which is "in the blood," which can be overcome only by cultural whitening. When he was president of Ecuador, Hurtado coined the term *indomestizaje* to refer to the populace of the country, but not those of his upper-class position. By so doing he consciously omitted all traces of African-descended peoples from the nation's cultural makeup (e.g., Whitten 1981).

It should be clear by now that the doctrine, or ideology, of *el mestizaje* is best regarded as a polarizing symbol (Donoso Pareja 1998; Jijón y Chiluisa 1997; Stutzman 1981; Tomoeda and Millones 1992; Whitten 2003a, 2003b). Perspective enters here. From the standpoint or perspective of elites and those who are upwardly mobile with aspirations to adopt elite values, *mestizos* are those on the middle to lower rungs of a social ladder who have shed indigenous- or African-descended cultural orientations, values, dress, speech, or physical features. For those in the middle, however, who choose to move upward, *blanqueamiento* is their aspiration and *mestizaje* is their stigma. To those self-identifying as indigenous or black, *mestizos* are those who have shed their cultural orientation for a position to which they aspire but which they cannot attain (e.g., Butler 2006; Donoso Pareja 1998; Whitten 2003a, 2003b; Wibbelsman 2004, 2005; chapter 3, this volume). This is the living dilemma of those who are aggregated into what many sociologists, political scientists, and journalists call the *clase mestiza*.

Counter Forces to "Whitening" Ideology and the Second Bolivarian Revolution

There are many forces that work contrary to the doctrine of *el mestizaje* in Latin American nations. According to David M. Guss (2000), *mestizaje* constitutes what many call the myth of racial democracy, the false nationalist premise promulgated by essentially white people (*los blancos,* or *blanquitos*) that Venezuelans do not have a perspective of "race": "The language of *mestizaje* masks unequal social relations between blacks and whites wherein *blanqueamiento* or 'whitening' is the unstated physical and cultural goal"

(Guss 2000:61; see also Burdick 1992 for Brazil). Not only have black people and people of African descent been subject to exclusion on the basis of *mestizaje* ideology in Venezuela, so too have its approximately fifty thousand indigenous people (see also Andrews 2004).

In 2001 the fiery and controversial president of Venezuela, Hugo Chávez Frías, changed the October 12 (Columbus Day) celebratory figure of speech from the "*día de la raza*" to "*el día de la resistencia indígena*" (the day of indigenous resistance). Here President Chávez seeks to conjoin those against elitism and classism to a movement against "whitening" as a key to upward mobility. He substitutes "indigenous" for "*mestizo.*" Thus far those so categorized seem to accept this imagery and constitute a formidable political base (about sixty percent of Venezuelans according to polls over the past few years and according to the national presidential elections of December 3, 2006).

Chávez prides himself on being of mixed heritage—black and indigenous—and he does not promulgate a doctrine of *mestizaje*. Rather, he regards himself as *pardo,* here meaning the mixing of Afro-descended people and indigenous-descended people. He proudly informs his followers, most if not all of whom are from lower classes and who are noticeably darker complected than those in upper socioeconomic brackets, that his father was mixed Indian and black and his grandmother was a Pumé (Yaruro) indigenous person (e.g., Kozloff 2005; Jonathan D. Hill, personal communication) from the *llanos* of the mid-Orinoco region. This is a significant change in Latin American perspectives on self and other for one at the pinnacle of executive power and privilege. This is the first time in Venezuelan history that a president has proclaimed himself to be *pardo* and to identify with those who have been and are *pardo.* The self-designation resonates with the pre-election self-representation by former Peruvian President Alejandro Toledo as *cholo* and with that of Bolivian President Evo Morales as *indio* or *indígena.* The Latin American world may indeed be transforming from the top down, at least as pertains to executive political power.

Chávez hails from the southern plains, called *llanos,* of Venezuela, an area long known for its black and indigenous mixtures and for its spirit of rebellion. The liberator Simón Bolívar with an army of Haitian black soldiers marched through these plains, where he collected an army of *pardo* warriors who swept through the Colombian *llanos* westward to Villavicencio, on up the Andes to Bogotá, and thence to a successful campaign, freeing what is now Venezuela, Colombia, and Ecuador from the yoke of colonial rule. But at the end, with independence, Bolívar promulgated a doctrine of *mestizaje,* fearing the force of the indigenous and black people—and their mixed congeners—upon whom he depended during the revolution. Slaves were freed, but they were neither socially nor culturally liberated. Rather, they were re-racialized (e.g., Andrews 2004; Appelbaum et al. 2003).

By bringing the power of the rebellious mixed-race *pardo* into the national scene, Chávez spearheaded a cultural-ethnic revolution, based on the actions of Simón Bolívar but divorced from the ideology of *mestizaje*. This is the cultural dimension of his *revolución bolivariana*. Other social movements resonate with that of Venezuela. For example, in Ecuador and Bolivia, indigenous people forcefully seek to exorcize the image of the whitening *mestizo* from their lexicon of self-liberation, and strive to change the national celebration of the *día de la raza* to the figure of speech "*500 años de resistencia*" (500 years of resistance). The polarization of the two perspectives—one a celebration of *mestizaje* and the other a celebration of indigenousness and resistance to assimilation—places in strong relief a major cultural tension permeating many Latin American countries at the end of the twentieth and beginning of the twenty-first century.

Interculturality and North American *Mestizaje*

Perhaps ironically, as the ideology of *el mestizaje* gives way to an ethos of *interculturalidad* (interculturality) in nations in Latin America undergoing transformations to an intensified respect for the plurality represented by, especially, those of indigenous and African descent, the early to mid-twentieth-century forces of cultural blending make inroads in the United States (e.g., Dávalos 2001). Near the end of her book on this subject, Miller writes:

> Mestizaje has repeatedly proven to be a flawed doctrine of Latin American identity that nonetheless continues to distinguish Latin Americans from their Northern neighbors. At the same time, it is newly mobilized and empowered through electronic diffusion that renders it ever more ubiquitous, so that its ideology is now pervasively felt in the United States, that same national and cultural power it was fashioned to repel. (Miller 2004:142)

My own sense of the transformation of *mestizaje* to interculturality in many Latin American nations and its transformative manifestation among Chicano, Latina, and Hispanic movements in the United States (e.g., Pérez-Torres 2006) is that the two phenomena of Latin American interculturality and North American *mestizaje* stem from the same roots and have merged to become the same overall phenomenon. I return to this below. Latin American *mestizaje* emanates from the top of social hierarchies and stifles creativity and the celebration of difference within a nation state. But in North America, the semantics change, as the ethos—probably born in the Mexican Revolution—is a bottom-up appreciation of the multiple experiences shared by peoples of other Latin American nations within the Anglo-dominated, racialist, and pluralist society of the United States.

In the 1997 afterword to *José Vasconcelos, La raza cósmica,* Joseba Gabilondo (1997[1979]) puts this matter in a complementary way when, while explicating what he calls the "Chicano reappropriation" of the Cosmic Race, he writes, "Vasconcelos' work reminds us that race exceeds modernity's institutions while constituting them. More than ever before, race is one of the sites, beyond scientific or political reification, at which the historical moment of contemporary globalization and capitalism can be politically grasped" (Gabilondo 1997:110).

The Discomforting Third Category of Mixture: *Zambaje*

Let us return now to the triangle-within-a-triangle figure shown above (p. 29) and the preceding discussion. The one category that has flummoxed the powerful from colonial times down to contemporary life is that of the indigenous-descended–African-descended mixture now called *zambaje* in many regions of modern South America. Such mixture, dating from the beginning of the sixteenth century, carries a double epitome of non-European people, African descended and indigenous descended. It is constituted of African descendants who fled slavery and established free communities, often called *palenques* in Spanish, *quilombos* in Portuguese, and of those indigenous descendants who also escaped slavery and who received their African congeners. The Mamelucos of Brazil, the Miskitu of Nicaragua and Honduras, the Garífuna of Central America, the black lowlanders of northwest Ecuador, and the *pardos* of the eastern plains of Venezuela are historical and contemporary illustrations of such people.

According to Schwartz and Langfur (2005), there were numerous stories about *mamelucos,* as mixtures of black and indigenous people were labeled in colonial Brazil. At that time, people in urban and rural areas, following Spanish Jesuit emergent doctrine of the sixteenth century, called such *zambo* or *mameluco* people "the devil's helpers" (Schwartz and Langfur 2005). The authors quote Nicholas del Techo (1897) as follows: "Satan, angry at seeing the progress of his enemies, united his forces, and then by himself or by the mamelucos, his allies in evil, he sought to destroy the nascent mission towns." The phenomenon of *zambaje* here is clearly one of colonial counterhegemony.

It is in this sense that we come back to it frequently. We need to understand this in some depth as we re-probe history for undergirding concepts that emerge in every century right up to the one in which we presently live.

Because of the prevalence of African-descended people and Indigenous American people in historical conjuncture over a very long period of time, Norman Whitten and Rachel Corr (2001; chapter 2, this volume) undertook a study to see how indigenous people conceptualized blackness in select areas of Venezuela, lower Central America, Colombia, Ecuador, and Bolivia. What they found was that indigenous people reject "slavery" as the embodiment or essence of blackness. Such a rejection clearly contradicts the dominant white perspective on slavery and its legacies as the defining features of blackness in the Americas. *Lo negro,* Whitten and Corr found, is full of images and representations of self-liberation, including power, cultural creativity, adaptability in the realms of the known and the unknown, knowledge of real history and historicity, and constantly emerging and transforming cultural systems (see also Pérez 1998; Whitten and Torres, eds. 1998). We take this imagery to suggest a corrective on the perspective of Wade (1997).

Developing New Concepts

In the twenty-first century, as in the late twentieth, the system of tripartite racial fixity (*lo blanco, lo indio, lo negro*) endures, wherein the categories *lo indio* and *lo negro* are framed by the hegemony of *mestizaje* and *mulataje* through the racializing construct of *blanqueamiento*. Fluidity plays off of this fixity through the rise of the ideology of multiculturality, a doctrine of valorization of blackness and indigenousness through national constitutional reforms, and by the growth of institutes, NGOs (nongovernmental organizations), and even land reapportionment movements and governmental grants of usufruct to peoples previously stigmatized as black or indigenous, or both, living on "unclaimed" land often called *tierras baldías*.

In contemporary Latin American nation-states, and in pan-nationalist ethnic and cultural movements, the phenomenon of interculturality has emerged to offer an alternative, perhaps, to the polarity of fixity and fluidity. Interculturality is very different from an ethos of hybridity or social or cultural pluralism. It is multicultural but it is also intercultural. Interculturality stresses a movement from one cultural system to another, with the explicit purpose of understanding other ways of thought and action, whereas social and cultural pluralism stress the institutional separation forced by the *blanco* elite on diverse peoples. The ideologies of hybridity and pluralism are national, regional, and static; formal consciousness of interculturality is local, regional, diasporic, global, and dynamic.

Concepts that relate specifically to interculturality include ethnogenesis, alternative modernity, and emergent culture, all of which are motivated by processes of transculturation (e.g., Uzendoski 2004). Ethnogenesis refers to the emergence of a people within recorded or oral history (Hill 1996; Whitten 1976a, 1976b, 1996a). Throughout the Americas people have surged into history as independent nationalities or ethnicities, sometimes as allies in wars of colonial powers or in later wars of independence. In the late twentieth century and early twenty-first, waves of emergent people in cultural alliance with other people are sweeping Latin America not only in protest movements but also in performances that celebrate their new, alternative modernity, as historically rooted peoples in new contemporary places (e.g., Wibbelsman 2004, 2005, 2009).

People have also been placed in various categories historically, whether or not they wanted to be in such categories or deserved to be there (Hill 1996). In the twentieth and twenty-first centuries, cultural systems are also emerging to confront nationalist ideologies of "racial hybridity" as signifying the oneness of the *mestizo* body of the nation and to reject or transform stereotypic categories such as the Spanish *indio* and *negro*. In such rejections, aggregates of people as multicultural or intercultural often come to the forefront of ethnic resurgence. During such resurgence, emphasis is placed on culture as interethnic and ethnicity as intercultural (chapter 2, this volume). Nonetheless, the racialized fixities often reemerge, so that Afro–Latin American peoples may claim to be "indigenous" in order to partake of benefits granted to those classed as *indios* by state hegemony. In the Dominican Republic, for example, black people are officially classed on their identity cards and in the national census as *indios*.

Jonathan D. Hill (1996:1) writes: "ethnogenesis can be understood as a creative adaptation to a general history of violent changes—including demographic collapse, forced relocations, enslavement, ethnic soldiering, ethnocide, and genocide—imposed during the historical expansion of colonial and national states in the Americas" (see also Whitten 1976b, 1996a, 1996b). In a recent article in the journal *Current Anthropology,* archaeologist Alf Hornborg (2005) argues that ethnogenesis was prevalent throughout the prehistoric Americas, but as destruction and devastation occurred during the European conquest and subsequent extended colonial period, ethnogenetic processes became increasingly important as catastrophic disruption occurred in the varied lifeways of the vanquished. Transculturation is part of the process of ethnogenesis. It refers to the appropriation of cultural features by people in one system from those in another for specific purposes. Such purposes include trade, alliance against enemies, and religious conversion, among many others.

Emergent culture confronts racial categories of the conquest and colonial eras of Latin America and draws upon previous moments of ethnogenesis for strength and self-assertion. This idea of emergent culture refers to how people present themselves in various settings, ranging from everyday greetings to stylized ritual performances for varied audiences. In the 1980s, for example, indigenous people in many nations organized themselves into nationalities to reflect their individual cultures grounded in specific localities and also their common identity by specific histories of oppression. By the turn of the twenty-first century, more than twenty different nationalities had emerged in Ecuador alone, each with organizations established in the coastal, Andean, and Amazonian regions of that country. With all this diversity, coastal, Andean, and Amazonian people of Ecuador have arisen as one to confront national leaders of that country, even contributing to the ousting of several national presidents in the past decade (e.g., Whitten 2003b, 2004).

Alternative modernity (Parameshwar Gaonkar 2001; Uzendoski 2004; D. Whitten and N. Whitten 1993) is the idea that one can live in the contemporary world but adhere to cultural values and social practices at odds with the dictums of dominant modernity in which racial stratification, profit seeking, and forced conformity define an ideal way of life. Indigenous nationalities reflect the notion of alternatives in modern life, as do, for example, North American celebrations of Kwanzaa by African Americans near the time of the winter solstice. Indigenous nationality is an alternative to standardized, Western nationalist life, and Kwanzaa is an alternative to Christmas and Hanukkah. Racial fixity reflects modernity from its early beginnings in the 1440s through its manifestations in the twenty-first century. As such, multiculturality and its transcultural motivations constitute alternative modernities. Alternative modernities, however paradoxically, are often racialized by fusing the antipodes of the modern fixtures.

Three prominent examples of this phenomenon are to be found among the Miskitu population of Nicaragua and Honduras (Conzemius 1932; Dennis 2004; Pérez Chiriboga 2002); the Garífuna people of Guatemala, Belize, Honduras, and Nicaragua (Gonzalez 1983, 1988; Kerns 1983); and the Pacific Lowlands people of the Darién of Panama south through Colombia and Esmeraldas Province, Ecuador (West 1952, 1957; Whitten 1965, 1974). Here I comment on some general, but highly salient, characteristics that stem from colonial history to emerge again and again in this century.

The history of the European conquest and colonization of the Caribbean region, including eastern South America, often revolves around two indigenous aggregates, Caribs and Arawaks. The former are inscribed as the fierce Indians, and the latter as the friendly or tame Indians. But complications of this orientation to fierce versus tame Indians arose from the outset due to three factors: the presence of African-descended peoples in the same region, the phenomenon of *cimarronaje* (self-liberation) by African-descended and indigenous-descended people, and the mingling and mixing of those classed as *negro* and *indio*. Throughout the colonial period, indigenous- and African-descended people and the mixed descendants of such people defended their emergent traditions and new territories on the fringes of growing capitalist enterprise (e.g., Taussig 1978, 1980a, 1980b:41–92, 1987).

Two peoples that became historically known (and feared) emerged in early colonial times as the Garífuna and the Miskitu. Each of these Central American populations has been studied from a variety of scholarly perspectives. The Garífuna are usually regarded as African American and the Miskitu as Indigenous American, but both share a deep history of *cimarronaje, zambaje,* ethnogenesis, transculturation, and emergent cultural orientations. Many of these features negate the facile, racialized Western polarity of African and Indian.

The Garífuna of Honduras, Nicaragua, Belize, and Guatemala have large local populations with specific cultural organizations in Los Angeles, Chicago, New Orleans, and New York City (England 2006). They were first known in the seventeenth century as the "Black Carib" because they came into historical being on St. Vincent Island in the Lesser Antilles through interbreeding between native people, known as "Island Carib" (who spoke Arawak, according to Whitehead 2002:52–53), and black maroons and perhaps enslaved Africans. The plural of the name Garífuna—Garinagu—which these Central American people call themselves, derives from "Kalinago," the name by which Christopher Columbus came to know the "Carib" of eastern Venezuela and the Guianas. The admiral dubbed all "Caribs," and other native peoples who resisted his profitable advances, "Cannibals" (from whence came the name "Caribbean"; see especially Palencia-Roth 1993; Whitehead 1988). When the "Carib" label was applied by the conquerors and colonials, reputedly fierce Indians were free game for slavery or murder (see, e.g., Gonzalez 1988; Hulme and Whitehead 1992). Thanks to Columbus, the word *cannibal* replaced *anthropophagy* in English.

The Miskitu people of Honduras (Pérez Chiriboga 2002) and Nicaragua (Dennis 2004; Hale 1994; Helms 1977) became famous during the U.S.-sponsored contra fight against the Sandinista government of Nicaragua. In

April 2009, a segment of this population living in and near Puerto Cabezas declared themselves to be a nation independent of the nation-state. Their name derives from their colonial alliance with the British, from whom they obtained muskets, which they used against the Spanish. "Musket" became transformed from the weapons to the weapon bearers as "mosquitoes" (like "musketeers") and thence "Miskitu."

Missing the major point of *zambaje,* the mixture of African-descended and indigenous-descended peoples without European "admixture," many anthropologists and historians have debated whether the Garífuna and Miskitu, among many other similar people, should be studied "as Africans" or "as Indians." Once such a debate is engendered, the tendency is to see what is "retained" from African heritage and what is "retained" from indigenous heritage. When this happens, colonial mentality prevails, and people living their ways of life are stifled in expressing their existence, presence, and emergent cultural systems to a global audience. To use the Spanish vernacular, they become *negreado*—darkened, blackened, diminished, and silenced by a spurious hegemonic, racialized, diffusionist debate (Whitten and Torres, eds. 1998).

Esmeraldas, the southernmost region of the Pacific Lowlands of northwestern South America became home to self-liberated African and Afro-Hispanic people in the mid-1500s (Cabello Balboa 1945[ca. 1583]; Lane 2002). This history is described in the introduction (pp. 14–16).

As the concept of Afro-Indigenous peoples also became salient in national discourse in Ecuador in the 1990s, the concept of *zambaje* reentered the literary lexicon (Rueda Novoa 2001a, 2001b). *Zambo(a)* (sometimes *zambaigo*) refers, as noted above in several sections, to the genetic and cultural blending of African and African-descended peoples with indigenous peoples. The epitome of such blending is embodied historically in the original painting of the three ambassadors and lords from Esmeraldas. Significantly, perhaps, in the restoration of the Museo de Américas's painting in or around 1992, the features of *zambaje* were transformed to very black, to unambiguous *negro,* denying thereby the representation and significance of the mixed heritage of the Afro-Indigenous *cimarrones.* Globalization of the hypostatic fixity of racialization that began in Iberia in the fourteenth century (Moreno 1999) was recreated in this art restoration at the end of the twentieth century in institutionalized Spanish aesthetic perspectives. This is over six hundred years of racialized fixity, a *longue durée* indeed.

Black, *zambo, mulato,* indigenous, and other esmeraldeños of color are, like others in the Americas, becoming *negreado* (darkened, blackened) through political-economic moves of the powerful, just as their diversity is increasingly recognized through processes of interculturality. Conversely, many

Ecuadorians express displeasure with the existence of black movements of self-assertion and often deny that Afro-Ecuadorians themselves ever asserted cultural constructs of blackness prior to the indigenous movement, which erupted in 1990 with the first Levantamiento Indígena (Whitten 1996b). Black pride, however, subsuming *zambaje* and *mulataje,* has long existed, side by side with self-deprecation (Rahier 2003). Here is a poem published by the late Esmeraldan Nelson Estupiñán Bass in 1954 to move the reader to a level of cultural appreciation of, and pride in, blackness and enduring freedom in the face of oppression:

> Negro, negro renegrido, Negro, hermano del carbon. Negro de negros nacido. Negro ayer, mañana al hoy. Algunos creen insultarme Gritándole mi color. Más yo mismo lo pregono. Con orgullo frente al sol: Negro he sido, negro soy, Negro vengo, negro voy, Negro bien negro nací. Negro negro he de vivir, Y como negro morir.

> Black, black, blackened. Black, brother of charcoal. Black of blacks born. Black yesterday, today and tomorrow. They insult me Mocking my color. But I myself proclaim it. With pride in the face of the sun: Black I have been, black I am, Black I come, black I go, Black real black I was born. Black black I must live, and as black must die. (Estupiñán Bass 1997[1954]:50, 53; N. Whitten translation)

There can be no doubt about the affirmation of the identity of blackness in this poem—"*negro soy, negro voy*"—it is first person, publicly personal, declarative, poetic, and moving.

In the next chapter we look at the poetics of representation of blackness from indigenous perspectives to appreciate the many ways by which powers of resistance permeate cultural systems of people subject to centuries of domination and attempted hegemony. Then, in chapter 3 we move directly into Ecuador to discuss from multiple perspectives the topology of *el mestizaje*.

Acknowledgments

My interest in this topic began in North Carolina, Ecuador, Colombia, and Nova Scotia in the 1960s, while doing research with African Americans—many of whom asserted indigenous ancestry—and continued through participant observation among black and indigenous people in northwest Ecuador. In undertaking ethnographic research in Amazonian and Andean Ecuador from 1970 to the present, much of which has been and is joint with Dorothea Scott (Sibby) Whitten, I continue to encounter the twin phenomena of racial fixity and racialized intercultural fluidity. Collaborative comparative research with Diego Quiroga, Arlene Torres, Rachel Corr, and Michelle Wibbelsman in the 1990s–early 2000s and their collegiality and intermeshing interests into the present also contribute to my sense of understanding of these allusive transformative issues. Jonathan D. Hill, Jean Muteba Rahier, Michelle Wibbelsman, and Sibby Whitten read early and later drafts and contributed important suggestions.

Prelude

Rachel, Sibby, and Norman met in Salasaca in 1992. We visited there, where we shared many friends, and then again in Puyo, where Rachel met some of the indigenous people with whom we had been working since 1968. At the time, we were running an "indigenous school of writing by computer" jointly with our *compadre* Alfonso Chango and *comadre* Luzmila Salazar. Alfonso had completed his booklet *Yachaj Sami Yachachina* (*Shaman Class Knowledge,* 1984), and we had worked through this manuscript with color illustrations in Urbana with Carmen Chuquín Amaguaña and Enrique Mayer to see how we could help provide the reader with reasonable consistency in Alfonso's prose. Like a shaman's many-voiced séance, his phrases and written cadence moved in and out of the Quichua- and Spanish-speaking worlds.

Rachel was interested in sacred topographies and related symbolism in Salasaca, and as we talked we realized that we also shared many interests in relationships between indigenous people of the Andes and those of abutting Amazonia.

Both Salasaca and the area around Puyo were (and are) inhabited by indigenous Quichua-speaking people in the process of defending their ways of life and their dignity vis-à-vis a national government and provincial officials that had, between 1970 and 1979, threatened them with ethnocide based on the ideology of *mestizaje*. Both Salasacans and Puyo Runa had interaction with one another on mundane levels (e.g., soccer games) and on mystical planes (e.g., shamanic encounters). Both held stereotypes of the other, but both held a respect for the depth of indigenous culture that each sought to retain and expand. In both areas, indigenous people expressed their views on the racial-cultural makeup of the different categories of people in Ecuador, and beyond, including forces of the spirit world.

Rachel came to the University of Illinois as a graduate student, and we talked a good deal about all these matters. Then we decided to develop a paper, commissioned by Jean Muteba Rahier for his edited book *Representations of Blackness and the Performance of Identities* (1999). While doing library research for this piece, we also continued our individual research in Salasaca and the area around Puyo, sharing ethnographic information as well as historical and comparative materials. To expand our perspective we presented part of this paper, in Spanish, to a very diverse audience at the Congress of Americanists held in Quito in 1996. To the best of our knowledge this was the first comparative study of indigenous views of blackness. Since its publication many people from Latin America and North America have written to us reporting similar or cognate information gleaned from ethnography and history.

Chapter 2
Indigenous Constructions of "Blackness"

NORMAN E. WHITTEN JR. AND RACHEL CORR

> Todo deve ser cosa provechosa (All of these things should be profitable).
> —Christopher Columbus[1]

> The naming of relationships marks the beginnings of moral sanctions.
> —Sir Edmund Leach[2]

Perspectives, Issues, and Concepts

Professional perspectives on "race" and "culture" capture something of the enduring imagery of anthropologists and historians. Most cultural anthropologists treat race as a profoundly cultural construct, something that is socially divisive and discriminatory. In biological anthropology, by contrast, until recently the attempt has usually been to define "race" by genetic criteria. In both endeavors it is common to find that professionals dedicated to the study of culture and biology nonetheless project their quotidian or vulgar concepts of race and culture onto the peoples of the world. Writing about scholarly traditions focused on Latin America, Peter Wade puts it this way:

> The study of blacks and indians in Latin America has, to a great extent, been divided into, on the one hand, studies of slavery, slavery-related issues and "race relations" and, on the other, studies of indians. . . . the roots of the split go back to the fifteenth century and have spread right through the colonial period, the republican period of nation-building and into the twentieth century. (Wade 1997:25)

This divide, as Wade calls it, generates a conceptual system of serious scholarship wherein historical and ethnographic treatises on native peoples, *or* black peoples, hermetically seal off the data of the alternative people from analytical salience. Indeed, some scholars debate whether the Seminole of the southern United States, the Miskitu of Honduras and Nicaragua, or the Garífuna of Honduras, Nicaragua, Belize, and Guatemala should best be viewed as "Indian" *or* "Afro-American."[3]

Five hundred and fifty years ago, during the early modern "reconnaissance" of Africa, Portuguese slavers (*negreros*), directed from Sagres, Portugal, by Prince Henry the Navigator, began to mark the diverse peoples of Africa as *negros* (blacks) and brought them to Iberia in the caravels (also called *negreros,* "black bringers") to be sold for profit as chattel slaves (Moreno 1997; Russell-Wood 1995). This cultural practice of glossing all of the people of a continent (previously known by their diversity) by a monochromic color term, *negro,* coincided, perhaps ironically, with the beginning of large-scale conversions of diverse Africans to Christianity in the region of the Congo (Russell-Wood 1995; Thornton 1995).

Fifty years later, and over five hundred years ago, Christopher Columbus—later known as the "Discoverer"—the first profit-seeking European slaver in the Americas, claimed to have reached the gateway to Asian markets. He had witnessed the expansion in the Portuguese-sponsored African slave trade and learned from it. He marked the beginning of moral sanctions by naming all of the people of the Americas *indios* (Indians), and he established European hegemony over all of their lands, thereby creating a system sometimes called "landed slavery" (Wey Gómez 2008; Wynter 1995).

As Western histories continue to celebrate the genius of Prince Henry the Navigator and the "discoveries" of Columbus—Bearer of Christ and Admiral of the Ocean Sea—the bifurcation of the two continental populations that they and their disciples defined as the "black" and the "indian" endures. This European-designed cultural polarity of antipodal "races" provided a simplified, color-coded map for the organization and exploitation of cheap labor (Wey Gómez 2008). It gave the capitalist world and its scholars two primary races, forever (it sometimes seems) to be separated as distinct cultures, distinct peoples with distinct histories, subject to the polarized learned scrutiny by professionals as cultural worlds that have little or nothing to do with one another.

Thus continue the legacies wherein, in some genres of Western scholarly discourse, African Americans share something of a less-than-authentic "African" worldview and "Indians" share a somewhat acculturated, but disappearing, preconquest cosmology. Most who study African American cosmologies studiously avoid Native American studies, and those scholars of Native-Americana see African-Americana as intrusive and perhaps polluting (exceptions to this are noted in this text and in the references, but see especially Forbes 1993; Miller 2009; Restall 2005).

Naming and the consequent instantiation of "moral sanctions" that began in southwestern Europe over five and a half centuries ago endure with remarkable resiliency in scholarship in Europe and the Americas and are especially manifest when one looks at the academic specialties focused on "Afro-Americans" *or* on "Indians." This imagery is part of an embedded paradigm that colors and nuances scholarship back to its roots of oppression of Africans and of Native Americans. It is the purpose of this chapter to chip away at the barnacles of binary deception by looking for perspectives on "blackness," or *lo negro,* within indigenous South American vehicles of expression and ethnic depiction.

Let us return to "culture"; it is here that the sense of festivity, ritual, mythology, and discourse resides. It is also here that the generative qualities of "race" may be found across the academic divides. Leach's perspective, cited in the second epigraph, emerges from a paradigmatic view of culture. It suggests Clifford Geertz's contribution, as stated in *Local Knowledge* (1983:1): "cultural phenomena ... should be treated as significative systems posing expositive questions" (see also Leach 1976). Such systems carry meaning and raise questions. They constitute what one needs to know to understand the individual and collective thought of people living a particular way of life. This definition undergirds the one offered in the introduction, where we wrote of culture as "a corpus and flow of symbols and meanings enacted in social life at a given time in a given place."

Significative systems that pose expositive questions are fundamentally tropic (Crocker 1977; Fernandez 1991; Sapir 1977:1–32): they are composed of figures of speech that themselves form and revolve around representations (Combs-Schilling 1989:27). The representations we seek here are those of *lo negro* as they arise in indigenous contexts of festivity, mythology, and stylized discourse. These are contexts wherein creativity and reflexivity, as well as tradition and structure, prevail.

> Imagery, creativity, and reflexivity ... constitute a tripartite construct of mental processes ... Imagery is the corpus of images—concrete and allusive, stable and changing, patterned and chaotic, mimetic and inventive—developed by individuals from many sources in the course of their interactions. People draw on this corpus to create; creativity is the execution or expression of imagery, the communication of inner imagery to others. Reflexivity is the inward-looking process that involves the incorporation, integration, and interpretation of social

interactional experiences. (D. Whitten and N. Whitten 1993:7; see also Babcock 1980, 1987)

This chapter deals with texts and images wherein indigenous people reflect on a theme that emerged in Western scholarship in the Americas in the 1500s. Texts and images are drawn from mythology and festivity, from discourses on shamanism, and from public performances of native people of South America.[4]

Substance and Paradigms

In this essay we draw from literature on native knowledge systems that are themselves historically embedded within Hispanic settings in northern South America. The concepts that subsume "blackness" in northern South America include those of phenotype (*negro, zambo,* and *mulato* in Spanish), those of self-liberation (*cimarronaje, palenquismo, liberación*), and those of social and political upheaval (*levantamiento, alzamiento, sublevación*). The metonymic and metaphoric relationships among the concepts of phenotype, self-liberation, and social and political upheaval constitute dynamic and transcendent cultural paradigms of ethnic quality, ethnic space, ethnic history, ethnic narrative, and ethnic tension.

Throughout this chapter we deviate substantially from vulgar ethnic categorization and assume that all culture is interethnic and that all ethnicity is intercultural. As such, the paradigms of the dominant may be embedded and transformed within cultural systems taken historically to be at the antipodes of scientific or humanistic anthropological and historical discourses.

We first discuss qualities of blackness as they are found in the historical text of the native Andean chronicler Guaman Poma de Ayala. Writing from the *chaupi*, or "in-between," position of a *ladino* writer in the indigenous colonial world (Horswell 2005), Guaman Poma expressed sympathy for the plight of black slaves and expressed resentment of race mixture. We then move to modern indigenous representations of blackness in the "texts" of expressive culture: ritual, myth, and festivity among the Yekuana of northern Venezuela in the Watunna myth cycle.

We next turn to the Emberá and Wounaan of western Colombia and Panama, here looking at their sacred topography that structures historicity. From these two lowland rain-forest areas (one Amazonian, the other Pacific coastal) we move back to the Andes to the contemporary Quito Runa of the urbane capital of the Republic of Ecuador to present information expressed during the Yumbada festival associated with Corpus Christi. Because the concept of esmeraldeños (black people from the Pacific-coast rain-forest province of Esmeraldas, Ecuador; see Rahier 1998, 1999) emerges in the Yumbada, as well as representations of Upper Amazonian (or *montaña*) people, we draw material from Chachi indigenous peoples of this coastal province for a glimpse of their view of "blackness" in historical and contemporary perspectives.

Remaining in the Andes, we turn to the Salasaca Quichua native people of central Ecuador, as *lo negro* is expressed in the festivals of Caporales and Carnaval that mark the turn of the new indigenous year. Finally, we move back to Amazonia to understand our subject as it is expressed among the Canelos Quichua of Ecuador, as it emerges in their cosmogony of human and spirit origins, with special attention to the Wayalumba Supai.[5]

Guaman Poma

In his chronicle, Guaman Poma defended the goodness of those men "imported from Guinea" and praised the strength of "their King in Africa" (Dilke 1978:162). While he did not challenge the institution of slavery, he argued for better treatment of enslaved black people, particularly for keeping the black family together. He drew a simplistic "good *negro*/bad *negro*" dichotomy and recommended punishments for the "bad" ones. Yet most of his writing on blacks was critical of Spanish abuse of these people: "these poor Christians are made by the mistresses to do without meat or treats of any kind. Yet they are only made of flesh and blood" (Dilke 1978:162–163).

Guaman Poma argued that black people should have their own mayors and, when accused of a crime, should be judged by their own officials. One of the most telling of Guaman Poma's statements concerns his views of phenotypic features of blackness. He wrote: "When mulattoes—a mixture of black and Indian—produce quadroon children, these children lose all physical trace of their black origin except for the ear, which still gives them away by its shape and size" (Dilke 1978:162). This statement reveals how supposedly "biological" features are embedded in cultural and social systems.

Guaman Poma was opposed to interracial marriage, particularly white or black men marrying indigenous women. Yet he appears to assign a greater "value" to black men in one statement: "A little religion and education makes a Guinean worth two Creole half-castes and in an extreme case he is capable of sainthood" (Dilke 1978:162). As in modern-day views of blackness presented below, Guaman Poma embodied some dominant stereotypes of blacks as slaves, but expressed sympathy for their mistreatment at the hands of whites. We turn now to the representations of blackness among modern-day South American indigenous peoples.

Locations of indigenous people mentioned in text

Yekuana, Amazonian Venezuela

In the famous Watunna myth originally recorded in German by Marc de Civrieux and edited and translated from the Spanish into English by David Guss, black people are associated with the black curassow ("*pava de monte*"), Kurunkumo. In this context, black people are dreamed into being by Odosha, evil brother of good creator Wanadi (the son of the sun), as slaves to the evil Spaniards (the Fuñuru) and also as agents of Spanish oppression, the soldiers of the army.

> With the Fuñuru came a people called Kurumankomo, the black people. They were servants of the others. Their father was a black man, named Mekuru. He was Kahiuru's servant. They were good, poor people too. The Fuñuru made them work. They didn't give them any money. Lots of them ran off to the jungle and mixed with the Iaranavi [the good Spaniards, with whom the Yekuana had good relations of trade]. That's how the Murunmatto, the mestizos [*mulatos*], were born. They have our color. They're our friends. (Civrieux 1997[1980]:156)

This tale-telling by the indigenous Carib-speaking Yekuana resonates well with tales of the only black people to have emerged from this area in historic times. Venezuelan ethnographer and historian Berta Pérez recently found that the elements of alliance among indigenous people, the problematic issues of emergent *mestizaje,* and the asymmetric power relationships that unfolded during the colonial era are expressed in Afro-Venezuelan tales of *la pantera negra* (black panther). This is the legendary ancestress of *cimarrones* (self-liberated people) who fled slavery in Dutch Guiana (now Suriname), traversed one of the most difficult and treacherous terrains in the world, emerged in the upper Caura River region in the eighteenth century, and migrated downriver to near the Orinoco by 1850, where they live today (Pérez 1997, 1998).

Where an indigenous myth cycle ends with the departure of Wanadi to the sky world, the Afro-Venezuelan myth of the mythical black panther woman begins with the ethnogenesis of the endurance of *négritude* in Venezuelan Amazonas. Similarly, with regard to the working of gold and *guanín* filigree and other jewelry, Friedemann (1974) found that contemporary legends of the black people of Guélmambí, southwestern Colombia, tell of how they took over the artistic work of native people on the demise of the latter (see also Whitten and Friedemann 1974). In Ecuador, historian P. Rafael Savoia (1988) traces a migration of self-liberated mixed black-indigenous (*zambo*) people from Esmeraldas to Bahía de Caráquez, where they continued the long-distance maritime trade for which the indigenous people of the area were famous, after the virtual demise of the Manabí native people of this area as a result of the European conquest.

Wounaan and Emberá, Pacific Lowlands of Panama-Colombia

Themes similar to those in Yekuana myth and cosmology about the forces of evil and good of contemporary life are salient among the stories told by the Wounaan and Emberá of the Darién of Panama and in the Pacific Lowlands of western Colombia (e.g., Velásquez Runk 2005). Here we find what Stephanie Kane (1994:107) calls a "scale of sentient beings" that includes people or beings called *libres* (free [people]) and *cimarrones*. *Libre* and *cimarrón* are two key Emberá (and Wounaan) categories for the merger of human and spirit power. *Libre* is a term that embodies the historical association of blackness with self-liberation.

Cimarrón, according to Richard and Sally Price (1993:283), comes from the Spanish language of the Americas, with Arawak language roots (the Arawak, specifically the Taíno, were the first people contacted by Columbus in the Bahamas on October 12, 1492). The term emerged in the Caribbean and mainland of South America around 1500, first to refer to feral cattle and then, shortly thereafter, to refer to runaway indigenous and black slaves taking refuge in the *haití*, or forested hilly region, of the large Caribbean islands (and of the interiors of the Guianas, Venezuela, Central America, and Colombia, which had different names; see, e.g., Civrieux 1976; Guss and Waxer 1994). The Taíno designation for such a refuge zone became the name of the western side of the island of Hispaniola, Haiti, when the people there successfully revolted against French colonialism in 1804 (e.g., Trouillot 1989).

Eventually, the concept of *cimarrón* became attached exclusively to runaway blacks. The imagery of *cimarronaje* or *cimarronismo* (see Jaramillo Uribe 1963:42, Zuluaga R. 1988) among the Wounaan and Emberá is that of mysterious, free, dangerous, spiritual, but also corporeal, beings (their footprints can still be seen) completely familiar with the deep forest and committed to free life beyond the confines or reaches of "white authority." These *cimarrones* may be other Emberá or Wounaan, or blacks, or a mixture of indigenous and black spirit people, called *zambos*. "As symbolic mediators between this and the other world," Kane writes,

> Black-Kampuniá are located between Emberá and all other Kampuniá (outsiders who have power to condition everyday life, despite their physical absence). As symbolic mediators between Emberá and the otherworld (outside as unknown), black-Kampuniá are located between Emberá and devils/animals/hai, who may take on Kampuniá guise. The duality of their roles is conflated in practice, making much social interaction with black-Kampuniá a paradoxical combination of appreciation and fear for Emberá. (Kane 1994:107)

Colombian ethnographer Luis Guillermo Vasco (1985) describes six stages of initiation of the Emberá shaman. In the fifth phase, a being called Onasi, described as both *negro y libre* (black and free), appears. This conjoined force of blackness and freedom becomes part of the route the Emberá shaman travels. After the shaman is liberated from the black *libre,* he is ordered to carve the *bastones de hai* (*bastón* is Spanish for "staff" and *hai* [*jai*] refers to "spirit" in Emberá and Wounaan). In one story of the origins of Emberá shamanism, Vasco narrates how the first *haibaná* (shaman) acquired his mystical powers.

The first *haibaná* was a woman who encountered spirits who invited her to their tree house. The woman was like a person drunk, or in trance, but she had drunk no *chicha* (home brew) nor had she taken *pildé* (*ayahuasca* or *yajé*—*Banisteriopsis caapi* with vegetal additives). She returned several times to the tree house of the spirit world. She eventually took her husband to this spirit dwelling. In this house, among other beings and things, there were many *negros,* which were neither indigenous nor human. They were "*como espíritus,*" "like spirits." The *negros* were adorned with crowns of flowers and they also danced to a different drumbeat than that familiar to the Emberá; when they rested they sat on seats of power like those of the Emberá. The woman gained power from the spirits, including the black people-like spirits. After a fight with her husband, she went on to teach others shamanism, embodying thereby the feminized spirit power of blackness and freedom in what was to become an indigenous male domain.

The Colombian ethnographers Gerardo Reichel-Dolmatoff (1960) and Arturo Muñoz (1996) both write of a master water spirit, called *pulvichi* in Wounaan and Emberá, or *la madre de agua* (or *madre agua,* "water mother-master") in Spanish. In spite of the feminine depiction in Spanish, *la madre de agua* is conceived of as a "fierce, Black man, [who may] overturn canoes and drag people into the water, drowning them" (Muñoz 1996:48). Reichel-Dolmatoff (1960) describes this being as a monster with a black face who drowns or swallows travelers in their canoes. According to Juan Córdoba (1983:73), an Afro-Colombian anthropologist from the Chocó, *la madre de agua* is a being who can be sent by Emberá or Wounaan indigenous shamans to cause harm (see also Losonczy 1997).

La madre de agua is prominent in the indigenous narratives about historical societies of *cimarrones,* among maroons themselves (e.g., Price 1983:70), and in West African tales (e.g., Nunley 1987), as well as in indigenous cosmology of Amazonia (Luna and Amaringo 1991; Whitten 1976a, 1985, 1988), where it is often known by the Quichua designation *yacu mama* (water mother-master). It is often seen as a chthonic force and may represent the power of the hydrosphere against social forces of oppression, as one author has argued elsewhere (Whitten 1988).

The emergence of three "distinct" systems of biocultural being—*negro, indio, blanco*—is part of a Wounaan creation myth that accounts for the origins of human races, just as in the Yekuana Watunna myth. In this myth we find that a master spirit, sometimes associated with the Christ God, became a "protector" for free blacks, *libres,* who came to the Chocó as *cimarrones* escaping white-sponsored commercial slavery. It also accounts for the emergence of the three "races" at the Upper Chocó, at Bahía Solano, as hierarchicalized spirit forces that generated hierarchicalized "*razas*" of the colonial era.

Quito Runa, Andean Ecuador

The Yumbada, which often takes place in Andean Ecuador during the period of Corpus Christi, now renamed Inti Raymi, offers a striking imagery of the antipodes of *el mestizaje.* During the Yumbada, the prominent human constructs are those of the white *prioste* (festival sponsor) offering the fiesta to the Catholic Church. Prominent stereotypic representations in the festival are the indigenous "Yumbo" from the forested Andean slopes (*montaña*) and the "Black," as "*molecaña*" (sugar-cane grinder), from the low, hot rain forest of coastal Esmeraldas Province. Through it all the performers refer to themselves as Quito Runa. *Runa* is the Quichua word for "fully human being." When used in Andean Spanish, it is often a pejorative term for an indigenous person, or even a dog. Frank Salomon describes the black imagery as portrayed by the Quito Runa in this way:

> Four *negros de Esmeraldas* or *molecañas,* men disguised as blacks of the north coast, guard the *loa* [little blonde girls in white dresses]. Their inky masks glitter with golden eyebrows and scarlet lips. Their clothing is that of the backwoods rough rider; their motif is the violence and raunchy humor attributed to coastal blacks. (Salomon 1981:166–167)

This heartily masculinized imagery of blackness contrasts totally with that of the *alumbrantes,* women who, "bearing giant white candles for the church, radiate a feeling of cleanliness, quiet, and modesty" (Salomon 1981:167). And, as protectors of the beautiful, blonde, white-dressed little female *loa,* these images of blackness in Quito Runa ceremony strongly suggest fertility, which begets the quality of being *zambo,* and thereby being from the Zambo republic of the mid-sixteenth century from whence the *molecañas* came to Quito (see, e.g., Cabello Balboa 1945[ca. 1583]; Lane 2002; Phelan 1967). One is reminded also, perhaps, of the black spirit-man, evil Odosha, who steals the wife of his brother, good Wanadi, in the tales of the Watunna among the Carib-speaking Yekuana of Venezuela, or of the free, dangerous, libidinal *cimarrón* of the Emberá and Wounaan of Colombia. This particular *negro* festival character of urban Quito seems to be the epitome of what the Chachi of Esmeraldas call Juyungo (e.g., Ortiz 1943).

Milton Altschuler (n.d.) describes the evocation of *lo negro* as a human-spirit quality of shamanic blackness in an unpublished manuscript developed from his doctoral dissertation. During a Chachi shamanic curing, the healer "speaks" power words: *moreno . . . indio . . . bravo . . . enfermedad . . . brujo* (dark one . . . indian . . . fierce . . . sickness). He also chants in Spanish, the foreign language of domination: "This man is sick, I know, I know, cure, cure, *negro.*" Altschuler explains that the use of terms such as *negro* and *moreno* during the mixed-language incantations is necessary because of the knowledge of powerful, killing magic of the contemporary black people of the region, and the "fierce indians" who left their mystical and dangerous powers behind in the pottery and stone artifacts that are common in this same region (Altschuler n.d.; see also Barrett 1925:353–381).

Milton Altschuler's revised doctoral thesis manuscript and the book by Eulalia Carrasco (1983) make it clear that while the black people and Chachi of Esmeraldas share the same universe, their origins are entirely different, their moralities are entirely different, and all of the contrasts between the Chachi and black people coalesce in the dangerous fusion of the "*razas*," in the persona of the Zambo, the fount of both danger and freedom. We return to this theme in our conclusions.

Salasaca Quichua, Andean Ecuador

In Salasaca, festivals transform the figure of the black from one epoch to the next. The same polar meanings of blackness in Yekuana mythology of oppressed slaves and the fierce soldiers emerge in two different Salasacan festivals: the soldier image in Caporales, celebrated in February (Chango and Jerez 1995; Guevara 1969–1970; Scheller 1972), and the slave image in pre-lenten Carnaval. The fiesta of Caporales is associated with the Catholic feast days of Los Reyes (the Kings, Magi) and the baby Jesus. In this representation, the blacks signify soldiers who guard the treasures brought by kings for the baby Jesus. These performances fuse images of different black peoples from both Spanish Catholic imagery and from Salasacan historical experience.

During Caporales each actor who portrays a black person enacts a stereotype of a man of color from the coast passing through Salasaca. This portrayal is often that of a soldier in the army of Eloy Alfaro Delgado during the time of the great Liberal Revolution of the mid–nineteenth century—the *alfarada*, as it is sometimes called, of 1895—that caused a national social transformation. Alternatively, a petroleum worker moving through this indigenous parish to the eastern oil fields of Amazonia during the recent epoch of economic transformation may be depicted.

Each *negro*, as the dancers are called, is paired with a *doña*, "woman of esteem," who is a robust boy or strong young man dressed as a Salasacan woman. In recent years, Salasacan girls have replaced the cross-dressing young men to perform as *doñas*. The *negros*, dressed in soldiers' uniforms and carrying swords, dance with the *doñas* while moving their swords up and down, up and down, in their scabbards. The movement suggests combat and sexual prowess. Exegetically, for the Salasaca, the blacks represent military and sexual potency. Young men who have performed as *negros* in this festival report that as they dance they shout, "¡hoyaaá! ¡como zambo! ¡como yana! ¡como negro!" ("like black!"). They claim to be from Esmeraldas, where black people live, or from Manabí, where blacks fought as *montaneros* in the Liberal Revolution. Some say that they are on their way to the Oriente (Amazonian) provinces to seek their fortunes in the petroleum camps. They say that they are taking a stroll (*el pasito*) through the parish of Salasaca, and they comment on the beauty and desirability of the women there. Some actors grab sexually and roughly at single women, who fiercely resist their advances.

The term *caporal* was used in other parts of Latin America to refer to the black administrator, labor boss, or slave master. In the seventeenth-century sweatshop of Pelileo (the town in which the parish of Salasaca was formerly incorporated), the *caporales* were the black workers who were ordered to assist in the punishment of indigenous workers. A 1666 report stated that the Indians were "held to the ground, with two hands, by their blacks, whom they call *caporales,* and they punish them with whips made of cowhide" (Archivo General de Indias 1666). Sweatshops, like mines, were sites where blacks and indigenous people were forced to work together under white domination (see Lane 2005). The tin miners of Oruro, Bolivia, enact a performance during Carnival called the *Morenada,* in which they reenact a rebellion against the black slave master, called *caporal* (Nash 1993:131–132). But this is not the meaning that the "black" characters have for Salasacans. Most Salasacans say that they dress up as black soldiers for Caporales because that is the tradition.

The black soldier image itself has polar meanings within the festival of Caporales. It can stand for a liberator or for an oppressor. The Salasacan actors smear cooking oil and soot from blackened iron kettles on their faces, carry swords, and wear soldiers' uniforms. The ritualized behavior of those mimicking "*negros*" enacts that of the soldiers once sent by the Spanish (and white) *hacendados* to harass indigenous women. The portrayal is homologous to the Yekuana mythic "agent of Spanish oppression." The "*negros*" are also portrayed by the Salasacans as the coastal black soldiers sent to protect president Eloy Alfaro, considered in Salasaca, as elsewhere in Ecuador, to be a liberator of black people and of indigenous people (e.g., Arteaga 1992). In some modern oral Quichua traditions, he is affectionately referred to as *yaya* Alfaro (father Alfaro; Harrison 1996). This protector role of the ex-president is analogous to that of the protector role of the esmeraldeño "*molecañas*" (each of whom also carries a machete on his hip) in the Quito Runa Yumbada, in which they protect the lovely young, female, white *loa*.

According to oral history, in the 1890s Salasacans collaborated with the black coastal soldiers to disguise President Eloy Alfaro as an indigenous woman so that he could safely travel northward through the Sierra to arrive in Quito (where he was later assassinated on January 28, 1912). In Salasaca people share a consciousness of the common struggle of Afro-Ecuadorians and indigenous people against oppression. As one Salasacan said:

> The dark people [*morenos*] were also on his side, on the side of Eloy Alfaro. They left slavery. They were also treated as children. [The *hacendado*] treated dark people [*morenos*], blacks, badly. Because of this Caporal [festival] is just like what happened with the black and the black is dressed with clothes [that are associated with the imagery of blackness]. The dark people have always walked together with the indigenous people. This was the time of the good president [Eloy Alfaro]. The festival of Caporales is thus a time to give thanks. Because he is part of the indigenes, of the dark ones. The indigenous people and the dark people are one.

The contra image of *lo negro,* represented as an embodiment of enslavement by whites, and conterminous with oppression of indigenous people, is also enacted in a Salasacan ritual drama during Carnaval. A Salasacan man and a boy paint their faces black to portray, respectively, the *tayta negro* (black father) or *yaya negro* (also black father) and the "*ashinegrito*" (roughly, funny black). The *tayta negro* "sells" the black youth to the Salasacan sponsor of the festival. Some people say that the *alcalde* (mayor) examines the youth for physical strength, sometimes checking his teeth as one would a bovine or horse, and sometimes asking him to show how he works with a machete. After the *alcalde* agrees to "buy" the youth, the *ashinegrito* throws capsicum (red pepper) onto the cooking fire, causing the women to run out of the *yanuna wasi* (dark, blackened, smoke-filled cooking house) so that the *ashinegrito* is able to escape with plenty of cooked meat.

Throughout Andean Ecuador the image of *lo negro* in the context of indigenous festivity and indigenous artistic portrayal fuses images of different black personages across many centuries. One of the best known and most publicized of these is the Mama Negra (Black Mother) festival held in the city of Latacunga in November (see, e.g., Weismantel 2003). One expression in this festival is that of the black wet nurse. Through her nurturing breast milk, the Black Mother turns the Christ Child (represented by a blonde, white doll) black (Weismantel 2001:257). Among other events celebrated is the liberation of black slave miners in Cotopaxi by indigenous people from that province. Other images of blackness in Ecuadorian Andean festivity include the Black King or Magus coming from "Abyssinia" to view the Christ Child and to guard his treasures; sixteenth-century Spanish imagery of Moors; black troops from the wars of liberation in the nineteenth century; and more. Still other images relate to indigenous historicity with regard to white enslavement of black people in the Andes and on the coast and to soldiers and runaways during colonial and republican times. Movements and migrations of black and indigenous people into ethnically defined spaces motivated by economic situations such as the nineteenth-century gold rush and Amazon rubber boom, and the twentieth-century petroleum boom that brought Afro-Ecuadorians from the coast, through the Sierra, and into indigenous Amazonian territories, are also portrayed. Analogous booms were those of cacao and bananas that brought indigenous people from the Sierra and Oriente to the coastal provinces. Any and all epochs and movements may be fused or separated in indigenous festival images of "blackness." These various texts are expressions of the intertwined histories of black and indigenous peoples in South America.

Canelos Quichua, Amazonian Ecuador

In the myth of Sicuanga Runa, the toucan liberator person in Canelos Quichua tales, Sicuanga frees two beautiful women, Widuj Warmi (black woman, from *Genipa americana*) and Manduru Warmi (red woman, from *Bixa orellana*), from a cage of spiny bamboo. They were enclosed in this snare by foreign monkey person, Machin Runa. This story of indigenous liberation is the opposite of a Canelos Quichua tale of the origin of blackness both as a spirit force and as a mystical forest person.

Blackness emerges as follows (Whitten 1985:84–87). Wayalumba Supai lives in a natural entanglement of spiny ferns deep in the Amazonian rain forest. He emerges from this entanglement with a different kind of drum, which he beats to attract children to him. Wayalumba is self-liberated. By his drumming and by his dancing he emerges as another force, called *zambu*, or *negro*. The Quichua word *yana*, "black," as in *yana runa*, "black person," or *yana supai*, "black spirit," is not used in these tellings. Wayalumba is black; the spirit (*supai* in Quichua) is of the various epochs of cultural time and dimensions of cultural space. He may come forth in beginning times-places, times of revolution of Eloy Alfaro, times of the grandparents, or present times.

His imagery is of the forest—spiritual, dangerous, and libidinous—but he resides near indigenous settlements. He is very similar to the conceptualization of the *cimarrón* in Emberá-Wounaan and Chachi cosmology. He is part of the indigenous biosphere, but he is not of the same original sources. Like the *negros* of the Yekuana, the Kurumankomo of their Watunna myth, the Wayalumba Supai is part of a creation that involves the Spanish conquest. He is not "Sacha Runa" (Whitten 1976a); nor is he "Yumbo" or "Auca." Wayalumba is of the forest, yet he is intricately connected to the history and legacies of the Spanish conquest, of the people of today, and to the emergence, within history and destiny, of blackness.

As we reach an end to this preliminary sojourn among the color signifiers of conquest as encountered in indigenous portrayals of blackness, we find that the connections between peoples beg for more complex signifieds. The colonial signifiers of conquest map poorly, if at all, onto South American humanity (the signifieds) in its diversity. Within systems of indigenous representation we find an embedded paradigm of conquest and capitalist signifiers and signifieds to be manifest in myth, discourse, festivity, and ritual, but the indigenous webs of signification within which *lo negro* is suspended dynamically, remain, as they must given Western polarized scholarship, problematic. What is clear is that among the indigenous peoples of northern South America, historicity engages with spiritual forces to conflate images from mythic times with past colonial and postcolonial encounters and mixtures of black and indigenous people.

In Pastaza Province of Amazonian Ecuador, the demonic figure of Wayalumba Supai transforms to a quotidian comparison with modern-day esmeraldeños (Whitten 1985), as indigenous people discuss their ofttimes competitors in gainful employment situations. Also, from time to time, imagery of a *negro supai* (black spirit) emerges. This spirit is portrayed with a tobacco pipe in his mouth and a large machete on his hip. Once again, we are reminded in all of this of the dramatic festival performances of the Andean Salasaca Quichua as they merge and separate images of slavery, black soldiers, and modern-day petroleum workers; of the way the Emberá place archetypical black imagery in their cosmological framework as a shamanic messenger; and of how the Yekuana origin myth cycles include blackness in multiple dimensions in their historicities.

Discussion and Contextualization

The West European concept of *raza* emerged from "obscure roots" in Spanish (and in Italian, French, Portuguese, and English) around 1500. At this time, the idea of distinct imagined systems of biocultural "beings"—*blanco, negro, indio*—empowered a vast system of colonial values of white supremacy and black and Indian subservience. In Latin American colonial, republican, and nation-state ideologies, this system of ethnic polarities has been and is said to be mediated by *mestizaje*, even to the point of bringing into being a *raza cósmica* through the biological and cultural transformation of *negros* into *mulatos* and *indios* into *mestizos* (Carballo 1989:13–16; Vasconcelos 1989:31–52, 93–99).

Key markers in a paradigm of dominance, and sometimes hegemony, that has been of fundamental importance in the Western Hemisphere from about 1500 are diagrammed in chapter 1, where concepts of mixture and hybridity are discussed. With the sets of symbols brought into being in the Americas more than five hundred years ago, cultural stereotypes and ethnic formations came to reflect, accept, and reject one another during the entire "modern" epoch of the West. The set of symbols that form images of segregated humanity and its embedded polarizations is paradigmatic. By this paradigm, evocation of one symbol, or one facet of one symbol, implies the others in shifting but discernible patterns of signification.

At the antipodes of class-status relationships emanating from the wealthy and fair of skin color to the poor are those people generally represented in northern South America in various walks of life as *negro,* on the one side, and *indio,* on the other. Literature on concepts of "indianness" within black historical narrative, ritual, and mythology is fairly well known to many specialists in Afro-Americana. However, information on the reciprocal embeddedness of the concept of *"lo negro"* in indigenous lore and ceremonial practice is most obscure. The reason for such obscurity may be that specialists in indigenous cultures of South America do not carry with them the same sort of imagery as do the peoples who are subject to their studies. This is not altogether so, of course, or we would not have been able to come to grips with Yekuana, Wounaan, Emberá, Chachi, Quito Runa, Salasaca Quichua, or Canelos Quichua concepts about blackness in their cosmologies and cosmogonies.

The professional imagery of anthropology is, all too often, part of a deeply embedded and remarkably persistent cultural paradigm with its roots in fifteenth- and sixteenth-century early modernist thought, wherein human commodities came to be known and expressed as racial categories. In the Americas, the most important of these categories became those of *negro,* for chattel slavery of African Americans, and *indio,* for the landed slavery of Indigenous Americans. Given this polarity, inadequate attention has been given to understanding the interethnic, intercultural character of such an embedded paradigm within indigenous local knowledge systems.

When we turn our attention to such systems, even with the sketchiest of data, as presented here, we come face to face with our own history and understand in a more complex manner the intercultural historicity of the original people of South America, whose legacies and destinies intertwine with those of blackness and whiteness. A search for such history, which historian Natalie Zemon Davis in unpublished presentations calls "braided traditions" (Davis n.d.), takes us far from the *mestizaje* of vulgar political discourse that characterizes the self-styled hybridity of prominent literary and scientific ideologues (e.g., García Canclini 1995, and see, contra García Canclini, Rosaldo 1995).

In this chapter we seek to cast initial comparative light on black imagery in indigenous cultures of northern South America and to sharpen our scholarly reflexivity vis-à-vis a cherished set of Western images of ancient cultural antipodes. To the best of our knowledge, comparative studies of such racial topography focusing on concepts of blackness in indigenous cultures of northern South America have not been undertaken. It is the purpose of this essay, then, to draw attention to some initial tracings in what remains a vast moral topography of entwined cultural awareness that ethnographers of "South American Indians" seem more often than not to ignore, and of which so many specialists in Afro-American diaspora studies seem unaware. We hope to increase interest in indigenous and African American hermeneutics through this brief demonstration, to expand thereby the horizons of serious ethnography and serious reading of the recorded historical texts.

Alternative Contextualizations

We have presented materials on indigenous views of *lo negro,* and our analysis to this point has stressed the legacy of racism in such views. But there is much more to be said, to which we now wish to contribute some seeds for thought. Throughout our discussion of indigenous concepts, issues of inner power, shamanic power, spiritual power, cosmic power, and ethnic power emerge. Writing of systems of power in Africa, Arens and Karp (1989) offer insights that fit nicely with systems of local knowledge in the Americas: "Transformation is the key to understanding concepts of power in African societies. A central cultural theme . . . is that the powers agents have allow them to transform the world. 'Transformative capacity' is a key element in people's understanding of power" (Arens and Karp 1989:xx).

One cannot read texts from the Yekuana, Emberá, Wounaan, Chachi, Quito Runa, Salasaca Quichua, or Canelos Quichua, or from the Saramaka, Garífuna, Miskitu, or black esmeraldeños, without coming away with this same sense of "transformative capacity" tied to peoples' understanding of power. Concepts of force that can be used for good or for evil seem to be generally embedded in cosmologies of people, especially in contexts where paradigmatic hegemony is manifest. Powerful forces, seen as spiritual bordering on the quotidian, affect bodies and souls, as in illness, impoverishment, and exploitation. Such powers can be tapped, in turn, to heal the body, to soothe the mind, and to resist dominance (e.g., ensuing chapters). Indigenous reflexive awareness of forces and powers as cultural phenomena is what we are presenting. Such awareness needs no boundaries, and cultural diversity is a generative feature. This takes us back to our early assertion that all culture is interethnic and that all ethnicity is intercultural.

We noted above, in several places, that the two polar ethnic paradigms of *negro* and *indio,* in Western modernist mentality, are offset by a nonhybridized concept of ethnic merger, the phenomenon of the *zambo* in colonial and contemporary discourse. The analog to *zambo* within indigenous cultures of Ecuador seems to be found in the concept of *yumbo* (see N. Whitten and D. Whitten 2008; Whitten et al. 1997). In metasymbolic terms, the image of the Zambo and that of the Yumbo may, during times of crisis, represent bodies of human beings with shamanic powers who come from the lowlands—"below" the pinnacle of bureaucratic control—to challenge that control system. The greater force is found in the unity of the Yumbo and the Zambo, a unity of diverse personages that rejects whiteness and *mestizaje* to form a union in the Americas devoid of racialist or racist classification. Here cultural diversity is crucial, but boundaries become transformed into braided legacies and intertwined destinies.

We can attest to the presence of fear, in the past (e.g, Salomon 1983) and in the present, among those high in class hierarchies in northern South America, of unities of indigenousness and blackness. The unification of the West European hypostatized ethnic antipodes, the African American and the Indigenous American, surging from "bottom" to "top" of class hierarchies implies the unification of spiritual and cosmological attributes, transformed to phenotypic attributes and their associated cultural characteristics. Out of early European colonialism, and enduring through republican and modern epochs, the associated social and political power of the nonhybridized unity of antipodal *razas* challenged and challenges the dominant societal model of the *blanco*, with its attendant *mestizo* and *mulato* categories as biological and cultural transformations within a *blanqueamiento* mobility system created during colonial rule (see, e.g., Whitten and Torres 1998; chapter 1, this volume).

Confining ourselves to Ecuador, with which we are the most familiar, it is certainly the case that the Indigenous Uprising of 1990 (chapter 4, this volume), the March for Land and Life of 1992 (N. Whitten and D. Whitten 2008; Whitten et al. 1997), and the 1997 Columbus Day March to Quito from Ecuador's four cardinal points stressed the fusion of powers of people of diversity against the materialist forces represented by hybridizing and whitening.

Conversations

At the Forty-ninth Congress of Americanists in Quito during July 1997, it was gratifying to find more than seventy people crowding into a relatively small room at 8:00 A.M. on a Saturday to listen to a twenty-minute presentation of our joint research and to comment meaningfully on it. Present, among others, were Venezuelan ethnographer and social analyst Nelly Árvelo de Jiménez, who worked for many years with the Yekuana; several scholars from Colombia and Europe with intimate, first-hand, extended experience based on years of field research with the Wounaan and Emberá; specialists in Afro–Latin American cultures in many nations; many Ecuadorianists with experience throughout the republic; Africanists, specialists in U.S. cultures, and at least one colonial historian from Spain.

The leader of the symposium, Jean Rahier, presented a very provocative paper on the image of the Jew in black esmeraldeño festivity. This, together with one by Isidoro Moreno on religious black brotherhoods from fourteenth- to eighteenth-century Spain (Moreno 1983) and another by Peter Sutherland on festival (and tourist) representations of American Vodun in the ancient slave port of Whydah (now Benin, once Dahomey), dovetailed nicely with our presentation. It became quite clear that the African diaspora is one of intertwined traditions that continue to span Africa, Europe, and the Americas. And it became most apparent that representations of power in the African diaspora are not confined to people with a particular skin color or other physical features. Blackness has to do with spirituality, with forces, with the known and unknown, with history and historicity, with cultural transformation and endurance. The collection of presentations made in Quito underscored all of these features, and much more. They presented a coherent statement about multifaceted reflexivity with its own transformative powers.

Members of the symposium commented favorably on the dimensions of *lo negro* that we presented from our reading of literature and from our own ethnographies. One repeated comment was that the myths, stories, discourses, and festivities that reveal something of *lo negro* in indigenous discourse are changing. Each scholar with experience among the Yekuana, or Emberá, or Chachi, attested to the fact that cultural phenomena are dynamic. They change and shift, new emphases enter, transformations occur. We certainly agree. We also asserted, however, that the racialist reference points of *indio, negro,* and *blanco,* mediated by a false projection from *blanco* as *mestizaje-*embedded *blanqueamiento* of racist hybridity, nonetheless endure, and those who discussed these matters agreed with us.

We all concluded on the note that when dealing with African American imagery anywhere in the Americas we certainly must read, reflect, and think about Indigenous American imagery on the same or similar subjects. And conversely, those seeking to understand indigenous cosmology must not ignore that which is well embedded in the various systems of négritude. There are many voices out there in the cultural worlds of Hispanic domination; the counterhegemonic social movements that we learn about now and then are but the most dramatic of enduring realities of interethnic, intercultural reflexive historicity and struggle. To listen more carefully to the multiple modes of alternative conceptualizations of power, hegemony, resistance, and defiance is essential to a necessary transformation of serious ethnography and serious history. On this chord we conclude this moment of our brief, but ongoing, conversation.

Acknowledgments

Part of the joint research contributing to this essay was funded by two Arnold Beckman Institute Grants through the Research Board of the University of Illinois at Urbana-Champaign (1994–1995 and 1996–1997). Funds contributing to research in Ecuador that turned up materials presented here came from a Research Grant to Corr by the Center for Latin American and Caribbean Studies of the UIUC. We gratefully acknowledge earlier assistance and related collaboration that led to facets of this essay provided by Diego Quiroga, Isabel Pérez, and Arlene Torres. We thank Jean Rahier for inviting us to the symposium at the Forty-ninth Congress of Americanists in Quito (July 1997), where an earlier and shortened version of this essay was originally presented, in Spanish, by N. Whitten, and for his encouragement and critical perspectives on the subject of this ongoing research and this particular contribution. Arlene Torres and Dorothea Scott Whitten read various drafts and commented significantly on what became our final submission.

Prelude

In 1990, at the invitation of the chief of the Schomburg Center for Black Culture in New York City, Arlene Torres and Norman Whitten developed a two-volume manuscript entitled "Blackness in Latin America and the Caribbean," and we published a condensed version of our introduction in 1992. The Schomburg project collapsed for lack of other manuscripts for a series that was to run to some sixty volumes, and thanks to Joan Catapano, Indiana University Press moved into the breach to publish a radically altered two-volume manuscript in 1998. In 1990 indigenous people had thrust themselves onto the national scene in their nationwide Indigenous Uprising (chapter 4, this volume), following that in 1992 with the March (Caminata) for Land and Life from Puyo to Quito. Black people had joined these events, and awareness of Afro-Latinity and indigeneity as strong forces for positive and progressive change was at an all-time high through all sectors of Ecuadorian society and throughout the hemisphere. In the meantime, Rachel Corr and I had worked on our "blackness in indigenous myth" piece (chapter 2, this volume), and I had developed the keynote address for a UNICEF-sponsored symposium on racism in Quito in 1997.

In 1999 I was invited to participate in a symposium entitled "Mestizaje and Créolité" at the University of Chicago, where Latin Americanists and Caribbeanists were brought together to deliver papers and discuss common perceptions of "racial and cultural blending." Michelle Wibbelsman, an Ecuadorian and U.S. citizen with field experience in Otavalo and family ties to Quito and Riobamba, was working with me on subjects pertaining to the persistence of views of *el mestizaje*. A confluence of research projects came together when I developed this chapter, with sustained assistance and critical commentary from Michelle.

Most important, however, was the ethnographic context of past and ongoing ethnography with Afro-Ecuadorian and indigenous people who continue to feel demeaned by elite projections that, on the one hand, glorify the processes of *mestizaje* as creating a oneness of a nation while, on the other hand, debase those who aspire to "whiteness" and those who fall outside of the ideology of racial and cultural hybridization. In all such models, black people and indigenous people are left in social, cultural, and ideological limbo. They seek to transform this state of being betwixt and between competing systems of power into a persuasive position in a nation-state with which they identify strongly. We could say that their collective aspirations are to develop powers of resistance.

Technical language notwithstanding, there are biases in this chapter that bespeak many years of living with black people and indigenous people who some of our one-time facilitators in Quito regarded as inferior beings. One distinguished Ecuadorian once told me that I lack dignity and gentility because I associate with *yumbos* and *negros* and not with "real Ecuadorians." Other Ecuadorians of the same rank and class, however, have supported our studies and continue to do so.

Michelle Wibbelsman's ethnography in Otavalo and her innumerable conversations with me helped put this in perspective by relating to me the graffiti of that area at a time of charged indigenous emotions directed against those who were once regarded only as *blancos* but since have been placed in the pejorative category *mishu,* short for "*mestizo.*"

Chapter 3
The Topology of *El Mestizaje*

In this chapter I (N. Whitten) consider the phenomenon of *symbolic inversion* (Babcock 1978) to contribute to the theme of ethnic dynamics that I began to explore in the early 1960s (Whitten 1965), continued to study in the 1970s (Whitten 1974, 1976a), and, with many others, addressed more fully in 1981 (Salomon 1981; Stutzman 1981; Whitten, ed. 1981; see also Whitten 1999).[1] Symbolic inversion refers to processes of resignification in multiple arenas such that hegemonic constructs become publicly re-cognized and thereby contested. The dynamics of symbolic inversion are, I argue, fundamental to the politics and poetics of local identity that contribute to transformed collective representations that, in turn, motivate social movements. Symbolic inversion involves mimetic equalization of power relationships that connect spiritual power to secular political power (Taussig 1993; Whitten et al. 1997).

My focus here is on the dynamics of *mestizaje* ideology in Ecuador. Such ideology—especially in its contested dimensions—is intricately tied to processes of inversion of domination and hegemony in quotidian and ritual settings (Babcock 1978; Gluckman 1962; Moore and Myerhoff 1977; Turner 1973, 1974, 1985). Ideological *mestizaje* and its multiple inversions are also tied to shifts in structural power (Wolf 1999:3–8) that develop out of symbolically motivated social action (see, e.g., Whitten 1988, 1996b, 2003a, 2003b; Whitten et al. 1997; N. Whitten and D. Whitten 2008).[2]

To discuss dynamics of *mestizaje,* I adopt the metaphor of topology and topography. Ecuador has one of the most complex geographical topographies in the world. In many ways, its cultural mosaic is mapped onto this complexity with the added dimension of a stratified social structure that features not only rigidities in class and ethnic categories, representations, and identities (e.g., Whitten 1985; Whitten and Quiroga 1998; Whitten et al. 2001), but also remarkable fluidity across the categorical boundaries. Rather than treat *mestizaje* ideology as a unified and unifying doctrine of *ecuatorianidad,* I choose to present a selective topography of *el mestizaje*—the blending of a national social body—as viewed in specific spaces where concepts of *raza* (race) are salient in particular contexts and arenas.

Let us begin with the Otavalo region of Imbabura Province. Otavalo is both a market-tourist town and a region of many villages in Imbabura Province, north Andean Ecuador (Wibbelsman 2009). Symbolically, in Ecuador, Europe, and the United States, indigenous people of Otavalo, referred to hereafter as Otavalans,[3] are praised for their indigenousness and industriousness and are often set out in public discourse and in publications as a model of what indigenous society could or should be (e.g., Colloredo-Mansfeld 1999). Within Ecuador, a myriad of discriminatory mechanisms are applied to them through "white-mestizo" subtle and blatant displays of racism. In his book *The Native Leisure Class* (1999), Rudi Colloredo-Mansfeld makes a strong and systematic case for sustained racism in this region directed specifically at Otavalans by their white-mestizo neighbors. He carefully and convincingly exposes Ecuadorian racism in lucid dimensions that range from concepts of illness and dirt ("hygienic racism") to white-mestizo attributes of indigenous wealth linked—wrongly and falsely—to the illegal cocaine drug trade:

> [M]odern racial ideologies in the Andes dehumanize subordinate peoples ... by making reference to the body. In Ecuador, though, race means more than skin pigmentation, genetics, and blood; it relates to bodies in an expansive sense. The physical world of native peoples—the foods of their gatherings, the fabrics in which they are clothed, the private spaces of their homes, the products made and exchanged through their skilled labor—contains many "micro-sites" ... where white-mestizo elites find signs of contamination. (Colloredo-Mansfeld 1999:84)

An Indigenous Space of Power and Counterhegemony

I choose a quotidian piece of graffiti to open this discussion. There is no question but that some readers will be amused by this; others will be offended; some may even be shocked. Such is the nature of counterhegemonic discourses and symbolic inversions; they are constructed to jar one's psyche from an acknowledged (if not accepted or acceptable) doctrine, to a public contestation.

> Meztizos babosos no son blancos. Solo son longos acomplejados.
>
> Drooling meztizos [misspelled] are not white. They are indians with an inferiority complex [neurotic indians].

In 1994 this epithet was painted on a wall facing the Pan-American Highway on the northern edge of Otavalo, a major market site in northern Ecuador and a favorite locus for international tourism. Obviously, *mestizo* is misspelled. We return to the misspelling below. In specific social and spatial context, initial explication based on ethnography (Colloredo-Mansfeld 1999) in this and other regions is not difficult: nonindigenous local people are pejoratively called or labeled "drooling half-breeds." The drool is that of social idiocy. They are not "white" (as they claim in self-identity). They are "Indian," rendered by the pejorative "*longo* with an inferiority complex."

In the Otavalo region, when used by those who self-identify as *blanco* (white), *longo* stands unambiguously and pejoratively for *indio*. Until perhaps twenty years ago when native Otavalans began a serious move to assert their economic power by buying up more and more prime commercial property surrounding the Poncho Plaza, which is the major attraction for international and national tourists, there were, according to nonindigenous residents, three "races" in northern Ecuador: *blancos, indios,* and *negros* (whites, indians, and blacks; for a detailed discussion see Colloredo-Mansfeld 1999; Stutzman 1981; Whitten, ed. 1981). Indigenous Otavalans added the national elitist projection of *mestizo* to the region, relegating all those self-identifying as *blanco* to the status of *mishu*, a Quichuaization of *mestizo*. It was but a short rhetorical step from *mishu* and *mestizo* to the adjective of animality or social retardation, *baboso* hybrid (*baboso* means "drooling" [or dripping]; it also means slimy and slug), and to the pejorative "*longo* with an inferiority complex." With this epithet an entire tropic inversion of *blanco* in superior relationships to *indio* as mediated by *mestizaje* is publicly constructed. The public construction of inversion provides a highly contested space for equalization in social action when people are confronted with the hard realities of a stratified system within which they strive.

From my interpretation of at least some indigenous Otavalan perspectives, an explication can be carried further to something like this: Otavalans know who they are—indigenous people; *runacuna* (fully human people); *gente* (real people); ¡*otavaleños!* Many are upwardly mobile people with no need for *blanqueamiento* (whitening) to progress. They are creators of an expanding space of indigenousness in a racist nation, and in this powerful creative process the nation is being transformed (see, e.g., Butler 2006; Colloredo-Mansfeld 1999; Meisch 1997; Salomon 1981; Wibbelsman 2009 for details on Otavalo).

To continue with the symbolic inversion in contrast to indigenous Otavalans in this explication, "*mestizos*" are part of the local social universe, but they constitute a culturally inferior part of it. They are part indigenous but with an inferiority complex that privileges *blanqueamiento* over indigenous culture and over indigenous history. *Blanqueamiento* belongs to the ideological domain of Western civilization; it is a process of cultural and biological whitening that is part and parcel of *mestizaje* processing (Torres and Whitten 1998; Whitten and Corr 2001; chapter 2, this volume). *Mestizos,* or people so categorized when placed in this context of symbolic inversion, become nothing more than inferior beings aspiring out of their stigmatized category to a racial and social status they cannot attain; this constitutes social retardation reflected in the pejorative epithet *mestizos babosos.* They have adopted a self-ascriptive hegemonic rhetoric of identity that is socially impossible to sustain.

To put this explication based on my interpretation of indigenous reflexivity in perspective, we take a radical leap "upward" in the topography of *el mestizaje* to the small and hermetically sealed space of political-economic power occupied by the Ecuadorian elite and would-be elites. We move to the realm of great wealth, self-perpetuated historical social esteem, and genealogies of power and influence.

The Elite Space of Power and Hegemony

People in the high and very small upper class divide loosely into two parts, one of which includes those who self-identify as *gente bien* or *gente de bien* (good, proper, righteous people) and also as *la sociedad* (the society; the definite article is crucial here). This elite sector constitutes part of the pinnacle of economic control, political power, and inherited social esteem. Parallel to them is another oligarchy, sometimes known as the *gente de bienes,* people of money, nouveau riche, whose position is a direct result of accumulated economic and political capital. These two sectors, *gente de bien* and *gente de bienes,* stand apart from other aspiring sectors, such as those that would be viewed as "middle class." All members of these oligarchies self-identify—and until recently were usually identified by others—as *blancos* (whites).

From these oligarchic positions emanate the concept of *el mestizaje,* the blending body of *ecuatorianidad. Mestizaje* is a projection of mixture "downward" from those who stand atop the class and ethnic pyramid. To move "upward" in wealth, power, or prestige is to engage in a process of *blanqueamiento,* "whitening." People who are moving toward the sector of economic success are sometimes known as *gente de categoría,* "prominent people."

Among themselves, elite men and women delight in using racialized or ethnicized terminology with or without diminutives for one another: *cholo, cholito,* and *cholita* (but not *chola*) and *negro, negrito, negra,* and *negrita* are not uncommon terms of address and endearment among those who share equal and very high status. Subtle references to a "tinge" (which speaker and listener know does not exist) of blackness may be alluded to within families or in-groups of the elite, such as when one is characterized as *un poco crespito* because of the curliness of his or her hair. I must stress here, though, that all elite fall within the range of their own concepts of white or very white. This sort of terminology percolates downward in class and status hierarchies, especially in Quito.

Among the elite, the terminology becomes instantly pejorative when directed to one of darker complexion or with known indigenous or black ancestry. Class mobility enters here, because those with such ancestry do not ascend by elitist definition to oligarchy status. Nor are they usually referred to as *gente de categoría*. According to elite discourse, people in the middle classes may be *la clase mestiza* or *la clase media* (the *mestizo* class or the middle class). Here, from elite perspectives, the middle class is conflated as "the *mestizo* class." The elite hegemonic imagery of *mestizaje* as forming the body of the nation—the mother *patria* (homeland) and the father *país* (country)—finds its locus in a vague concept of being in the middle sector (the solar plexus?), a space of blending or hybridity, where *blanqueamiento* in a cultural and biological sense should be taking place. The elite designations and ascriptions for what they take to be the genuine body of the country are often termed *la clase blanco-mestiza* or just *la clase media mestiza,* "white-mestizo middle class" or "the *mestizo* middle class."

Here white genes mingling with Indian genes produced a "half-breed" (*casta,* breed) race of *mestizos*. As diagrammed in chapter 1, white genes "mixed" with those of black Africans produced *mulatos,* people analogous to the cross between a horse and a donkey that produces a mule (Forbes 1993:131–220; see also Oxford English Dictionary [3rd ed., rev.]; Webster's International Dictionary [deluxe 2nd ed.]). Both of these mixtures were governed by the racist construct of "hybridity" wherein the higher status in racialist rank (the white, *blanco*) gave superior genetic stock to the lower (Indian, *indio,* or black, *negro*) to serve thereby as a "civilizing" cultural factor (Forbes 1993; Whitten 1999). Black and Indian mixes produced the *zambo,* or "black indian," a cultural status that permeates colonial accounts of dangerous people (Whitten and Corr 2001; chapter 2, this volume; Whitten et al. 1997). The danger emerges due to the lack of genetic mediation of whiteness and consequently a blend of savagery or barbarism in a conjoining of ethnic antipodes (e.g., Cabello Balboa 1945[ca. 1583]; Lane 2002; Rueda Novoa 2001a, 2001b; Savoia 1988). Please note here that I am offering my interpretation of an elitist model of racialized humanity that comes down from the sixteenth century, and is affirmed today by modern dictionaries, not my own model of "race."

We return to the so-called middle class of Ecuador below. For now we can simply say that the confusing and contradictory discourses of *mestizaje* are currently in vogue in literary and journalist circles in Ecuador, producing sets of identity referents that one author (Donoso Pareja 1998) calls "schizophrenic," while another (Jijón y Chiluisa 1997) argues in his self-styled "irreverent analysis" that "all Ecuadorians are *longos.*" To explicate something of the ethnic nuances of Ecuadorian discourse, the latter-cited author's name is a pseudonym. Jijón as in "Jijón y Caamaño" is a truly elite name, something coming out of the *gente de bien.* By changing the post-hyphen surname to Chiluisa, the author creates a socially unacceptable category by substituting an indigenous name strongly associated with poor indigenous people of Cotopaxi Province (Chiluisa) for the elite name (Caamaño). If a union between a Jijón and a Chiluisa should occur, no one would advertise the fact by adopting the hyphenated surname. Probably no clerk or political official in a parish registry office would inscribe such a surname, even if a parent brought it to him.

We now make another radical leap from the elite *blanco/a* identity system to the racialized space where *lo negro* (blackness) is salient.

A Black Space of Tentative Power and Cultural Counterhegemony

Penetrating statements about *mestizaje* emanate from specific locales where, by national stereotypes, "blackness" taints the province: Esmeraldas on the north coast and the Chota-Mira Valley of Carchi and Imbabura in the northern Andes. Black people live all over Ecuador, with sizable populations in Quito and especially Guayaquil. People from these urban centers wonder why they are asked whether they are from Esmeraldas or the Chota-Mira Valley. The answer lies in the pejorative localization of blackness in the topography of Ecuadorian ideology, wherein black people are, or should be, restricted to their proper place, to their rural villages in either Esmeraldas or Imbabura-Carchi (Rahier 1998, 1999, 2003). When people are regarded as *fuera de su lugar,* "out of their place," they are regarded as analogous to dirt (Colloredo-Mansfeld 1999:57–86).

Let us take the restricted space of a small park in the city of Esmeraldas, capital of the province of Esmeraldas. There, people who could be represented by the above paradigm as *negro/a, mulato/a, zambo/a,* or *moreno/a* but who uniformly now identify as *negro/a, moreno/a,* or *afroecuatoriano/a* gather daily in a small park that they have named Mandela. Prominent in their highly localized discourses are tropic analyses of Ecuadorian elitist racialized hegemonies as these are manifest in stereotypes that directly affect the quality of blackness (*lo negro*). For example, a common discourse revolves around the trope *mejorar la raza,* "to improve the race," which refers to cultural orientations and to phenotypic features. The park-goers counter this with *hacer valer la raza,* "to validate the race" (to assert one's right to one's "race"). By this is meant that blackness, for dark people and for all other people, is to be of worth, of value, and it is quite clear in their own explications that discriminatory language at all levels, including those of lampoons and ironies in newspapers, magazines, and especially television, must end. They seek, they say, an end to the interminable symbolic container of *mestizaje,* because of its implied "whitening" in upward mobility and its clear deprecation of those who are "tainted" with the stains (*manchas*) of indigenous or African darkness in culture as in phenotype (Colloredo-Mansfeld 1999; Whitten and Quiroga 1998).

One of the most powerful counterhegemonic tropes to come out of these discourses and make its way into the mass media, into academic symposia, and even to the floor of the national legislature is *rescate de la dignidad nacional,* "the rescue of national dignity." This first emerged on January 30, 1988, during the formal establishment of La Asociación de Negros del Ecuador (ASONE, the Association of Blacks of Ecuador). This rescue is that of a dignity of *la nación, el estado, el gobierno, el país, la patria,* and even *la clase dirigente* (the class that directs; those in political power, the ruling class) that cannot exist while racism prevails. All cherished entities and even the disliked powers of Ecuador, by this analysis, lack dignity, and hence the homeland lacks it too. Without dignity Ecuador suffers as an infirm social body and as a dysfunctional nation.

El mestizaje, the blending body of *ecuatorianidad,* from this perspective, defeats all attempts of multicultural accommodation and respect for difference. Without respect for national cultural and phenotypic diversity, as this tropic analysis goes, the nation is deprived of its dignity. The elitist theme of *mestizaje* from this perspective renders the nation tainted in its physical and cultural makeup. We are reminded now of our earlier quote:

> Meztizos babosos no son blancos. Solo son longos acomplejados.

Earlier, I explicated this epithet from my interpretation (based on the work of many other scholars and indigenous spokespersons) of the inverse symbolism and reflexivity of an indigenous, Otavalan, collective perspective. I treated it as an epitome of symbolic inversion. But to those who read the inscription, it was not clear who authored it. For some, at least, attribution to indigenous Otavalans was too facile; the attribution lacked the intrigue of Ecuadorian micro-political action. To begin with, *mestizos* was spelled "*meztizos.*" Jerome Windmeyer (University of Leiden) and other researchers told Michelle Wibbelsman, who was carrying out a study of ritual performance and representation in several communities there, that a local *mestizo* could have written this with the intent of presenting indigenous people as racist, thereby discrediting them at a time when the indigenous economic, political, and social spaces were expanding rapidly. When social inversion is occurring, it behooves those in the category being inverted to strike back.

The misspelling in the graffiti by this interpretation would be so placed as to make it appear that a poorly educated indigenous person was to blame. The syntagma of poverty, indigenous, illiterate, racist (and even dirty; see Colloredo-Mansfeld 1999), and resistant coalesces here, and supposedly, in this analysis (which I take to be far-fetched), indigenous space of integrity contracts in regional perspectives. The "misspelling" goes further. When some Ecuadorians extend a trope such as "drooling," they may speak as though the drool itself was interfering with their pronunciation. Here *mestizo* would be rendered "*meztizo*" so that the negative inverted power of *meztizo baboso*, as drooling (and thereby unable to speak clearly) hybrid person, is indicated.

The graffiti also fits the black inversion of *mestizaje*. Ambiguity over what possible sector of northern Ecuador may have generated the graffiti perpetuates the conflictive discourse that permeates the ontology of nationwide *mestizaje* discourses, counterdiscourses, or their silences. Let us make another radical leap from explication of vulgar graffiti to the space of academic discourse. We move to an urbane place where scholars and learned writers assemble to come to grips with the subject of "understanding racism: the Ecuadorian case."

Theatrical Spaces of Controversy

On November 18, 1998, the UNICEF-funded symposium sponsored by FLACSO, the Facultad Latinoamericana de Ciencias Sociales, Quito, entitled "Entender el Racismo: El Caso de Ecuador" (Understanding Racism: The Ecuadorian Case) opened with a panel of journalists, mediated by two social scientists, who discussed whether or not racism exists in Ecuador. As expected by the audience, the speakers referred to themselves as *mestizo*, "mixed," although mixed toward the white end of the white–light brown spectrum. One prominent speaker alluded to himself as "*mestizo pero pintadito con la brochita blanquita*," *mestizo* but painted with the little white brush (note all the diminutives). What was not expected was the audience reaction. Quickly, one after another of the black people present—about thirty-five in all among an audience of more than one hundred—rose to address the enduring syntagma in which *blanqueamiento* and the endeavor to *mejorar la raza* generated such pejorative stereotypes as *mestizo pero un poco morenito* (*mestizo* but a little on the dark side) unless one were *negro* and hence, by the Ecuadorian criterion of enduring contrast, *bien negrito* or *negro azul* (very black or blue black). (For a discussion of the use of the Spanish diminutive in discourses of whiteness and blackness, see Whitten and Torres, eds. 1998.)

For the indigenous people present—about twenty of the one hundred—the issue was cultural discrimination and sociopolitical exclusion, the lack of national respect for differences, and the rude attitudes of the *mishus*. The topography of the Ecuadorian *razas* became rough as discussants entered a dangerous and near-threatening terrain. There was an Afro-Ecuadorian–Indigenous-Ecuadorian unity, however, in audience reaction, because those from the black sector and those from the indigenous sector were roundly denouncing *mestizaje* while the journalists and "others" in the audience defended it.

While black and indigenous people talked past each other, the former stressing color prejudice, the latter lack of respect for distinct indigenous cultures, those of the opening panel manifested increasing astonishment at the polarized discourse that had taken on theatrical qualities (black and indigenous on one side, the panelists as proponents of a nation of *mestizos* on the other). The indigenous and black people voiced their unity in opposing the ideology and praxis of *mestizaje*. This unity resounded with a consensus of rejection of the journalistic positions and an accusation that the journalist fraternity of Ecuador kept people of color out of the media, while strategically utilizing the pejorative concepts of "*raza*" to diminish the inherent value of blackness and indigenousness. The response of the journalists was that if there were no black or indigenous writers in the country, it was due to lack of ability. The polarization widened, as "ignorant" was implied as an adjective for both black and indigenous people (there are, in fact, many black and indigenous authors in Ecuador, but very few journalists).

Finally, in frustration, but with levity in the midst of a rather heavy confrontation, one prominent journalist began demonstrating his versatility with such tropes as *lo que no tiene del inga tiene de mandinga,* "that which is not of the Inca is of the Mandinga" (see, e.g., Cornejo 1974). Coming from the coastal city of Guayaquil, the journalist was proud of his ability to lampoon the various "mixtures" that he perceived as constituting a substantial field of phenotypes and cultural orientations. Basically, he implied, those people without indian blood (Inga) have black blood (Mandinga). They surely are not white! They are all hybrids. He did not use the first-person singular or plural in his representations. He was not speaking of his identity, or the identity of others, in his racialized topological space; he was speaking of *los otros,* "the others," not of *nosotros,* "ourselves."

Two other phrases that he delighted in were *quien no toca la flauta, toca el tambor* (who doesn't play the flute [*indio*] plays the drum [*negro*]) and *¿y tu abuela 'onde e'tá?* (and your grandmother, where is she?, meaning "you may not look black but [the speaker knows] you descend from blackness") (see Torres 1998).[4] Why this journalist chose this opportunity to display his knowledge of these tropes is far from clear. It appeared that he wished to amuse his fellow panelists and those not of indigenous or Afro-Ecuadorian background in the audience with populist refrains. His remarks, however, created and sustained an aura of growing tensions—disturbed racial terrains—and aggressively projected a negation of ethnic dignity onto more than half of the audience. He certainly widened the ethnic spaces to re-create an elitist topology of racialized exclusion (see Whitten 1999). The theatrical polarity of multiculturality for the indigenous people and Afro-Ecuadorian people in opposition to *mestizaje* ideology and rhetoric came to dominate the "discussion" part of the evening conference.

Social Praxis and Symbolic Inversion

When we move in the topography of Ecuadorian racialized culture to indigenous sectors, we encounter sustained pragmatic social action in public spheres. The first Levantamiento Indígena in Ecuador's modern history occurred in June 1990 (see Whitten 1996b; chapter 4, this volume). The Spanish trope *levantamiento indígena* was used by indigenous people and others to connote a "rising up" in a spiritual as well as physical sense. It implied a heightened consciousness of the repressive world in which they live. Most journalists and people from upper sectors who chose to publicly comment, however, referred to it as *alzamiento indio*, an indian revolt. *Alzamiento*, as in *indios alzados* or *negros alzados* (indians out of control or blacks out of control), refers to actions of people getting out of place, lacking consciousness, and acting in an unruly manner. There is no trope in the Spanish language that could be presented as *blancos alzados*. Only black people and indigenous people (and animals, such as in a cattle stampede) can be so categorized and stereotyped. The first Levantamiento Indígena was triggered by an indigenous sit-in in the Santo Domingo church in Quito, but the uprising, once under way, did not touch the capital city. Quiteños, however, witnessed the "taking" of some Sierran cities on national network television.

After a second uprising in specific sectors of the Sierra in 1994, July 1999 bore witness to the third Levantamiento Indígena in Ecuador's history. This uprising, unlike the first two, fused indigenous demands for national transformation with working-class demands for specific economic reforms and restorations. A new millennial body of diverse people was forming and enacting a new sense of transformed *ecuatorianidad*. Significant events included the cutting of all communications in Ambato, the Andean link between coastal and Amazonian lands, and between the northern and southern Andes, and the "taking" of Quito and other cities by an estimated ten thousand native peoples—men, women, and children—most wielding ten- to twelve-foot-long defensive staffs. Foremost in the rhetoric of the leaders of the "taking" of Quito was the stress on the peaceful nature of the urban occupation, in contrast to the epistemic and social violence of the government in maintaining a political-economic structure to the detriment of indigenous people, Afro-Ecuadorian people, and poor working unemployed people of many walks of life and ethnic origins.

The fourth Levantamiento Indígena occurred in conjunction with a military coup resulting in the ouster of President Jamil Mahuad Witt. This event has become known as *el golpe del 21*, "the coup of the twenty-first." The name commemorates January 21, 2000, when the military and police guarding the legislative palace parted to allow thousands of indigenous people (and others) to "take" the governing body of the nation. Many of these guards were former Heroes of Cenepa, fighting men who had defeated Peru to claim a major military victory for Ecuador. A salient feature of the *golpe del 21* was that officers of the Ecuadorian military, when ordered to use *la mano dura* (literally, heavy hand, or military force, but in context, killing force) against the *indios,* disobeyed the order because, their leaders said, these were "Ecuadorian people." What happened next is history recorded not only in books, periodicals, and newspapers but also in videos (e.g., CONAIE 2000; Dieterich 2000; Hernández et al. 2000; Lucas 2000a, 2000b; Mendoza Poveda 2001; Ponce 2000; Selmeski 2000; D. Whitten 2003).

For two and a half hours, a junta—known as the Junta de Salvación Nacional (the junta of national salvation)—ruled Ecuador. It was composed of army colonel Lucio Gutiérrez, CONAIE (Confederation of Indigenous Nationalities of Ecuador) president Antonio Vargas, ex–supreme court justice Carlos Solórzano, and, shortly after its formation, military general Carlos Mendoza Poveda. For the first time in Ecuador's history, an indigenous person—Carlos Antonio Vargas Guatatuca—assumed a role at the pinnacle of executive power in the republic (Dieterich 2000; Hernández et al. 2000; Lucas 2000a, 2000b; Mendoza Poveda 2001; D. Whitten 2003).

The fifth Levantamiento Indígena, also known as *el paro indígena* (the indigenous strike), took place in February 2001. Again led by Antonio Vargas, then third-term president of CONAIE, the uprising lasted more than two weeks and ended only when the government of Gustavo Noboa Bejarano, who assumed the presidency from his position of vice president the day after the *golpe del 21,* agreed to twenty-three separate points including, as first and foremost, to reduce the price of cylinders of gas and not to increase the price of diesel fuel and gasoline. Many of the rest of the agreed-to demands revolved around increasing the economic opportunities for indigenous people, marginal people, and poor people, including expansion of the Consejo de Desarrollo de los Pueblos y Nacionalidades del Ecuador (CODENPE; Council of Development for the People and Nationalities of Ecuador), which is the organization established after the election of Abdalá Bucaram Ortiz to promote opportunities for the progress of indigenous and black Ecuadorians. Nothing concrete was decided on the economic front as it affected indigenous people, black people, rural people, or others, except that representatives of *el gobierno* would discuss matters with representatives of *el pueblo,* beginning in March 2001. The discussion continued sporadically. This theme is picked up briefly in the conclusion of this book to bring the situation up to date through 2010.

The three *levantamientos* (1998, 1999, 2000) prior to the 2001 strike were supported by unions whose members and sympathizers blocked all major roads of every city and town. These actions forcefully conjoined indigenous people, rural people, and working-class people in large-scale collaborative movements heretofore unknown in Ecuador's history.

The 2001 Levantamiento, like the first in 1990, was clearly indigenous, almost to the point of ethnic autonomy of collective action. Both of these indigenous uprisings made a sustained statement about *el pueblo unido* against *el gobierno* (the united people against the paternalistic but corrupt government). Salient concepts of nationality such as *la nación, el (padre) país, la (madre) patria,* were voiced everywhere and within these constructs was embedded the emphasis on *multiculturalidad* and *multinacionalidad* as synonymous with *ecuatorianidad.* The one concept that did not receive attention anywhere was that of *el mestizaje,* the blending. People united and they respected one another. They did not "blend" or become "embodied" into some malleable middle sector. Diversity was respected and even intensified throughout.

The common chant "*el pueblo, unido, jamás será vencido*" (united people will never be conquered) carried absolutely no connotations whatsoever of "blended people." Unity was found in diversity and mutual respect for this very diversity. As Dr. Luis Macas, former president of CONAIE and the first indigenous national legislator elected in 1996, put it in his presentation on September 7, 2001, at the Latin American Studies Association Meeting in Washington, D.C.: "*estamos unidos pero no revueltos*" (we are united, but not scrambled).

Ritual and Political Spaces of Counterhegemony

In April–May 1992, a protest march of indigenous Amazonian people began in Puyo, the capital of Pastaza Province, and ended in a prolonged campout in El Ejido Park in Quito. As the drama of this highly dangerous ethnic-cultural performance unfolded, striking resemblances were noted by marchers and outsiders to the north Andean Corpus Christi ritual called "Yumbada." These events have been described in published works elsewhere (Salomon 1981; Whitten 1988; Whitten, ed. 1981; N. Whitten and D. Whitten 2008; Whitten et al. 1997), as has the first Levantamiento Indígena of 1990 (chapter 4, this volume), which clearly established an active, political space of indigenousness and indigenous people within the nation-state of Ecuador. In each macro upheaval—the first Levantamiento, the Caminata, and the third, fourth, and fifth Levantamientos—as in the Yumbada ritual and other comparable festivals and rituals, the ideology of *mestizaje* is dismissed and the concept of Ecuador as an *estado* or *país* or *nación de multinacionaldades* is (or was) affirmed.

By 1992 and subsequently (but not constantly and not consistently), large numbers of nonindigenous, nonblack Ecuadorians cheered on the embattled native people. They brought them food and drink and united with them against the *gobierno*, viewed in each case by the supporters as paternalistic but corrupt. The numbers of self-identifying *ecuatorianos* who vigorously supported indigenous peoples seemed to increase in 2000 and 2001. Again, this intense uniting of Ecuadorians from different ethnicities carried no representation of *mestizaje*. While many Ecuadorians through the early 2000s have been quite uncomfortable with the concept of nationalities (*nacionalidades*), most today seem to accept the cognate concept of *multiculturalidad* (multiculturality), and the idea of Ecuador as a state of multiple nationalities is now not only accepted but also written into the constitution of 1998 and strengthened in the new constitution of 2008. Constitutionally, Ecuador is now an "intercultural" and a "plurinational" state (see the translation of the opening words to the 2008 constitution given in the introduction to this book, p. 6).

Where then does the ideology of *el mestizaje* reside in Ecuador's racialized social topography? Can this racialized topography be mapped? As stated above, the concept continues to emanate from the very small and very powerful elite sector, which is, to repeat, hermetically sealed in its hegemonic imagery of "blending" for the body of the republic that exists "under" them in "lower" statuses. It is also manifest within military training barracks and bases (with some notable exceptions) and finds a highly ambiguous locus among students in such universities as the Catholic University and the Central University of Quito.

An Expanding Space of Resignifications or Contradictions: Nationalism and Racism

It would seem that, in 2001—the new millennium—the ambiguous but recognized (or re-cognized) space of *mestizaje* is being confronted constantly by that of multiculturality. The character of this confrontation, however, is anything but clear. In spite of the location of the fount of *mestizaje* ideology within the elite sector, the contrast is not one of elite/others. There are too many complications. The hegemony of *blanqueamiento* down through history has had its profound effects. Across the class and ethnic lines of many walks of life in modern Ecuador, rhetoric of *indio, negro,* and *mestizo* has long been deployed, often in pejorative manners, particularly in contexts of economic competition. Racialized tropes used by those in a favored economic position vis-à-vis their competitors are many: *indio, negro, mulato, mestizo, chagra* (rural bumpkin indigene or *mestizo*), *cholo* (crude term for *mestizo*), *chulla* (smooth and slippery lower-class urbanite with rural characteristics), *longo, mono* (monkey, coastal person), *mocho* (half *mono* and half *longo*), *montuvio* (person from Manabí or Guayas province, unruly coastal person), and even *moti* and *pescao* (hominy for Andeans and fish for coastals). Individually and collectively, they reinforce the structure of racism in modern, nationalist Ecuador. As Ronald Stutzman (1981) argued convincingly over two decades ago, "*mestizaje* is an all-inclusive ideology of exclusion." When "plural-cultural" or "plural-national" is used within a framework of *mestizaje,* the paradoxical trope connotes the bringing of the "races" together as distinct "nationalities," but not as social constructions still cast as "racial groups" in the process of *blanqueamiento*.

Since 1999 some journalists have argued for adopting the common term *indigenous* (*indígena*) for "all" Ecuadorians, reserving the pejorative *indio* for the indigenous people heretofore identified and represented in nationalist space as *indígenas*. This rhetorical stratagem would, in effect, substitute *indigenous* for *mestizo,* and leave the "primary races" in their fixed colonial categorical positions. The pejorative terminology radiating from the middle class, whose economic situation is worsening, is confronted everywhere in offensive epithets hurled in self-defense by ethnically separated peoples. These include, among many others, *blanco mesquinador, blanco enganchador, blancura basura, mishu manavali, mestizo baboso, mestizo de mierda, mashca pupu, cibulla sicucta, chupa sangres,* and many more. These terms are symbolically charged and vary considerably in the meaning conveyed, but a cryptic translation of this list would include "white mess-maker," "white enslaver," "white trash," "no good *mestizo*," "drooling *mestizo*," "shitty *mestizo*," "barley gut," "onion ass" (or "onion balls"), and "bloodsucker." This is the domain of street language, the language that is used as graffiti—*malas palabras,* dirty words. It further contextualizes our vulgar epigraph:

> Meztizos babosos no son blancos. Solo son longos acomplejados

Terms such as those given above in the first set (*indio, negro, mestizo, longo*) are used as epithets in the loosely constructed middle class, where they constitute a system of epistemic violence (Taussig 1987) that defines lines of conflict that can be transcended by creating new lines of conflict, or identifying fields of contradiction. Of late, the lines of conflict have been most effective when those at the antipodes of the elitist and hegemonic nationalist paradigm of *el mestizaje* confront those at the pinnacle of power, economic wherewithal, and social esteem, and when they are enjoined in such confrontation by aspiring, socioeconomically lower-middle-class activists, students, teachers, and unionists. Such class consciousness, or at least collective class enactment, treats the powerful as the enemy of the nation, and in the name of the "homeland" (*la patria*), a call for their "expulsion" from office is often made.

In 1997 such a confrontation occurred. Native peoples, Afro-Ecuadorians, and others of the aspiring classes—all collectively self-identifying as *ecuatorianos,* with no overtones of *mestizaje*—joined together against the president and his policies. They were buttressed by the power of the congress and by a unified press, and, at the crucial moment, by the military, to force the president of the republic, Abdalá Bucaram Ortiz, out of office and out of Ecuador to exile in Panama. In 1999, a scant two years later, the combined strike of many social sectors and a third national indigenous uprising had as one of its goals the ouster of President Jamil Mahuad Witt. Within the rhetoric attendant on these movements of presidential ouster and transformation of the nation-state, the term *clase* became especially salient. People in all walks of life called for the end of the "*clase política*" and the "*clase dirigente*" (the political class and the directing ["leading," "ruling"] class). Each of these tropes refers to the same people, depicted as "the class that lives off politics," which is the same as "the directing class" (the class that "directs" the nation, the economy, the formation of policy, the execution of policy). As noted above, Mahuad was ousted in the *golpe del 21* in 2000, and a subsequent extended Levantamiento or the strike of 2001 seems to have accomplished multiple goals while maintaining the strong contra force to "the directing class."

These national and nationalist collective movements require us to consider nationalism and its relationships to racism. Benedict Anderson, in his second edition of *Imagined Communities,* writes: "Nationalism thinks in terms of historical destinies, while racism dreams of eternal contaminations transmitted from the origins of time through an endless sequence of loathsome copulations: outside history" (Anderson 1991[1983]:149). According to Michael Herzfeld, whose cultural reifications may be instructive when combined with those of Anderson,

> The nation-state is ideologically committed to ontological self-perpetuation for all eternity. While it may seek to embrace technological or even social change ... it maintains to the semiotic illusion of cultural fixity and may well try to impose a static morality on others ... The technology for the construction of this timelessness pragmatically connects a mythological notion of pure origins with respect for perfect social and cultural form; innovations are coopted by being treated as the realization of an eternal essence. (Herzfeld 1997:21)

In *Cultural Intimacy,* Herzfeld's ultimate hypostasis with regard to what he calls "social poetics" is that "cultures have national boundaries." To this I would add (Whitten 1999) that in Ecuador, and elsewhere in the Americas, cultures have socially constructed racialized boundaries. When nationalism in its essentialist and epochalist dimensions (see Geertz 1973; also Herzfeld 1997; Whitten 2003c) is challenged within the global economy, as is the case in Ecuador today, then the national boundaries and the racialist boundaries clash.

La Familia and *"Las Razas"*

The epigraph to chapter 2 from Sir Edmund Leach, which states the power of "naming" and thereby framing people, resonates with the analysis of Trouillot (1995:115). Leach was referring to the *indio/a* trope, but we could equally well refer to that of *negro/a* as it emerged in the mid-fifteenth century in Africa and Iberia (Berlin 1996; Forbes 1993; Jurado Noboa 1995; Moreno 1997, 1999; Russell-Wood 1995; Thornton 1995, 1998a, 1998b; Wynter 1995; chapter 1, this volume). *El mestizaje,* as racial or ethnic "hybridizing," constitutes a fundamental proposition in the networks and lattices of blood relationships in the nation-state. Nevertheless, the people classified, socially constructed, or named or referenced as "*indio/a*" and "*negro/a*" exist in the same national rhetoric as manifestations of biological beings—imagined beings and real social beings—in families, households, communities, and regions, and at national levels, from which emanate ontological and ideological affirmations and negations. Both the affirmations and the negations mark what Leach (1982) called the beginning of moral sanctions, and they led Trouillot (1995:115) to write that "names set up a field of power." The field of inclusive *mestizaje* ideology, with the power of "whiteness" that it both reveals and obscures, incorporates the paradigm of ethnic exclusion of named racializations, the most salient and exclusive of which are *indio/a* and *negro/a*.

We turn now to the Ecuadorian concept of *la familia,* which is one of the most salient social constructs of political-economic and social mobility. The concept shares an ontological construction in many sectors of complex Ecuadorian social structure. Within the intimacy of *la familia,* in Ecuador, whether among the elite or the aspiring classes (upper-middle, middle, working), reference to and representation of various nuances of social being, in racialist terms, abound. *Familias* in this sense are personal kindreds and stem kindreds (e.g., Arensberg and Kimball 1940; Whitten 1965, 1974) of considerable ramification. People reckon from multiple perspectives just what their ties are and the ways by which those ties can be acknowledged through intimacy and in the broader contexts of quotidian life in a system that, for the middle sectors, is characterized by both fluid class boundaries and fluidity of boundary transcendence through upward and downward mobility.

It is within families that one hears, in intimate conversations that clearly convey moral sanctions, strategic use of pejorative terminology, used somewhat "endearingly" but also as a warning. From the *un poco crespito* trope for a person with slightly kinky hair—here, unlike the elite usage, connoting a tainted ancestry—to little ditties such as "*rojo con verde matita de ají, solo las cholas se visten así*" (figuratively, red and green hotly blended, only the *cholas* dress this way; which refers to bad mixtures of colors in one's dress that "only *cholas*" [roughly, market women; Weismantel 2001] wear), we find mini-representations of the macro system of Ecuadorian racialized or ethnicized tropes, all of which, ironically, fall into the general elite category of *mestizaje*. A family member who dresses in a manner taken by the teens to be off the *de modo* mark may be chided with the reference of *chagra,* a rural bumpkin connected to the soil, not far from a stereotypical image of indigenous life. Again, with regard to clothing, a family member might say "*¡qué chagra!*" (what a bumpkin!, how rural!) to indicate dress that suggests a "throwback" to premobility status of the kindred. Family language ramifies through peer groups from early periods into college, and into the founding of new affinal families who, through transformed terminology, perpetuate the application of moral sanctions.

The language of casual chastisement within families often draws from Quichua, pidgin Quichua, or Chaupilengua morphs. The Quichua *wambra,* "youth," is sometimes used to designate or stigmatize a child who is dirty, as in *wambra mocoso,* "snot-nosed kid." Another example would be *wawashimi,* from the Quichua "baby talk," or *wawashina,* which means "baby-like" or "brat." *Carishina* chastises a "woman who is like a man" as an insult to a woman who manifests aggressive behavior. "Racialized" or "Quichuaized" (the latter being "indianized," as in *longo*) language used to describe characteristics of individuals within families may draw from Quichua or Chaupilengua terms—and the meaning of these terms may or may not be known by the speaker—to suggest undesirable, negatively ascriptive characteristics mapped onto a transparent and pejorative category *indio*.

We return now to the "macro" or nationalist interpretation that leads to the contradiction of a collective body of *el mestizaje*. To "be" *mestizo* represents an ontology that is rejected roundly by those whose mobility involves indigenousness. Such indigenousness is all too often suggested by the pejorative terminology sketched above, which itself is, perhaps ironically, part of the broader picture of *mestizaje* in its exclusionist dimensions.

To take a leap from the micro to the macro, over a decade ago I argued (Whitten 1999) that the transformation of socially constructed hypostatic biological antipodes as *"las razas"* syncretized with the hegemony of nationalist identity in the nineteenth century. The conquest and colonial mentality of distinct "races" fused with nationalist rhetoric of cultural circumscription in manners that were quite impossible socially though quite convincing rhetorically to power wielders. *El mestizaje,* the political body of nationalist modernity in Gran Colombia, and later in Ecuador, Colombia, and Venezuela, fused with the conquest and colonial mentality to create distinct cultures within a discourse of "foundational racialized contrasts." The resulting circumscription and cultural hermetics, or elitist intimacy—the structure of *nosotros*—fused with the nationalist ideology, based on conquest and colonial mentality, to generate again and again a persistent cultural structure of hypostatic racialized contrast—the structure of *los otros*—and, in this way, we encounter the generative fount of racist rhetoric that represents those "named" as *indios* and *negros* in opposition to the interminable genesis of the *mestizo* vis-à-vis the process of *blanqueamiento*.

Within *familias,* oscillation of representations and identities between racialized reference points—however nuanced they may be—within a continuum of intimacies, clarifies and/or obfuscates social constructs of *nosotros* and *los otros,* us and the others. In a given family, people may all be *"mestizos"* according to elite rhetoric; and most or many of them may regard themselves as *blancos* according to upwardly mobile class-bound criteria. But family members may also treat one another as slightly ahead or behind the *blanqueamiento* identity or representational processing: some are too far ahead, taking on "airs"; others lag, as *longos* or *chagras* (or even *cholo-longo*). Here we encounter the contemporary genesis of continued reenactment of racialist thought, which reaches its pinnacle with the reification of all of the ambiguities of *mestizaje*.

Transformations and Reproductions

Today, in modernizing and millennial Ecuador, the elite adhere to the pure essence of Iberian descent for themselves and espouse a lightening model of *el mestizaje* for the aspirants in the upper-middle, middle-class hierarchy, where fluidity of movement is matched by the relative fluidity of economic, status, and political-arena boundaries. Looking at modern Amazonia for dramatic immediacy we quickly find the following millennial phenomenon: indigenous people in Amazonia now clamor to enrich their ethnic space by legislating a new fixity of Amazonian territory (they won 1,115,574 hectares in 1992 after the March for Land and Life), a fixity that could require removal of all petroleum companies, all timber companies, and all agricultural developmental agencies. This essentialist ethnogenetic reaffirmation of native Amazonian space confronts the nationalist and nation-state's need for financial revenues that come heavily from this geographic zone (N. Whitten and D. Whitten 2008). This recent movement again raises the specter of frontal conflict in Amazonia, at the very time when the sovereignty of the Ecuadorian military there is being challenged by Colombian guerrilla and paramilitary expansion and expansionism and by the U.S. political-military hegemony of Plan Colombia and its (previous) military base of the Southern Command in Manta (chapter 5, this volume).

To be black in modern Ecuador can be dangerous. After the assassination of black Esmeraldan congressman Jaime Hurtado and his two bodyguards in 1998 in front of the legislative palace, and the subsequent accusations of his alleged linkages with the Fuerzas Armadas Revolucionarias de Colombia (FARC), the Ecuadorian military occupied the black areas of the interior of Esmeraldas Province, especially the Ónzole River region. In this occupation, an association was made between an unconfirmed accusation of a congressman's involvement with radical Colombian politics and an Ecuadorian region known for its "blackness" and its "remoteness." In the face of this military action, publicly espoused blackness, as ideological *négritud,* retreated into local and regional discussion groups.

South of Esmeraldas Province, *costeños* (coastal people) in all walks of life, of all classes, and of all ethnic sectors—who collectively constitute slightly over half the population of the nation—have on several occasions over the past few years burned the Quito flag and threatened secession from the nation. In such movements, the call goes out for the return of Abdalá Bucaram from his exile in Panama as savior of the nation or as savior of coastal dignity contra the Quiteño elite and political class.

In the Andes, indigenous leaders regard themselves as "ready" (*listo, shayana,* or *jatari*) to rise up as one indigenous body to join with any group in ousting the paternalistic *gobierno* and its entrenched political class and to reform the republic on a model of horizontal, community-based, semi-autonomous "indigenous" organizations. The above is offered to indicate something of the internal conflicts within modern Ecuador before returning to an extended explication of the topology of *mestizaje*.

Mestizaje and Multiculturalism: Corporate Symbol and Social Enactments

What we can say about topographies and topologies of race is that the doctrine of *mestizaje,* silent though it may be at times in public discourse, certainly competes with multiculturality in many spaces and arenas. A glance at the books and scholarly chapters recently written on the subject of *mestizaje* in Ecuador and in sister countries underscores its enduring quality and ideological tenacity (see especially Donoso Pareja 1998 and Espinosa Apolo 1997).

Mestizaje ideology is most evident in elite discourse about the body of the nation. This discourse ramifies from time to time through journalistic circles, particularly when indigenous and Afro-Ecuadorian people raise issues about their mutual exclusion. In middle-class, social-economically aspiring kindreds, we find intrafamilial application of verbal sanctions by use of references to the alleged vulgarity of *mestizaje,* illustrated here by such concepts as *longo, chagra,* and *cholo.* These familial references and verbal sanctions are part of the peer-group systems of high-school and college students.

The resulting paradigms offer conflicting models of resignifications and contradictions of everything discussed above. *Mestizaje* certainly exists as a national emblem and as a nationalist trope. But the trope is sometimes silent, as it is today in most sectors where confrontational drama exists. Silence nonetheless may be salient (e.g., Trouillot 1995). Multiculturality becomes ascendant in national and regional contested arenas when classist and indigenous interests overthrow, for a while, elitist and developmentalist strategies and plans. We are reminded here of Michael Taussig's statement: "From the represented shall come that which overturns the representation" (Taussig 1987:135). In 2001, near the Avenida de los Granados, where CONAIE has its headquarters, this piece of graffiti appeared:

> *Indios luchando, Quiteños bailando* (indians fighting [joining in a struggle for rights], Quiteños dancing [engaging in festive or frivolous activity]). (CONAIE 2000)

Michelle Wibbelsman (personal communication 2001), reflecting on these issues from Otavalo, put it this way:

> I would add that from the representers have come the instruments of their own downfall. The actions of indigenous people during these [2001] marches and their ongoing efforts to improve the national situation, not only for themselves as an ethnic group but for all Ecuadorians, have begun to cast off the epithets of "lazy, ignorant indians." We now have "*Quiteños bailando*," disinterested, lazy, frivolous, not participating in these momentous political and social struggles, and "*indios luchando*," negotiating solutions for current crises across the board, offering informed, long and short-term economic, social and political proposals, physically enduring the marches and dangerous confrontations with police and the military.

To go back in time before the public indigenous movements of the late 1990s and early 2000s, symbolic processes of ritual and rhetorical inversion were well under way. Around 1984 the indigenous movement came forth with the Imperial Inca greeting *ama llulla, ama shua, ama quilla,* "don't lie, don't steal, don't be lazy." With this emblematic trope they hit verbally on the "governing class" wherein rampant corruption was, and is, publicized nearly daily by the media. The graffiti above, *indios luchando, Quiteños bailando,* underscores the dynamics of symbolic reversal and inversion, particularly when conjoined with the prevarication, theft, and reluctance to carry out socially beneficial projects that those in power manifest.

Another phrase that came out of the 2000 Levantamiento that ousted President Mahuad in the *golpe del 21* is this:

> *El poder es un instrumento que permite cristalizar los sueños de los pueblos* (power is an instrument that lets the dreams of the people crystallize). (Salvador Quishpe Lozano, Ecuadorian indigenous leader, *El Comercio,* February 20, 2000)

From the power of the state and the corrupt forces of *el gobierno,* Quishpe takes us to the dreams of the people. A *sueño* in Quichua is a *muscui,* in this context an image of the desirable, a future value that might be attained through collective social action. This is a truly millennial statement; its rhetoric represents a total reversal of Ecuadorian institutional (or structural; see Wolf 1999) power. By *millennial* here I do not refer to the classic definitions of *millennial* as the change of the millennium or the second coming of Christ.

Rather, these medieval Western ideas are transformed into the historical and modern Quichua concept of *pachacutij*, the transformation out of an unhealthy present to a healthy future reminiscent of, but certainly not identical to, a one-time healthy past (see Whitten 2003c).

In 2001 yet another slogan emerged to contribute to the processes of symbolic inversion:

> *El pueblo también dispara* (the people also shoot [figuratively, the people strike back])

Here symbolism again converts to a call for collective social action. Those engaged in goal-oriented sociosymbolic action assert themselves as *el pueblo*—the people—in their diversity. This assertion is especially evident in the trope used as the title of a recent book, *Nada solo para los indios* (Acosta et al. 2001), "nothing only for the indians." What this means is that what indigenous and other people acting to remake the world do is for *all* people, not just for those undertaking the transformative enactments. This completes, for now, the explication of symbolic inversion with which I began this essay. The people of Ecuador, led at times in the 1990s and early 2000s by those who self-identify as *indígena*—and at times in public discourse as *indio*—have turned the tables on the perpetrators of the blending *mestizaje* ideology. They assert themselves as *el pueblo,* the people, united in their diversity. The new millennium of Ecuador is perhaps transforming out of a past modernity of ethnic and class oppression.

In closing this chapter, I simply want to say that the significata of both *mestizaje* and multiculturalism (as *multinacionalidad,* multinationalism) compete today in modern Ecuador and both multivocalic metatropes—which sometimes serve as polarizing symbols and sometimes as condensing symbols (e.g., Turner 1973, 1974)—constitute the emblematic stuff from which fragmented and localized discourses generating social contradictions emanate. From those contradictions, as explained long ago by Africanist social anthropologist Max Gluckman (e.g., 1958, 1962, 1965), come sustained, collective action at regional and national levels. This collective action, in turn, rotates on the respect for diversity created out of processes of ethnogenesis and sustained through the dynamics of symbolic inversion that contribute to the formation of alliance structures that, in turn, stress perceived horizontal social relationships for the common good of *el pueblo.* Who is to be identified as *el pueblo* at any given event, in any given context, in any specific arena, during the contemporary conjuncture, depends, in part, on the ways by which the macrotropes of *el mestizaje* and *multinacionalidad* play out on the stages of millennial transformation now ongoing in the Republic of Ecuador.

Acknowledgments

Michelle Wibbelsman extended considerable assistance during the development of this chapter, including information on the Otavalan opening graffiti and the various ambiguities involved in its interpretation and explication. She also provided insights from Otavalo and Quito before, during, and after the 2001 uprising. I greatly appreciate her many insights and critical responses to various drafts of this chapter. Her own ongoing research on ritual in the greater Imbabura and Pichincha area (and elsewhere), in its shifting system of significations set in nationalist praxis, contributes greatly to issues raised herein (Wibbelsman 2009). Dorothea Scott (Sibby) Whitten read several drafts and contributed to my thinking in many ways. She also shared (and shares) many experiences with me as we jointly thought about the issues presented above. Previous work with Ronald Stutzman, Kathleen Fine-Dare, Mary Weismantel, Isabel Pérez, Arlene Torres, Diego Quiroga, Rachel Corr, and Jean Muteba Rahier has also contributed to my thinking about some of the sensitivities sketched. I must, however, accept the responsibility for all interpretations. I thank Andy Orta for a most penetrating critique of this essay, which served to help me in the final revisions and will set a scene for future research and publication.

Prelude

In the mid-1980s the idea of transformative dynamics had formed in my mind, but it had not been "named." Thinking of our experiences in Ecuador during Andean festivals, Amazonian aesthetic creations, elitist discourse about "race" and "culture," and unfolding Ecuadorian politics, I wrote, in 1988, "the power of enacted tropes is so strong . . . that one thinks of the [Ecuadorian] nation as a body divided." The subject here was the Quito headship of wealth, power, and "national culture" in contrast to the Amazonian native people as a faraway body capable of great transformations.

Sources of insight for this statement came from stories in Amazonia of the body of an anaconda moving toward its severed head—often expressed in ceramic symbolism and song—and from the indigenous Andean performance of "killing the *yumbo*" in Quito and elsewhere in the Andes during Corpus Christi. Great transformations, expressed metaphorically in indigenous ritual and art, were ubiquitous in Andean and Amazonian Ecuador in the 1980s. In the closing chapter of Jonathan D. Hill's edited book *Rethinking History and Myth,* I wrote, "It is as though the collective body of forest natives is growing toward the Quito head, itself transformed by conquest to something alien yet attainable" (Whitten 1988:300).

In early summer 1990, Andean and Amazonian native peoples rose up as one body to cause transformative upheavals, and by 1992 in the indigenous march from Puyo in Amazonia to the Andes, the body of indigenous Amazonian peoples undulated toward Quito and there united with the alien head in another upheaval of millennial dimensions.

We did not get to Puyo in 1990 until well into July because of the Levantamiento Indígena during June, followed by massive earthquakes and landslides that blocked passage between the Andes and Amazonia. Indigenous people with whom we visited and worked said that this was a real-life contemporary enactment of the mythic upheavals that led to the near demise and then the transformation of the ancient people in beginning times-places (D. Whitten and N. Whitten 1988; chapter 7, this volume). By the time we reached Puyo, people's orientations were awash in millennial symbolism.

Master potter Santa Gualinga, from Sarayacu, made two European–Andean style goblets, each with a raised anaconda on each side, mouths wide open, and said that this was emblematic of the ancient *tupaj amarun* rulers. Alfonso Chango wrote a story about a ruler named Tupaj Amarun and illustrated the story with a series of color drawings. One of the drawings was a goblet just like the one made by Santa. Achuar Juana Castillo, from Numbaime, took us to a spot on the edge of town where strong "peep peep" sounds came from a hole in the ground and explained to us that this was a cutter ant (*ucui*) hiding place under which dwelled a huge *tupaj amarun*. Other women made raised anacondas in their drinking bowls, and though we had never seen emblems like this before, they did not surprise other indigenous people to whom they were shown. All agreed that this "return of the anaconda of its body to its head" signaled the beginning of new transformative powers, called *pachacutij,* attached to their own lifeways now in a sustained political conjuncture with Andean power systems.

These events, both mighty (the uprising) and small (the icons of drinking bowls), triggered the retrieval of information about indigenous American and also African American systems of identity, representation, and revolt. Reflection on these and other matters led to this essay. This is the oldest chapter of the book and the source of one of its principal themes, expressed in the introduction as "to remake the world."

Chapter 4
The Ecuadorian Indigenous Uprising of 1990

In the mid-1970s, I argued for a perspective that could encompass processes called ethnocide and ethnogenesis. These processes were taken to be complementary features in systems of radical change. My focus was on the Canelos Quichua people of Amazonian Ecuador, who were among the first indigenous people in the moist tropics of South America to be declared "Christians" (Pierre 1983:188) and who have sustained a rich cosmology and cosmogony from colonial history through today (see, e.g., D. Whitten and N. Whitten 1988, 1993; Whitten 1976a, 1985; Sullivan 1988). In the late twentieth century and early twenty-first, they are at the forefront of movements of political self-assertion as part of an indigenous nation of native Quichua speakers in ideological alliance with all other indigenous nations. Between mid-April and May 12, 1992, the Canelos Quichua people marched from Amazonian Puyo to Andean Quito to claim and attain legal rights to ancient indigenous territory (N. Whitten and D. Whitten 2008; Whitten et al. 1997).

This essay continues my interest in ethnogenesis: the public, historical emergence of culture (Hill 1996; Whitten 1996a, 1996b). To express this in technical language, processes of ethnogenesis subsume both the expansion and condensation of contrast sets among and between human aggregates. These processes manifest all of the structural properties of symbols, as set forth by Victor Turner (1973, 1974), including multivocality, condensation, associational unification, and polarization. Consciousness of an ethnic-bloc formation, as manifest in public discourse focused on us/other (or us/them), is fundamental to ethnogenetic processing of aggregate contrast sets into culturally meaningful systems of social movement (see chapter 7, this volume, for further development).

Ethnogenetic processes are profoundly symbolic and value laden; however we conceive of them, we must always bear in mind that these cultural processes move people to action. To come to grips with ethnogenesis in the late twentieth/early twenty-first century, we must strive for a broad frame of reference that includes nation-state nationalist domination and hegemony, ethnic-bloc nationalism as a culturally constitutive process, strife between peoples over ethnic-bloc agency of development and survival, processes of counterhegemony, and enduring structures of racism and racialism. The resulting frame of reference that encompasses these processes should provide a basis for understanding oppositional processing and patterning of discourse formations and social movements. The general purpose of this contribution is to work toward such a framework.

The specific purpose of this essay is to explore, in a preliminary way, dimensions of ideologies of interethnicity manifest in racialist discourse and in collective action. As a conceptual guide to what follows, please consider these two quotations:

> Whatever else ideologies may be—projections of unacknowledged fears, disguises for ulterior motives, phatic expressions of group solidarity—they are, most distinctively, maps of problematic social reality and matrices for the creation of collective conscience. (Geertz 1973:220)

> Practice ... has its own dynamics—"a structure of the conjuncture"—which meaningfully defines the persons and the objects that are parties to it. And these contextual values, if unlike the definitions culturally presupposed, have the capacity then of working back on the conventional values. Entailing unprecedented relations between the acting subjects, mutually and by relation to objects, practice entails unprecedented objectifications of categories. (Sahlins 1981:35)

Nation-State Sociocultural Structure of Ecuador

The Republic of Ecuador in western South America is a modern OPEC/NOPEC nation that won its independence from colonial rule in 1822 and became in 1830 El Ecuador (the equator). Salient features of its tumultuous history are sustained ethnic clashes and equally sustained domination by a white minority. Mainland Ecuador is divided into three parts, Coast, Sierra (or Andes), and Upper Amazonia (Región Amazónica; El Oriente); the vast majority of its twelve to thirteen million people live in the Coast and Sierra. Ecuador is now, as it has been since at least the early nineteenth century and perhaps since the sixteenth century, in the ongoing process of social reproduction and cultural transformation of strongly represented ethnic categories that signify segments of its ever-expanding population (e.g., Salomon 1981, 1986; Whitten 1974, 1976a, 1985, 1988; Whitten, ed. 1981). To even begin considering these processes, it is necessary to sketch the well-known, highly dynamized concepts of *indio* and *negro* as set against the national hypostasis of supremacy of the *blanco* and ideological redemption of the middle and lower classes and the "masses" through an elitist imagery of *mestizaje*.

Ecuadorian social structure may be considered as a class pyramid within which the siphon economy of center–periphery developmentalist capitalism operates. An oligarchy, previously described, constitutes the pinnacle of political power, economic control, and social esteem. Ecuador has a significant "middle class" of professional, commercial, and service people who also generally self-identify as *blanco*.

Further down the class hierarchy we find people dependent for their livelihood on commercial transactions of varying scale, none of whom self-identify as *mestizo*, except under exceptional circumstances, but who are politely tagged with various labels meaning "mixed" by those above them or with the labels of the antipodes—*indio, negro*—when discourses reflect interaggregate or interpersonal anger signaling open conflict. Sometimes, under conditions of severe stress, those in superordinate positions use common metonymic associations for the ethnic antipode terminology—*salvaje*, "savage," or *alzado*, "out of control"—in heated discussion reflecting social conflict. Upward mobility is conceived of by those in superordinate positions of power and wealth as a process often called *blanqueamiento*, "whitening," in Ecuador, as in Colombia and Venezuela. Within what some call the "masses" and others call the "popular classes," processes of *mestizaje* are often called by the vulgar term *cholificación* in Ecuador, as in Peru and Bolivia.

At the real antipodes of class-status relationships are those aggregates of people represented by power wielders as *negro*, on the one side, and *indio*, on the other. I have noted elsewhere (e.g., Whitten 1985) that, in power politics, the endeavor is made by indigenous leaders to move a discourse about the *indio* potential for revolt directly into the realm of the status-conscious rhetoric of the oligarchies. Spokesmen and spokeswomen of the *negro* potential for insurrection aim their discourse of pending disorder at middle levels of the class and status hierarchy. When discourses of ethnic "disorder" or "revolt" reach the mass media, all subtleties of ethnic categorization are dropped in favor of condensed, multivocalic, polarized, and associationally unified re-presentations of human beings. In this process, synthetic symbolic units of racialist ideology that emerged in the Americas soon after its European "discovery"—*blanco, negro,* and *indio*—bring forth a predicative link that carries the double act of assertion and denial. I explore this proposition below.

An Ethnic-Enacted Sociocultural Event of National and Regional Salience

Sibby and I arrived in Quito on Sunday evening, May 27, 1990. We had a research grant from the Wenner-Gren Foundation for Anthropological Research to study the ethnointerpretation of salient features of Canelos Quichua and Achuar Jivaroan culture in the Amazonian region, and we planned to work through materials suggested to us by indigenous people from Pastaza Province. On the day of our arrival, Quichua-speaking indigenous people from various Andean provinces occupied the Catholic church of Santo Domingo (built between 1581 and 1650) in the colonial part of Quito. Just before the occupation, the Instituto Nacional de Patrimonio Cultural del Ecuador, which until recently had its offices across the street from the church, announced that under the Plaza Santo Domingo was an ancient indigenous burial site of the first urban Ecuadorians, those who predated the Inca and took the initial steps toward genuine indigenous Quiteño urbanity.

June and July in Andean Ecuador is a period of intense indigenous festival activity. A central feature of indigenous ritual during this period is an ongoing, highly stylized (but sometimes violent) battle for the sacred urban spaces of regional administrative centers (Fine 1991; Weismantel 1998[1988]; Wibbelsman 2009). Additionally, national elections for Congress were upcoming in two weeks after our arrival, and the indigenous vote was considered to be critical to the fate of contending parties throughout the Sierra and Upper Amazonia.

When the president of the Republic of Ecuador, Dr. Rodrigo Borja Cevallos, refused to enter into a dialogue with those occupying the church or with their clerical spokesmen, eleven indigenous protesters (three women and eight men) announced on Saturday, June 2, that they would begin a hunger strike in the church on Monday.

With the church occupation ongoing, the first nationwide Indigenous Uprising began about 2:00 A.M. on Sunday, June 3, in Salasaca, and spread throughout the Sierra by that night and in sectors of the Coast and Oriente soon after.[1] By Monday morning, Riobamba and Latacunga were "occupied" by indigenous people. Ambato was sealed off, and there was no access by major or minor roads between Coast, Sierra, and Upper Amazonia. Word came on the radio at 10:00 A.M. that there was a *paro* (national strike, standstill) and that the president would not enter into a dialogue with anyone disrupting national life. By 7:00 P.M. of the same day, the nationwide special news network (La Cadena Nacional) of television and radio announced to all Ecuadorians that according to the Confederation of Indigenous Nationalities of Ecuador (Confederación de Nacionalidades Indígenas del Ecuador, hereafter CONAIE) a Levantamiento Indígena (Indigenous Uprising) had begun and was taking place on a national scale. The national television and radio network also announced that the president would be "dialoguing" with the leaders of indigenous organizations as soon as the "strikers" allowed traffic to pass on the major highways (the Pan-American and its branches to the Coast and Upper Amazonia) and left the "Sacred Quiteño Temple" (as it was now being called) of Santo Domingo.

By Tuesday things were really getting rough: thirty military and police were held hostage by indigenous people in Riobamba; one indigenous leader was shot and killed in Riobamba by the military; haciendas were ransacked throughout the Sierra and the southwestern coastal region; *hacendados* were physically abused in a number of ways (one was held without clothes during the subfreezing night). Indigenous people sacked part of the Ambato market. In Upper Amazonia, road-construction machinery was confiscated, and the only plane to fly that day was also confiscated. The president, who had steadfastly refused to dialogue with indigenous people up to noon Tuesday, suddenly agreed to a national dialogue to address the sixteen points of the Acuerdo de Sarayacu (the Sarayacu agreement) presented to him in 1989 by CONAIE as a condition to resume transformed relationships between indigenous Ecuadorians and other Ecuadorians. The points had been drawn up initially in a confrontational setting in the Amazonian region and the president had not acted on them, or even mentioned them, for slightly more than a year. These points included (among others):

1. delivery (surrender) without charge of appropriated land to the indigenous nationalities;
2. end of property taxes for indigenous people;
3. cancellation of all debts owed by indigenous people;
4. a constitutional change to designate Ecuador as a multinational, multiethnic state;
5. federal allocation of funds for the indigenous nationalities to allow them to develop their own priorities and to carry them through by sustained indigenous agency;
6. tax- and duty-free import and export for indigenous artisans and artists;
7. legalization of indigenous medical and curing practices;
8. the placing of all archaeological investigations and the wherewithal to carry them out in the hands of CONAIE and affiliated indigenous organizations;
9. expulsion of the Summer Institute of Linguistics/Wycliff Bible Translators;
10. recognition of the Acuerdo de Sarayacu and implementation of the points of the *acuerdo*.

Discourse Structures, Reference Points, and Interethnic Salience

Throughout our three and a half months in Ecuador in 1990, the most salient features of indigenous discourse involved the Levantamiento Indígena, which came to be called *el alzamiento indio* by most of the media commentators and by political analysts. The contrast in terminology is instructive. Whereas *levantamiento* carries the meanings of conscious raising and sublimity, and even rebirth, as well as insurrection, *alzamiento* means unruly behavior, as well as insurrection. There is no sense of consciousness in the term *alzamiento;* loss of control is implied, and the term may be used for animal behavior. Indigenous people perceived in their *levantamiento* (or, in Quichua, *jatari,* though it was in Spanish discourse that the macrocategories were utilized and contrasted) a raising of culture to a new level; those using the term *alzamiento* saw indigenous peoples as "lowering" their cultural potential to that bordering on animality, and they saw and described indigenous behavior as "like sheep." An *alzamiento* implies that, by definition, the indigenous peoples do not have the cultural potential to engage in a *levantamiento;* therefore, they are *fuera de su lugar,* "out of their proper place," or *indios alzados,* "unruly Indians."

For indigenous people, the fundamental public pronouncement in the Andes and in Amazonia was "¡Despúes de 500 años de dominación, autodeterminación indígena en 1992!" (After 500 years of domination, indigenous self-determination in 1992!). The year 1992 was chosen as the epitomizing symbol of a raising up, in a cultural as well as political-economic sense, in clear and confrontational opposition to the elitist rhetoric of the quincentennial celebratory activities to be undertaken in that year to commemorate the European "discovery" and conquest of ancient indigenous territory and the establishment of hegemony over contemporary indigenous people. That territory included, according to indigenous discourse reflecting on recent scientific and humanistic pronouncements, the colonial center of Quito, which was also taken to be the precolonial and pre-Incaic center of indigenous civilization. As the polarities increased between nonindigenous ideologues in very active and sustained public discourse (which was reported daily in newspapers, magazines, and tabloids and on radio and television), black spokesmen and spokeswomen of Esmeraldas and Carchi provinces also joined the national debate through the communicative vehicle of *négritud,* a concept developed in the francophonic Caribbean (as *négritude*) and recently adopted by some leaders in the Ecuadorian *comunidades negras* directly from

Colombian racialist politics. The term *mestizo* is not one normally heard in intraindigenous discourse or in indigenous discourse directed to nonindigenous audiences. But during and after the Levantamiento Indígena, it was commonly used by indigenous and black spokespersons to refer to cultural barriers to ethnic, social, economic, and political advancement.

In the rhetoric of the Levantamiento Indígena, including as it did the central postulates of *autodeterminación indígena* (indigenous self-determination) and *autogestión indígena* (indigenous self-management), and in the rhetoric of *négritud, liberación de las comunidades negras* (liberation of black communities), and *liberación del pueblo negro* (liberation of black people), discourses that could be described as racialist continued (and continue) to swirl and eddy within the Republic of Ecuador. From nonindigenous and nonblack standpoints, the media and political analysts stepped up the rhetoric centering on the conjoined concepts of *el problema indio* (the indian problem) and *el problema negro* (the black problem). As such, commentators on both sides of the escalating confrontational discourse presented rich racialist imagery in a paradigmatic way: mention in any context of any of the key racialist signifiers such as *blanco, negro, indio,* and *mestizo,* among others, automatically evoked imagery of the opposites and the syntagmatic associations with these opposites (see, for background, Fine 1991; Weismantel 1998[1988]; Whitten 1985; Whitten, ed. 1981).

The field of racialist discourse in this modern Latin American nation, in other words, became central to both nation-state nationalist discourse and ethnic-bloc nationalist discourse, just as the denial of such discourse became located in the same centralities. For example, the president of the Cámara de Agricultura del Primer Sector, Ignacio Pérez, said that "los indígenas están cayendo en el nazismo de la raza pura" (the indigenes are falling into the Nazism of pure race), to which the president of CONAIE, Cristobal Tapuy, responded, "Quién habla de racista es el primer racista" (he who speaks of racism [racist] is the primary [or first] racist). Let us consider for a moment the concept of *el problema* as it is used in Ecuador. Mary Weismantel (1998[1988]) has argued that *problema* in Ecuador suggests the concept elaborated upon by Victor Turner as a cultural "arena," "the concrete settings in which cultural paradigms become transformed into metaphors and symbols with reference to which political power is mobilized [and] in which there is a trial of strength between influential paradigm bearers" (Turner 1974:17). "'Social dramas,'" he writes, "represent the phased process of their contestation" (Turner 1974:17). A social arena has the following explicit characteristics: (1) a framework, a "setting for antagonistic interaction aimed at arriving at a publicly recognized decision"; (2) "an explicit frame; nothing is left merely implied" (Turner 1974:134); and (3) "a scene for the making of a decision . . . [t]here is a moment of truth when a major decision is made, even if it is the decision to leave things temporarily undecided" (Turner 1974:135).

An illustration of this *problema* as arena within a larger setting of charged symbolic fields occurred in the Gold Room (Salón Amarillo, also called the Reception Hall) of the National Palace on August 22, 1990. There, in the well-appointed room where foreign diplomats are received by the president, the president of the Republic of Ecuador received a *planteamiento histórico* (a document in the form of a proposal with the implication of history in the making) from the regional organization of indigenous peoples of Pastaza (Organización de Pueblos Indígenas de Pastaza, OPIP).

Prior to the meeting with indigenous leaders from the Sierra and Upper Amazonia, the president had met with his unofficial but very prominent advisor on indigenous affairs, Alfonso Calderón Cevallos, who then left the building. Then President Borja met with the assembled indigenous leaders. There followed a public confrontation carried live on all the national news channels (La Cadena Nacional). The president was clearly angry and quite authoritative about a serious legal and political breach that he and his technical advisor on indigenous affairs perceived to be caused by the explicit language of the document presented to him.

The basis of the perceived indigenous breach of national sovereignty was especially evident in the third chapter of the report submitted on the territorial rights of the Quichua, Shuar, Achuar, and Shiwiar people of Pastaza Province. The key terms singled out were *autodeterminación, autogestión,* and *autonomía* of the indigenous people of Pastaza Province, together with the proposition of *autogobierno* and the claim to the wealth of their territory, including all rights to the revenues to be reclaimed from the exploitation of all subsurface deposits, including petroleum.

It appeared that the president, on the righteous nation-state nationalist side, and the Amazonian indigenous people, who seemed to call for an ethnic-bloc nationalist state in Pastaza Province, were not previously aware of each others' positions. But a little probing reveals that a key role in this confrontation was played by Alfonso Calderón Cevallos, first cousin of the president (their mothers are sisters), who was not only advisor to the president on indigenous affairs but also informal technical advisor to OPIP and the Confederation of Indigenous Nationalities of Amazonian Ecuador (CONFENAIE) during the writing of the indigenous proposal.

Much of the "indigenous rhetoric" that so infuriated the president was taken directly from Calderón's own well-known book, *Reflexiones en las culturas orales*. Moreover, Alfonso Calderón had been at the confrontational meeting in 1989 in Upper Amazonia when the controversial Acuerdo de Sarayacu was drawn up, and he had worked with the president of CONFENAIE, Luis Vargas Canelos, on the very document presented to the president by OPIP.

Prior to his election as president of the Republic of Ecuador, Rodrigo Borja Cevallos had stated in public campaign speeches that the nation-state of Ecuador was most clearly one of "multiple nationalities, multiple cultures, and multiple ethnic peoples" (Serrano 1993). The rhetoric of Ecuador as a multinational, multiethnic state emanated directly *from* the espoused ideology of the then-aspiring presidential hopeful, Rodrigo Borja Cevallos. One finds the very same rhetoric in all five editions of the small but influential book of his first cousin, Alfonso Calderón Cevallos.

We can conclude from this that elitist rhetoric (as manifested by Borja at the presidential pinnacle of power of the ethnically entitled white *gente de bien*) is not transformable or transferable to the indigenous (or black) antipode of discourse of the indigenous social movements. Borja's own rhetoric could not be used, as the elite and wealthy saw the matter, in the polarized arena wherein indigenous discourse appropriated a paradigm of liberation from the charged field of nation-state nationalist political ideology. Borja, prior to his election, engaged in a persuasive discourse of ethnic gratuities; his appropriated rhetoric, as part of ethnogenetic processing by indigenous people from Amazonian Ecuador, was repulsed with a presidential self-righteous fury born in and backed by nation-state power, domination, and hegemony.

For their part, the indigenous people from Pastaza Province perceived a serious breach within the National Palace, a breach of social contract inscribed in the enduring relationships of kinship and bureaucracy. They had worked on that critical chapter with future historic implications for more than two years, grounding it in the principles set forth in *Reflexiones en las culturas orales*. Indeed, sections of this history-making document are taken word for word from Calderón's book, with only specific geographic locations inserted.

This dramaturgical conflict was televised nationally from the presidential Gold Room. For a time it brought negotiations between indigenous people and representatives of the central government to an end. This event and the polarized public reaction indicate that Ecuador is characterized by a system of vertical articulation of conflict that complements that of a horizontal articulation of conflict. By this I mean that schisms at the highest levels of government ramify systemically to grass-roots sociopolitical movements. In the process of downward ramification, the liberal-leftist rhetoric of ethnogratuities confronts, at the grass roots and at the ethnic antipodes, the same symbols. But these symbols move people to action as an ethnogenetic counter-rhetoric, thereby feeding the process of oppositional processing and contributing to the paradigms that become increasingly rigid in the charged field of racialist discourse.

When, it seems, the pinnacle spokesman for nationalist pride, propriety, and righteousness, the president of the republic, encounters in indigenous discourse the familiar conflict generated in his own discourse (or that of Calderón Cevallos, his cousin and advisor on indigenous affairs) about democratic reform and recognition of multiple nationalities within a nation-state, severe conflict between his office and that of the indigenous nationalities is again sparked.

The charged fields of cultural paradigms electrifying Ecuador in 1990 that influenced the oppositional processing within clear-cut sociopolitical arenas of conflict were denied to indigenous people. In turn, it was precisely to those fields of symbol- and metaphor-laden discourse that indigenous people turned. The replication of a system of oppositions across the antipodes of ethnic and class awareness in Ecuador in 1990, as in previous years (see Whitten, ed. 1981) and in the present, continues to motivate systems of ethnogenesis just as it motivates increased forms of domination and hegemony.

Ideologies of racialism that spawn such vertical articulation force unending oppositional processing between the white spokesmen for one nation and the indigenous and black spokesmen and spokeswomen for ethnic freedom. Such ideological forces undergird discourses in many Latin American nations. Such discourses have led to hemisphere-wide paradigmatic imagery focused on the highly charged and evocative epitomizing symbol of "1492–1992" (e.g., Rivera Cusicanqui 1991).

Culture and Agency

Between 1990 and 1991, the symbol of 1992 and the praxis of the Levantamiento Indígena in Ecuador conjoined discourse structures from the highest level of Ecuadorian society to the dynamic antipodes of blackness and indigenousness. The processes this essay has considered, though illustrated by events in Ecuador, should allow us to think more broadly about indigenous and black autogenous "uprising" ongoing throughout the Western Hemisphere. Ideologies of racialism that have framed discourse in many Latin American nations have led to hemisphere-wide paradigmatic imagery focused, through 1992, on the highly charged and evocative epitomizing symbol of 1992. What has been unfolding subsequent to the passing of 1992, and its international prolongation during the 1993 International Year of Indigenous People, is beyond the scope of this essay, but is addressed in ensuing chapters. The foci in 1993 changed, but the ethnogenetic processes discussed are expressed in myriad public performances and in countless genres with common paradigmatic underpinnings.

What I would like to do now is reflect on culture, ethnicity, race, domination, hegemony, resistance, and related concepts that emerge in considering the highly charged epochal epitome of the 1992 "celebration" of people throughout the Americas of the "discovery" or "encounter" of the New World by Cristóbal Colón. Colón, the "Discoverer," insisted to his death that he had arrived in India in 1492. The black and indigenous perspectives on 1492 focused on an epochal event five hundred years ago when all native people were tagged with the image of *indios* with lands to be conquered and commodified and souls to be appropriated and turned into ecclesiastical commodities.

The commercial conquest of the Americas itself, stemming from this focal ideological event, was undertaken by trafficking in *negros bozales* (black people in bondage) from the *negrería* (black land) brought by *negreros* (slavers in black people) (see Forbes 1993; Hyatt and Nettleford 1995; Rout 1976; Whitten and Torres 1992; Whitten and Torres, eds. 1998). As such, the epitomizing symbol of 1992 signaled a public, transnational cultural contest between the celebration of European hegemony for the *blancos* and the spontaneity of a rising up of indigenous and black people and a raising of indigenous and black cultures with a new imaging of a future for a new millennium.

Let us turn again to "culture," not so much for disciplinary reasons but because it is a tremendously important concept to indigenous and black people throughout the Americas. Clifford Geertz tells us that "cultural phenomena should be treated as significative systems posing expositive questions" (Geertz 1983:3). To this let us add the definition recently deployed effectively by Greg Urban: "culture is localized in concrete, publicly accessible signs, the most important of which are actually occurring instances of discourse" (Urban 1991:1). So let us begin with *cultura*. In Spanish, the feminine definite article *la,* as in *la cultura,* elevates the concept to something refined, European, civilized. When one goes to an expensive opera in Bogotá, Colombia, for example, wearing fine clothes and speaking in a refined manner, one is participating in *la cultura* and one is *muy culto,* very civilized. The *gente de bien* (or *gente bien*), Ecuador's old social oligarchy, regard themselves as "the most civilized." Today, in most Latin American societies, to affix *cultura* to blackness or "Indianness" without the definite article *la* is to demean traditions and lifeways to something vernacular or popular, worthy of study by folklorists but insignificant in the processes leading to higher and higher levels of Latin American civilization.

Still worse, *cultura indígena, una cultura indígena, cultura negra,* or *una cultura negra* is something to be viewed as unrefined, inchoate, confused, fragmented, stagnant, and static. One studies *una cultura popular* or *una cultura vernacular* to find something of antiquity retained and an enormous amount of culture lost. During the 1990 Levantamiento Indígena in Ecuador, indigenous people insisted on the concept of *las nacionalidades indígenas* (the indigenous nationalities) as the appropriate designation of representation for their collectivity. In each indigenous language, the concept of "our culture" (e.g., *ñucanchi yachai, ñaupa yachai* in Quichua) is embedded—by a juxtaposition of signs—within the Spanish concept of *la nación*. *La nación* implies culture, sovereignty, and viable territoriality. *Las nacionalidades* is an older term of respect for indigenous cultures ("high civilizations") of the Americas. Attributes of *las nacionalidades* included differentiation of humanity according to language and territory; shared status in terms of exploitation beginning, ideologically, with the arrival of Cristóbal Colón in 1492; and a continuous strain toward hemisphere-wide indigenous cultural advancement truncated by *mestizaje* thereafter.

A hemisphere-wide black movement, similar to the indigenous one, began in a centralized fashion at the Primer Congreso de la Cultura Negra de las Américas (First Congress of Black Culture in the Americas) held in Cali, Colombia, in 1977 (which I attended) and continued through the Fourth Congress held in 1991 in Paris. At all four congresses, black people, well aware of the power of racist symbols and stereotypes, insisted (and still insist) on the definite article *la,* as in *la cultura negra,* for black cultures: black, sophisticated, existential, experiential, and adaptable—entwined processes of tradition, history, and modernity moving toward higher and higher levels of black civilization in the Americas.

Geertz's concept of cultural phenomena as something to be treated as "significative systems posing expositive questions" can be combined with one derived by the historian Daniel J. Boorstin (1983) that resonates well with the insistence of Latin American indigenous and black spokesmen and spokeswomen for *las nacionalidades indígenas* and *la cultura negra*: "'Culture' (from Latin *cultus* for 'worship') originally meant reverential homage. Then it came to describe the practices of cultivating the soil, and later it was extended to the cultivating and refinement of mind and manners. Finally, by the nineteenth century *'culture' had become a name for the intellectual and aesthetic side of civilization*" (Boorstin 1983:647, emphasis added).

Indigenous and/or black culture, as I am coming to understand the polarization of the signification of confrontational discourse, is that which is worthy of reverential homage by indigenous people and by black people within their communities, regions, and nation-states; it is also the means by which the cultivation and refinement of mind and manners has been nurtured, developed, and adapted in the New World for nearly five hundred years. It is an aesthetic side of the raising of civilization, which may be found explicitly or implicitly in any domain or context of social life. Survival itself, as in the cultivation of the soil, figuratively and literally, is a critical concept contributing to the sense and reference of indigenous culture (undergirding the concept of *nacionalidades indígenas*) and black culture (undergirding the concepts of *négritud* and *las comunidades negras*).

Black culture and indigenous culture, as such concepts are manifest in practical and spiritual conflict, are characterized by reverential webs of signification that are illuminating to black people and to indigenous peoples in any given time and place, and through them to others who will read, reflect, and think about ethnic-bloc formations and ethnic transformations and reproductions in settings of white domination. This concept of culture is also reflected in, and contributes to, subsistence and commercial survival strategies and is adaptive to a myriad of structures of domination encountered and overcome in the Americas.

In coming to understand racialist rhetoric in Ecuador and elsewhere, one finds that the same terminology transcends the polarities in the symbolic fields where paradigms develop and are elaborated. For the moment, I would like to discuss some relatively invariant postulates of racialist discourse in charged political settings, separating the macro symbols of "race" as they seem to emerge in nation-state nationalist discourse and in ethnic-bloc nationalist discourse.

Nationalism, Ethnic-Bloc Formation, and Ideologies of Racial Cultures

We begin with the idea of nation-state nationalism. Although clearly rife with ambiguity, the term refers to the identity of the majority of people within a nation-state with the republic, nation, or national society as the primary reference group. A nation-state must, above all else, retain all power of sovereignty and all power of territoriality. Ideologies of nation-state nationalism are located within the cultural space of nation-state control. In Latin America and the Caribbean in the 1990s, we find two complementary and one competing nationalist ideology of racial culture, often denoted by one of these symbols: racial mixture, Indianism, blackness. I present each of them briefly, by reference to the terms in the language with which they are most commonly associated (i.e., *négritude,* in French, which has become a Spanish term, *négritud*), but always with a focus on the ways by which they are currently used as signs and symbols in Spanish.

Mestizaje, the ideology of racial intermingling, is an explicit master symbol in all Latin American countries. *Indigenismo* is a dual concept reflecting, on the one hand, a search for the creative dimensions of nationalism through the symbolism of an indigenous past and, on the other hand, a sociopolitical–literary symbol that conveys the mood of remorse over the living conditions of contemporary "acculturated Indians." Both of these meanings seem to run through American Romanticism and American Realism (e.g., Sacoto 1967). The ideology of *mestizaje* embraces both senses of *indigenismo* (e.g., Bourricaud 1962; Pitt-Rivers 1967, 1973). Indeed, *indigenismo* may be thought of as a key support for the exclusion of contemporary native peoples from nation-state affairs. A related component of *mestizaje, blanqueamiento*, is discussed below because it is not an explicit component of nationalist ideology.

Négritude is a concept that denotes the positive features of blackness among people classed as, or self-identifying as, black. This specific term was introduced into French literary usage in 1947 by the black Martiniquan poet Aimé Césaire (Coulthard 1962:58; see especially Trouillot 1989:124–136). It provides a single term by which to assert the positive power inherent in, and positive aesthetic forces of, "blackness," leaving many avenues open for the definition of what and who is, and what and who is not, to be considered black. Within the Americas, only Haiti has adopted an explicit nationalist ideology of *négritude*, and the literary and artistic roots of this concept provide the basis for Césaire's and others' (such as Frantz Fanon) literary and political creativity (Coulthard 1962:58–70).

Nationalist ideologies develop not only symbols of internal oneness based on concepts of racial classification but also ideas of oppositions using the criterion of "cultural exaggeration" as discussed by James Boon (1982). It is perhaps the case that, throughout the Americas, the *mestizaje/négritude* contrast represents a symbolic opposition reflecting cultural exaggeration of ideologically conjoined social constructs of race, civilization, nationalist patrimony, and social movement. There is, perhaps, no room in explicit nation-state nationalist discourse for *autodeterminación étnica* or for *autogestión étnica* except as an elitist political ploy.

Let us now turn for a moment from nationalist ideologies with key racialist symbols to ethnic-bloc nationalist formation. The New Nations program at the University of Chicago turned up information that sustained ethnic-bloc nationalist formation characterized the consolidation of nation-state nationalism (Geertz 1973:234–310). An ethnic bloc constitutes a conscious reference group for those who share recurrent processes of self-identification.

Ethnic-bloc formation is a political-economic manifestation of cultural ethnogenesis. Ethnic blocs, and expressions of ethnic-bloc nationalism, may be based on any criteria such as common residence, language, tradition, and custom. Indeed, the bases for bloc identity may sort of slip and slide around the criteria themselves, as the bloc itself becomes increasingly strong. The concept "bloc" is taken from politics (as in a political bloc); whatever its bases, power of identity, power of representation, and power of discourse structuring are crucial. Such powers (or powers of resistance; see Whitten, ed. 2003 and the conclusion chapter herein) come into being when ethnic exclusion takes place, as when indigenous people or black people are ethnically disfranchised from full participation in the dominant society.

Such powers of resistance within ethnic blocs also derive from a collective, inner sense of the oneness of a people, in contradistinction to nation-state racialist hegemony. The two generative power sources are related, but the nature of such a dynamic relationship requires careful, empirical study. Ethnic-bloc nationalist formation may be seen as a process of contra–nation-state nationalism, and the symbolic processes of ethnic-bloc formation seem similar to, or the same as, those identified as fundamental in processes of nation-state nationalist consolidation. The relationships created by these generative powers permeate the political-economic fabric of any social order. Ethnic-bloc formation, and hence ethnogenesis, in other words, is as international or global in scope as it is local in origin.

One would anticipate that black-based ethnic-bloc formations would use the ideology of *négritude* and, in so doing, be perceived as a threat to nationalist sovereignty and nationalist territoriality. This certainly seems to be the case in Colombia, Guyana, and Venezuela (e.g., Friedemann and Arocha 1995; Friedemann and Cross 1979; Wade 1993; Williams 1993; Wright 1990). In the processes of ethnic-bloc nationalist formation in the Americas, three master symbols of racialist ideology emerge, the latter two of which are potentially complementary: phenotypical, cultural, or ethnic lightening (or whitening); black liberation; and indigenous self-determination.

Blanqueamiento refers to the processes of becoming increasingly acceptable to those classified as and/or self-identified as "white" or "light." This is an ethnic strategy (however unconscious it may be) now coterminous with socioeconomic advancement governed by the ideology of "development" that depends upon socioeconomic and political assistance and loans from the developed (i.e., highly industrialized, highly energy-dependent) countries. *Blanqueamiento* essentially accepts the implicit hegemonic rhetoric of the United States with regard to white supremacy and often blames those classed as black people and indigenous people for the worsening state of the nation.

Ethnic or cultural lightening may occur as an ideological feature among people self-identifying as black (e.g., Wade 1993; Williams 1993). One example of the former would be in nineteenth-century Haitian literary circles, wherein the positive attributes of blackness (via Egypt and the Sudan) were juxtaposed to French civilization. *Blanqueamiento,* an enduring ethnic-bloc complement to the nationalist ideology of *mestizaje,* is an ephemeral feature of enduring *négritude.* To the extent that people in the Americas accept, however implicitly, standards of whiteness as attached to "developmental potential," the phenomenon of hegemony may be said to exist.

Négritude may express the same sets of meanings in ethnic-bloc rhetoric that it does in nation-state rhetoric, as discussed above. Indeed, the Haitian ethnologist Jean Price-Mars (1928), during the extended U.S. occupation of Haiti from 1915 to 1934, conscientiously turned to the voices of Haitians for concepts of blackness, Africanness, and being Haitian. Price-Mars sought to liberate nationalist ideology from its European francophonic bases in "whitening," in which the powerful, literate elite of Haiti saw themselves as mulatto (analogous here to *mestizo;* for an extended analysis of such terminology, see Trouillot 1989; Whitten and Torres, eds. 1998). *Négritude,* and its implicit and explicit cognates, from the writing of Price-Mars (1928) onward, must be considered to have two senses: in its nationalist sense it may or may not reflect a process of lightening, but in its ethnic-bloc sense it is profoundly populist and rejecting of nonblackness as a criterion for sophisticated self-awareness (see especially Trouillot 1989:124–136).

Autodeterminación indígena is predicated on the assertion that indigenous people, who were deposed and disfranchised by the Euro-American conquest of the Americas, must articulate to New World nation-states in modern, indigenous ways, which they themselves will determine. It is a proclamation of indigenous sovereignty and territoriality. *Autogestión* adds indigenous agency as the central ethnogenetic dynamic to sovereignty and territoriality. This multivocalic, condensed symbol of liberation (self-determination) specifically looks to contemporary indigenous cultures in multiple communities and societies across the Americas. It rejects the literary-based ideological components of *indigenismo,* just as early twentieth-century ethnographers such as Price-Mars (1928) in Haiti and Fernando Ortiz (1940, 1947, 1960) in Cuba turned away from elite academician definitions of national culture and sought out the voices of the culturally rich black poor in both urban and rural areas. Today indigenous self-determination appeals to black people in many areas. *Négritude* and *autodeterminación indígena* are complementary constructs of ethnic-bloc ideology, both of which are contrary to *mestizaje* as nation-state nationalist ideology and ethnic-bloc nationalist ideology (see Whitten and Torres, eds. 1998).

To return to nationalism and racialist ideology for a moment, in the non-Anglophonic world today, Peru-Ecuador-Colombia-Venezuela, on one side, and Haiti, on the other, constitute polar nationalist opposites. In the former nations, the colonial dream of overcoming the barriers of racialist classification linked to economic opportunities became transformed into a nationalist, democratic ideology of racial mixture. In the latter, blackness inundated a formative New World gene pool to create the first self-liberated democratic island republic in the Americas with collective, self-conscious roots in its African and European past.

Structures of Domination

Nationalism represents, for indigenous and black people in nation-states governed by any racialist ideology, a structure of domination (e.g., Dolgin et al. 1977). Structures of domination intensify culturally by simple rhetorical devices. The first of these is simile. When a person says "s/he sure doesn't look like a black" (el [ella] no parece como negroide[a]) or "s/he sure doesn't talk like an Indian" (seguro que el [ella] no habla como indio[a]), a powerful statement has been made that some other people will "look like" someone who "is" black or "talk like" someone who "is" Indian. The "like" (*como*), in other words, signals a conscious or unconscious awareness that there are agreed-upon commonalities or properties that attach symbolically to the salient cultural representations of *indio* and *negro*. Put another way, the symbolic denial, by simile, of an individual's adherence to dimensions of a putative racial category is a powerful assertion of the enduring existence of the synthetic category itself.

Metaphor is the second rhetorical strategy, as when someone says "s/he is Indian"; "s/he is black"; "s/he is *mestizo(a)*"; "s/he is mulatto(a)." With metaphor the person, class, aggregate, group, community, or region is tagged with the cognitive and symbolic associations of a nonwhite or culturally "darkened" resemblance. These symbolic associations constitute properties of Indianness and blackness that convey meaning. Metaphor concretizes properties that are categorical and provides the rhetorical wherewithal to all people to label other people with such properties, as though physical features, genealogy, and heritage have some real correspondences among people, representations, and categories. People who "are" *negro* or *indio*, in other words, are signified by qualities and resemblances that belong to signifiers that stem from racialist and racist cultural constructs. These constructs, to repeat, carry the twin predications of affirmation and denial in public discourse.

Structures of domination are given form, meaning, and power of repression by the rhetorical strategy of reification. Reification occurs when people consciously read symbolic, religious, moral, or ideological properties into categorical social relationships, as though these properties actually exist. In a chapter entitled "Humanity and Animality," Edmund Leach (1982:107) referred to this in terms of the power of names and the way by which they begin the structuring of moral sanctions. This is the process of signification wherein meaning is constructed by strengthening the relationship between the signified (individuals, aggregates, groups, or categories of people) and the signifier (cognitive and symbolic associations that constitute the properties of representations and categories).

When nation-state nationalist ontology and ideology reify racial mixture not only as an ideal but also as a reality, they create objectifications of outsidership (*los otros* as opposed to *nosotros*) among indigenous and black populations within the nation-state. People in communities and regions so objectified and morally sanctioned by undesirable attributes self-consciously reflect on such reifications and attempt to overcome the barriers imposed by racialist structures of domination. This involves symbolic as well as practical dimensions of actions of moral inversion in society. The result is a reordering of visions that people hold of humanity and spirituality in the world perceived and in the world imagined. When such actions spark social movements of self-liberation and cultural resistance, they may be said to raise the issue of nation-state nationalist domination to one of transcendentalist ethnic-bloc nationalist formation.

In the process of formation and strengthening of structures of domination and the inevitable forces or powers of resistance to them, we must consider the phenomenon of hypostasis. This concept, which entered the English language in 1529, literally means "that which stands under"; that is, a support or foundation (for other concepts). If we take structure to be a set of relatively invariant reference points that remain after a series of transformations has occurred, hypostatized structures are those that are taken to be enduring realities. They are structures with deep historical underpinnings and supports that unite concepts of humanity and divinity and separate both from animality (see Leach 1982). In the ethnic formation of New World structures of European colonial domination, three relatively invariant reference points were the categories of the white (European) in superior relationship over the black (African) and the native ("Indian").

When a structure of domination—such as a pyramidal class structure of a given nation-state with white people on top, masses of pluralized *mestizo*, mulatto, and white people in the middle, and poor, pluralized black, *mestizo*, and indigenous people on the bottom—is assumed to be an unchanging, static reality by people at the pinnacle and in the middle of the structure, then the full power of bureaucracy is wielded to solve the "black problem," find new ways to overcome the "Indian problem," and accelerate the processes of *mestizaje*. While such solutions to hypostatized problems are being sought, national, regional, and local political, social, and economic resources flow to the top, are partially redistributed in the middle, and deprive those on the bottom of the class–ethnic hierarchy. This is a process of the reproduction of underdevelopment of Fourth World people in underdeveloping Third World nations and the production of increased distance between Third World poverty and First World wealth (see Comaroff 1985; Worsley 1984).

Processes of ethnogenesis flow from the structures of oppression and also subvert such structures. In the processes of downward flow from elite, *blanco* control, through those represented by upper echelons as striving toward whiteness, and in the processes of populist and ethnic subversion, the paradigm of *blanco, negro, indio,* and *mestizo* that emerged five hundred years ago in the Americas is strengthened.

Within any given structure of domination, we seem to find that those in power endeavor to maintain hegemony over those immediately below them by blaming those on the bottom (especially ethnically distinct indigenous and black people) for the lowly "undeveloped" condition of regions and communities that can be easily designated by reified ethnic terminology. The hypostatized "reality" is often inscribed in developmental reports, plans, and educational materials and in scholarly publications. At the same time, this symbolic but negatively concretized "reality" is challenged by powerful, dynamic counter-ideologies and social movements that seek to spark recognition of the falsity of the hypostatic ideological racialist structures. Ethnic-bloc formation undertaken under the ideological aegis of *négritude* and/or *autodeterminación indígena* strongly illustrates the challenges mounted in the late twentieth century to false yet hypostatized "reality" that has been with the New World since 1492. No wonder, then, that many black people (and *mestizo* people) in Latin America joined their indigenous congeners in the cry, "¡Despúes de 500 años de dominación, autodeterminación en 1992!"

Processes of Liberation

The Levantamiento Indígena that took place in Ecuador in 1990 may be understood, at least in part, as a process of liberation from structures of domination that are bundled into the epitomizing symbol of 1492. Understanding processes of liberation involves us with dominance formations that constitute structures of power. Structures of domination and the ways by which class, ethnicity, and political blocs coalesce, change, and are expressed, maintained, and transformed are dynamic and volatile. While hegemony may come into being, it is extremely difficult to maintain, for people are conscious actors attuned to their life situations.

When discussing structures of domination, I introduced the idea that people are signified by signifiers as they become parts of categorical webs of signification in modern nations. Rhetoric attendant on the Ecuadorian

Levantamiento Indígena, which rapidly reached the national congress and the office of the president of the republic, Dr. Rodrigo Borja Cevallos, contained a rich embodiment of enlightened and insightful indigenous representation of the entwined histories, presents, and futures of conquest, domination, and self-liberation. This reminds us again of Michael Taussig's phrase, "From the represented shall come that which overturns the representation" (Taussig 1987:135). This statement relates directly to the idea of people remaking the world and being in a world refashioned from the conquered one that the European "discovery" or "encounter" of 1492 began.

In the concept of the unity of *las nacionalidades indígenas,* within Ecuador and across the Americas, one finds the embodiment of the transcendental concept of being indigenous as *bound to survival for nearly 500 years.* The ultimate transcendence, or transformation, or cultural metamorphosis is to reproduce, in an entirely new manner, indigenous unity of the twenty-first century.

In July 1990, while the president of Ecuador was still engaged in public "dialogue" with indigenous spokesmen and spokeswomen, a Pan-Indigenous Congress was held in Quito. The theme of the congress, which had been established a year before in Bogotá, Colombia, was manifest in its title: Primer Encuentro Continental: 500 Años de Resistencia India (First Continental Encounter: 500 Years of Indian Resistance). The unity resulting from the sustained resistance was expressed as a reuniting of the condor and the eagle, symbolizing the union of the inner essence of Latin American indigenous spirituality, bound to shamanism, with the outer essence of North American spirituality, bound to public indigenous ceremony. The key to the unity lies in the collective sense of indigenous healing of foreign-inflicted illness. The identity of the power to heal serves as one of many reverential symbols worthy of macro-indigenous identity. This is an aesthetic quality that people self-identifying with human indigenousness find and appreciate across the boundaries of specific communities, regions, nations, and traditions.

Blackness at the Primer Congreso de la Cultura Negra de las Américas in Cali in 1977 and at the subsequent congresses of black culture also referred (and continues to refer) to that epitomizing symbol worthy of a macro identity to which communities, regions, and even nations could aspire. Such a referent is also transcendental; it comes from black people in black communities but it is the polar opposite of popular culture. In the United States, and elsewhere in the Americas, the epitomizing symbol of blackness in its transcendental character is expressed as "soul." This is an aesthetic quality that people self-identifying with human blackness and/or with black cultures find and appreciate across the boundaries of specific communities, regions, nations, and traditions (Whitten and Torres, eds. 1998).

1492–1992 as Epitomizing Symbol

The tripartite ideological structure of white power and moral righteousness, a coverlet of *mestizaje* to cloak flagrant racism, and the enduring praxis of forced *indio/negro* subservience to the church, state, and secular holders of land and people was established in the early sixteenth century in Europe and in the Americas. The epitomizing symbol "1492" expresses the inherent evil of this foreign hegemony to black and indigenous people in the Western Hemisphere.

For a while, the symbol *1992* represented the movement to counter this evil, to raise blackness and indigenousness to new counterhegemonic levels of civilized discourse in multiple languages within relatively old modern states. These nation-states, of which Ecuador is clearly one, are constituted of complementary and contradictory ideological processes of transformation and reproduction that reveal, in their sparked interethnic oppositional rhetoric, a concern with emergent and traditional "culture" as sets of structures of conjuncture. The emergence of cultures within and between these sets fits well the definition of ethnogenesis introduced in the introduction and other chapters of this book.

Jean Comaroff (1985:196; following Hebdige 1979:17) has put forth a persuasive perspective, which strikes me as especially helpful in understanding these processes. This is the sense that we may continue to understand more and more about ideological clashes within and between the structures of conjuncture (and disjuncture) in history and in ethnography, and especially by their combination, by reference to "*an unending struggle for the possession of the sign*" (Comaroff 1985:196; emphasis added).

Much of the public rhetoric of the Levantamiento Indígena in Ecuador in 1990 focused on making 1992 the year when the tragedy of Euro-American conquest would become transformed into a triumph wherein a new nation of indigenous peoples, including all peoples with indigenous backgrounds and all people who identified as indigenous, would regain their lost freedom and assert their cultural and political autonomy (e.g., Macas 1991).

From about 1989 through the first half of 1992, the symbolism of "1492–1992: 500 Years of Resistance!" in indigenous and black discourse in Ecuador was framed by the cosmogonic polarities that Lawrence Sullivan (1988) calls the *Primordium* and the *Eschaton*. These concepts pertain to the pre-beginning of everything (the *Primordium*) and the end of everything, with new life occurring out of death (the *Eschaton;* chapter 7, this volume). Midway through 1992, the public rhetoric of ethnic and class schism shifted from millennial to practical, from cosmic–nationalist (hemisphere-wide) to local and regional.

In Ecuador a shift toward local-level violence occurred wherein indigenous and black people appropriated land by force, pledged alliance to one another's movements, and became pitted against one another in an arena of increasingly violent local-level political-economic maneuvering by power wielders. Nationalist rhetoric as manifest by the public statements by the new president, Sixto Durán Ballén, from August 10, 1992, on has vigorously stressed the ideology of *mestizaje* and the black and indigenous "problems" that only governmental agencies (often unspecified) can "solve." The major change in national praxis has been the denial of direct access by indigenous people to the president of the republic and to his immediate advisors. Indigenous people, under the regime of Durán Ballén, have become increasingly analogous to their black congeners.

Current ethnic and class clashes in the Americas define a structure of conjuncture entailing "unprecedented objectifications of [ethnic] categories" (Sahlins 1981:35) cast in increasingly rigid racialist terms (see also Sahlins 1994). Ethnogenetic processes and the discourses that emerge from such conjunctures provide a profound cultural critique on Western thought. Dimensions of such a critique have been set forth with learned elegance by the comparative religion specialist Lawrence Sullivan (1988) and by the anthropologist Michael Taussig (1987). In this essay, I have endeavored to embed a sense of such a cultural critique within my overall specific theme of interethnicity manifest in racialist discourse and in collective action.

Acknowledgments and Notes as to Context

This essay draws, in part, from two collaborative projects. One, joint with Arlene Torres, focused on blackness in Latin America and the Caribbean (Whitten and Torres 1992; Whitten and Torres, eds. 1998). The second, ongoing, project with Dorothea (Sibby) Scott Whitten focuses on the Ecuadorian cultural transformative events and processes within a research framework that has developed over a number of years. This framework includes intensive work with indigenous people in Puyo, capital of Pastaza Province (see D. Whitten and N. Whitten 1993; N. Whitten and D. Whitten 2008). A sequel to this essay is on the Caminata from Puyo to Quito in 1992 (Whitten et al. 1997). I am most grateful to Arlene Torres, Diego Quiroga, and Sibby Whitten for critical and productive readings of early drafts of this essay and for the collaborative work that made the essay possible. Although the chapter reflects joint research and joint publication, only I am to be faulted for any errors of omission or commission, and I am entirely responsible for flaws in interpretation.

Prelude

It was through a potter's quest for expanding indigenous horizons of mythopoetic knowledge to guide her design elaborations while decorating polychrome drinking bowls that we came to draw together the information on a moment of Ecuadorian time to write this chapter under pressure of strict deadlines.

Jean Muteba Rahier, editor of the *Journal of Latin American Studies,* asked me (N. Whitten) in March 2004 to prepare an op-ed article for publication in November of that year. The article was to be based on information about ongoing events in Ecuador between June and September, and would be a model for others in the new section Actualidades. I agreed but asked Jean, "What if nothing special is going on in Ecuador, or nothing special happens?" "You'll think of something," he immediately replied.

First in Quito and then in Puyo we did the usual things in addition to our field research: we read newspapers and magazines, listened to the radio, watched TV, listened carefully to what people were talking about. Sibby kept track of the frequency of topics, and we discussed multiple items, seeking out the "novel" for publication. Although lots of interesting things were going on, nothing seemed especially noteworthy for an article in a distinguished journal; moreover, the arrays of information we were collecting did not hang together except that they were taking place within the Republic of Ecuador during a short span of time. Actually, life seemed sort of messy: social movements were pretty depressed, there was conflict but nothing seemed to result from the scrimmages, and national events bordered on the frivolous except for bursts of information on violence in Colombia and U.S. hegemonic endeavors in culture and politics.

A year earlier, in Puyo, Marta Jobita Vargas Dagua, daughter of master potter Jacinta Estela Dagua Malaber, had asked us whether we knew the story of the *cutu amarun,* and we replied we did, but in bits and pieces. She said that she had found a new "aunt," who was Achuar from the Río Bufeo region northeast of Montalvo, who "really knew the story," and she proceeded to tell it to us. Then, midway through the summer of 2004 she began to paint drinking bowls decorated with all sorts of anaconda designs, one of which was the *cutu amarun*. As she worked, she talked of these mythical power sources, relating case after case of stricken people who ran afoul of evil *pajus* in various parts of the Oriente (especially Tena, Montalvo, and Puyo). As we thought about this story and its thematic structure, we began to "see" that core motifs of the "howler monkey [sounding] anaconda" could serve as a unifying feature for the span of time in modern Ecuador about which we were soon to write. And so we used it to draw together this piece that, with exceptions noted late in the chapter and in the conclusion of the book, fits Ecuador in 2010 as well as it did in 2004.

Chapter 5
Ecuador in the New Millennium

Twenty-five Years of Democracy

Diez de agosto, 2004, formally marked the twenty-fifth continuous year of democracy for the Republic of Ecuador, and the media and scholarly reminiscences and projections of its pathway since emerging from nine long years of dictatorship (two civilian, seven military) constituted significant public and private commentary from May 2004 on. As the rebirth of democracy was celebrated, so too was the death of the populist president, elected in 1979, mourned. On *24 de mayo,* 1981—Ecuador's independence day—Jaime Roldós Aguilera, his wife, Martha Bucaram de Roldós, and a small entourage perished in a plane crash in Loja. At his inauguration in 1979, Roldós spoke in Quichua, a language understood by at least one-third of the people. "*Kunan punchaka, mana pushaita japinchik* (Today we are no longer entrapped [as in the year past])," he said, and he went on to name, and thereby recognize, the indigenous, Afro-Ecuadorian, foreign, and other people of Ecuador. His last words in 1981, delivered in a speech in Quito an hour before he boarded the military Beechcraft plane especially designed in the United States for mountain flying and landing in difficult terrain, were "*Ecuador amazónica desde siempre y hasta siempre, ¡viva la patria!* (Amazonian Ecuador forever and ever. Long live the homeland!)."

In its twenty-fifth year of democracy, it was very widely acknowledged throughout the country that the nation-state of Ecuador in 2004 seemed to be turning in on itself, going nowhere, and that it had lost all sense of direction. Seen from Amazonia, the nation seems to be moving on a trajectory characterized in the Quichua dialect of Pastaza Province as *mana tuparina ñambi,* a path or road that leads into the unknown where strange and powerful forces reside and from which no one knows how to return. Forks, mazeways, switchbacks, and spirals exist to confound the traveler; there are few if any signposts for guidance, turning back is impossible, and the end is anything but what it may be envisioned at the outset of the journey. This pathway constitutes a labyrinth within which the seeker encounters the possibility of *paju,* dangerous powers beyond his or her control. To move into the realm of *paju* is to encounter enshrouded and fearsome imagery of unrecognizable and unknown entities. *Paju* can cause severe illness, and even death.

Two interrelated consistencies that enshrouded this path in 2004 and continue to cast their pall in 2010 are the increased presence of Colombian drug traffickers, paramilitaries, and guerrillas and the dominance and hegemony of the United States of America—both seen by indigenous, among other, Ecuadorian people as analogous to great *pajus.* Reports, editorials, and commentaries in the national media from May 2004 on stress, in order of magnitude of information, Plan Colombia; the escalating drug scene emanating from Colombia; Colombia's policies and interpretations of its southern neighbor; divisiveness among Ecuadorian members of the "political class" and among indigenous people; Ecuadorian emigration, most of it expensive and illegal; U.S. dominance and hegemony; petroleum exploitation in Amazonia; attempts to overthrow the government; racism; and the protest movements of the *jubilados* (retired people with pensions).

These are all intertwined and constitute the labyrinth of conjunctures through which one can move only with caution and with danger on all sides. The way out may come through a great and wrenching change, known in Quichua as *pachacutij,* taken here as an episteme of transformation from one space-time system to another. In Spanish the verb *recambio* (to change again) was used repeatedly in the media and in quotidian discourse to reflect this need for radical change. It emerged from the concept expressed by the trope *refundar el país* (to refound the country) that was a millennial element in the 2003 assumption of office of President Lucio Gutiérrez Borbúa (Whitten 2003a).

Interculturality

Beneath the surface of the public publications, radio broadcasts, and television presentations lies the indefatigable social movement toward *interculturalidad* (interculturality) together with its seemingly paradoxical complement of reinforced cultural and ethnic boundaries. Interculturality is very different from an ethos of hybridity or social or cultural pluralism. It is multicultural but it is also *inter*cultural. There is no hybridity involved. Interculturality stresses a movement from one cultural system to another, with the explicit purpose of understanding other ways of thought and action, whereas social and cultural pluralism stress the institutional separation forced by the *blanco* (white) elite on peoples. The ideologies of hybridity and pluralism are national, regional, and static; formal consciousness of interculturality is local, regional, diasporic, global, and dynamic.

The ideological focus of *interculturalidad* is the polar opposite of *el mestizaje*. More than a quarter century ago, Roldós picked up the then inchoate concept of *interculturalidad,* and after his tragic death it was again suppressed in the national ideology of *el mestizaje,* the blending and "whitening" of phenotype and culture, until reemerging vigorously in public discourse during the Levantamiento Indígena of 1990 and then again in the Caminata of 1992 (N. Whitten and D. Whitten 2008; Whitten et al. 1997). I will not review here the phenomenon of *mestizaje* as an ideology of exclusion (Rahier 1998; Stutzman 1981; Whitten, ed. 1981). Suffice it to say that interculturality specifically opposes this doctrine (e.g., Salomon 1981; Whitten 2003a, 2003b).

In 1995 during the war with Peru, multiculturalism gained strength within the military, as well as in the more depressed sectors of the expanding populace. Abdalá Bucaram Ortiz was driven to exile in Panama in 1997 by an indigenous–populist movement that engaged people in all classes and walks of life, and the dramatic ouster of Jamil Mahuad Witt by a combination of indigenous and military rebellion on January 21, 2000, further strengthened interculturality in some sectors, while promoting class and regional divisions in others. The conjoined idioms of military victory, rebellion, and multiculturality carried the principal colonel in this rebellion, Lucio Gutiérrez Borbúa, into a victorious presidential race in 2002 (Whitten, ed. 2003).

After an enlightened moment in early 2003 that witnessed the president's appointment of two indigenous people, Nina Pacari (Cotacachi, Imbabura) and Luis Macas (Saraguro, Loja) to prominent cabinet positions—together with four hundred or so members of the Pachakutik social movement to positions nationwide—the president completely reversed his millennial moves. He embraced global hegemonic forces represented by the International Monetary Fund, the World Bank, and high-level representatives of the United States such as Otto Reich and George W. Bush, and as promulgated by his previous archrivals to move Ecuador to the heart of neoliberalism. These included, especially, great coastal barons and power wielders of Guayaquil epitomized in the persona of León Febres Cordero, called by many *el dueño del Ecuador,* and lauded by the late Ronald Reagan as a "champion of free enterprise" (Corkill and Cubitt 1988:77).

On August 6, 2003, Gutiérrez rescinded all four hundred or more of his Pachakutik appointments and reestablished a nation based on a rudderless ship of state foundering on reefs of capitalist modernity and neoliberalism.

He took the country into the *mana tuparina ñambi,* which features, especially, a rising and record-high price of oil in a country for which this is the number-one revenue source, together with serious indigenous and populist protests about present, past, and future petroleum exploitation.

Recent Events: Ecuador on the Global Stage, 2004

Recent salient public events in Ecuador include the most recent of a number of quick visits by General James Hill, chief of the Southern Command of the United States; the Miss Universe contest and multiple ceremonies taking place in May and June; the meeting of the Organization of American States in June; and the indigenous parliament of the Americas and an indigenous forum on racism, neoliberalism, and interculturality at about the same time. Officials of the International Monetary Fund came and went, Chevron-Texaco initiated a lawsuit against Petroecuador to counter the ten-year suit against Texaco brought by indigenous people of Ecuador, and Robert Zoellick arrived to chant the virtues of the Free Trade Agreement and was met and confronted by sustained indigenous and popular resistance.

The grand finale of the Miss Universe spectacular featured Donald Trump's appearance on the night of the crowning, which prompted the U.S. ambassador to Ecuador, Kristie Kenney, to say on national television, "with more events like this Ecuador could enter the modern world" (*El Comercio,* June 1, 2004). Trump's presence is significant for this glimpse of modernity since the debt for the "misses" amounted to 13.5 million dollars, with no tangible benefits noted by the vast majority of spokespeople of Ecuador. If anyone knows how to sell and profit from debt, it would seem to be Donald Trump (e.g., O'Brien and Dash 2004). Social commentator Raúl Vallejo (2004), in an editorial entitled "Neocolonizados" (Neocolonized), referred to the event as an "*embobamiento colectivo*" (collective stupefaction). A caller to a newscast the next morning commented to announcer Andrés Carrión that the event celebrated "Miss Misería and Miss Corrupción," the twin features of modern Ecuador represented by barely concealed female flesh: misery for the masses and corruption at the top and in the middle of the class-prestige pyramid.

In sharp contradiction to the Miss Universe rhetoric was the indigenous parliament and forum in which, among other things, an alternative to neoliberal debt-oriented development and wealth for the rich was promulgated. Here the model offered to people of the Americas and the world was that of an intercultural portal to globalization, one in which understanding across cultural lines would help to construct transformative radical changes toward a democracy that allowed the real voices within the vast majority of nation-states to be heard, and new actions to be initiated. These included the rejection of U.S. domination and hegemony, the end of corruption in all branches of government and especially in banking establishments, and a respect for human livelihood, social justice, local-level and regional welfare, and human diversity.

The visit by Secretary of State Colin L. Powell on the last day of the meeting of the OAS was dramatic and decisive. Only a few days before his visit, U.S. Ambassador Kristie Kenney had publicly proclaimed that the president of Ecuador would soon terminate his term of office. But Powell came to Ecuador with another message: he proclaimed the United States to be an aggressive supporter of democracy in Ecuador (if not in Venezuela). He was seen by many as saving President Gutiérrez from indigenous and other political forces that could lead to his early demise. The difference between the U.S. ambassador's take on Ecuadorian affairs and that of the U.S. secretary of state could not be more striking.

Hyper-Racialization in Public Spheres, 2004

Pernicious racism through the Ecuadorian media was explicitly revealed following Powell's brief visit. Writers for the weekly satire page of *El Comercio* referred to Powell as *negrito* and *azabache* (ebony, jet black), as well as *negro, afroamericano,* and *afrodescendiente.* In a cartoon (reprinted in this chapter), Pancho Cajas captures the obsession manifest in the Quito press about Powell's race.

On the left in the cartoon is a cannon that has just backfired, its smoke and black powder covering the faces of past presidents León Febres Cordero and Rodrigo Borja, who fired it. Behind them indigenous leader Leonidas Iza comes running with a big rock. Looking annoyed at these characters is Colin Powell, garbed in angel wings and a flowing white robe. He holds Lucio Gutiérrez to protect him from the firepower of ex-presidents–as–*caudillos* and the rocks of the indigenous movement. President Gutiérrez, dressed in white pants and striped jacket, looks back over his shoulder and sticks his tongue out at his adversaries. He carries a shepherd's crook to guide the white-faced black sheep of his PSP (Partido Sociedad Patriótica) party. Powell is portrayed here as the black Dominican lay brother San Martín de Porres of Peru who, while in jail, fed his own meals to the dog, cat, and rat, ancient enemies who sat together to sup at his feet. "Saint Powell" now protects the president of Ecuador from his various enemies, including the rat, cat, or dog behind the cannon.

Cartoon portraying Colin Powell as San Martín de Porres guarding the president of Ecuador. (Actualidad, *El Comercio*, June 11, 2004, p. A2, reprinted by permission; Copyright © Pancho Cajas/*El Comercio*/June 11, 2004, All Rights Reserved)

The "family" magazine section of this same newspaper on the same day featured a whole page of advice about how and what to do to avoid *mal olor*, bad (body) odor, which is mentioned eight times. In the center of the page is a prominent color photograph of Dr. Condoleezza Rice jogging. No mention is made of her in the text: the juxtaposition serves effectively to racialize body odor.

The rhetoric of racialization, illustrated above, snakes through the public discourses of publicists and politicians. Blackness is especially salient in 2004 (for background on this subject see especially Rahier 1998, 2003; Whitten 2003a). At the Miss Universe gala, two former Miss Ecuadors tagged as "black" were excluded from the invitation list, causing protests alleging deliberate prejudicial planning against people of color. In interviews on national television with black spokespeople and politicians, the focus invariably zooms in on the lips of the speaker, especially if a regional dialect is spoken.

Editorials about Canciller (Secretary of State) Patricio Zuquilanda often refer to him as "Suquilanda (con Z)" to lampoon him as having indigenous background (Suquilanda is a Saraguro surname, whereas Zuquilanda is what the canciller insists on as the "proper" spelling). For his part, Zuquilanda recently removed from the Ecuadorian embassy in Washington, D.C., the only two representatives of blackness and indigenousness of any Andean nation, ever—Mae Montaño (Esmeraldan Afro-Ecuadorian) and Silvia González (Saraguran Indigenous Ecuadorian)—both of whom are highly qualified for their positions. They were appointed by the Ecuadorian ambassador, Raúl Gangotena, with the approval of President Gutiérrez.

Intraindigenous rhetoric, especially attendant on the appointment of Antonio Vargas as Minister of Social Welfare (p. 129) falls into this pattern of racialization, as does the press's systematic denigration of Vargas as an "unqualified" and "unprepared" person, without discussing his accomplishments in endeavoring to build a new democracy in Ecuador and with no reference to the expected qualities one requires to be "qualified" or "prepared."

Colombia, Plan Colombia, and U.S. Hegemony

Michael Taussig (2004:145), in his postmodernist discourse on Colombian realities, uses his literary license to characterize Ecuador as follows: "cleanliving Ecuador, the Switzerland of South America, safe haven of the U.S. imperium complete with its dollarized currency and spanking new U.S. Air Force base on the Pacific Coast at Manta to make strikes into Colombia." If one compares the average income of different Swiss socioeconomic classes and the poverty levels of Switzerland and Ecuador, Taussig's flippant and gratuitous comparison becomes highlighted in its absurdity. Switzerland has one of the lowest poverty and unemployment rates in the world, Ecuador one of the highest; income distribution in Switzerland is quite equitable, whereas the differential between the extraordinarily wealthy and the seventy percent or more poor in Ecuador is enormous, and increasing regularly. Moreover, Swiss banks are internationally known as safe depositories, whereas Ecuadorian banks are notoriously risky and seem to be run by corrupt manipulators. Today in Ecuador the trope *banquero corrupto* (corrupt banker) is standard parlance. Ecuador is no Switzerland.

Ecuador is not Colombia writ small, either. It is, however, increasingly tied to the fate of that country through a highly porous and unstable border region and through the U.S.-coopted Plan Colombia, with its military base in Manta and with its use of various regions of coastal and Amazonian Ecuador for training special troops. The borderland between Ecuador and Colombia, going west to east, includes the coastal province of Esmeraldas, the mostly Andean province of Carchi, and the Amazonian province of Sucumbíos. Together, these border provinces constitute about one-third of the territory of the nation. The Colombian military has no permanent base along this entire region, which is controlled in Colombia by the Autodefensas Unidas de Colombia (United Self Defense System of Colombia; AUC), the Fuerzas

Armadas Revolucionarias de Colombia (Revolutionary Armed Forces of Colombia; FARC), and the Ejército de Liberación Nacional (Army of National Liberation; ELN). The Ecuadorian military, reduced in budget after the war with Peru in 1995 by ensuing presidents, has the responsibility of patrolling the entire region but lacks bases and must develop new tactics to fight narcoterrorist activities. Just south of these provinces lie Manabí (Coast), Imbabura (Sierra), and Napo and Orellana (Oriente); these provinces are also affected by ongoing processes attendant on the spread of drugs, crime, and terror.

The most aggressive and dangerous aggregation of terrorists is the AUC, which controls the entire sector of the rain-forest–riverine Nariño Department that abuts Esmeraldas and Carchi. While images of horror and death abound, no one from the northwest sector of Esmeraldas—inhabited primarily by Afro-Ecuadorians and Chachi and Awá indigenous people—can forget the day that the AUC came to the small settlement of Mataje, near the San Juan River that forms the border between Colombia and Ecuador, captured the Teniente Político (local appointed parish administrator) of the community, ordered all people present to watch as they tied his arms and legs to a tree, so that his head and torso faced the gathering, and cut him in half from head to crotch with a chainsaw. In September 2004, news came to us that the AUC had also entered the Oriente province of Sucumbíos to spread terror and death.

Colombian President Álvaro Uribe Vélez, long a friend of the AUC movement (e.g., Hristov 2009:142–143), worked hard to grant amnesty to allow a sizable number of the 13,000-member movement to reenter civil society and probably engage in activities including military operations and private guard duties. In late July 2004, three members of the AUC, Salvador Mancuso (a prominent leader and drug czar, whom the United States wished to extradite for his shipment of seventeen tons of cocaine), Ramón Isaza, and Iván Roberto Duque, visited the national congress by invitation to expound on the sacrifices the AUC had made in freeing Colombia from the grips of the FARC and ELN. They were flown there in a military helicopter. William Wood, U.S. ambassador to Colombia, called the event a "scandal" and United Nations Secretary General Koffi Annan said that Colombia ought not permit general amnesty or de facto impunity for crimes committed by the *paras* who, since 1980, have protected narcotraffic (*El Comercio,* July 4, 2004, p. A10; Leech 2004).

Coca growing, marketing, and export have come under the auspices of the AUC, whose members may also control about one-third of the Colombian congress. According to Peter Canby (2004:34), "Diego Fernando Murillo [the successor as an AUC leader after the disappearance of Carlos Castaño] [is] known as Don Berna, a man who once took a giant step up the slippery cocaine slope by betraying his boss, Pablo Escobar." At least in western Nariño, Cauca, and Valle, cocaine traffic is virtually synonymous with the AUC's operations, which move inexorably into Ecuador. To the east, the FARC prevail, with their own cocaine trade, which uses routes into and out of northern Ecuador as the major conduit to foreign markets.

Plan Colombia was conceived by Colombians and U.S. personnel in 1999 but soon was coopted by the United States to move its strategic Southern Command base from Panama to Manta-Manabí. This base is far more sophisticated in its surveillance apparatus than was the Panama base, and it is coordinated with Tres Esquinas deep in the rain forest of southern Colombia, in Caquetá Department, just north of the Putumayo River region that forms the border between Ecuador and Colombia. Manta is the key in a U.S.-controlled triangulation around Colombia that includes the base of Palmerola in Honduras and Reina Beatriz in Aruba. Its original mission was to interdict Colombian cocaine trade and to destroy coca gardens and plantations, especially by massive spraying of coca fields with Monsanto's Ultra Roundup (or Roundup Ultra) mixed with a powerful Colombian toxicant called Cosmoflux. This deadly herbicide combination kills all plant life, including the rain-forest canopy and subsistence crops, pollutes rivers, and causes innumerable illnesses in people and animals. Ironically, the first plant to recover from such spraying is coca. The spraying reaches into Ecuador at times, and even when it doesn't, the fallout does. After 9/11, 2001, the United States mandated that the war on terrorism be expanded to include Colombia's FARC, ELN, and even AUC, the result being a U.S. military and U.S. contract mercenary soldier and espionage buildup in many areas of Colombia. The buildup continues.

This whole system of severe disruption penetrates at least one-third of Ecuador's territory. Moreover, President Uribe has developed a program called Plan Patriota that calls on all five abutting countries—Panama, Venezuela, Peru, Brazil, and Ecuador—to defend with vigor their boundaries with Colombia, and where possible to pursue paramilitaries and revolutionaries into Colombia itself. Ecuador has vigorously and vociferously rejected this plan, even to the point of nearly breaking diplomatic relations with Colombia. In turn, Uribe blames what he calls a corrupt Ecuadorian military for supplying the FARC with weapons and explosives.

When Ecuadorian military and diplomatic spokespeople requested U.S. military assistance, as part of Plan Colombia, and pursuant to the base at Manta to help with its buildup of police and military along its northern border, they were curtly refused. Secretary of State Colin Powell said, in Ecuador, and this was repeated and reiterated by Ambassador Kristie Kenney, that Ecuador would have to take care of its own borders. As the U.S. presence escalates in Colombia and its budget for the internal war there increases, and as the United States uses Ecuadorian bases in the Coast and Amazonia for training special forces, and as the base in Manta grants all kinds of privileges, including imports and exports without customs intervention, it denies Ecuador the very aid required to maintain its sovereignty. Moreover, as the United States steps up its financial aid to Colombia, mostly for military activity, more and more AUC and FARC personnel enter north Ecuador (and perhaps elsewhere) to continue their plans and activities, ranging from assassination and kidnapping to growing coca, making cocaine paste, and shipping refined cocaine out of Ecuador in various ways to various destinations in South America, Central America, Europe, and the United States.

In 2004 the fact came to light that not only does the United States deny support to Ecuadorian sovereignty but it also seems to have taken action against Ecuadorian vessels on both the high seas and in sovereign territorial waters (albeit in the disputed two-hundred-mile limit radiating out from the mainland and from the Galápagos Islands). Specifically, the U.S. Coast Guard, operating out of Manta, is alleged to have intercepted ships carrying illegal migrants north from Ecuador to Guatemala, and then sunk the ships after evacuating the migrants back to Manta or Guayaquil. The issue waxes and wanes only to rise again. But the sovereignty of the Ecuadorian national territory and possessions seems threatened by the United States as well as by Colombia. Vallejo (2004:A4) ends his piece with this phrase: "National Sovereignty? For the neocolonized this is an obsolete concept."

Indigenous Politics and Divisions, 2004

Contrary to some popular and academic opinions and positions, indigenous people are Ecuadorians and subject to the same forces as are other members of civil society. Their reactions to being placed in a *mana tuparina ñambi* are varied and sometimes appear to be contradictory when they are lumped together as a monolithic bloc of *indios* by unreflective commentators and analysts. The indigenous movement has three focal organizations, ECUARUNARI (Ecuador Runacunapac Riccharimui, "Ecuadorian Indigenous People Awaken") in the Sierra, CONFENAIE (Confederación de Nacionalidades Indígenas de la Amazonía Ecuatoriana, "Confederation of Indigenous Nationalities of Amazonian Ecuador") in Amazonia, and COICE (Coordinadora de Movimientos Sociales, "Social Movements Coordinator") on the

Coast. All three are coordinated by CONAIE (Confederation of Indigenous Nationalities of Ecuador), which has its centralized office in Quito.

There has long been a wide division between the leaders of ECUARUNARI and those of CONFENAIE, and the new coastal organization seems to take a lot of clues as to its movements and positions from indigenous people of the Oriente. In the Sierra, dominant blocs of indigenous people come from every region. All speak Quichua and most are bilingual in Spanish. The coastal nationalities include the indigenous Awá, Chachi, and Tsáchila, all speaking Barbacoan; the Spanish-speaking Afro-Ecuadorians and Epera (who also speak Siapedia); and the newly organized "Montuvios." In the Oriente are Cofán (unclassified), Siona (Western Tucanoan), Secoya (Western Tucanoan), Waorani (Huaorani, unclassified), Naporuna (Napo/Quijos Quichua), Canelos Quichua (Pastaza Runa), Zápara (Zaparoan), Andoa (Zaparoan), Shiwiar (Achuar, Quichua, maybe other languages), Achuar (Achuar), and Shuar (Shuar). People from these nationalities range from subsistence-oriented to urbane; many are bilingual or multilingual; intercultural, interlanguage marriage is not uncommon.

The Amazonian and coastal nationalities in their diversity would seem intuitively very difficult to coordinate, but their ethos of interculturality emerges strongly at times of perceived collective crisis, when they bind together with Andean indigenous people to form a powerful intraethnic (indigenous) bloc capable of remarkable mobilization. This was first evidenced during the Levantamiento Indígena of 1990 when indigenous peoples from the Sierra and the Oriente rose as one to occupy the rural sectors of the Sierra and much of the Oriente and to block all access to roads in and out of the Sierra, Oriente, and Coast. This movement involved political coordination greater than any seen in the entire history of the republic. Again, as 1992 approached, and the epitomizing symbol "1492–1992" reached high salience, word went out from Puyo to all Canelos Quichua, Shiwiar, and Achuar people that they must march on Quito now or lose their opportunities to regain their lands. One of the leaders of this march was Carlos Antonio Vargas Guatatuca, a Canelos Quichua man from Unión Base, one of twenty-three hamlets of the Comuna San Jacinto del Pindo, just south of Puyo.

Subsequently, Antonio Vargas was elected president of CONAIE, in Quito, serving for two terms, during which time presidents Abdalá Bucaram (1997) and Jamil Mahuad (2000) were expelled by combined indigenous–populist (Bucaram) and indigenous–military (Mahuad) forces. In the latter expulsion, Antonio Vargas teamed up with Lucio Gutiérrez to create a triumvirate (including the coastal judge and lawyer Carlos Solórzano), which lasted for about three hours until the crushing political-economic weight of the United

States intervened (e.g., Whitten 2003b). After the coup, indigenous fragmentation was reported by the media, and active and public white racism, sometimes attributed to a shadowy Legión Blanco (white legion), reemerged. Sierra–Oriente schisms became salient as the election of 2002 took place, and Antonio Vargas, who had run for president of the republic in 2002 on his Jatari Amauta party, was expelled from the organization. He moved his base of operations to Guayaquil, on the coast, where he continued to organize people into a movement for an "alternative government."

In 2004 the elected president of CONAIE, Leonidas Iza, from Chimborazo, was returning to his office from a trip to Cuba with his wife and son when an attempted assassination took place in front of the CONAIE building. He and his wife escaped and survived, but the fate of his son, the most gravely wounded from the gunshots, is not known. Some blamed the Legión Blanco, others Colombian *sicarios* (professional assassins), but the case has not been resolved.

The indigenous movement is tied in its modernity to national politics, to which it is often opposed. At the level of the national *clase política*, also known as the *clase dirigente* (the political class or the class that directs), enormous ferment is under way. The *mana tuparina ñambi* is constructed constantly by the incredibly narcissistic clashes of powerful *caudillos* operating in their own self-interest. In breaking with the transformational agenda of his campaign and dismissing indigenous people and the Pachakutik social movement, which sometimes acts as the political arm of CONAIE, Gutiérrez allied himself and his Sociedad Patriótica party with the Social Christian party, dominated by León Febres Cordero and Jaime Nebot Saadi.

As this alliance took place, Febres Cordero was also allied with his one-time political enemy, Rodrigo Borja Cevallos, leader of the Democratic Left party. Before long, Borja and Febres Cordero decided to remove Gutiérrez from the presidency—constitutionally, if possible—and Iza and CONAIE went along with these *caudillos* as the storm troops-to-be (see the above cartoon). Iza, as president of CONAIE, with strong support of leaders of ECUARUNARI, called for a *levantamiento indígena* to do away with the wrongs of the country, seemingly attached full force to Gutiérrez and his family, friends, *compadres*, and military colleagues involved in the *"golpe del 21 de enero."* As the May 31 day for the uprising and coup approached, it became clear that the bases of support for CONAIE were not mobilizing, and just why CONAIE should do the bidding of *el dueño del Ecuador* was anything but clear.

Moreover, neither CONFENAIE nor COICE subscribed to the *levantamiento* idea in 2004. In the face of all of this, Iza and some ECUARUNARI leaders continued to assert their ability to force the government from office and create a new form of democracy. Rhetoric echoed that of the public indigenous ideology of early 2000, late 2002, and early 2003—especially as promulgated by Antonio Vargas—but it failed to motivate those who had to undertake considerable risks to join a transformational social movement in a time of great uncertainty. Gutiérrez was working with leaders of indigenous bases in all three mainland regions of the republic by granting rights, giving tractors and farm tools, and making contracts with and promises to grassroots organizations.

Finally, perhaps as a trump card in the unfolding dissatisfaction with the government and with the pinnacle of indigenous leadership, the president appointed Antonio Vargas to his cabinet as Ministro de Bienestar Social, the Minister of Social Welfare. This position was vigorously and in some cases viciously attacked by the president of CONAIE and by spokespeople for ECUARUNARI. One young indigenous woman from Chimborazo, speaking in highly articulate Spanish on an early morning television newscast, affirmed that although Vargas was an "indigenous person," he was also an "Amazonian Indian" (*indio amazónico*) who lacked consciousness of the social movement, indigenous democracy, and the indigenous ideology of change. With words such as these, the long-standing rift between Amazonian and Sierran indigenous people reemerged with high salience, and pernicious racism, discussed above, entered the intraindigenous system straining toward transformation but caught in its national modernity. The day of the announced *levantamiento* came and went without incident, and those of CONAIE and ECUARUNARI who came to stand in the Parque El Arbolito in Quito soon dispersed. Ecuador remained on a course of *mana tuparina ñambi*, the trail into the unknown full of strange and frightening dangers from which one cannot find one's way back.

Internal (National) Politics and Divisiveness, 2004

Divisiveness characterized the narcissistic moods, motivations, and modus operandi of political activity. Appointments intended to heal enmities or win allies frequently backfired, as in the case of the almost constantly changing ministers of education, health, and social welfare. During 2004 the infighting among prominent men (less so women) of the *clase política* underscored the extraordinary *caudillismo* of coastal and Andean politics. Not only did former political enemies, or at least rivals, Borja and Febres Cordero, align to destroy Gutiérrez "constitutionally," but also Febres Cordero became involved in a very public and very nasty dispute with his one-time strongman, Renán Borbúa, first cousin of the president and a prominent figure in 2004 politics.

One cartoon portrayed "the lion" (León Febres Cordero) as shouting in fury that Borbúa (portrayed as a mouse or rat) planned to kill him and then sue him. This is how ridiculous these fights are, but they are part and parcel of Ecuadorian egomaniacal rhetoric within the "class that directs" the country.

Such rhetoric permeated a remarkably successful social movement by the elderly and the retired. The revolt of the *jubilados* that took place from June through August and cost eighteen lives due to hunger strikes conjoined with closing of health facilities succeeded in achieving a minimal retirement salary that exceeded the terminal work earnings of thousands. But as success occurred, political-class–like bickering broke out at high levels, and the *jubilados* began to fight one another over what sort of scale would be applied; as they did so, pension checks ceased arriving. The issues here are unresolved but attract considerable media attention.

Migration

Mary Weismantel (2003:331) writes: "The *mestiza* nation . . . is simultaneously imploding and exploding: imploding as the rural indigenous population takes over the centers of white urbanity and exploding as Ecuadorians from all walks of life abandon the land of their birth for the United States [and Europe])." Not only are poor people hocking everything they, their relatives, friends, and neighbors have to make the treacherous journey, but skilled laborers from Ambato and Cuenca are also making such a sacrificial journey. As Ecuador's skilled labor force diminishes, jobs are filled by Peruvian immigrants. Of a population estimated at thirteen million, seventy percent live in poverty or subpoverty, and seven to ten percent, maybe more, live abroad (e.g., *Hoy,* August 7, 2004; Miles 2004; Spencer 2003; Weismantel 2003). Probably seventy percent of the diaspora population is in another country illegally. Some years ago we were surprised to learn of fees of from $6,000 to $10,000 paid to "coyotes" who arrange passage to another country and thence, through extraordinary time and travail, into the United States. But now we learn of fees from $12,000 to $18,500 for this service. Payment comes not just by up-front money but by obligations to pay a percentage of one's wages once one finds work; mortgage of every piece of property of the migrant and of his or her relatives, friends, *compadres,* and inlaws is also common or standard.

Remittances returned to Ecuador by its swelling diaspora population exceed every single other legal source of revenue in the gross domestic product except that of petroleum. The earnings of the illegal coyotes nearly equal those of the illegal drug exporters. The latter amounts to an estimated fifty million dollars per year, and the traffic in illegal emigrants comes to forty million per year (*Hoy*, "Blanco y Negro," Saturday, August 7, 2004). Ecuador is not only a petroleum-exporting nation, it is also a poverty-exporting nation. Profit has immense human costs, and Ecuadorians in their diaspora have established an organization called *llactacaru* (distant territory) to press their rights as human beings and as Ecuadorians. *Llactacaru*, with its own international newsletter and web site (http://www.llacta.org/organiz/llactacaru/) and e-mail address (llactacaru@llacta.org), stretches from the United States to Spain, where Ecuadorians constitute the second-largest immigrant group after Moroccans (*New York Times*, April 19, 2002) and includes smaller aggregates in Italy, France, Germany, Holland, and Canada.

Illegal migrants endure incredible dangers, from being captured prior to departure, to capture on the high seas or in territorial waters, usually by U.S. Coast Guard vessels. On board ship, hunger, thirst, and sickness are compounded by robbery, abuse, and rape of women by coyotes and boat captains and crews. Then come the arduous journeys into and through Guatemala and Mexico and across the border into the United States and, with luck, travel within the United States to a remunerative destination such as Queens, New York (Miles 2004), or Danbury, Connecticut (Spencer 2003), among many other destinations. Many are turned back at one point or another in the journey, often after considerable abuse, only to try again—and if they don't make it, again. In detention centers, such would-be emigrants compete with others from South and Central America as well as from India and China. Here danger abounds, as the packed surroundings in detention put the Ecuadorians seeking livelihood in competition for space, food, and dignity with drug smugglers and those engaged in other illegal activities (e.g., Spencer 2003:22).

Dominance and Hegemony by the United States

The possibility of dollarization was first raised by then president Abdalá Bucaram in 1996. The Argentine model of pegging the dollar to the sucre (the Ecuadorian currency until 2000) led to great consternation in the republic. Yet movement in that direction continued. Jamil Mahuad suggested actually adopting the Yankee Greenback, for which he was severely criticized, but then Gustavo Noboa Bejarano, who became president following the *golpe del 21 de enero*, 2000, operationalized Mahuad's plan, and the dollar—at a twenty-five thousand sucres per dollar conversion rate—became the only Ecuadorian currency in that year. Imagine the shock to the poor and the rural residents, those whose use of money revolves around the equivalent of thirty thousand sucres per day for wage laborers and much less for those balancing subsistence and cash economic life. Suddenly one earns a dollar and perhaps a few cents a day; this in a country where the price of gasoline in 2004 ranged from $1.50 per gallon for "extra" to $2.10 per gallon for "super."

The logic of the U.S. coins, which are used in most Ecuadorian transactions below the middle sector, was initially incomprehensible: the fifty-cent coin is larger than the dollar, which is about the size of a quarter; and the five-cent piece is much larger than the ten-cent piece. It should not take much imagination to figure multiple ways to swindle the unsophisticated: "Here's the *jatun* (big) dollar (the fifty-cent coin); please give me two of the *ichilla* (little) dollars (one-dollar coins)," et cetera.

For those with money in a bank, ranging from the equivalent of a few hundred to hundreds of thousands of dollars, the radical devaluation of the sucre reduced savings by seventy-five percent. Then the banks closed, accounts were frozen, and several banks crashed and never reopened. The largest, Filanbanco, a national state bank, has yet to reopen, and the scandals involving who took the money where and how it is to be returned seem legion. Consensus in Ecuador seems to be that for the wealthy and the middle-class, adoption of the dollar has been beneficial, but for the rest of the country the question of benefit remains open. As the macroeconomy has improved significantly in its neoliberal framework, the livelihood of the vast majority of Ecuadorians has worsened proportionately.

The U.S. Air Force base at Manta is complemented by its alleged use of U.S. Coast Guard ships to interdict and sink private Ecuadorian vessels in territorial waters as well as on the high seas. When the Latin American Association of Human Rights broke this news publicly in June 2004, Canciller Patricio Zuquilanda said there was no evidence for it just as Ambassador Kristie Kenney announced that this was standard U.S. policy backed by Ecuadorian requests. The reason usually given for such sinkings was the transport of illegal emigrants and/or of illegal drugs. While Ecuadorian navy officials denied knowledge of these events and stated that the United States had no rights to sink Ecuadorian ships, joint Ecuadorian–U.S. commissions declared that such activities were requested by the Ecuadorian navy.

The ongoing collective negotiations among Venezuela, Colombia, Ecuador, Peru, and Bolivia with the United States, and those individual negotiations going on "bilaterally" between each of these Andean nations and the United States, are championed and led by the minister of foreign commerce, Ivonne Baki, and supported by Zuquilanda. It seems, at times, that for Baki and Zuquilanda, anything that benefits the colossus to the north benefits Ecuador. Baki argues strongly that even without an easing of internal subsidies to agriculture in the United States, together with a removal of Ecuadorian subsidies, inflows of cheap foods to Ecuador will benefit the people of the republic.

She cannot be thinking of the poorer of Ecuador's citizens, the seventy percent or more who live on far less money than their daily lives require. It is this same high-profile woman who once served as ambassador to the United States in the Mahuad regime, who returned to run for president within her own Metamorphosis party in 2002, and who insisted and insists that Ecuador reaped great benefits from its 13.5-million-dollar debt to host the Miss Universe contest (called in some vulgar street settings "Miss Putita"). And, she is a personal friend of Donald Trump. Add to this the statement by Ambassador Kristie Kenney that Ecuador could enter the modern world with more such events and the allegedly unauthorized (by the Ecuadorian military) sinking of Ecuadorian ships by U.S. ships on the high seas and in territorial waters, and the structure of U.S. imperialist hegemony should emerge clearly.

There is more to the *mana tuparina ñambi* story. It is appropriate to elaborate here with the United States in mind. One of the *paju* powers to be encountered is the *cutu amarun,* the "monkey [sounding] anaconda." One takes an unknown fork, comes upon an unknown lagoon, and is completely lost. Moving to another trail on another fork one comes to an area enshrouded by dark clouds; above is the tail and lower body of the great constrictor, but one cannot see this. The head of the *cutu amarun* is in the earth in a dangerous cave occupied by dangerous spirits, *juctu supais*. What brings the person to this place is that the boa constrictor knows how to make the sounds of the red howler monkey, which is food for the indigenous Amazonian people. But the gift of monkey meat from the forest spirit master is an illusion, for above it all is the great constrictor, the great *paju,* that in seeming to offer food actually presents great danger, the awful threat of being crushed and devoured.

This and other stories are used as tropes of simile or metaphor for the deceptive tactics and devouring potential of the United States of America by many indigenous people of Amazonia, but still some voluntarily take the trail that leads them to such conjunctures of political and economic life. As I wrote elsewhere, "Between the promise of wealth and the reality of poverty lie dynamic symbol systems to enhance critical insight and to sustain movements into and out of liminality and into new dimensions of social relationships" (Whitten 2003a:29; see also Quiroga 2003).

This takes us again to relationships between indigenous and national politics (and the conjuncture of the two), set in the *mana tuparina ñambi* enshrouded by the two great and interrelated *pajus* of Colombian guerrilla, paramilitary, and terrorist activity and cocaine production and distribution, and the hegemonic policies, strategies, practices, and effects of the United States and its international affiliates. We turn now to the arena of petroleum exploration and exploitation.

Petroleum Exploration and Exploitation

Oil was rediscovered in the northern Oriente (Amazonian region) of Ecuador in the mid-1960s and within a few years exploration companies blanketed the area. This followed widespread exploration by Royal Dutch Shell Oil from the 1920s to the early 1940s that featured considerable disruption throughout the central Amazonian region. In 1992 Ecuador became the first country to leave the OPEC cartel with plans to greatly increase production and hence revenues. But while petroleum brought in wealth for the few, the situation for the majority of the country worsened. Ecological and environmental damage has been catastrophic. According to Suzana Sawyer, "Between 1972 and 1990 the Texaco-operated Trans-Andean pipeline spilled an estimated 16.8 million gallons of crude into Amazonian headwaters—over one and a half times the amount spilled by the Exxon Valdez" (Sawyer 2004:101). Other spills in the northern sector affecting especially Cofán, Siona, Secoya, and colonists receive daily attention in Ecuadorian media. The suit against Texaco (Chevron) by the Cofán and a coalition of colonists is not resolved, and a decade later Texaco now blames and is suing the Ecuadorian Petroecuador corporation that has the dual and contradictory roles of both making and increasing profits for the state and policing the pipelines and oil companies.

For Amazonian indigenous people and coastal and Andean colonists, petroleum is nearing its fortieth year of severe and dramatic influence, either direct or indirect, on their lives. This constitutes a human span of over two generations of real people of the Upper Amazon–Andean piedmont. It is part and parcel of the road that seemingly leads nowhere, where great promise of economic wherewithal and wealth for some combines with utter destruction of natural resources, ecological systems, and environmental management systems that have characterized the Amazonian region since time immemorial. Sawyer (2004) documents some of the Arco–OPIP (Organización de Pueblos Indígenas de Pastaza, "Organization of Indigenous Peoples of Pastaza") interactions over issues of oil exploitation in Pastaza Province during much of the 1990s. The subject is of highest salience today in Ecuador, as a major moneymaking company, Occidental Petroleum (OXY), may have 150 million dollars in state-withheld taxes returned to it because petroleum is a natural product, not one manufactured. This case comes at a time when the state is desperate for revenues to cover its ever-increasing external and internal debts.

There is a dramatic indigenous–oil company standoff in Pastaza Province that threatens to break into a "war" between allied indigenous people—Quichua speakers of Sarayacu, Achuar of the Pastaza drainage, and Shuar from the Macuma River region to Taisha—and the forces of petroleum companies—CGC (the Argentine Compañía General de Combustibles) in the north and Burlington in the south. Each of these was once a subsidiary of Arco.

The indigenous people who reside in two blocks of territory wherein subsurface rights have been ceded to the companies are also stewards of the land, forest, and rivers ceded to them in 2002 and guaranteed to them by the national constitution of 1998. The only legitimate force that the companies can draw on is that of the Ecuadorian military. The interaction of indigenous forces, petroleum forces, and the military of the Oriente are of critical importance to the entire nation. During the March for Land and Life in 1992, some twelve years ago, the indigenous people, specifically Canelos Quichua, Achuar, and Shiwiar, gained the national concession of 1,115,574 hectares in their rain-forest–riparian zone of Pastaza Province, about sixty-five percent of their initial request. This territory, originally granted to OPIP and the Evangelical organization, became divided up among different nationalities, including the Waorani, Zápara, Shiwiar, Achuar, and Amazonian Quichua of different organizations. Other organizations and ethnicities (Andoa, most recently) emerged to claim portions of the redistribution of surface land. But the subsurface rights to exploration and exploitation were retained by the state. In 2004 the state has its rights to wealth that lies beneath the surface and by the constitutional change of 1998 the indigenous people have their rights to health, welfare, and a satisfactory life in their territory, which includes healthy and uncontaminated flora and fauna of forest and water systems.

In this situation, people struggle with the paradoxes and contradictions before them on their unknown trails in modernity, just as those guardians of *la patria*—the military—increase the numbers of indigenous people in their ranks and enter at every level into the debate about whether or not they should be placed in a killing situation vis-à-vis their cultural congeners and family members. Throughout the military, it is recognized that the collaboration of indigenous Shuar people in the Cenepa River region of southeast Ecuador was crucial in Ecuador's victory over Peru, so the idea of killing indigenous people over the rights of foreign oil companies rankles and divides.

The analog to the petroleum situation is that of logging, and especially illegal logging. The people of northern Esmeraldas, mostly Afro-Ecuadorian and Chachi, have been subject to large-scale illegal logging since the 1970s. To make things worse, like the indigenous people of the Oriente, their lands were long declared *tierras baldías,* unoccupied lands, even though, in northern Esmeraldas, as in the Pacific Lowlands and the Chocó of Colombia, these were the most densely populated of the moist tropics of the Americas prior to industrialized exploitation of marginal territories. In response, Afro-Ecuadorians have been organizing their land into indigenous-like *comunas* for many years, as have the Chachi and Epera; indigenous and Afro-Ecuadorians have also cooperated in a myriad of manners and have developed organizations to resist illegal and some legal logging (the line between the two is at best hazy). Added to this is the explosive expansion of shrimp farming in the past quarter century that has devastated the mangrove forest swamps, some of the largest and most biodiverse in the world (e.g., Quiroga 2003).

In Amazonia great tragedy has befallen small groupings of indigenous people in Pastaza Province. On May 26, 2003, a well-known group of Waorani living on the Vía Auca, a road built and named by Texaco from Lago Agrio south to the Tigüino River, made a well-planned raid on a long house, or several long houses, of what were thought to be Tagaeri people but seem to have turned out to be the legendary Taromenane (Taromenga) people near the Curaray River region. The known results were the corpses of eight women, five children, and an uncertain (if any) number of men and the severed head of one man brought on a pole by Waorani raiders back to the "Auca Road" to be photographed by journalists from Quito and Guayaquil (e.g., Cabodevilla et al. 2004; Proaño García and Colleoni 2008). *Auca,* by the way, when used in national Spanish-speaking contexts, is a very pejorative word meaning "savage" of the forest.

It turned out that the Waorani making the raid did so at the behest of illegal Colombian loggers in the zone. An investigation was made at a national level confirming this, but the Colombian loggers are still operating illegally along the Tigüino River, using the Vía Auca as their roadway to industrial wealth by the illegal exploitation of the tropical forest of Amazonian Ecuador. For their part, the Waorani organization, ONHAE (Organización de la Nacionalidad Huaorani de la Amazonía Ecuatoriana, "Organization of the Waorani Nationality of Amazonian Ecuador"), whose president, Armando Boya, is the brother of one of the Waorani raiders, and other organizational leaders from OPIP and CONFENAIE, blamed the petroleum companies for the massacre and asked state officials to invoke the concept of "indigenous justice" to exonerate those who raided and speared to death unknown and threatened Taromenane people. As of February 2010, the illegal logging continues and the raiders live at home, unmolested by internal or external legal sanctions.

A Long Road Going Nowhere?

It would seem to be a long road—a *mana tuparina ñambi*—that twists and turns from the colossus of the United States to a rain-forest setting of death and terror in the region between the Curaray and Tigüino rivers of Amazonian Ecuador. But the road connects in a serpentine manner—even if few U.S.

citizens and none of the surviving Taromenane are aware of it—the huge and mighty and those threatened with extinction by cultural congeners speaking their own language. Two great *pajus* signify danger and possible death on the road of modernity in contemporary Ecuador. Some Colombians, who are at the periphery of their own violence, introduce and sustain terror and death in Ecuador. They play an increasingly important role in constructing this labyrinth. They would seem, in 2004, to represent the covert dimensions of the *cutu amarun* that complement the overt dimensions of the distant but powerful *norteamericanos*—the second great *paju*—who seek to control land, life, and destiny of diverse people of a small and beleaguered nation.

These are some of the actualities of modern Ecuador in their morbid dimensions. Since 1990 indigenous people (with others) in intercultural unity have made sporadic breakouts from this road to nowhere, but their heroic endeavors to transform the republic in peaceful ways have again and again been enshrouded by the forces sketched above.

Thirty Years of Democracy

Major events occurred after this piece was published in 2004. In 2006 Rafael Vicente Correa Delgado, who holds a Ph.D. in economics from the University of Illinois at Urbana-Champaign (and who received the International Alumni Award, 2009) and who descends on his mother's side from the great nineteenth-century *caudillo* and leader of the 1895 Liberal Revolution, Eloy Alfaro Delgado, was elected president of the Republic of Ecuador. A prominent slogan in his campaign, which carried through his first two years in office, was "¡*Dale Correa!*" This translates as "whack 'em Correa!" or just "belt 'em!" This condensed populist political trope refers to the man—Rafael Correa—and to a belt (*correa*) with which the man is to whip (and thereby punish) the elites and leaders of political parties to liberate the country from the twin yokes of corruption of its leaders and dependency on the United States.

Correa pledged to bring about a constitutional convention to not only rewrite the statutes that would govern Ecuador in the foreseeable future but also reorient the entire worldview of this nation to one stressing the "good life" (*buen vivir* in Spanish, *sumak causai* in Quichua; the trope appears in both languages in the constitution each time it is mentioned). He also pledged to eliminate the U.S. military base at Manta by November 2009 and to send the U.S. Coast Guard packing. The president took a very strong hand in the convention's proceedings and was bolstered by a substantial majority of delegates. A new 150-page constitution was drafted with greatly increased powers allocated to the executive branch. It was voted into law in a national referendum by an overwhelming majority, and then edited for coherence.

On March 1, 2008, while the convention was in full swing, a Colombian army commando unit invaded Ecuador and bombed an Amazonian FARC encampment, "Angostura," in Sucumbíos Province near the Colombian border. In this "Operation Phoenix" (Operación Fenix), twenty-six to twenty-eight people, including FARC leader Luis Edgar Devia Silva (a.k.a. Raúl Reyes) and three or four Mexican students who were visiting there during a lull in an international socialist convention in Quito, were killed. The attack was launched from Tres Esquinas, the covert U.S. military base deep in Colombian Amazonian territory (and on the border of the FARC-controlled zone of San Vicente de Caguán). Two Brazilian-made Embraer EMB 314 Super Tucano attack planes, also called ALXs or A-29s, made a night raid, dropping ten "smart bombs" on the base. Then the commandos came in from helicopters and snatched the corpse of the FARC leader "Raúl Reyes" and one other person thought to be a Colombian. The rest of the bodies were left to decompose and the wounded (including one surviving Mexican female student, Lucía Andrea Morett) left to suffer prior to rescue by Ecuadorians. The second snatched body turned out to be an Ecuadorian from Quito, Franklin Aisalla, who was running a FARC ring in the southern sector of the capital city and who perhaps set up the visit by the Mexican students as part of their trip to a socialist conference in the same capital city (see e.g., Tibanlombo Salazar 2008).

Now the story gets a bit murky and iffy, because of alleged United States involvement. The night of the raid, President Álvaro Uribe of Colombia called President Correa and lied to him, telling him that there would be action on the Colombian side of the border. U.S. CIA personnel, however, were completely briefed by the Colombians on the cross-border raid well in advance and were kept informed throughout the operation. High-ranking Ecuadorian military were also kept in the loop by the CIA, without the knowledge of the president. Also, a specially equipped U.S. military or CIA aircraft, never before seen in Ecuador, landed at the Manta air base three days before the raid, took off for night flights two or three times before the raid, and was airborne during the raid. Two days later it left and never returned. No other night flights have ever been reported out of the Manta air base. The Mexican student who survived the attack described how she was led to the camp as a side trip from her conference, which raised questions of whether Ecuador was knowingly playing host to Colombian rebels. Each of these items has a series of full-blown stories behind it and many secrets seem to be embedded in each of the stories.

Correa broke diplomatic ties with Colombia and, on learning that his own military intelligence had been informed by the U.S. CIA about the pending attack, he expelled the CIA from Ecuador. The constitutional assembly (the "*congresillo*"), functioning in lieu of a congress, adopted a provision in the new constitution prohibiting foreign military bases and personnel on Ecuador soil once the current contract with the United States expires, and all U.S. personnel left the Manta base sooner than specified in its contract with the government.

A year later, in 2009, the United States consolidated its position in South America by gaining access to seven Colombian military bases, including both navy and army installations. This led U.S. historian and journalist Greg Grandin (2010), writing in *The Nation*, to declare Obama's "new Monroe Doctrine." During this same year, Ecuador, with its new constitution, saw the reelection of Correa for four more years (he had to rerun after his second year because of the new constitution), his own party's majority in the new "congress," and a vow to "radicalize" the "citizens revolution." To celebrate his reelection; his presidency pro tem of the Union of South American Nations (UNASUR), with its headquarters in Quito; and the two hundredth anniversary of the shout for national independence, a gala celebration took place in the Atahualpa Olympic Stadium.

Following various meetings and festivities throughout the day in Quito, Correa played host to presidents Hugo Chávez (Venezuela), Raúl Castro (Cuba), Manuel Zelaya (Honduras), Evo Morales (Bolivia), Luis Inacio Lula da Silva (Brazil), Michelle Bachelet (Chile), Cristina Fernández de Kirchner (Argentina), and Fernando Lugo (Paraguay), among other dignitaries. At the inauguration of the president in the Atahualpa Olympic Stadium, Correa, Chávez, Castro, and Zelaya (all now members of ALBA, the Bolivarian Alliance for the Americas) took the stage to sing and speak. Finally, they joined hands to sing "¡Venceremos!" to the cheers of ten thousand attendants. "¡Venceremos!" (We Shall Triumph!) is a protest song used by the Unidad Popular movement in Chile during the 1970 election campaign of Salvador Allende, whose career ended on September 11, 1973, when the right-wing military, backed by the U.S. CIA, bombed the national palace, which led to the death of the socialist president. Conspicuous in his absence from this Union of South American Nations (UNASUR) meeting and festival was Álvaro Uribe Vélez, president of Colombia, with whom diplomatic relations were severed right after the 2008 attack on Angostura and not reestablished until twenty months later in November 2009, on Friday the 13th.

By February 2010, it became clear that the indigenous movement and Correa's action plans and policies were separating at an accelerating pace.

By mid-spring, indigenous mini-uprisings occurred in various areas of the Sierra. Escalation of the schism occurred in June as CONFENAIE called for a March from Puyo to Quito to commemorate twenty years since the great Indigenous Uprising of 1990 (chapter 4). Called the "Minga for a Plurinational State," frequent slogans were "We are sons and daughters of the National Indigenous Uprising of 1990" and "We continue the struggle following in the footsteps of 1990," and names of past indigenous heroes from Atahualpa to Palati were shouted.

This March coincided with a new "Condor and Eagle" meeting in Quito among Indigenous Ecuadorians and Indigenous North Americans, which also included representatives from many other countries. Following that, the nations of ALBA held a large-scale meeting in the coliseum in Otavalo. No representative from CONAIE was invited and, while affirming a strong platform of indigenous rights, the delegates were confronted by over two thousand indigenous people from all over Ecuador who clamored for their own real rights, as specified in the new Constitution, and loudly accused Hugo Chávez, Evo Morales, and Rafael Correa of failing to develop real change in the plurinational character of their respective nation states and of subverting genuine socialist reform in favor of neoliberal policies of capitalism and mineral extraction. By the end of June, CONAIE formed the Gobierno de los Pueblos y Nacionalidades (Government of Peoples and Nationalities) to begin meeting in October in Quito.

Acknowledgments

I thank Sibby Whitten for working with me on the project that resulted in this chapter. Without her painstaking attention to events, nuances, and innuendoes of Ecuadorian actualities this contribution would have suffered. In Puyo and Quito, she undertook the organization and structuring of materials collected. I also deeply appreciate her reading and editorial help on several earlier drafts. Thanks to Marta Jobita Vargas Dagua, whose creative mind transformed the concept of *mana tuparina ñambi* to intricate designs on *mucawas,* fine pieces of Amazonian ceramics made to serve *asua* manioc brew to family, friends, and guests. In a timely e-mail communication of September 10, 2004, Linda Belote clarified the journalistic "Suquilanda (con Z)" trope and the removal of two Ecuadorians from their embassy in Washington, D.C. I appreciate the prompt permission given by Francisco Cajas Lara (Pancho Cajas) to reprint his cartoon taken from *El Comercio* and thank Julie Williams for preparing it for publication. I am grateful to Santiago Gangotena, Carlos Montúfar, Diego Quiroga, and Nancy Orellana of the Universidad San Francisco de Quito for providing and sustaining a productive infrastructure from 1990 to the present for our ongoing research. This chapter builds on analyses in *Millennial Ecuador* (Whitten, ed. 2003) and precedent publications, but its focus is on events taking place in 2004, updated slightly for this book through February 2010.

Prelude

Sometime in the 1970s, we became attracted to paintings by itinerant artists from Tigua, a sector of Zumbagua parish, high in the *páramo* of Cotopaxi Province. We had collected several by 1979, when the late Olga Fisch gave us a large painting by Julio Toaquiza. Undated, it typifies the early style of painting described in this chapter. During the mid to late 1970s, we bought paintings from native artists walking the streets of Quito, and from some shops.

By this time, a number of artists had found their way to the Quito home of the late Joe Brenner, where they described and sold their works to *gringo* and other foreign visitors who also hung out there. Sales records in our files indicate that we purchased paintings from various Quito galleries and from North American dealers as early as 1981.

While we were "stuck" in Quito because of the Levantamiento Indígena of 1990, Diego Quiroga introduced us to the new outdoor Art in the Park, held Saturdays and Sundays in El Ejido, a large park in north-central Quito. There we met and bought from painters, some of whom we had previously known and with whom we have had continuing relationships over the past two decades.

For years painters were highly concentrated in their assigned area in the park, and they offered a dizzying array of products. A number of painters now sell their wares at the popular tourist market of Otavalo. Others venture to tourist sites in Cuenca and even Guayaquil. They have been reported on the Galápagos Islands, and some have visited and exhibited in the United States and Europe. Recently, a temporary move to El Arbolito, a small park across the street from El Ejido just south of the Casa de la

Cultura Ecuatoriana, seems to have reduced the available art in Quito. At this writing, the artists have returned to El Ejido and the overall market seems to be picking up somewhat, but it is nothing like it was from 1990 to about 2000. Some master painters, however, now working out of the gallery in Tigua proper, have illustrated several beautiful books on Andean and Amazonian subjects, and are working almost exclusively through commissions with wealthy buyers from many nations.

Disclaimer: I have visited but never done ethnography in Tigua. Rather, I let the artists present through their paintings the Ecuador they know so well, and about which we constantly seek to learn.

Chapter 6
Indigenous Ethnographers Portray Their World

DOROTHEA SCOTT WHITTEN

During the 1990s, active political participation and a series of public protests by various indigenous groups of Ecuador propelled them into the international spotlight. Amazonian and Andean organizations are now regarded as exemplary of indigenous-rights movements in South America. For an examination of the development of these movements and their considerable historic background, see Becker 2008.

Participation in politics and protests has been artistically recorded by a number of painters from the Tigua area of Cotopaxi Province high in the Andes. They also have recorded the breadth and scope of shamanic practices throughout Ecuador, as well as international and global events that touch on indigenous life such as ecological destruction and perceived threats of terrorism. Increasing recognition of the distinct ethnic identity of the artists strengthens their ability to communicate imagery to national and international audiences. To a striking degree, their artwork reflects the transformational dynamics of Ecuador, as analyzed in other chapters of this book. Before describing specific topics of the paintings, I offer a review of the development of this popular new art form.

Just as the women potters of Pastaza incorporate graphic references to their experiences and observations into their traditional ceramics (D. Whitten and N. Whitten 1988; N. Whitten and D. Whitten 2008; chapter 7, this volume), men and a few women Tigua artists portray ancient, historical, and contemporary themes in their relatively new art form. For untold years, some men from Tigua painted leather drumheads and carved and painted wooden masks to be used in their own festivals. Julio Toaquiza Tigase, generally credited as the first to paint in the new format, at one time sold old drums to antique dealers in Quito but later switched to selling drums he made and painted himself. His version of how he began to paint on square or rectangular dried sheep hides stretched over wood frames is presented in Colloredo-Mansfeld 2003 (see also Colvin and Toaquiza 1994; Ribadeneira de Casares 1990). According to the late Olga Fisch, a well-known collector and promoter of Ecuadorian arts and crafts, she suggested the change and provided him with the initial frames.[1] Her version, of course, does not negate Julio's memory of a shaman's vision and a subsequent dream that originally led him into the art world. His paintings had a naive charm and became popular among tourists and some nationals. Soon other men from Tigua were producing *cuadros,* as the paintings are known in Ecuador, as well as masks and drums for the tourist market.

From its birth in the early to mid-1970s, a highly popular and economically successful style of painting emerged from a relatively obscure native craft.[2] The new paintings rapidly transformed from an inwardly directed craft to an outwardly directed ethnic-arts market, in Nelson H. H. Graburn's (1976) terms. In aesthetic style and scope—scope here meaning the range of topics portrayed—paintings have moved from local to cosmopolitan orientations, in sociologist Robert Merton's (1957) terms. Merton examined the relation of mass communication to patterns of orientations of influential members of a small community. We have adapted his concepts as a means by which to review the range of orientations of paintings from "local," circumscribed, content toward "cosmopolitan" national or international content. The repertoire of subjects now includes examples of global political and economic events and their repercussions within the nation. The paintings themselves have become internationally recognized.

The first indigenous art cooperative was formed in 1989 by Julio Toaquiza and his sons; it was rebuilt in its present structure with Swiss aid following the earthquake of 1993.[3] Paintings from the Toaquiza-based and other cooperatives (see Bielenberg 1996, 1997; Colloredo-Mansfeld 2003, 2009; Colvin and Toaquiza 1994; Muratorio 1999) as well as those produced by a number of independent artists have been "discovered" and promoted by Ecuadorians, North Americans, and Europeans, who have sponsored exhibitions in Ecuador, the United States, Canada, France, Brazil, England, and Germany.[4] Two prestigious exhibitions of paintings by members of the Toaquiza family were held in Quito. One, presented in the presidential palace (Carondelet) in 2001, was the first such occasion organized by the national palace and was roundly endorsed by President Gustavo Noboa Bejarano. The Guayasamín Foundation opened a striking exhibition in its galleries in July 2002.[5]

Drums used in the festivals of Corpus Christi were decorated with important Corpus characters, such as the *danzante* (dancer), or motifs from the *danzante*'s costume, and these Corpus themes were transferred to many of the earliest *cuadros*. In 1979 Olga Fisch commissioned over fifty paintings from Julio Toaquiza and exhibited them in Germany (Scheinman 1981:15). I suspect that some paintings from this batch were those included in her 1981 exhibition of Corpus Christi costumes at the Renwick Gallery of the Smithsonian Institution (Muratorio 1981a:32, 1981b:13, 1985:54–55). Early topics also portrayed the celebrations of Christmas, variously called "Christmas Night," "Celebration of the Child," and "the Three Kings." Other *cuadros* depicted quotidian chores: planting and harvesting crops, spinning and weaving, or tending sheep and llamas. Some painters combined so many elements of pastoral, agricultural, and festival activities into one scene that I refer to them as "slice of life" paintings.

The largest, most expansive slice of life painting is a mural approximately eight by four feet by Juan Luis Cuyo Cuyo. It graces the wall of the entrance to La Bodega, a gallery in Quito, and contains scenes from every conceivable quotidian and ritual activity in the artist's experience and memory. Juan Luis carefully labeled and described each segment and periodically updates the mural in keeping with current national events, including the 1990 Levantamiento Indígena (chapter 4, this volume) and the 1992 March for Land and Life (N. Whitten and D. Whitten 2008; Whitten et al. 1997).

In 1985 Mary Weismantel analyzed and described seventy paintings and drums; she noted fine details (such as earrings, lace on petticoats) and, in the earlier paintings, three levels or fields from top to bottom, with some integration or interchangeability between the middle and lower levels in later paintings (Weismantel 1985). She later referred to the levels as three distinct spatial zones (Weismantel 1998[1988]) that correspond to human activity in the foreground, the physical setting (houses, churches, fields) in the middle ground, and, in the upper level, the mountains and sky of the *páramo* that provide the cosmological and mythical settings for imaginative portrayals. The levels, or spatial zones, are still evident in many paintings in today's market, but they are diminished or absent in cases where the painter concentrates on a full-frame interior or on relating a particular scene or event, such as the Nativity taking place in a cave.

In the earliest paintings, festival characters were lined up against an Andean background that usually included a volcano, churches, and houses. Dancers, people in animal masks and costumes, and musicians, particularly drummers, were presented face on, staring at the viewer with Orphan Annie–like eyes. Over the years, painters developed their techniques and skills into styles that show greater depth perspective, much more sense of motion and action, and greater refinement in details. One young artist, Rodrigo Ugsha Cuyo, has mastered techniques of rendering visual, dimensional perspectives and additionally employs the sequential perspective of a roving camera, changing location and adjusting focus. A pair of his paintings show, for example, bulls being rounded up by the famous Chagras (cowboys) of Machachi, with the Pan-American Highway and the Cotopaxi and Tungurahua volcanoes in the distant background. In closer focus, we see the Chagras and their helpers loading cattle into a truck parked alongside the highway. In two views of the same house, the artist shows commercial activities—weaving, mask making—in front of the house, agricultural work behind it, with cattle and sheep in nearby fields.

Along with this evolution came an expanded repertoire of themes ranging from the ones already mentioned to mythology, to reflections on the cosmos, to other Andean festivals such as La Mama Negra and the New Year's celebration of Año Nuevo, to the national sport, *futbol* (soccer). Portrayals offer commentary on modernization, ecotourism, ecological destruction, and the social hierarchy of the world of the painters. They include Bible scenes, markets, weddings, baptisms, funerals, and shamanic practices, including blessing the llamas for luck. Current paintings are lessons in the multinationalism and multiculturalism characteristic of modern and millennial Ecuador. No longer purely local in orientation, the artists paint the nation as they see and experience it. Prominent people who visit an indigenous community are likely to be painted into history, as is the case with ex-presidents Rodrigo Borja Cevallos, León Febres Cordero, Abdalá Bucaram Ortiz, and Jamil Mahuad Witt. The current president, Rafael Correa Delgado, was recorded in his famous postinaugural meeting in Zumbagua with his allies, Presidents Hugo Chávez and Evo Morales, all decked out in matching striped ponchos.

The remainder of this chapter is based on the recordings—the paintings—by the artists whom I regard as native ethnographers of fellow Ecuadorians. Their observations of political events and protests, shamanic practice, ecological destruction, and global threats are particularly informative. These portrayals illustrate the dynamics of interculturality and reflect a clear sense of alternative modernities.

Politics and Protests

Expanded indigenous representation and participation in national affairs accompanied the escalation of economic and political crises that occurred throughout Ecuador toward the end of the millennium. Their organizations, leaders, and spokesmen and spokeswomen have become established voices of power in government policies and actions. Various protests of the past two decades have been graphically recorded by artists who more likely than not were also active participants.

Two paintings, quite similar in content and composition, portray different views of the political ascent of Dr. Luis Macas. Both scenes are set on the Panecillo ("little bread loaf," a landmark hill that overlooks the colonial center of Quito), where Macas is surrounded by colleagues and supported by throngs of other Andean indigenous people. Before he took the oath of office in August 1996 as national congressman—the first indigenous person so elected—he and other newly elected indigenous representatives were cleansed by shamans on the plaza atop the Panecillo.

Francisco Vega Ugsha shows the group assembled under a wide Pachakutik banner (plate 1). They sit around a table where the shamans kneel and blow tobacco smoke toward them. Guatemalan Nobel Prize–Laureate Rigoberta Menchú Tum, who accompanied Macas during his investiture and the presidential inauguration, sits to the right of Macas and another newly elected congressman, Miguel Lluco. Music is provided by a drummer, several flautists, and one *bocina* (six-foot-long hide horn) player. A shadowy sky spirit blows its curative breath toward the gathering. The Virgin of Quito rises above the Pachakutik banner; Carondelet (the national presidential palace), the national flag, and the statue of Independence are in the left background.[6] Two *gringo* tourists with backpacks start to climb the steep, winding road. They are followed by groups of supporters carrying more rainbow banners, which echo the real *arco iris* seen in the sky and identify the marchers as being indigenous people from Cotopaxi, Tungurahua, and Imbabura.

Another banner, adorned with the archaeological gold sun mask found in La Tolita (Esmeraldas) and adopted as the emblem of the Central Bank of Ecuador, hangs from a building where people cheer on the marchers. At the base of the hill, more people, some with llamas, pour out of small houses and join their compatriots to begin the ascent to the congregation of indigenous power at the top. The volcano Cotopaxi looms in the right background, its spirit observing the rising sun and the huge rainbow that links a Tigua-Quilotoa setting to the political center of the nation. The widespread support by indigenous people of Luis Macas and the Pachakutik movement is reflected in the five signs carried by actors depicted by the artist as well as by his inscription on the back of his painting: "The Quichua people of Ecuador have transferred power to the elected indigenous congressman of Pachakutik. For the first time they have participated in the political arena."

Julio Toaquiza places Luis Macas and other indigenous leaders (two men, three women) on a Panecillo-like hilltop. Behind them a huge rainbow arches across the sky. Macas holds a large book of indigenous justice to be transformed into national law; in the distant clouds is a spirit book, the source of his traditional knowledge. Men and women, one carrying a rainbow banner labeled "Movimiento Unidad Plurinacional Pachakutik Nuevo País," start to climb the hill. They are followed by two women bearing baskets of bread or perhaps cheese and by a few men wearing fedoras and ponchos; a couple of them play flutes, one beats a drum, and another holds a bottle and a glass. They appear to be leading a multitude of people, most of them in red ponchos and all of them in white, round hats. Carondelet again is seen in the background, the national flag flying from the cupola. At the bottom of the hill, a nonindigenous man—identified as Abdalá Bucaram—runs away from the oncoming indigenous crowd, while looking back at it over his left shoulder. This painting, as the artist's son Alfredo Toaquiza explained to us, documents the strong role that Luis Macas played in uniting indigenous power with the voices of other segments of Ecuadorian society to force the ouster from the presidency of Abdalá Bucaram by vote of the National Congress in 1997.

The recent political upheavals within Ecuador have been witnessed and recorded with the same detailed attention given to the natural eruptions of volcanoes Guagua Pichincha and Tungurahua during 1999. Many authors have documented and are documenting the development of indigenous organizations and the actions of indigenous peoples throughout Ecuador as they have united in social movements and in public protests to change the course of participatory democracy and to enhance their role within it (e.g., De la Torre and Striffler, eds. 2008; N. Whitten, ed. 2003). Indigenous involvement in major political events has been chronicled by observant artists.

Julio Pallo depicted supporters of CONAIE marching through an Andean town, perhaps Salcedo, to join the 1990 nationwide Levantamiento Indígena; they are burning tires, and some women hassle police while another policeman trains his gun on the demonstrators. Juan Quindigalle presented two versions of the Levantamiento of 1994, the largely Sierran protest over land problems still unresolved since the agrarian land reform of 1964–1965. In both scenes, members of the indigenous organization of Cotopaxi march over a bridge and into a village, holding their defensive field staffs high as police try to stop them. Again, tires are burning in the street. In one scene, a policeman tugs at the poncho of one man while the leader shows a written petition to another officer.

As Amazonian marchers progressed into Andean territories in 1992, they gained national media attention, mostly favorable, and political and moral support from their highland compatriots when community after community of indigenous Quichua-speaking people joined the ranks. Men and women of the Tigua-Zumbagua area of Cotopaxi Province not only participated in the march but also recorded it in their paintings. Julio Pallo shows throngs of men and women heading down the narrow, winding road that links Tigua with the "Pana," the Pan-American Highway, at Latacunga (plate 2). One group walks ahead of a truck, which is packed with people; men sitting atop the cabin hold a sign, "Comuna Tigua Chimbacucho." A small group following the truck includes a drummer and two flute players, and still more people walk toward the truck from a side road. In the distance, buses and a truck are blocked by boulders that other indigenous people have rolled onto the middle of the Pana.

The theme of a painting by Bernardo Toaquiza V. is "El Levantamiento Nacional del 7 de Febrero de 2001,"[7] a sustained protest of the economic policies of the president. Under the canopy of a large volcano, indigenous people raise poles as they march toward a distant cluster of high, red-tiled buildings. Men in ponchos and women in skirts and shawls all wear shoes and white hats with turned-up brims. Two women carry a rainbow banner reading "MICC" (Movimiento Indígena y Campesino de Chimborazo) and "Viva el Levantamiento." Behind this central group is a man wearing fur chaps, a poncho, and a Pachakutik scarf; he holds a long rod with a rope attached. He is followed by musicians, one of them beating a drum, another playing a flute, and a third blowing a very long Cotopaxi *bocina*. With them is a man in a *vaca loca* (crazy cow) costume; he has a white band around his head and carries a bottle. An ancestral spirit, probably Pacha Mama, gains strength from the rays of the rising sun and sheds her tears to earth.

A confrontational scene is described by another artist, Ernesto Ugsha C.: "This is the indigenous strike, made to depose the corrupt president of Ecuador, Jamil Mahuad . . . some indigenous people are in the bus en route to Quito." The people indeed appear angry in the painting. They have blocked the highway with boulders and huge tree trunks and are burning more tree limbs to stop a bus with indigenous and nonindigenous passengers. On the front of the bus is a small rainbow flag with the words "Viva el Paro" (long live the strike). A red-ponchoed man standing on top of the bus holds up a sack in a threatening gesture and he seems to be shouting to a woman standing directly in front of the bus and to the people behind the rocks. The protesters appear to be from Cotopaxi, Chimborazo, and Saraguro. They hold a white sign that says, "El Pueblo, Unido, Jamás Será Vencido" (the united people will never be conquered).

Rodrigo Toaquiza presents before-and-after perspectives of the demise of Jamil Mahuad. His first theme is "Seizure of the government palace by indigenous people on February 5, ousting Jamil." Carondelet looms large against the background of purple, blue, green, and brown mountains. The national flag flies overhead and a number of Ecuadorians, most but not all wearing ponchos and white hats, wave red, blue, and yellow flags and hold a tricolor banner from the balcony of the palace where they stand. On the street below, two buses, one marked "Congreso Nacional de Ecuador" and the other "Turismo," are blocked by three tree trunks and a camouflaged army truck. Between the logs and a barbed-wire fence, a group of soldiers faces an indigenous crowd. The military wear helmets and brown berets; they carry rifles with bayonets, and canisters of tear gas are attached to their belts. Antonio Vargas, leader of the indigenous protesters, holds a written statement out to the soldiers. He is flanked by women and men from Otavalo and others from Chimborazo or Cotopaxi. Behind them are stereotypical *yumbos,* bare-chested men wearing feather headdresses and body paint. People in this mixed crowd wave both tricolor and rainbow flags that symbolize, respectively, the nation of Ecuador and the nationalities of its constituent members. They bear signs with clear messages: "Long live indigenous unity. Long live the blockade. Down with corrupt politicians. Away with robber bankers. Jamil, we want justice for the people, enough fraud of the Ecuadorian people."

The second theme of Rodrigo Toaquiza is "The destitution of the ex-president of the republic, Dr. Jamil Mahuad, the fifth of February 2001, in which all of the indigenous people of the country participated in the Indigenous Uprising." Here the artist places Antonio Vargas in the middle of indigenous people on the balcony of Carondelet. They wave small Ecuadorian flags while the full-size flag flies over the palace. A bus and car are blocked by logs on the street. A crowd of indigenous men and women in white hats and colorful ponchos and shawls demonstrate with Pachakutik flags and signs that again express opposition to corrupt politicians, naming "Jamil," "Noboa," the *diputados* (congressmen), and corrupt bankers, and affirm a resounding "no" to privatization. On a rural hillside setting that overlooks the protesters in central Quito, a couple from the Sierra is being cleansed and cured by two shamans, one a *yumbo,* the other an Andean woman. A third shaman, apparently from somewhere in the Sierra, blows his magical breath toward new indigenous leaders on the palace balcony. The underpinnings of shamanism mediate the contrast of rural–urban interests and places and of indigenous/governmental opposition.

José Eduardo Cayo Pilalumbo, who with his brother Abelardo Cayo Pilalumbo visited the Anthropology Museum, University of British Columbia in 1998 for an exhibition and sale (Muratorio 1999), painted and described the mood of Ecuador in 2000. Two finely detailed, seemingly similar paintings show grim-faced indigenous people with round-brimmed hats—men in ponchos, barefoot women in pleated skirts and shawls—confronting uniformed soldiers who carry rifles and stand near their military truck labeled "Fuerzas Armadas de Ecuador" (Armed Forces of Ecuador). The artist wrote his themes and descriptions on the back of each scene. The first title is "Indigenous Uprising," the second is "The military detains the indigenous people." The artist's words accurately describe what is going on in each picture. The first scene shows the indigenous people of Cotopaxi Province arriving in the city of Latacunga, having been summoned by CONAIE to protest against the government of Gustavo Noboa Bejarano because of the economic crisis of the country: "Soldiers with arms begin to confront indigenous people who defend themselves with poles." In the second scene, the army begins to detain indigenous people in different provinces of the country, and Cayo writes, "and for this reason the indigenous people unite more strongly to advance to the capital of the republic, Quito."

Through the lens of the painters one can trace the history of indigenous protests that have occurred over the past twenty years, protests that are taking place more frequently, with an increasingly broader regionally based constituency. They are also met with more governmental use of military and police control. The 1990 national indigenous uprising was settled with the help of church and government mediators. Local police actually escorted and protected marchers as they moved from one town or area to another during the 1992 Caminata. Military in full riot and combat gear tightly controlled the "500 Years of Indigenous Resistance" demonstration of October 12, 1992, and prevented many, many people from joining those already in Quito (Meisch 1992). One exception to the increasing use of force was seen in the 2000 ouster of President Mahuad. Portrayals by Tigua artists of recent, successful protests that have launched indigenous people into legitimate participation in national political life remind one of a phrase from the Ecuadorian national anthem (written in 1865 by Juan León Mera): "After the struggle, victory soared; liberty followed triumph."

Intercultural Knowledge and Power

Powers that derive from conquering geographic, psychological, and social, hegemonic distances contributed to the success of the 1992 March for Land and Life. Its success was also due to several other factors: the insistence of the indigenous leaders on *peaceful* demonstration; the careful, though delayed, negotiations of representatives of President Borja; and the opportunity for citizens of Quito to become acquainted with, and thereby support, fellow citizens from Pastaza. People from the Oriente tried to explain the nature of tropical rain-forest ecology and the meaning of their desire to protect their ancestral lands. Men taught Quiteños about their ancient shamanic beliefs and practices, while women gave demonstrations and explanations of their traditional pottery manufacture.

The strength and confidence to lead indigenous people into new realms of political participation appear in some cases to be associated with a close relationship with a shaman and a familiarity with shamanic knowledge. The paternal grandfather of Antonio Vargas, Eliseo Vargas, was a powerful shaman who spent his last years in Unión Base, near Puyo. We have been told by collaborators in Puyo that other leaders from Amazonia and the Sierra also are the sons, grandsons, or nephews of shamans (see Vickers 2003).

To date, I lack information about the relationship of active female political leaders to the relatively few female shamans or to male shamans. Among the Canelos Quichua, the feminine counterpart of the male shaman is a master potter who is grounded in the symbol system of shamanism and who clarifies and specifies the images that surround the male shaman. Such ceramists learn the imagery of the cosmos from their fathers, grandfathers, or husbands. Master potters also share the experiential knowledge and insights of powerful male relatives who are not shamans. *Sinchi yachaj,* "powerful shaman," *sinchi curaga,* "strong leader," and *sinchi muscuj,* "strong visionary," are Quichua terms that link the spheres of shamanic knowledge, political leadership, and master Amazonian potters (D. Whitten and N. Whitten 1988; N. Whitten and D. Whitten 2008; chapter 7, this volume).

Destruction: Ecological and Other

In addition to recording ongoing activities, native ethnographers also reflect the growing concern with the very real threats of ecological pollution and destruction and the perceived threat of international terrorism.

The long-simmering feud between promoters of economic interests (especially revenues from petroleum and mining extraction) and defenders of biodiversity received international media attention through the efforts of Al Gore and Sting in July 1997. Gore organized the worldwide, simultaneous broadcast of Sting's concert, "Live Earth," to protest petroleum exploitation in the Yasuní National Park (*El Comercio,* July 7, 2007, section 2, p. 20). The Yasuní is home to the Waorani indigenous people, who are in sustained or sporadic interaction with those outside their immediate environment, and to the Tagaeri-Taromenane indigenous people, who prefer to remain "isolated."

The Yasuní is also "home to the most diverse array of plants and animals in South America and possibly the planet" (*New York Times,* January 26, 2010, p. D8).

National and international interest in protecting the Yasuní, especially the more heavily populated ITT (Ishpingo-Tambacocha-Tiputini) section, apparently inspired a young artist, César F. Ugsha, to paint his vision of destructive forces. In the center, hunters fire double-barreled shotguns and a lever-action rifle at flying birds and at a growling jaguar. An indigenous man holding a palm-wood spear raises his other hand as if to stop the hunters. Signs are posted, in English, "Yasuní National Park" and "Animals in dangers of extinction." The painting is titled "Kawsaymanta, Cuando el última jawar muere . . . ¡Que!" (From life, when the last jaguar dies . . . What?). This artist reminded us in 1997 of human destructive forces beyond petroleum exploitation.

Also in 1997, Gustavo Toaquiza portrayed the scene of the long-standing legal battle between Ecuadorian indigenous people and Chevron (then Texaco; see, e.g., Sawyer 2004). From one of several huge oil storage tanks marked with Texaco signs, a stream of black crude oil flows into an Amazonian feeder river in the northern Oriente. Indigenous residents of the adjacent village look hopelessly at the dark smoke polluting the air and at the dead cow lying among the barren tree stumps atop contaminated soil. This stark rendition of ecological destruction in northeastern Ecuador has been widely copied by other artists; it is one example of abuses of intellectual property rights, such as copying or signing another artist's unsigned work, as discussed by Colvin (2004:141–143).

Alfredo Toaquiza, again in 1997, painted a nighttime scene of a woman kneeling before a big jar broken by an emerging hummingbird-like spirit. His description: "luck [life force, in Quichua] abandons man because of the causes of contamination, eruption, and because of the use of chemicals in mother earth. Because of this we live in poverty."

While the above examples of ecological degradation deal with current situations (the ethnographic present), a couple of imaginative young artists tackle what may be thought of as the ethnographic future. They interpret the 9/11 attacks in the United States and the continuing threats of terrorism by Osama Bin Laden as possibly happening in Ecuador.

Multiethnic interconnections encompassed by global events confronted us head on when we returned to El Ejido Park on June 2, 2002, and greeted *comadre* Juana Cuyo and her son, Rodrigo Ugsha Cuyo. He had just put a painting, finished the night before, in the center of the family's sale booth (plate 3). We were first attracted to his presentation of the basin of Quito, filled with white and blue buildings that expanded into the surrounding hills and mountains. Then his central focus hit us with breathtaking force. He had placed the Panecillo with the Virgin of Quito statue in the heart of modern Quito, and out of it rose the Twin Towers of the World Trade Center in New York City, black smoke billowing from the top floors. Behind them, to the right, are two smaller towers, both on fire. A jet plane, also belching smoke, is headed toward the ground. It is flight 93. On a hillside overlooking the scene, people from various ethnic groups and a *mestizo* couple watch and talk about the unfolding tragedy. In the extreme right foreground, Rodrigo painted the Mitad del Mundo monument like a giant tombstone. On it he inscribed this title and message: "Twin Towers. In Quito?!"[8]

During 2002 and 2003 another young artist, Rodrigo Toaquiza Cuyo,[9] produced a series of surrealistic paintings of indigenous uprising and conflicts with special government armed forces, as well as futuristic portrayals of repercussions of Bin Laden's actions for South Americans. One of the latter bears the theme "the indigenes attack Bin Laden." Bin Laden stands on a flat-topped hill in mid-picture; he raises a flag, green and white with a yellow emblem, while directing the World Trade Center attack seen on the left. He is pursued by angry Andean indigenous people armed with long sticks. Icy water flows from the mouth of a mountain spirit into a lake. Two large spirit faces, a female and a male, emerge from constellations in the night sky.

Another stark painting shows the explosive attacks on New York as a background to a bleeding indigenous man fastened to a pole that emerges from Ecuador. The artist's theme is "Crucifición de América Latina." He interprets the suffering of New Yorkers as comparable to that of indigenous South Americans. His uncanny vision is reflected in a statement released by Bin Laden in January 2010. Switching from religion and holy wars to climate change, Bin Laden sets his sights on U.S. corporations as "the true criminals against the global climate" and blames them for the global economic crisis, driving "tens of millions into poverty and unemployment" (*The News-Gazette*, January 30, 2010, p. A-6).

The Art of Healing

The multinational, multicultural, and intercultural nature of Ecuador is clearly articulated in portrayals of shamanic healing. While these paintings appear on the market frequently, with a great deal of repetition and copying, some stand out in their communication of patterns of interaction among healers, patients, and agents of illness and health. These layered connections exist across great social, topographical, and physical distances and extend from antiquity into modernity.

PLATE 1. Francisco Vega Ugsha: *Shamanic Cleansing of Dr. Luis Macas, Congressman* (25½" × 21¾")

PLATE 2. Julio Pallo: *Caminata for Land and Life of 1992* (13¾" × 9½")

PLATE 3. Rodrigo Ugsha: *Twin Towers in Quito!* (25½" × 21¾")

PLATE 4. María Ermelinda Cuyo: *Amazonian Yumbo Shaman Visits an Andean Festival* (9⅜" × 6¼")

In the summer of 1996, we took several shaman scenes to Puyo to obtain Amazonian indigenous perspectives on the Andean paintings. We particularly sought the interpretations of our long-time collaborator, Alfonso Chango, who has traveled fairly extensively in the Ecuadorian Andes and lived for two years in Riobamba, the capital of Chimborazo Province (see Chango 1984; Whitten et al. 1997). As he and his wife, Luzmila Salazar, studied the paintings, they realized that they needed the help of her father, Domingo Salazar, a powerful shaman who has treated numerous Andean patients in his home near Puyo and in their own locations in the highlands. His knowledge of the network of shamans and shamanic practice was a source of much of the following four interpretations.

In the first painting, Rodrigo Cuyo portrays the interior of the large house of "*un curandero amazónico, sinchi yachaj,*" a powerful Amazonian healer who employs standard Canelos Quichua shamanic techniques. After drinking the hallucinogen *ayahuasca* (*Banisteriopsis caapi*—soul vine), he gains insights into the worlds of powerful spirits during a nighttime séance. Spirits guide his diagnosis of the cause of illness; once he "sees" the evil source, which resides in purple mucus inside the victim, he can suck it out and dispose of the harmful element while retaining the spirit force.

The healer, his assistants, and family members are identifiable as Amazonian residents by their stereotypical feather headdresses and grass skirts. Through a window we see two more people, similarly dressed, searching in a river for *carichamas,* a type of catfish found under rocks. Another feather-bedecked man poles a canoe bearing an Andean couple toward the big house. A cross-section of Ecuadorians awaits treatment. An Otavalo husband and wife drink *trago* (cane alcohol), a Salasaca woman bundles up for a nap, and people from Cañar and Esmeraldas appear to be next in line to be cured.

The shaman is seen blowing on an Achuar woman to protect her from illness caused by mystical injections from two green spirit snakes coiled about overhead rafters. He also uses power stones and a staff made of *caña brava,* a special, strong riverbank cane that contains the power to defend against all sorcery or witchcraft. The patient's husband assists; he stands behind her, holding another *caña brava* staff and touching her with what appears to be a cutting of *ayahuasca* vine.

Family members gather sacks of potatoes, corn, and peanuts brought to the shaman by his patients, while someone cooks for them. A large, round fish tank is guarded by an assistant holding a *caña brava* staff. Another green snake clings to the outer wall of the tank, which harbors a source of food (fish) as well as a source of illness—fish bones—that some people regard as evidence of magical darts blown by a shaman.

In contrast to the first painting, where the site was generalized, Domingo Salazar immediately pinpointed the location depicted by Francisco Vega Ugsha as Quindigua, also called Maca, high in the *páramo* near Guaranda, Bolívar Province. The shaman here learned his secrets in the nearby hills of Yanaurcu and Cariurcu. In this moonlit scene, an Andean shaman holds a power stone and blows *trago* breath and candle smoke on a woman standing in an icy fast-flowing stream, while his assistant also blows on her and cleanses her with an herb bundle. The three principal mechanisms of curing here are the use of spirit stones, sweeping-cleaning, and drinking *ayahuasca*. The woman's soul, stolen by evildoers, has been hidden in a small crevice in Cariurcu. The shaman instructs the patient's husband to place a bright pink handkerchief in the crevice, which is portrayed by the artist as the mouth of a mountain spirit (*urcu mama* in the Andes, *urcu supai* in Amazonia). The frigid water and the power of the shaman force the mountain spirit to "vomit" the woman's soul into the handkerchief, which the husband returns to the shaman, who restores the soul to the patient, thereby curing her. As this curing takes place, some Andean people depart, more arrive, and others await treatment in nearby houses with both tile and thatch roofs.

In a third painting, according to the interpretation of Amazonian shaman Domingo Salazar, Francisco Vega Ugsha again creates a curing scene in a specific location: Tonchigüe, a coastal town that is halfway between Esmeraldas and Punta Galera. The raised bamboo and thatched-roof houses in the background are identified as those of Afro-Ecuadorians of Esmeraldas Province. The central figure, a powerful shaman, is far from his home, for he is A'i (Cofán), from the Upper Agua Rico area of the northern Oriente. He is identifiable by his collar of jaguar teeth and his green cotton kerchief. Part of his curing apparatus includes a *jatun rumi yacu tian,* a big stone (depicted as a human head) that contains water inside of it. An unseen person is said to be cleansing, or "sweeping," the big water stone.

The Cofán shaman has traveled here to acquire two powerful material adornments: a collar of shells from the Pacific Ocean and whalebone. He wears a characteristic headdress, but the feathers are from the coastal red parrot. He acquired his staff in Sua, en route to Tonchigüe. He blows *trago* breath and candle smoke to cure an Andean woman, who is accompanied by a female relative or friend. Other people, husband and wife pairs from Cañar and Otavalo, have come to Tonchigüe with a variety of illnesses, which the shaman, through his coastal-Sierra-Oriente mergers of powers, can cure. A couple wearing ponchos and round white felt hats departs in a canoe that is paddled by a *costeño* with a wide-brimmed straw hat. According to Domingo

Salazar, "The people in the canoe are from the Sierra, and are being taken down the Sua River to a wedding by a '*montuvio de Manabí*,' probably from Punta Galera."

A fourth painting, by Jorge Toaquiza Ugsha, takes us back to the Sierra, this time to Guaranda, in Bolívar Province, central Ecuador. The shaman here is well known to Domingo Salazar; his nickname is El Chino, or Juanito el Chino, and his permanent residence is in Riobamba, Chimborazo Province, on the Plaza de San Alfonso. His Christian name is Victor Chambo. The curing here is being done in Pasa Grande, which is near Guaranda. Specifically, it is in "San Fernando, *frente de* Chirolliris." Parenthetically, this shaman also cures, in the Shuar language, on the Vía Macas, south of the Pastaza River in the Upper Amazon in Morona-Santiago Province. He is said to travel through "all of the Andean, Interandean, and Amazonian regions." The wife of the shaman cooks for the patient, who has not eaten in days. He lies on a straw mat and is covered by a blanket. He is accompanied by his wife and a friend who acts as a *suplicante* (supplicant) to formally request treatment by the shaman. The shaman's *mesa*, "curing table," is set with paraphernalia that embody and mediate powerful forces: a human skull, *supai rumi* (spirit stones), candles, a mystical deer skull, a leaf bundle, a bowl of *huayusa* (*Ilex* species), a cup to drink this native tea, and another cup to drink *ayahuasca*.

Through a small opening in the wall of the house, a huge green boa flickers its tongue as it stretches toward El Chino. This is the embodiment of the Tslamanga *supai* or spirit that inhabits an ice-cold lake contained in a large rock that exists somewhere within the extinct volcano of Cotacachi, Imbabura Province. The Tslamanga image is another representation of the big stone with water inside seen in the third painting.

The following paintings were not analyzed by Domingo Salazar but are included here because of their vibrant presentations of the multicultural, multiethnic context and content of shamanic performance.

In 1988 and 1989, Julio Toaquiza T. produced contrasting scenes, one of a Tsáchila shaman curing in his house near Santo Domingo de los Colorados (now Tsáchilas), the other of a "Yumbo" *yachaj* treating a woman from Zumbagua in a home in that area. Both healers have elaborate *mesas* replete with skulls, frogs, snakes, candles, stones, and other spirit devices. From a small drawer in each table, a little white demon emerges, while a large dark devil image appears hovering over and behind each shaman. The Tsáchila *curandero* holds a wood staff in his right hand and a devil's pitchfork in his left; a green boa is draped across his stomach and over his shoulder. The Oriente curer has a long staff of authority, similar to the one held by the woman patient, who also wears a Christian cross around her neck. Both shamans blow tobacco smoke on their patients, as does the Tsáchila's assistant, who treats a man holding a pair of femurs. Two other patients in this scene undergo special herb steam baths in a side room. Andean and Afro-Ecuadorian people have traveled to both locations to seek treatments for a variety of afflictions.

Jorge Toaquiza carried out the devil theme in a starkly surrealistic setting that places tiny people in a huge room. Stars shine in the night sky seen through a window; inside, the room is lighted by a Coleman-like lantern hanging from a nail in the wall. Near the bed of a patient, a small dark devil figure raises a spear over its head. Perhaps it is directed across the room toward a *yumbo* shaman who cleanses and treats an Andean patient. Looming large behind the *yachaj* is a second, much bigger devil. He holds his spear at his side. His tail rests over the handle of an enormous fire-blackened *paila* (cauldron). In the center of the room, a dog sits on a yellow chair painted with the same floral decorations seen on the bedposts and on a trunk. The animal must represent a spirit mascot, since it is highly unlikely that it would occupy the choice, and only, seat in the house.

María Ermelinda Cuyo, one of the first women artists known to us, painted two variations on a theme in 1991. The theme is that of an Oriente shaman in the midst of a full-blown festival that features masked, costumed characters, musicians playing flutes and *bocinas* and beating drums, and other participants in Andean dress (plate 4). The shaman, wearing white pants, a blue shirt, and a feather headdress and necklace, sits on a simple log seat of power (*bancu*) and holds a long staff of authority. María Ermelinda identified him as "Domingo Salazar from the Oriente," the very same person who gave interpretations of the first four paintings described above. Not only did she transpose people and settings, as have other artists, but she also collapsed historic and geographic time and space by placing several *conquistadores* (one holding a Bible) on a hill overlooking the fiesta while their sailing vessels are anchored in the ocean west of the Andes.

Very similar scenes of a *yumbo* shaman seated in the midst of an Andean festival were painted by Jorge Toaquiza Vega and Manuel Cuyo Vega. I originally assumed that the shaman was curing, but on closer examination there is no patient to be seen. In each painting, the shaman is flanked by aides who hold a curing wand, a bottle, or both. The shaman's presence may indicate that he is blessing the fiesta, overseeing it, or perhaps both. His centrality to the festive activity stresses the significance of the powerful outsider's visit. Corr (2010) discusses the power that Salasacan shamans impute to "*yumbo*" Amazonian shamans, especially the Canelos of Pastaza Province, and to a lesser extent to Tsáchila shamans from Santo Domingo de las Tsáchilas, Pichincha Province.

The array of masked characters depicted in the *yumbo* shaman paintings indicates that these fiestas are performed in the Zumbagua-Tigua area, as described by Umajinga (1995:261). Such central Andean festivals are not conflict-free, but the seeming tranquility and even playfulness shown in Cuyo's painting contrast radically with the violent rituals of northern Ecuador analyzed by Wibbelsman (2009).

In a multicultural country such as Ecuador, illnesses and the powers to cure them come from many different, distant sources. Power resides in the acquisition of distant knowledge, according to Mary Helms (1988:58–59):

> In terms of the sacred or symbolic significance of geographical distance, the uncertainty or variability associated with distance, that is, the sense of "distance" as constituting some kind or degree of obstacle, may be as significant as the association of distance with concepts of the unknown or the "known about." . . . if distance is an obstacle, he who overcomes, "controls," or "conquers" distance may evidence superior ability, power, wisdom, and worth.

Julio Vega Llaquichi brings us into contemporary time in his portrayal of the other, "Western" side of medical-care delivery—a clinic staffed by a nurse and an assistant who wear caps marked with red crosses. They dispense medicines to Andean patients. This represents a type of medical care that coexists with traditional and alternative treatments but, in recent years, has been curtailed or altogether nonexistent due to lack of government funds for the medicines, personnel, and facilities.

The failure of government agencies to provide adequate medical care is counterbalanced by the government's constitutional recognition and active encouragement of the rights of indigenous people to practice their traditional forms of curing, shamanism, and by its promotion of shamanic endeavors as tourist destinations. Once considered illegal and practiced clandestinely, at night, shamanism has come out of the closet and is performed in broad daylight in public places open to all who choose to watch and partake. Several years ago, the city of Quito organized bus tours to the famous archaeological site of Cochasquí, high in the mountains between Quito and Otavalo, where a veritable "shamans' supermarket" was held about the time of the summer solstice.[10] Tourist agencies and enterprising individuals advertise trips to various points in the Oriente where visitors can enjoy ecotourism by day and shaman-led *ayahuasca* sessions by night. The latter can be a dangerous experience for the uninitiated, or for one who does not understand the language of his or her shamanic guide. In spite of such occurrences, traditional shamanism continues very much as it has for centuries and exists along with a mixture of fakes, phonies, and *hechecería* (witchcraft).[11]

According to the *El Comercio* web site of November 6, 2001, the first national conference of shamans was held in Ambato in November 2001. Regional associations proliferated and by July 2002, the First International Encounter of Shamans convened. It included eighteen delegates from Andean, Amazonian, and coastal Ecuador along with others from Colombia, Venezuela, and Peru. The growing organizational developments were accompanied by attempts to regulate practices, fees, and dress. The president of the Shamanic Curacas of Tungurahua announced at the 2002 international meeting that "the shamans will remain here (Santo Domingo) through next Monday to undertake cleanings and cures; costs begin at six dollars for a *limpieza* (cleansing)" (*El Comercio,* July 20, 2002, p. D1). Suggested fees have risen now to a reported "legitimate" range of $25–$45 per session, but people report far higher fees.

The most visible product of regulation, dress, has been well documented in media coverage of various meetings of shamans. The standardization of the all-white attire (shirt and trousers), sometimes with the addition of a colorful belt and/or headband, has been recorded by several artists. An unsigned painting, possibly by a Toaquiza family member, shows a shaman clad in white with red collar, belt, and headband curing an Andean man high above a volcanic lake. He cures with a leaf bundle and curing wand while he blows alcohol breath toward the patient.

Luis Cuyo shows a white-dressed shaman standing in the icy stream that flows from the sacred waterfall at Peguche, near Otavalo. With a leaf bundle in each hand, he directs his efforts toward an Otavalo woman standing on the right bank. Another Andean couple watches the action from the left bank. The standardized white clothing appears to be used by shamans throughout the country.

When facing problems of health, pending death, or even a run of bad luck, people turn to shamans. Through their travels, both physical and virtual, shamans seek and exchange knowledge of distant others, thereby creating broad networks of people and ideas. These expanded multicultural and intercultural networks form a basis for knowledge, respect, and identity shared by multiple ethnic groups.

Tigua artists' painted observations range from mundane, quotidian tasks through international, globally stimulated events. Their most profound ethnographic contributions are in the areas of political participation and shamanic performance. The former paintings document the modernity of the nationwide indigenous involvement that continues into today's charged political climate. Shamanic paintings record practices derived from ancient beliefs that underlie contemporary healing systems throughout Ecuador.

Acknowledgments

I wish to thank all of the Amazonian and Andean artists mentioned above for sharing their knowledge directly and indirectly. Additionally, Marcelo Santi Simbaña, Faviola Vargas Aranda, Delicia Dagua, Alfonso Chango, Luzmila Salazar, Domingo Salazar, and Estela Dagua have given continuing insight into Canelos Quichua culture. Research has been facilitated in Puyo by Absalóm Guevara, César Abad, and Felipe Balcázar R.; in Quito by María del Carmen Molestina and Diego Quiroga; and in Salasaca and Otavalo by Rudi Masaquiza and Julio Chicaiza. Rudi Colloredo-Mansfeld has shared his knowledge of the painters as well as a slide of an early painting. Pilar Cano, Gogo Anhalzer, María Fernanda Valdivieso, and especially Napo Albán provided history and hard evidence of the early paintings. We are indebted to the late Olga Fisch for her generosity and encouragement of our interests in Ecuadorian arts.

The research on which this chapter is based has been an ongoing joint endeavor. Funds have been provided by the National Science Foundation (GS-2999), the Wenner-Gren Foundation for Anthropological Research (3287, 4405, and 5232), and the Graduate College, The Research Board, and the Center for Latin American and Caribbean Studies of the University of Illinois at Urbana-Champaign. Research in Ecuador has been conducted under the auspices of the Casa de la Cultura Ecuatoriana, the Instituto Nacional de Antropología e Historia, the Instituto Nacional de Patrimonio Cultural, the Museos del Banco Central del Ecuador, and the Universidad San Francisco de Quito.

Prelude

In December 2007, Rachel Corr invited me (N. Whitten) to deliver one of two keynote addresses to the newly formed Society for Amazonian and Andean Studies. I began early drafts by reflecting broadly on relationships between three vast regions of South America—Amazonia, Montaña, and Andes—beginning with the archaeological insights offered by scholars of Chavín de Huantar in north-central Peru and San Augustín of Tierra Adentro, southern Colombia. Here extraordinarily complex ancient stone monumental art signaling multiple transformative dimensions of Amazonian–Andean cultural confluence are found. But as I worked, my attention returned repeatedly to the transformative mythopoetics of indigenous thought to which we have been drawn since about 1973 on completion of eighteen months of ethnographic research among the Puyo Runa and their cultural congeners to the north, south, and east.

Concern has been growing for some time about the journalist and academic portrayals of Amazonian Quichua speakers as somehow "marginal" to life in this region of the moist tropics. Then, in June 2008, Laura Rival wrote to invite me to develop a piece to "problematize the distinction between 'lowland' and 'highland' South America." Apparently this issue came up at the Cambridge-Paris meeting that summer of the members of the Society for the Anthropology of Lowland South America (SALSA), which publishes the journal *Tipití*.

By summer 2008, I became saturated in rereading early works on these issues while trying to stay current with recent expositions. My broad quasi-synthesis was narrowing rapidly into the memories (bolstered by notes and recordings) from such people as Marcelo Santi Simbaña and the stories he told while we trekked. We thought of his sister Clara Santi Simbaña and her traditional expressive songs loaded with metaphors of modernity. These were transformed into drawings and narratives by our *compadre,* her son, Alfonso Chango. What we have learned from the pottery-making sessions with interspersed songs and deep conversations from Apacha Vargas, which also moved back to the deep pasts and distant places to connect with the immediacy of her history and the here and now, flooded our consciousness. The shamanic voice of the late Virgilio Santi and the contemporary insights of master ceramists Estela Dagua and Delicia Dagua stayed with us.

The result was a deeper appreciation of Marshall Sahlins's expositions on "the structure of the conjuncture." In rereading Sahlins juxtaposed to Runa modes of presentation and performance, and with an undergirding of history and archaeology, I could envision a transformative synthesis in Sahlins's early addiction to cultural evolution, later conversion to structuralism, and then a creative and productive emergence that began with *Historical Metaphors and Mythical Realities* (1981). The lessons of Clifford Geertz's admonishments in *The Interpretation of Cultures* (1973) were also uppermost in my mind as this essay took shape.

This chapter completes a hermeneutic circle within which we hope a horizon of knowledge continues to expand. Above all, it plumbs the strength of the perspective of transformative dynamics as a theory-constructive and culturally empowering ethnographic endeavor.

Chapter 7
Indigenous Modernity

I want to call attention to the emergence in the late twentieth–early twenty-first century of the indigenous–global conjuncture set within the Andean–Amazonian interface. Marshall Sahlins, a specialist in the ethnohistory and ethnography of Oceania, offers a perspective on the structure of the conjuncture that should be useful for both Andeanists and specialists in "Lowland South America." In *Culture in Practice* he writes:

> [V]arious indigenizations of modernity undertaken by people who have escaped the death sentence imposed by world capitalism now offer a whole new manifold of cultural variations for a renewed comparative anthropology. (Sahlins 2000:271)

My focus is on interculturality and "indigenizations of modernity"—both of which contribute to "alternative modernities"—manifest by the Canelos Quichua, Napo Runa, Andoa, Zápara, Achuar, and Shiwiar people of Pastaza Province, Amazonian Ecuador. By zooming down on the Canelos Quichua contemporary indigenous people, I seek to combine shared information from peoples speaking languages from three distinct families in three distinct classes of the Andean stock of the Andean-Equatorial language family (Greenberg 1960)—Quechua, Jivaroan, and Zaparoan—to understand some of the dynamics of alternative modernity as it emerges from time to time in a dynamic regional cultural system.

Cultural Topography

Before we get to *inter*culturality, let us take a glimpse at culture by reference to meaningful mythology, significant festival performance, nation-changing suasive ritual drama, and persuasive indigenous political action (e.g., N. Whitten and D. Whitten 2008). Topography is a good place to begin, especially if we are to problematize the "lowland/highland" bifurcate. Throughout Amazonia, when indigenous people signal their view of their near and distant spaces, they place west on top, east on the bottom, and north and south to the right and to the left (e.g., Sullivan 1988; Whitehead 2003). As a cosmograph, this orientation focuses on the dynamics of the sun rising out of primordial water on the eastern edge of the earth to begin its journey over land, forest, rivers, and mountains, tilting first slightly northward at midday to cross the vertical apex at the center—forming the cosmic *axis mundi*—and then back westward, where it goes underwater at the western edge and travels slightly southward and then eastward at night (e.g., Sullivan 1988). Day's end signals a dangerous cooling and the emergence of nocturnal forces of chaos and predation controlled by the moon. The moon itself, as we shall see, represents fertility and fecundity, of people and of plants.

The cosmology, cosmogony, and modern cosmography of the Canelos Quichua indigenous people who live in the Upper Amazonian–piedmont region of east-central Ecuador fit this pattern perfectly. Indigenous tellers quickly point out that in beginning times-places—times of great transformations in specific places—the sun did not make its appearance until well after the moon had committed incest with his sister, the whippoorwill-like Potoo bird.

An Amazonian Origin Myth

In mythic time-space, the "ripe" or full moon (*pucushca* Quilla) would descend on a sky ladder to visit the nocturnal Potoo bird, Jilucu.[1] Jilucu wanted to see her lover and so, one night, she cooked a seed from *widuj*, the *Genipa americana* tree, and later painted Moon Man with its juice to make him beautiful and so that she could "see" just who this handsome person was. In the early, nearby, predawn skies that he illuminated, Moon Man appeared, beautiful to be sure, but recognizable as her *turi*, her brother. How she cried when she realized that she had committed incest. Her sisters, *Genipa americana* (Black Woman) and *Bixa orellana* (Red Woman), cried with her; down came the rain as the stars joined in with their weeping. And then came the dreadful merger of torrential rain, earthquake, and flood. The rivers swelled, volcanoes erupted, and the earth shook and shuddered. The emerging earth people in beginning times-places were all swept eastward toward the great river sea, and perhaps also to the ocean sea, traveling on hastily constructed balsa rafts on which they had placed mounds of manioc and other goods.

With chaos and violence all around him, Indi, the sun, came out of his cave at the base of the Andes and hurtled skyward, going straight up; as he broke out through the deluge, thousands of bubbles exploded around him and fell to earth. As they fell, the colored bubbles congealed into seed beads and the white bubbles crystallized into salt. As the flood subsided and the earth calmed down to its current periodic rumblings and shakings, Indi created order by establishing the east–west regularity we know today. The emerging fully human beings, Runa, trekked homeward, going from east to west toward the Andean foothills, now rich in volcanic ash and ripe for tropical swidden gardens, always following the path of the now consistent sun trails. This east-to-west trek initiates an important dimension of *callari rucuguna,* beginning times-places. The Runa recognized ancient habitation sites by the *chontaduro* (peach palm) and *huayusa* (*Ilex*) trees planted by their pre-human shamanic forebears. In their treks, they also resurrected "lost" brothers through experiments with the edibility of bracket fungi, and they arrived at their original destinations with expanding populations and deep knowledge of Amazonia.

Let us return to Indi. In today's world, the world of fully human beings and transformed spirits in what we call culture and nature, manioc is the life-sustaining staple crop. Manioc must have strong solar illumination to propagate, to grow, to mature, and to produce large edible roots. It was hummingbird (Quindi) who, as younger brother of Quilla, the moon, was transformed into Indi, the sun, by Nungüi, the undersoil feminine spirit of manioc-producing garden soil. This occurred after episodes of violence, desire, and jealous spite and envy that resulted in the transformation of beginning-times spirit woman Nungüi to contemporary master spirit of garden soil and pottery clay. However these stories are told by Jivaroan-, Zaparoan-, or Amazonian Quichua–speaking people, east–west directionality from beginning times-places orders a system in which, during the day, masculine Indi provides the energetic illumination for manioc to grow, while at night, overseen by the masculine moon, undersoil feminine Nungüi nurtures the manioc stems—who are her daughters—to promote growth. Planting manioc stem cuttings, *lumu jichana,* is done by women at the time of a full moon so that each new manioc garden enjoys an ontogeny of *quillu pachama,* the ancient fecund yellow illumination without the dangerous burning powers associated with the sun. The mythopoetic cultural-ecological phylogeny of mythic time-space (*unai*) to beginning times-spaces (*callari rucuguna*) through times of destruction to times of the grandparents to now times is represented in their respective domains in the ontogeny of the manioc garden.

The Topographical Reorientation

A reorientation occurred in indigenous political topography in northern South America with the coming of the Inca, and then the Spanish. The Inca cosmological orientation was east–west, focused on the rising and the setting sun (e.g., Rowe 1946:300). But in the Incaic conquest of the Andes, the political-economic orientation adjacent to Upper Amazonia subverted this east-west primordial directionality in the Tahuantinsuyo Empire and imposed a south–north orientation that in many ways attenuated Amazonian systems from the centers of emerging Andean political economy (e.g., Richardson 1994). The Spaniards, intrigued as they were by the possibilities of exploiting the gold in the Land of El Dorado and the profitable products of American cinnamon, tobacco, capsicum, broom fiber, calabashes, bottle gourds, cotton, and dyes in the Land of La Canela to the east, nonetheless maintained the south–north primary directionality so contradictory to Amazonian and pre-Incaic cosmovision. Furthermore, active indigenous resistance to conquest and colonial exploitation, beginning in the Quijos territory and in the Jivaroan territory as early as 1579 (Santos-Granero 1993:215), set up barriers to highland–lowland political-economic integration and exacerbated the fission between Andes and Amazonia. Actual social relationships, however, among Amazonian and Andean peoples perhaps intensified during Incaic and later Spanish hegemonic reorientation of space-time.

The Canelos Quichua

The Canelos Quichua people of east-central Ecuador are an Amazonian people who live on the fringe of Western Amazonas, in an Andean nation. They are of the Upper Amazon canopied rain forest, one of many indigenous people of Ecuador whose cultural orientations resonate with one another, different though they may be in specifics. From time to time, the indigenous people from both "lowlands" and "highlands," along with others in various socioeconomic classes, have moved as a chiliastic Amazonian–Andean political force united by intersecting cultural systems to change the face of the nation. Many Canelos Quichua people intermarry with Achuar and Shiwiar Jivaroans and, less so, with Shuar Jivaroans. Probably twenty percent are bilingual in Achuar. Their name derives from the widely dispersed settlement of Canelos, into and out of which Dominican friars moved from time to time to temporarily nucleate segments of the people and to launch their mission *visitas* hither and yon in a vast and rugged mountainous rain-forest territory to which Spain laid claim over Portuguese pending domination.

Culturally, Canelos Quichua territory includes regions of the Bobonaza River system, especially, in addition to Puyo and Canelos (moving east), Pacayacu, Sarayacu, Teresa Mama, and Montalvo, down to Nuevo Andoas in Peru, where other ramifications of culture are encountered. Northward, Canelos Quichua have long lived on the edges of Waorani territory in sectors of the Villano and Curaray river regions (Cabodevilla 1994; Reeve 1993–1994, 1994, 2008). Within their territory, the Canelos Quichua people seem to "emerge" out of a confluence of Zaparoan people (especially Zápara, Andoa, and Shimigae) and Jivaroan people (especially Achuar) in the Bobonaza River region. To the north of the Bobonaza and to its south, enmities between Zaparoan and Jivaroan peoples escalated in mutual hostilities, but were buffered through an emergent and expanding culture whose carriers spoke a dialect of the Quechua language identified as "Canelos Quichua."

Ethnogenesis—the emergence of a people in specific times and places, in indigenous historicity and in Western history—clearly came to define the Canelos Quichua people in the sixteenth, seventeenth, and eighteenth centuries as a sustained cultural identity forged by a synergy of mutually hostile Zaparoan and Jivaroan people communicated through the Quichua language. They again emerge in indigenous memory in several languages as a cultural force of Amazonia at a time when the Liberal Republic of Ecuador appears on the world capitalist stage in the 1890s. This period is appropriately remembered as *alfaro rucuguna,* one of many "times of destruction." The name "*alfaro*" comes from the great liberal *caudillo* Eloy Alfaro Delgado, sometimes known as "*el indio alfaro.*"

Amazonian and Incaic Quechua

Turning to language, Bruce Mannheim's (1991) clarification of two divisions of Quechua helps clear the way for setting aside common erroneous stereotypes. Our first difficulty in understanding ethnogenesis is the sheer fact that Quichua is related to Quechua, best known as the language of the imperial Inca. All Quechua dialects, including those known as Quichua (Kichwa), are frequently, although erroneously, associated exclusively with the high Andean regions of Ecuador, Peru, and Bolivia. Mannheim makes it very clear that Canelos Quichua belongs to a northern branch of "Peripheral Quechua" and Incaic Quechua belongs to a southern branch of "Peripheral Quechua." Both diverge radically from "Central Quechua." Canelos Quichua and Incaic Quechua are related, but one probably did not derive from the other. Peripheral Quechua borne by the Inca was a language of conquest in Andean Ecuador in the fifteenth century, but its entry into what has become Canelos Quichua territory and its eventual domination over Jivaroan and Zaparoan languages in parts of Ecuador's Amazonian regions remains an intriguing problem. It may have been introduced from the southeast (Amazonian) region of San Martín, Peru, as I suggested in *Sacha Runa* (1976a) back in the 1970s, a position that Mannheim (1991) supports. Its southeastern to northwestern flow would be through the Marañón Valley region. Although clearly related to Andean Ecuadorian Quichua dialects, there are conservative features of the Amazonian Quichua dialects that perhaps relate to Amazonian Peru more closely than to the Ecuadorian Andes.[2]

Defining Features of the Canelos Quichua Indigenous People

The Canelos Quichua manifest features throughout their territory that, in their specific configuration, are but partially shared with their neighbors. I want to sketch these to show why I am not simply lumping them together as "rain-forest Quichua," as has now become fashionable in some quarters. These include the following aggregated cultural themes and complexes.

* *Extraordinary interculturality,* not just "multiculturality." Once one moves culturally inward, below the patina of surface proclamations, in Spanish, to outsiders to their lifeways, a deep historicity of relationships to Zaparoan peoples (Zápara and Andoa-Shimigae) and to Jivaroan peoples (especially Achuar and Shiwiar) comes forth. In the 2000s, these historicities have been ethnogenetic in the emergence of Andoa, Zápara, Shiwiar, and Achuar in a re-territorialization of ethnicities, as separate—though intercultural— entities. In this cultural dimension, indigenous people of the Vaupés of Colombia come to mind, as do the cultural ramifications of the multisocial Upper Xingu region of Brazil and the Arawakan-Tukanoan nexuses of the Río Negro and adjacent regions. Gow (1993) explores the dynamics of such systems for sectors of Western Amazonas in Peru and Ecuador.

I want to elaborate a bit here. Canelos Quichua men and women seek to balance experiential knowledge (*ricsina*) with cultural knowledge (*yachana*) and visionary experience (*muscuna*) with learning (*yuyana, yuyarina*). Central to the transformative paradigm involving these critical concepts is the *yachaj,* the "one who knows," the "possessor of knowledge." This concept often means "shaman" when applied to males, but may also be used to refer to master potters, who otherwise are known as *muscuj warmi,* or *sinchi muscuyuj warmi,* strong visionary woman. This paradigm pertains to two realms of existence, one called *ñucanchi yachai* (our cultural knowledge) and the second *shuj shimita yachai* (other cultural knowledge). As shamans and master potters show us again and again, one cannot understand one's own people's perception without understanding something of the lifeways and thought processes of other peoples. This translates perfectly in the modern Spanish *interculturalidad,* one of the hallmarks of the contemporary Ecuadorian indigenous movement and a concept now written into the new Ecuadorian constitution of 2008. A particular paradigm of knowledge, power, vision, and reflexivity does not map readily onto other Amazonian or Andean systems, but is reminiscent of many of them when generalized into "interculturality."

Let's return now to the list of particular complex features that have long characterized Canelos Quichua culture.

* A kinship system with strong emphases on intergenerationality and affinity, wherein people continuously rework their affinal ties so as to "consanguinize them," so to speak. In this system, a marriage, whether by arrangement or elopement, is eventually cognized as some replication of affinity resulting in descent from grandparental generations. And in these generations, the historicity of interculturality is again confronted, absorbed, and elaborated.
* A system of cultural transmission of knowledge and imagery in a parallel way through men and through women. Men pass cultural imagery and knowledge on to other men, through shamanic gnosis, while women pass imagery and knowledge to other women through Amazonian ceramic design, decoration, and imagery probably of Tupi origin. One cannot overemphasize the importance of ceramic techniques and imagery in cultural transmission in Canelos Quichua culture, something that is not shared with other peoples of Ecuadorian Amazonia or of Ecuadorian Andes.[3]
* A festival system that has elements of performance from Amazonian societies and from Andean societies, but that nonetheless emerges repeatedly in historical sources and perseveres in the present as unique in its configuration. Critically important here is that this kinship festival, which recounts in performance the origin of the people before and after destruction, while leading toward destruction, also connects the living people to the historical and contemporary dominance from the outside world and enacts a resistance to that dominance that, in its very enactment, threatens to unleash the awful transformations that led to and lead to the end of the world. This festival epitomizes the dramatic action of what Lawrence Sullivan (1988) calls the *Primordium* (the beginnings of everything) and the *Eschaton* (the ending of everything). Here, as is characteristic of other systems of Amazonian cultures, ritual enactment to express the end of everything—the *Eschaton*—precedes the mythic origins of the world and people—the *Primordium*.

With this sketch, I return to the themes of ethnogenesis and the indigenization of modernity.

Ethnogenesis and the Indigenization of Modernity

In the spring of 1992, the Canelos Quichua, Achuar, and Shiwiar marched collectively to Quito in a moving social drama known as the March for Land and Life, reinterpreted by some Andean indigenous leaders—who fused the event with the Levantamiento Indígena of 1990—as "the revolt of Inti Raymi," a rebellion of the sun festival. Initially following the east–west path of the sun, three thousand trekkers bedecked in feather- and animal-skin headdresses—women carrying pottery drinking bowls and men beating snare drums, blowing pottery cornets, playing vertical and transverse flutes, and in a couple of cases carrying and beating slit gongs—started up the Andean slopes. The first night was spent in Río Verde in the veritable *montaña*, where groups of shamans collectively took *Banisteriopsis caapi* and communicated about ancient ties to ancestors and spirits. Next came a reunion of Andean and Amazonian people in Andean Salasaca, where intercultural communication between diverse humans and diverse spirits never before experienced by living peoples was reported. As the procession swelled in numbers and moved northward toward Quito, it was described as *jistashina*, "like a festival," and *amarunshina*, "like an anaconda." Arrival in Quito, a camp-out in El Ejido Park, and myriad activities ranging from shamanic curing by men and pottery demonstrations by women to dramatic acts of civil disobedience forged a system within the heart of power of Quiteño experience that resulted in the grant of over one million hectares in Amazonia to be divided among indigenous ethnicities—some still emergent and inchoate—of Pastaza Province.

The full story of the millennial trek to Quito is a long and involved one (e.g., N. Whitten and D. Whitten 2008; Whitten et al. 1997). But my point should be made: indigenous people created their niche in the modern nation as an alternative to Western capitalism. An indigenization of Amazonian modernity was demonstrated in the heart and cerebrum of the power system of Ecuador—Andean Quito—from which it ramified nationwide and worldwide.

This indigenization of Amazonian modernity quickly became imprinted on the face of the Andean republic, just as Jilucu's *Genipa americana* was imprinted on the face of the moon. Building on the triumph of 1990 when an indigenous uprising occurred nationwide, in 1992 the myriad of non-indigenous people of Ecuador and an Amazonian segment of indigenous people were able to view each other in rather stark relief. Interculturality was and continues to be underscored across the Andes and through Ecuadorian Amazonia in public declarations since 1992. This surge of ideological interculturality gained enormous impetus during the undeclared war with Peru in 1995 when prominent members of the Ecuadorian military acknowledged key roles played by people of Shuar and Afro-Esmeraldan cultures of eastern and western Ecuadorian regions. Unmentioned was the role of the IWIAS special-service indigenous unit, stationed in Shell, comprised heavily of Canelos Quichua soldiers, plus Shuar soldiers. (The name Iwias comes from a Jivaroan cannibal monster.)

Self-Essentialization

The Canelos Quichua, Achuar, and Shiwiar marchers and protest campers clearly essentialized themselves. One example was the telling of collective intercultural mythohistories to those who would try to listen in El Ejido Park in Quito. Short stories told to reporters referred to previous treks from the Upper Amazon to Quito, and the camping Runa were specific on just which of the "old ones" from the times of the grandparents made such a trek, where they stopped to rest, and how in some cases the ancestors of the old ones accompanied them as returned spirits in the form of living great jaguars. By relating this not-so-distant history, tellers wanted listeners to know that trekking westward and northward to Quito to avoid catastrophe was well within the ethnogenetic modernity of this living indigenous body. By the time they reached Quito, the trekkers numbered about ten thousand people and included coastal and Andean Afro-Ecuadorians.

A Transcendental Myth of the Creation of Pottery Clay

A mythic episode from beginning times-places was also told, but was harder to follow for most listeners. This episode is one that Claude Lévi-Strauss, in his book *The Jealous Potter* (1988), calls the "essential myth" in "Jívaro" cosmology (he is referring only to the Shuar). The myth is central to Canelos Quichua cosmogony, though Lévi-Strauss scarcely mentions these people or their pottery. Indeed, when Rafael Karsten (1935:99–100; also D. Whitten 2003:85; N. Whitten and D. Whitten 2008:102, 169) wrote about how the Quichua-speaking people of Canelos brought their ceramic art "to a remarkable degree of perfection," he emphasized the quintessential cultural focus on this pottery in contradistinction to that of the Shuar ("Jívaro"). The omission of Canelos Quichua pottery is particularly odd in Lévi-Strauss's extended discourse, in that pottery manufacture, imagery, symbolism, and quotidian, festival, and ritual use constitute a transcendental place in Canelos Quichua cosmovision, cosmogony, and historicity in ways not evident at all among the Shuar. The fact that Lévi-Strauss himself turns to Karsten for information on pottery and cosmology makes this emphasis on the "Jívaro" and near negation of the Canelos Quichua even more puzzling.[4]

This takes us to the story of Squash Woman and Moon Man, one of many such tales told by indigenous men and women in El Ejido Park in Quito in the spring of 1992. Here I offer some key elements before returning to reasons for their omission in Lévi-Strauss's oeuvre (see also D. Whitten and N. Whitten 1993; for Achuar versions see Descola 1986, 1994 and Taish 2004; for lower Napo Quichua see Goldáraz 2004, 2005; the information in note 1 to this chapter also applies here).

Squash Woman and Moon Man

In beginning times-places (*callari rucuguna*), beautiful voluptuous Squash Woman, oldest of five or six daughters of the Widow Bat Woman (the others in birth order are *Bixa orellana, Genipa americana,* Corn Woman, and Nitrogen-Fixing Bean Woman), was living deep in the forest in a great oval house surrounded by a huge garden. The woman would feed her husband green, uncooked squash, which he loathed. He accused her of saving the ripe squash and cooking them for herself, but she showed him that she had sewn up her lips and said, with her mouth closed, "how can I eat cooked squash, I cannot even open my mouth" (this is spoken with lips closed by the teller). But he tricked her and witnessed her cooking ripe squash and opening her mouth wide, stretching the elastic-like threads.

In great anger he cursed her, walked to a sky-ladder vine, called *chaca* (or *chacana*), on which he had descended in the previous story. This ladder is a nitrogen-fixing *Bauhinia* species of vine, a contemporary rain-forest icon of a mythical *axis mundi*. He began to climb, playing sad songs on his three-hole transverse flute. Quickly now, Squash Woman scurried around the great oval house, which was precisely oriented to east–west with a central axis going straight up and straight down. She picked up everything and put her feminine paraphernalia, including items for pottery making, into a huge net bag or basket that she slung over her back. She began to climb, and climb, and climb. But Moon Man reached the sky, saw her coming up, and in great anger said to her, "you defamed me when you tried to deceive me." He cut the vine ladder and she and all of her household and garden belongings fell to earth with a great thud, and she broke her back, and she defecated. Then Quilla blew on the woman with his magical breath. "Suuuuuuuuu Jilucu," he said, "you become Jilucu [the common Potoo bird], and your feces will become special pottery clay."

The ladder is also a bridge, growing from the roots of the forest trees, where it fixes nitrogen, toward the sky, where the moon, sun, and stars live as ancient people.

When the moon is full, the song of Jilucu echoes through the forest:

Jilúuu-cu-cu-cu-cu-cu-cu-cu.

The Annual Ayllu Jista (Kinship Festival)

During the March for Land and Life from Puyo in Amazonia to Quito high in the northern Andes, indigenous participants described the event as "like a festival." Mary-Elizabeth Reeve, after eighteen months of intensive ethnographic research in Curaray, wrote this about festival significance in Curaray: "history shares with ritual the process of reaffirmation and potential renegotiation of a shared social reality" (Reeve 1993–1994:19; see also Reeve 1985:138–178, 1988a:121–156, 1988b, 2008; Whitten 1976a:165–202; N. Whitten and D. Whitten 2008:119–166). The Curaray Runa are part of the cultural system I have been discussing. The Canelos Quichua hold an annual (or sometimes semiannual) festival in every territory and hamlet where there is a manifestation of the Catholic dominion—a chapel, or even just a niche with a cross. While men trek on a two-week hunt for forest game and fish, women make highly significant arrays of pottery, and gallons and gallons of *asua*, a brew made from masticated cooked manioc. The festival is divided along lines of a central myth of beginning times-places, that of the union of Quilla, the male moon, and Jilucu, the female Potoo bird who transforms mythically into Nungüi, the master spirit of garden soil and pottery clay.

The array of creative imagery imparted to ceramic vessels is enormous (e.g., D. Whitten and N. Whitten 1988), but in every festival someone makes an effigy of the moon and someone makes one of Jilucu. The very division of the festival is into two parts, the male moon part and the female Potoo part, each represented by a festival house oriented on a precise east–west axis. As the festival proceeds, with participants moving en mass back and forth between the two houses, joining with each other and then breaking apart, men and women sing in falsetto about their ancestors, about beginning times-places, and about *unai*, the time of amorphous chaos when everything was sentient but those creatures who were to become historical and contemporary humans crawled on their hands and knees like babies and spoke only in two-tone hums, $^{mm}{}_{mm}$ $^{mm}{}_{mm.}$ This hum, by the way, is used by the shaman in séance to evoke mythic time-space (*unai*) prior to bringing to himself the spirit masters of the river and the forest in the form of the giant anaconda and the great black jaguar. While dancing, women toss their heads so as to make their hair fly back and forth as a feminine Nungüi analog to this male shamanic hum.

The festival culminates in a ritual summoning a bamboo-pole simulacra of the great multicolor anaconda from the river; it is borne by four Runa men who represent black jaguars. They lurch through the Catholic chapel, if there is one, and symbolically destroy it, bringing about the potential for the great upheaval of volcanic activity, flood, and darkness in which the indigenous people are swept eastward toward and into the river sea. *Tucurina,* "ending everything," is enacted. This is where this chapter begins (after discussion of the area). And this is where the festival ends, in an enactment of what Lawrence Sullivan (1988) calls the *Eschaton.*

In El Ejido Park in Quito, in the late spring of 1992, indigenous people tried to impart such imagery to those who were interested in their arrival. And they failed. Rather than listen to the assembled indigenous people from Amazonia, questions were raised about them, questions that may be considered to be epistemic distortions that could prevent our understanding of the many manifestations of indigenization of modernity.

Epistemic Distortion

"Who are these Indians?" many asked. "Where did they come from?" They are not Jívaro (Shuar); they are not Auca (Waorani). Others answered, "They are the *yumbos,* ancient acculturated *indios* from the Oriente, who used to come to Quito to cure and to trade." Some Quiteños remembered that there is an Andean ritual performance during the time of Corpus Christi in the small indigenous communities surrounding Quito, and in south Quito, in which the enactment of the arrival of a Yumbo troupe takes place. The Yumbos arrive, dance, and transform the open performative arena into a tropical forest drama in the space of Amazonian death. The dancers signify the wild and free shamanic power of the naked savages, and the trading power of Andean–Amazonian connectivity of the acculturated market-oriented "Yumbo." Two *yumbo* dancers divide into predator (*auca* hunter-with-lance) and prey (*yumbo*-as-peccary-person). The peccary person flees through a forest of swinging palm lances borne by the other male performers, but is caught hiding in a *tambo*—Amazonian shelter or resting place—by the hunter, and killed. Then, after payment of a fee to a shaman, the peccary person is resurrected and transformed to the Yumbo, and the Andean dance of delight begins. This is what Lawrence Sullivan (1988) calls the *Primordium,* where life arises out of violent death.

While the Yumbada is a festival in which people play (*pugllana*) with images and symbols (e.g., Fine-Dare 2007; Salomon 1981), the Amazonian people in El Ejido Park in Quito in 1992 were pragmatically *en*-acting. There was no play here. The camp-out was most serious. Indeed, indigenous people in El Ejido Park raised the question of whether they would live to return to their own territories, or whether *tucurina* (ending everything) might be imminent. Many passersby near the park looked away, and said that their city was in a state of contamination. These are *"indios alzados,"* they said, "indians out of place." We are reminded of Mary Douglas's (1966) analysis of anomalies and dirt as matter out of place. Following her mode of thought, Rudi Colloredo-Mansfeld (1999) wrote of the stereotypes of "dirty indians," referring to *mestizo* notions of "*indios fuera de su lugar,*" indians out of place.

The March for Land and Life resulted in indigenous people of Pastaza Province being awarded over one million hectares of surface territory, beginning a struggle for legal and quotidian possession that continues today in ever-escalating dimensions because of the state control of subsurface oil and minerals. The struggle resulted in the temporary abandonment by the Runa of Sarayacu in 2002 and, for a few years thereafter, of their kinship festival and a substitution of guerrilla-like encounters with petroleum-company people over subsurface rights. In 2007 one of the leaders of the anti-petroleum movement, Marlon René Santi Gualinga, was elected president of the Confederation of Indigenous Nationalities of Ecuador, CONAIE, with its headquarters in Andean Quito. He is the third Amazonian president of this national organization, which is usually associated only with the Andes.

Colonial History and Ethnogenesis

According to the governor of the province of Maynas, Francisco de Requena y Herrera (1991[1784]; also Cabodevilla 1994:476), the Puyo-Canelos sector of the Andean foothills–Upper Amazon was the jumping-off point for travelers to the Jesuit-controlled Huallaga-Marañón Spanish territory of the Mission of Maynas, with its locus at the confluence of the Huallaga and Marañón rivers, founded in 1638 (the Jesuits were expelled in 1767). By the eighteenth century, and probably before that, Canelos was the cultural switchboard not only between Andes and Amazonia but also for the Zaparoans of the Napo, Curaray, Conambo, Bobonaza, and Ishpingu river systems, the Achuar of the Capahuari and Copataza river systems, and some of the Shuar to the south, then and now known as the Chirapa. Over thirty years ago, Marcelo Naranjo (1977) argued that Canelos emerged and endured as a refuge region for people from all of these areas, and as such was the site of preference for traveling curates and explorers seeking labor and knowledge.

The concept of ethnogenesis does not only refer to a people's own sense of coming into being; in Western history it refers to the symbolism of "being" as a social and cultural "fact" of history. As such, signification looms large. People are remembered and so inscribed not as whom they say they are, but as they were or are named, framed, and written down. What the name for a people "stands for" is what symbolism is all about. As noted previously, Edmund Leach (1982:107) argued persuasively that "the naming of relationships marks the beginning of moral sanctions." For the early Church in this region—the Dominicans in the late 1500s—the symbolism of "Canelos" was that of a *reducción*, reduction (nucleation), to control the "savage" Jivaroans and Zaparoans, among others. The *reducción*, after all, was what the mission was expected to accomplish, and it could only do so if it claimed that it had, indeed, executed the task of semicivilization of colonial Christendom as a wedge between savage peoples. In short, maintenance of a Western polarity between tame and wild, acculturated and pristine was essential to the mission of these men of the cloth. On each side of the dichotomy, we find not "humans" but *"indios"*; an appellation of multiple stigmata originally applied to all native peoples of the Americas by Columbus in 1493 and subsequently elaborated as early modern Western mercantilism transformed into modern capitalism.

By the time the concepts of "indians" and "Canelos" and "Jívaros" become imprinted in history, all "indians" have been separated out of Western development and have been divided into—and contrasted as—the "reduced Christians," on one side of the polarity, and the "heathen savages," on the other—the tame and the fierce. François Pierre (1983[1889]) documents convincingly that the Dominicans carefully divided the territory of Macas-as-Jívaro from Canelos-as-Quichua—the former as savage and the latter as semicivilized—and strove to maintain this distinction even though using the same techniques of reduction and evangelization in both "savage" and "semicivilized" sectors of their dominion. Although classed in perpetuity as heathen—wild savages—some Jivaroan people were also baptized from time to time. Indeed, the renowned warrior Sharupe, leader of the Chirapa, who waged constant war against the people of the Puyo-Canelos area, was baptized with great ecclesiastical pomp and circumstance as José María Sharupe in Andean Riobamba in the 1890s (a time of *alfaro rucuguna*, one of many periods of destruction). Jivaroan people were also nucleated as the Canelos remained essentially dispersed and resistant to proselytization.

Historicity—high salience given to past events and people in indigenous discourse—again enters our anthropological understanding. The concept of "Runa," as "fully human being," reemerges as focal in several territories of Upper Amazonian Ecuador in the 1890s. The fact that territory and Runa run together through time and the fact that the Shuar, Achuar, Shiwiar, Caninche, Andoa-Shimigae, and Zápara people in various locations often use the word *Canelos* to refer to people from the Runa territories led to a focus on the term *Canelos* as a multicultural and intercultural ethnogenetic way of life that developed out of antiquity and projected into specific histories of a nation-state and three vast regions: Amazon, Andes, and their complex Andean–Amazonian interface.

Epistemic Distortion, Academic Structuralism, and the Structure of Conjuncture

Structuralism, in its Lévi-Straussian "classical" renditions as manifest, for example, in the four-volume *Mythologiques* series, or in its "neoclassical" renditions, is foundational to one prolonged theoretical moment of Amazonian studies (e.g., Carneiro da Cunha 2007:xii; Fausto and Heckenberger 2007:8). The other moment or movement is that of "cultural ecology," which often seems bent on removing "culture" from the process of analysis. Marshall Sahlins (2000:17) writes of structuralism and cultural ecology as creating a "theoretical schismogenesis, an atmosphere of irreconcilable difference." Following Lévi-Strauss, though challenged extensively by such scholars as Jonathan Hill, Terry Turner, and Neil Whitehead, to name only three, the Lévi-Straussian notion of "cold" societies inextricably tied to endless mythic cycles and so unable to become part of Western history motivates all too many colleagues (e.g., Taylor 1999:194–196) to regard people such as the Canelos Quichua and the Napo Runa as exemplars of a pervasive Ecuadorian Amazonian conundrum. Rather than understand their system as it has emerged in history and has engaged (and engages) in the national political economy from time to time, Taylor (1999) applies many labels that specify or imply marginality, hybridization, "acculturation," and anomaly.

Simply stated, the Canelos Quichua are just "too hot" to treat "structurally." Turner (1988:238) calls this the "fallacy of misplaced fahrenheit." Instead of attempting to understand Canelos Quichua and Napo Runa systems of social order and cultural orientations, Amazonian Quichua speakers are labeled "incaized," "hybridized," "Christianized," and other appellations that contrast with "authentic Jívaros." The shades of Dominican dominion cast a pall over ethnographic or ethnohistoric enlightenment about peoples and their transactions in this region.

But structure there is to be found if one seeks structure in conjunctures, as long advocated by Marshall Sahlins (e.g., 1976, 1981, 2000). Sahlins draws the concept of conjuncture from historian Fernand Braudel (1980[1958]), for whom a conjuncture is a period of dynamic time of from ten to one hundred years. The idea is to understand the cosmological scheme of a given people as it articulates to the pragmatics of changing political economy. For Sahlins, the particular reference points of indigenous cosmological schemata and quasi-hegemonic political economy constitute the "structure" (see also Ohnuki-Tierney 1990:9).

To understand structures of conjuncture, we drop the Western assumptions of structure standing apart from history and events, and take people as they are. Salient relationships that constitute a dynamic conjunctural structure of Canelos Quichua lifeways may be revealed in exquisite relief in situations in which symbols within their mythology and mythohistoric metaphors become manifest in ritual drama and fuse with quotidian knowledge and pragmatic action. Fusion, often expressed in song and ceramic art, occurs through male shamanic gnosis and through female pottery manufacture and imagery. We must explore this a bit.

In the four-volume Introduction to the Science of Mythology series (the *Mythologiques*), we learn, in *The Raw and the Cooked* (Lévi-Strauss 1969), what was suggested earlier in *Structural Anthropology* (Lévi-Strauss 1963a), in *Totemism* (Lévi-Strauss 1963b), and especially in *The Savage Mind* (Lévi-Strauss 1966): that myth is a relatively pure key to the workings of culture because it survives radical change or transformation. Mythical work breaks the continuous flow of culture into segments that, while not obvious to natives themselves, nonetheless can be understood by the Western analyst savant in terms of recombinant binaries through expansion and contraction of the oppositions, their classifications, and their imbricated hierarchies. Eventually we come to the structure of mind that culture obscures (e.g., Geertz 1967). In the fourth volume, *The Naked Man* (Lévi-Strauss 1981), we get to ritual, which, opposite to myth, tries (apparently in vain) to remake into continuities that which is cut into discrete segments of meaningful relationships. Both myth and ritual are extractable from cultural matrices to be studied comparatively "in their own right" (e.g., Handelman and Lindquist 2004).

The structuralist exercise is always interesting; but it ahistoricizes all tellings, often excises tellers who seem to the analyst to not represent the "authentic language" anticipated in anthropology (Jívaro being favored, Quichua marginalized), and the actions and praxes of people involved in specific events become nonexistent. Indigenous people do engage in political activities that actually alter the structure of the nation-state. In the case presented above, they describe their activity as "like a festival"; they bring their mythology through playful discourse, song, melody, rhythm, and ceramic imagery into strong consciousness; and they endeavor to educate people "of other cultures" (*shuj shimita yachai*) of the durability and even adaptability of their ways of life. By so doing, they indigenize modernity by placing themselves and their cultural orientations into coeval juxtaposition with the dominant system (contra Johannes Fabian 2002[1983]).

The energy so radiated within the nation-state is analogous to the sunlight nourishing manioc by day. This is easy to grasp. What is more difficult to understand is that within this same system of mythopoetics exist the sense of the fecund moonlight governing planting of manioc and the powerful feminine image of undersoil powers of fertility allowing the manioc to grow and to do human bidding rather than exercising its inherent feminine power of predatory blood sucking from human children. If we are to understand the indigenization of modernity, we must move into the deep metaphors of indigenousness itself—the *longue durée* undergirding the conjuncture—not transform these systems of signs and symbols into a Western mode. In short, we must explore indigenous hermeneutics within multiple dynamic modernities, eschewing Western hermetics of unified developmentalism and systemic binaries of savage and semicivilized. One salient antecedent for this endeavor is Karl Marx, who wrote, "As people express their life, so they are" (Marx 1998[1845]:37); Michael Uzendoski takes this perspective in his ethnography of the Napo Runa: "the people of Napo speak . . . through the voice and poetics of *pachacutic* —destroying, recuperating, and transforming society and history" (Uzendoski 2005:165).

The concept of *pachacutij* involves transformation (*tucuna* in Quichua), which in turn involves articulation of indigenous cosmological schemata to the extant political economy. The simile "like an anaconda" was used in 1992 by indigenous marchers to refer to their collective indigenous body undulating toward the Quito power-head. Runa in this culture hold to a cosmic truth that is comparable in its ineffable power to that of the doctrine of consubstantiation of the Eucharist and the corporeal resurrection of Christ in Roman Catholic Christianity. This is the deeply held cosmic postulate that the anaconda of the water realm is related to the male penis in the household domain, a conjuncture of fertilization mechanisms that can penetrate the nation-state and cause a dangerous rebirth. This root metaphor fits very well with Sullivan's concept of the *Primordium* of South American religious systems.

When a boa constrictor is encountered among the Canelos Quichua, it is first bludgeoned with a pole, and then, after death, its head is severed, its still-beating heart removed, and the body buried well away from water. The head and pulsing heart are taken home, processed into magical substances, and the remains buried far from the body. The body forever endeavors to grow toward the head, and if it connects, an explosive life-restoring phenomenon known as *tupaj amarun* takes place, causing massive upheaval and at times evoking *pachacutij,* a return of space-time of a healthy past to that of a healthy future. In indigenous discourse, we can abstract a strong sense of an intensification of the union of our culture–other cultures (*ñucanchi yachai-shuj shimita yachai*). In nationalist orientation, as expressed by a myriad of intellectual and media commentators, we come upon a veritable renaissance of interculturality.

The Duality of Ethnogenesis

To return to ethnogenesis, symbolism—the key to the semiotics of structuralism—is also our key to the structure of the conjuncture. Cultural emergence constitutes a signifier. In indigenous discourse, what is signified is oneness out of—or even into—diversity and interculturality. Beginning times in different places, *callari rucuguna*, is stressed in what sometimes seems like an epiphany of insight into cultural rebirth out of the death of collectivities, in a great transformation (*tucuna*) from its own reflexive ending (*tucurina*).

Ethnogenesis in history (what is written down), however, may often signify a-culturation (see Whitten and Whitten 2008:251–255)—the movement of culture from one ethnic system to a new one—and hence loss of culture from the donor. This is the position of Philippe Descola (1994) and Anne Christine Taylor (1999), among many others. Herein lies the genesis of epistemic distortion. The Canelos Quichua "cannot be" if their pristine roots have been so intertwined as to negate the false historical assumption of bounded tribes speaking distinct languages and traceable through multiple contacts with outsiders, what Michel-Rolph Trouillot (1995) calls the "savage slot" of anthropology and the mass media. Thierry Saignes's definition of culture fits this slot perfectly. He writes: "colonial native culture . . . lacks the attributes traditionally associated with the phrases 'a culture': internal consistency and outer boundedness" (Saignes 1999:61). The characteristics of Canelos Quichua culture, listed above, do not fit either Saignes's or Taylor's idea of Andean culture or Amazonian culture, so the attributes of culture loss, a-culturation, hybridization, Incaization, Quichuaization, and more are heaped on to create a murky miasma of misunderstanding.

When people are simply human beings, Runa, speaking Quichua, falsely associated solely with the Andes, and finding their identities not only in Achuar and Zápara antiquities but also in Andoa, Shimigae, Caninche, and even Cocama descent systems, then there is a polarity wherein indigenous ethnogenesis of a people, of fully human beings, is opposed to a Western historical ethnogenesis of a-culturated "indians" as inscribed, for example, in the section "Tribes of the Peruvian-Ecuadorian Montaña" in the *Handbook of South American Indians*. In the first—indigenous ethnogenesis—a vigor of oneness and a turn to mythohistory for future understanding are epitomized; in the second—historical ethnogenesis of a-culturated indians—a stupor of diversity-into-hybridity leading to cultural *mestizaje* creates national and perhaps anthropological ideological order by silencing indigenous voicing (e.g., Brown and Fernandez 1991:213).

Michael Uzendoski in his book *The Napo Runa of Amazonian Ecuador* challenges the epistemic distortion promulgated by Anne Christine Taylor (1999) (a student of Claude Lévi-Strauss): "Taylor's otherwise simulating piece . . . continues this stereotype in arguing that Amazonian Quichua speakers are 'assimilated,' *manso* (weak), and 'generic' natives with 'linear and periodized historical ideologies very different from those of the "traditional" groups of the region'" (Uzendoski 2005:165). Such structuralist stereotyping is doubly unfortunate, inasmuch as a case can be made for the homeland of at least a large sector of the Jivaroans as lying in the Andean piedmont of eastern Loja, according to Maurizio Gnerre (1973), while the Canelos Quichua (but not the Napo Runa) may have a homeland in San Martín, Amazonian Peru, in the southern Marañón basin. Even without such a polarity that plays the game of "who is more Amazonian or more Andean than whom," it is obvious that Jivaroans and Amazonian Quichua speakers have had vertical ties to sub-Andean and Western Amazonian systems for a very long time, and that their cultures have long intertwined to form a region of braided traditions.

Return to the Indigenization of Modernity and Interculturality

By now I am sure that some readers are thinking of my proclivity here to essentialize, a process thought over the past two decades or so to be something of a substantive anthropological disease akin to theoretical eclecticism. Marshall Sahlins helps us here. In a chapter called "Goodbye to Tristes Tropes," Sahlins (2000) bemoans the strong tendency of contemporary anthropologists to eschew all forms of essentialism—to turn away from people who self-consciously want the world to know who they are and in the process reinvent "tradition" or, as we might put it, reemerge into the World Culture–of–cultures as distinct peoples. He cautions us as to this tendency by historical hegemonic analogy:

> In the fifteenth and sixteenth centuries, a bunch of indigenous intellectuals and artists in Europe got together and began inventing their traditions and themselves by attempting to revive the learning of an ancient culture which they claimed to be the achievement of their ancestors but which they did not fully understand, as for many centuries this culture has been lost and its languages corrupted or forgotten . . . They created a self-conscious tradition of fixed and essentialized canons . . . All this came to be called the Renaissance in European history, because it gave birth to "modern civilization" . . . What else can one say about it, except that some people have all the historical luck? When Europeans

invent their traditions ... it is a genuine cultural rebirth, the beginnings of a progressive future [ethnogenesis]. When other peoples do it, it is a sign of cultural decadence, a factitious recuperation, which can only bring forth the simulacra of a dead past [acculturation]. (Sahlins 2000:478–479)

Summary

I have tried to demonstrate in this final chapter that the sharp distinctions made by scholars in many disciplines among myth, history, ritual, and political action are Western, not Runa, ones. My mode of presentation here is to see these dimensions of thought and action as cultural correspondences, ways of constructing and reconstructing symbolic templates in multiple systems of signification.

To address the central theme of this essay, the indigenization of modernity, I move to illustrate pervasive mythic cosmology to orient the reader to Canelos Quichua Amazonian perspectives on the very edge of the northern Andes. The relationships that obtain in language, culture, and even topography between the "lowlands" and the "highlands" are heightened as we move through culture and interculturality and take up the subject of ethnogenesis in indigenous thought and in written historical portrayal. Building toward an indigenous structure of conjuncture, I treat "epistemic distortion" in various academic sectors and attempt to counter or deflect what I take to be such distortions by reference especially to Sahlins (2000) and Uzendoski (2005).

Indigenous modernity has clear millennial proclivities (e.g., Whitten, ed. 2003). By "millennial," one evokes an English metaphor for the Quichua concept of *pachacutij* (Uzendoski 2005:ix) as "the return of space-time (chronotope) of a healthy past to that of a healthy future" (Whitten, ed. 2003:x). Indeed, the intertwining of modernity and its indigenization, the genesis of alternative modernities, and emerging culture generate a myriad of intercultural systems to which, it is hoped, more and more ethnographers will turn their attention, working—again it is hoped—with historians, linguists, literary professionals, and above all spokespeople for those in motion in the maw of Western modernity who endeavor to appropriate modern accoutrements of life through counterhegemonic and transformative systems of indigenous meaning.

Acknowledgments

A brief version of sections of this essay was prepared as the second keynote address for the first meeting of the Society for Amazonian and Andean Studies in Boca Raton, Florida. I greatly appreciate the invitation by Rachel Corr to deliver this address, and her comments on an abbreviated version of it. Kathy Fine-Dare and Mary-Elizabeth Reeve read early drafts of the keynote address and its expansion and made significant comments that helped me frame this version. Michelle Wibbelsman read an early and a penultimate version and offered valuable comments. To clarify some points on history and language, respectively, I wrote to Kris Lane and Bruce Mannheim, both of whom replied quickly and with accurate and detailed information, which I greatly appreciate. I am particularly indebted to Sibby Whitten, whose careful and critical reading vastly improved the later versions. My greatest debt is to the people of Canelos Quichua culture, and their Achuar, Andoa, Zápara, Caninche, Napo Runa, and other relatives, who have guided Sibby and me through intricacies of their lives and patterns of thought for a very long time.

Well after this essay was completed, I received a copy of the book *Time and Memory in Indigenous Amazonia: Anthropological Perspectives* (2007), edited by Carlos Fausto and Michael Heckenberger. Except for a couple of references to "neostructuralism," I have not been able to incorporate materials from it into this essay. A serious critical treatment of Taylor's work published in this book is in press in Hornborg and Hill (2011).

Conclusion
Ethnography and Theory in Cultural Life

> [B]eyond functionalism, beyond structuralism, beyond poststructuralism, beyond postmodernism, global ethnoscapes and the latest twist on human rights discourses, there lies the bedrock of anthropology—ethnography, our enduring gift to the world, a gift that sometimes enables readers to understand the wisdom of others, which, in turn, can open their being to an increasingly complex and interconnected world.
> —Paul Stoller[1]

Theory, as explanation, must be constructed from phenomena. A phenomenon, in turn, is nothing more and nothing less than a fact, event, or circumstance that can be observed, induced, or deduced. Theory construction, then, is the building up of explanation based on observable, inducible, or deducible phenomena. In anthropology a combination of these constructions is used, just as in everyday life. In the cultural anthropology of the late twentieth–early twenty-first century, and to some extent in other social sciences, we can apply the definition of the Oxford English Dictionary (3rd ed., rev.) to our endeavors at understanding human action: "A conception or mental scheme or system of ideas or statements held as an explanation or account of a group of facts or phenomena."

Let's back up a bit. We do not move from "observation" or "observable phenomena" in a direct line of "description." Rather, we rely on words, sentences, and mental constructs voiced or written or otherwise constructed and communicated. Ingrained tropes, images, and syntagma pile up, quite unconsciously. Without intersubjectivity born of sustained ethnography, we may build mental schemes that obscure or deny other perspectives, especially, at times, those we seek to reveal. Examples abound in Latin Americanist and Caribbeanist literature and we have sought to expose many of these in the preceding chapters.

Most cultural anthropologists do not deploy "theory" as a noun very often, choosing instead to use adjectival forms such as "theoretical perspectives," "theoretical issues," and even "theoretical dilemmas." This relates to the simple fact that as humans, we construct facts and interpret phenomena through our symbolic templates in specific social contexts. We construct what Geertz (1973) called not only "models of" but also "models for" phenomena. The former is a set of first-level generalizations based on our observations; the latter is an action plan to construct phenomena in the world, an example of which would be "race" as an explanatory principle. Addressing issues of "race" has permeated many of the chapters of this book. Moreover, issues of race constitute a set of the strikingly salient issues addressed repeatedly by members of the American Anthropological Association. Such issues have again reached a high salience throughout the world following the election of Barack Obama as president of the United States.

Obviously, to construct theoretical perspectives we must, at all times, deconstruct theoretical (read "cultural") paradigms extant in the ingrained propositions of our everyday and sacral lives (our symbolic templates, our models of and models for what we may take to be "facts" or common-sense deductions). In this sense, anthropology, with ethnography at its core, is of necessity iconoclastic.

Chapter 1, especially at the outset, constitutes an exercise in such deconstruction. The next chapter uses indigenous constructions of "blackness" to deconstruct many white-dominated Western notions, some of which have become hypostatic in a vast literature and even segments of academic disciplines that relate "slavery," or "the plantation," or "plantation slavery" to "blackness" or "black culture" in a fixed, linear, and causal manner. Chapter 3 fleshes out the paradigmatic clashes in racialist thought to expose historical roots of such hypostases, especially the Latin American ideology of *el mestizaje* and the challenges to it by "the represented." This leads to the Ecuadorian Indigenous Uprising of 1990 (chapter 4) and a review of the constructs that may connect the perspectives of people in motion in a real place—Ecuador—to disciplinary constructs on ethnogenesis, alternative modernity, emergent culture, structures of conjuncture, and transformational dynamics.

Chapters 5, 6, and 7 illustrate different but complementary features of contemporary ethnography. In chapter 5, we focus on the sovereign nation-state of Ecuador as a conflicted and at times beleaguered cultural system. In chapter 6, Dorothea Whitten reviews the art images through which native Andean people project their nation's legacies and radical changes. Norman Whitten then draws on indigenous Amazonian mythopoetics to conjoin ethnography with theory construction and deconstruction. Taken together these three chapters reveal a multidimensional set of Ecuadorian cultural worlds beset by local, national, and global forces.

In the introduction to his book *The Interpretation of Cultures,* Clifford Geertz (1973:3–30) made major theoretical contributions stemming from his ethnographic research carried out in Indonesia and Morocco. Such ethnography was set in, and confronted, a framework of productive theory developed from works by Max Weber (e.g., 1947; Gerth and Mills 1958[1946]), among many others, as filtered through his sociological mentor Talcott Parsons (1937; Parsons and Shills 1959) and motivated by the intellectual-political acumen of Clyde Kluckhohn (e.g., Geertz 2002:4–5). By developing a systematic alternative to French structuralism, on the one side, and American cognitive anthropology, on the other, and by weaving his way through and around a myriad of other perspectives, Geertz offered ways by which to sort "levels of signification" to create greater sophistication when presenting ethnography and in searching for historical matrices by which to understand continuity and change in culture. He also eschewed a focus on reconstruction of cultures ("historical distributionalism"), to emphasize the transformative dynamics of contemporaneity of people acting and communicating through culture. In the process of his illustration, he gave a superb encapsulation of interculturality of Berber, Jewish, and French colonial transaction (Geertz 1973:7–10).

The next year, Geertz published an article entitled "From the Native's Point of View" in the *Bulletin of the American Academy of Arts and Sciences* (1974), which was reprinted in his second book on interpreting culture, entitled *Local Knowledge* (1983). Focusing on his own ethnographic experiences and contributions to theory construction, Geertz stresses "the characteristic intellectual movement, the inward conceptual rhythm, in each of these analyses, and indeed in all similar analyses, including those of Malinowski—namely, a continuous dialectical tacking between the most local of local detail and the most global of global structure in such a way as to bring them into simultaneous view" (Geertz 1983:69). This perspective on "tacking" between local and global characterizes all of the essays in this book, and perhaps is especially evident in chapter 7.

> This is the now familiar trajectory of what Dilthey [e.g., 1996] called the hermeneutic circle, and my argument here is merely that it is as central to ethnographic interpretation, and thus to the penetration of other people's models of thought, as it is to literary, historical, philological, psychoanalytical, or biblical interpretation, or for that matter to the informal annotation of everyday experience we call common sense. (Geertz 1983:69)

Enter Victor Turner, whose work is pivotal to our presentation in chapter 4 and is evident in the first three chapters. In his book of essays entitled *Dramas, Fields, and Metaphors,* published one year after Geertz's first collection of essays, Turner (1974), following Charles-Arnold Kurr van Gennep (e.g., Van Gennep 1960[1909]), wrote of processual structure and social action. By this he meant an abstract sequence involving an event, processes leading to a crisis followed by a "liminal" period of confusion generating egalitarian camaraderie (called *communitas*) among actors, until finally reaching a resolution, which may promote either continuity (reproduction) or change (transformation), or some combination of the two. This processual structure, which is also dramaturgical, could be adapted for either ritual or political processes, fusing the analysis of the Western dichotomy between the sacred and the profane (e.g., Godelier 2010). Turner then took the abstract Western model (developed under the tutelage of Max Gluckman in Manchester, England [e.g., Gluckman 1954, 1962, 1965]), and reinserted it into ethnographic and historical contexts to demonstrate its viability, and to appropriately revise and refine in terms of the ethnographies and historical narratives themselves.

Later, emerging from an evolutionist mode of presentation and theoretical assemblage, Marshall Sahlins transformed both structuralism and Marxism by reference to historical clusters of events and the forces of history to deepen our concept of structure while retaining the focus on human action and agency. In *Historical Metaphors and Mythical Realities,* Sahlins (1981) drew on his own ethnography and ethnohistory undertaken in Fiji and then Hawaii to develop an interface for diachrony and synchrony by transforming Fernand Braudel's (1980[1958]) trichotomy of "*longue durée,*" "conjuncture," and "event" into a concept of a dynamic "structure of the conjuncture." Concepts developed by these scholars, each of whom is known for his substantive contributions to both ethnography and ethnohistory, pave a way by which we make first-level synchronic generalizations derived directly from intersubjective encounters in ethnographic contexts and juxtapose them to our disciplinary theoretical alternatives based on an interpretation of layers of signification. They also provide the means by which we may move to diachrony through an interpretation of indigenous cosmological premises vis-à-vis political-economic transformations within cultural spheres of action and knowledge. This latter mode of interpretation is especially evident in the preceding chapter 7.

Interpretation here is critical to both ethnography and theory construction. Geertz, Turner, and Sahlins (among many others) underscore the creativity involved in merging or juxtaposing indigenous interpretations with those of Western analysts working through the development of theoretical premises and constructs from disciplinary engagements. In Geertz's words: "[T]here are three characteristics of ethnographic description: it is interpretive; what it is interpretive of is the flow of social discourse; and the interpreting involved consists in trying to rescue the 'said' of such discourse from its perishing occasions and fix it in perusable terms" (Geertz 1973:20).

If the description and analysis of the lifeways of a given people is "perusable," then other analysts can, through hermeneutics, draw from comparative ethnographies and competing theoretical perspectives to come to a rich, nuanced, dynamic, and changing interpretation of the ethnographic information. To the extent, however, that perusability is not possible, as in some presentations by cultural materialists and structuralists, hermetic phenomena occlude our abilities to understand, interpret, and compare. Geertz (2000[1984]:60) expressed this as follows: "Wiring your theories into something called the Structure of Reason is as effective a way to insulate them from history and culture as building them into something called the Constitution of Man."

Let us return to "culture," as used in the preceding chapters. In the introduction, we defined culture dynamically as "a corpus and flow of symbols and meanings enacted in social life at a given time in a given place." We noted in that chapter that Michael Uzendoski emphasized the proposition, which is fundamental to anthropology and anthropologists, that "'culture' transforms our perceptions of the world." In chapters 1 and 2, we asserted "that all culture is interethnic and that all ethnicity is intercultural." We returned to Geertz (1983) again in chapter 2, where we added his definition of culture, as stated in *Local Knowledge*: "cultural phenomena . . . should be treated as significative systems posing expositive questions" (Geertz 1983:1; see also Leach 1976). We went on to argue that "[s]uch systems carry meaning and raise questions. They constitute what one needs to know to understand the individual and collective thought of people living a particular way of life."

Power, a subject that Geertz studiously avoids, enters here. Sahlins and Turner and their predecessor Peter Worsley, and more recently Michael Taussig, demonstrate convincingly that the Western dichotomies between "politics" and "religion" simply do not work when we undertake serious ethnography and through it work to develop a hermeneutics of interpretation of power (see also Godelier 2010). Earlier in this century, Max Weber (1947:152; also Gerth and Mills 1958[1946]:180) argued that power is the ability of actors to assert their will, against the resistance of the people participating in the field of activity of such "will." Here we paraphrase and include the concept "field," taken from the work of Victor Turner (e.g., 1974). In the late twentieth to the turn of the twenty-first century, the field of power includes nation-states, corporations, and armies, among other such entities. The late Eric R. Wolf (1999) called these fields "structural power." In chapter 2, we brought in the work of William Arens and Ivan Karp (1989) who, in their edited book *Creativity of Power,* wrote that "[t]ransformation is the key to understanding power in African societies. . . . 'transformative capacity' is a key element in people's understanding of power" (Arens and Karp 1989:xx).

In *Millennial Ecuador,* Norman Whitten drew on Victor Turner's (1974:272–299) concepts of "anti-structure," "contra-structure," and "restructuring" to refer to the forces contrasting with and sometimes opposing these macro entities (the state, international corporations, supranational organizations such as the World Bank and the International Monetary Fund, foreign governments, the United Nations) in Ecuador as "contrastructural power" (Whitten 2003a:29–30). Turner (1974:273), in writing of the power and agency of ritual action, defined "anti-structure" as the "positive, generative center" of social relations. Transforming Turner's focus on social structure and ritual processes to the realm of power, our "contrapowers" coalesce as ongoing "powers of resistance," discussed in the introduction. Michel-Rolph Trouillot (1995:xix) wrote of this process: "History is the fruit of power, but power itself is never so transparent that its analysis becomes superfluous. The ultimate mark of power may be its invisibility; the ultimate challenge, the exposition of its roots." After the indigenous rebellion of January 21, 2000, that deposed President Jamil Mahuad Witt, indigenous leader Salvador Quishpe Lozano (*El Comercio,* February 20, 2000) stated, "Power is an instrument that lets the dreams of the people crystallize." And immediately after the taking of the legislative building, Antonio Vargas, the president of CONAIE, stated, "the people are empowered" (Vargas Guatatuca 2000; Whitten 2003a:1).

By powers of resistance (also called "counterpower" by Graeber 2004:35–37), we refer to *sociosymbolic forces that coalesce as transformative dynamics in the face of structural power fields.* The forces are always present in contemporary society, but their coalescence is sporadic. The concepts are developed by special reference to the pioneering work of Victor Turner (1974) and Eric R. Wolf (1999; see also Uzendoski 2005 on the Napo Runa for more illustration and elaboration, and Whitten, ed. 2003).

Alternative modernities, a concept suggested but not so named by these scholars, constitute contested domains generated by these same sociosymbolic processes within a nation-state that come to epitomize modernity in such a manner as to make life uncomfortable, unbearable, or simply unthinkable for some of the people within its confines (Parameshwar Gaonkar 2001; D. Whitten and N. Whitten 1994). Under such circumstances, millenniarity may emerge. By *millennial* we refer to the Quichua concept of *pachacutij,* "the return of space-time (chronotope) of a healthy past to that of a healthy future" (Whitten, ed. 2003:x; see also Uzendoski 2005:165). These concepts permeate all of the chapters in this book.

One prominent task of ethnographers flagged by many but drawn together by Geertz (1973) is to set forth sociosymbolic processes in unfolding, transculturating, and transforming chronotopes to facilitate understanding across, within, and beyond national borders. Processes of intersubjectivity, expanding hermeneutic horizons, fusing or juxtaposing the "native's point of view" with generalizations and abstractions of the ethnographer, and sustained reflexivity are central to ongoing ethnography (N. Whitten and D. Whitten 2008).

Ethnography may offer insights to potential empowerment manifest by people in innumerable locations around the world and communicable increasingly by the potential interculturality of horizontal globalization, or "globalization from below" (e.g., Appadurai 2001:16–20; Colloredo-Mansfeld 2008; Ntarangwi 2009). Such a potential requires careful scrutiny that involves not only an inner view of symbol systems, communicative tropes, and the boundaries set up with other systems, but also an understanding of such *transformative systems in action within shifting world frameworks* (e.g., Geertz 2002; Scott 2005). Understanding of interculturality and its potential for communication globally requires interpretation of contemporary history and ongoing life that eschews the warps of condensed and highly distorted ideologies such as those of millennial capitalism (Comaroff and Comaroff 2001) and millennial fundamentalism (Hopkins et al. 2001) and their confluence. It is through ethnography and its attendant historicity that such understandings may emerge. And it is through ethnography that the multiple and often competing theoretical perspectives and paradigms may receive constant scrutiny so that choices made in explanatory modes may be based on those of explicative flows of information from people in action in a plethora of cultural and power-laden fields and arenas.

Consider the following statement, with which we opened our fourth ethnography focused on indigenous people of Amazonian Ecuador:

> The Puyo Runa people of Amazonian Ecuador tell us that to learn something of significance one must be prepared to "see" [*ricuna*]. Through their ancient and contemporary ceramic art, women potters show us how to "see" into their lives, their cosmos, their pasts, and their futures in the time of *cunalla*, "right now." Shamans, who are men, create seances in which blurred visions arrive as spirit images, called *muscui*, and it is the women, again, who clarify the images so that people may "see," "right now," just what is emerging that unites pasts, presents, and futures with different places. Images are controlled by "one who knows," *yachaj*, shaman; and by "one who 'sees'—owner or possessor of images"—*muscuyuj*, ceramist. The imagery of the cosmos includes the place of humans and all other beings in it, as well as that of other people, who think and speak through other cultures, *shuj shimita yachai*. To be fully human is to

> know other cultures, because through this knowledge one comes to know one's own. Power emanates from imagery.
>
> Imagery and power do not exist in a vacuum. They are grounded in many realities. Among them are the physical founts of daily existence—the cultural traditions and their dynamic creativities that allow people to wrest a livelihood from their environment. Other people, living and dead, constitute that environment, as do their souls, souls of others, spirits, and the imagined and real mysteries that such forces entail. Life itself, *causai*, as it is experienced and remembered, and the actions that it engenders, constitutes the power, the imagery, and the central feature of all knowledge.
>
> The phrase *causáunchimi!*, which means "We are living!" in Amazonian Quichua, sums this up: We are living! (as fully human beings). Listen to us! (Whitten and Whitten 2008:vii)

When writing this we thought deeply about experiences with people we have known a long time, and we often disagreed about phrasing and even intent. We drew on our knowledge of sectors of cultural anthropology and sociology. The statement, although ethnographically induced, links a number of propositions that have been tested, improved upon, and enriched through the work of scholars over the past century. The perpetuating dynamic in these processes is summed up by Karen Ho in her ethnography of Wall Street investment banking culture: "What seems like an abstraction can actually be culturally decoded" (Ho 2009:34).

In the above statement, we write of blurred male shamanic imagery and the clarification of such imagery by women who "see" (*ricuna*) that which the shaman "knows" (*yachana*). We enter a realm of *ineffability*. Some dimensions of culture, as all sensitive ethnographers learn or have learned, are simply ineffable. They cannot be described in words, or they constitute a domain about which we must not or cannot speak. Here we modify Geertz, whom we earlier brought into the three dimensions of ethnography, one of which is the rescuing of the "said" of social discourse. There is more to human culture within which discourse flows than the "said." We turn here, as we did in several chapters, to comparative religion, and especially to the work of Lawrence Sullivan (1988).

Early in our introduction, we wrote of "cosmography" and "chronotopes." *Cosmography*, a term used professionally in anthropology by Franz Boas (e.g., 1940b[1887]), sets the ethnographer's goal as understanding and writing about interactions among people in the known biosphere and the environing cosmogonic and cosmological noösphere, the sphere of culture that includes deities, spirits, apparitions, devils, demons, visions, and what have you. This is the realm of the ineffable. A chronotope is a conception of space-time. We have found, through anthropology especially, that concepts of space-time vary greatly and that human beings may enter and leave such temporal-spatial concepts and entities in many ways. This process, too, involves ineffability. By setting out broad dimensions of indigenous and Afro–Latin American cosmography early in the introduction to this work, we hoped to implant a readiness in the minds of our readers to appreciate alternative views of the history and events that are presented in subsequent chapters.

In an intriguing, captivating, and highly readable memoir, Paul Stoller, in *The Power of the Between: An Anthropological Odyssey* (2009), while never mentioning "hermeneutics," nonetheless contributes (perhaps in a parallel fashion) to the points we have been making. "Anthropologists," he writes (and here he clearly means ethnographers), "are the sojourners of 'the between'" (Stoller 2009:4). His "between" exists at many levels, and passes through many matrices, beginning with a Songhay saying about how people do not know their back side from their front side and so wind up in a state of confusion and inaction, and extending to being somewhere between life and death as in a noncurable cancer patient in remission. His key "between," where power is generated, though, is that between ethnography, which he calls "being there," and the academy where he works, referred to as "being here." Once we move into this "between" realm, usually after an extended period of ethnographic field research, we never leave it; what we strive to do is to learn from it and expand the between realm of being here and being there: "If . . . we find a way to draw strength from both sides of the between and breathe in the creative air of indeterminacy, we can find ourselves in a space of enormous growth, a space of power and creativity. For me, that is the power of the between and the subject of this book" (Stoller 2009:4).

For us, this is the power of an expanding hermeneutic horizon, to which we hope our book contributes. We come to the conclusion that two dynamics of culture are the inescapability of power and the inevitability of transformation. These dynamics were underscored by Sir Edmund Leach (1964[1954]) over a half century ago (see also Firth 1964; Wolf 1982:190–191). Let us turn now to see whether the "between" helps us to understand current systems of power and transformation, remaining within the Republic of Ecuador subsequent to the election of Rafael Vicente Correa Delgado as president for his second term.

Ecuador: Culture, Power, and Race in the "Between"

Early in the introduction to this book, we wrote that Ecuador is a land that lies athwart the equator in northwestern South America. Ecuadorians not only live in a land characterized by a rugged and varied geophysical topography, they also exist in local, regional, national, diasporic, and global political-economic polarities through which flow a plethora of shifting currents and forces. In 2010 this sovereign republic also lies athwart the increasingly cold-war–like left/right, socialist/capitalist divide that is exacerbating the bellicose movements that range from the United States through all of Latin America and the Caribbean. In 2010 it is also caught on the horns of a political polarity of centralizing power that features populist rhetorical ideals and an authoritarian executive reality. President Rafael Correa has exercised considerable power of persuasion to curtail the maneuvers of political parties. He has demonstrated his power of political acumen in strengthening the presidency and weakening congressional and judicial authority. And he continues to appeal mightily to large sectors of the populace in the Andes and Coast.

Against his extraordinarily effective *caudillismo* and populism are the majority of Amazonian peoples, who continue to back deposed president Lucio Gutiérrez. The indigenous movement, after a four-year period of dormancy, again emerged in late September 2009 as a force with which to be reckoned, and people within the movement are increasing their pressures on the president, in spite of internal conflict, in 2010 (chapter 5, p. 139–140).

Correa straddles the aforementioned divides through a socialist–capitalist mix that features state-controlled populism under the banner of a "citizens' revolution" and "twenty-first-century socialism" that, on August 10, 2009, he declared to be "radicalized" (chapter 5). At the geological base of his plan lie the subsurface petroleum and minerals, now including, especially, copper. Large-scale capitalist exploitation of mineral and petroleum resources is to be undertaken through contracts with foreign companies, especially Canadian and Chinese. Capital flowing back to the state will provide the dollarized infrastructure of a new socialist nation. In 2009 his influence resulted in a law wherein mining companies could appropriate water from local sources, thereby, in the eyes of many, privatizing water in the name of socialism.

An indigenous uprising occurred and persisted through October 6, 2009. Upper Amazonia became the primary locus of the power of resistance as the Shuar confronted the military and the police and in the process lost a bilingual schoolteacher, Bosco Wisuma, who was killed when one errant pellet entered his brain. The source of the pellet is still contested. After heaping contempt on the protesters, the president agreed to meet with the aggrieved parties, whom he then hailed as his "brothers," and did so in Carondelet on Monday, October 5. By spring 2010, however, the indigenous movement again broke with the president, leaving future relationships in limbo but with the promise of a "progressive series" of *levantamientos*.

Mobility within the pyramidal class and ethnically stratified social structure is supposed to come from redistribution of the nation's wealth, and clear deprivation of the elite and the formerly powerful neocapitalist operators. The superstructure ramifies from the affiliation of Ecuador with ALBA, the Bolivarian Alliance for the Americas, that, in 2009, included Cuba, Saint Vincent and the Grenadines, Dominica, and Antigua and Barbuda in the Caribbean; Honduras (before the coup) and Nicaragua in Central America; and Venezuela (the prime initiator), Ecuador, and Bolivia in South America. Argentina moves in and out of the sphere of influence of ALBA. ALBA also allies with Iran, a possible source of future nuclear expertise. Weakening of north–south domination radiating from the United States through Colombia and the strengthening of east–west relations with China, Iran, and Russia are stressed. A key to the infrastructure is the alliance among *caudillos,* with Hugo Chávez and Evo Morales the most forceful, Ecuador somewhere between leftist rhetoric and moderation, and the presidents of Brazil, Chile, and Argentina playing moderating roles.

The growing powers of resistance are seen in the oil-rich Amazonian territories of Colombia, Ecuador, Peru, and Bolivia, and in the indigenous movements that are increasingly linked across this tropical-forest zone of Western Amazonas. Within each of these countries, indigenous people point out that although the state lays claims to the subsurface exploitable wealth, real people live on the real surface and must have a hand in deciding whether or not petroleum, mineral, timber, and water exploitation will ruin their environments and lives (e.g., N. Whitten and D. Whitten 2008:241–247). These people share a heritage set forth in the introduction, and they also share the interculturality that emanates from experiences vis-à-vis people who enter their territories for a myriad of exploitative purposes.

For his part, Correa segregates the social domain of Ecuadorian life into Freudian-like categories. Indigenous people and Afro-Ecuadorian people (among others) who resist his proclamations are called infantile, primitive, and sometimes psychotic—concepts taken from Sigmund Freud's notion of the id (e.g., Freud 1918, 1955[1930]). Others who resist or go against his wishes are labeled infantile, liars, corrupt bureaucrats, neoliberalists, corrupt bankers, traitors, and even "terrorists." The president states that their motivations stem from conspiracies to destabilize his government, often adding that such plots emanate from the elite, corrupt bankers, corrupt bureaucrats, and previous president Lucio Gutiérrez and his loyal followers.

This imaginary aggregate would be a Freudian alter ego or contra ego. The central ego and its dominating superego reside in his own activities, thought processes, strongly held convictions, and extraordinary verbal acuity. Some take this structure to represent the ultimate in corporate narcissism with solipsistic statist tendencies. Media people and scholars with right, central, and leftist orientations have offered this analysis and criticism, with many elaborations. Within this mix, Correa's most energetic public diatribes target the media, the educators, the indigenous people, labor movements, and the academies, the sources of public information and verbal powers of resistance.

The subjects of "culture, "power," and "race" all move into this set of macro contrasts, the manipulation of which so often motivates large-scale exercises in structural power. The charisma of the president and his abilities to forge his will on a previously wobbly set of sometimes weakly balanced legislative, judicial, and executive powers has resulted in a diminished judiciary and legislature and strong executive structure. Ecuador's social structure is essentially that which has been described and analyzed since the 1920s (Becker 2008) and especially since the petroleum era beginning in the early 1960s. Its fundamental reference points are those discussed in chapters 1, 2, and 3 in terms of a *longue durée* dating from the Spanish conquest, through multiple historical conjunctures that reemerge with each new nation-altering transformative event.

The power behind insidious racialization flows up and down the Ecuadorian Sierra, lurking especially in urban areas, and spilling over into the Coast and Upper Amazonia. Upper-class people who regard themselves as white and others "below" them as "*mestizo*" nonetheless label such people in pejorative terms such as *cholo, longo, chulla* (now more often *chullo* for males), and *chagra*, among other epithets (chapter 3). In her recent book, self-styled "middle-upper class" Ecuadorian author Karem Roitman (2009:239) confirms this, stressing the point made by Michael Herzfeld (1997) that cultural features characteristic of people (in this case racialization processes) are the very kinds of information withheld from outsiders, and most vociferously denied when outsiders "notice" or "identify" such features. Herzfeld—whose long-term ethnography with "Cretan sheep herders" of modern Greece is exemplary of processes we are discussing—calls this national phenomenon "cultural intimacy."

Many Ecuadorians, although they often deny this, use the concept "*primo/a*" (cousin) to draw a distinction between themselves and those classed as *indio* and *negro*. This collateral reference is in terms of quasi-evolutionary "theory" in which those who fall outside of the mainstream of racialized Ecuadorians, the indigenous people and the Afro-Ecuadorian people, are said to be on a different line of development, a different evolutionary branch of Ecuadorian humanity. Against these forces is the cultural affirmation of *ecuatorianidad*, being Ecuadorian, and in the twenty-first century this macro-encompassing identity more often than not prevails in a spirit of interculturality.

With a white elite on top of a socioeconomic and classificatory pyramid with black people and indigenous people on the bottom, the middle sector (the "popular classes") represents a mass of people who seek upward mobility in a capitalist economy in which "improving the race" and removing the "stains" of indigeneity and blackness are short- and long-run goals. Correa's strategy of twenty-first–century socialism is to position himself in the middle of this imaginary social pyramid of upwardly flowing families (chapter 3). From this ideological vantage point of "the between," he verbally lashes upward (toward the elite) and sometimes downward or outward (toward indigenous and black activists), preserving his concept of the middle in what, to date, seems to be a system of decreased distribution of wealth and power in need of socialist "radicalization." He stresses *ecuatorianidad* against all other ethnic references.

As the chapters in this book should demonstrate, any theory construction of contemporary and historical features or events and movements in Ecuador must dig deeply into the interrelated factors of culture, power, and race. Race is a cultural construct, one fortified by the exercise of power. A cultural construct, which frames powerful images and representations of the value of real people, we will recall, may be thought of as an interpretation of "a corpus and flow of symbols and meanings enacted in social life at a given time in a given place." The cultural construct deployed throughout Latin America, and elsewhere, is bounded by the negative reference points of "*indio*" and "*negro*" that emerged in the fifteenth century as categories of subordinate status wherein those so categorized and stigmatized were seen by conquerors and colonials as a labor force to be exploited for capitalist advantage (chapters 1 and 2).

Nowhere in South America is there a concept in an indigenous language remotely resembling that of "*indio*." The word *indigenous* does not mean "indian," a point often missed throughout the Americas and Europe. In South America, "*indio*" is not a historical identity referent; it is an appellation of inferiority—an opposition to "*español*" (Spanish) that originated with Christopher Columbus in the Caribbean and Spain in 1493. *Indigenous* means native of a country or land or landscape, or something born to a person, something innate or inherent in a person or population. This meaning was denied by the Admiral and by colonists. In English the word is an adjective (the noun, which is seldom used, is *indigene* in its singular), so *indigenous* must modify something. "People" is or should be the most frequent referent. *Negro,* a term that has its origin in the mid-fifteenth-century Iberian slave trade in Africans, is used throughout Latin America to refer to people of (long ago) African descent, although it is not a term to be employed by people who are not so identified vis-à-vis African-descended peoples. People so named identify in myriad ways, often by reference to their territories and landscapes (Whitten and Torres, eds. 1998).

Indígena, as a noun in the Spanish language, concretizes the place of a given people by adding the preposition *de,* as in *indígena de la sierra* (indigene of the mountains, or better, indigenous person of the mountains). *Indio* became part of print language in 1493 in Columbus's famous letter to Santángel, the Spanish prince in the court of Queen Isabella, known as Isabel la Católica.

Indígena locates people while *indio,* used by the "Discoverer" to assert his arrival in India, dislocates people. Displacement and dislocation constitute the key to understanding *indio,* a term that, while pejorative in most senses, is sometimes used by indigenous people in their social movements for self-affirmation and self-determination, and especially in their claims to land (a process of symbolic inversion; chapter 3). Otherwise, *indio* connotes inferiority, peonage, inability to speak "correctly," illiteracy, lack of culture, marginal rurality, and social deterioration. As a noun, it is often accompanied by a very demeaning adjective such as "dirty," "unruly," "wild," or worse (chapter 4).

During colonial times, an elite of Spanish- and Americas-born people, all of relatively "fair" European complexion, emerged, and until the Ecuadorian Indigenous Uprising of 1990, people throughout the country thought of and spoke of contemporary elites as *"blanco."* After 1990 people without the quasi-European complexions moved into positions of power and prestige, including presidents Abdalá Bucaram, Jamil Mahuad, and Lucio Gutiérrez, the first two deposed by indigenous uprisings and the third by the human forces of united Quiteños of all classes and complexions.

We come, once again, to the middle of the social pyramid—the huge space of the "between"—and to the elite-projected trope of *el mestizaje.* Rafael Correa, to the best of our knowledge, never uses the term *mestizaje* and he has never spoken of or implied "improvement" of races or "whitening." He does not refer to a "white-mestizo class" as constituting a middle of Ecuadorian society. His discourse is in terms of power of people, the *pueblo,* and of Ecuadorian people in particular, *los ecuatorianos.* His negative contrast reference points are the United States and Colombia. In the process of egalitarian sociality across all perceived boundaries (except those of the "elite," or the "oligarchy," whom he constantly excoriates), *he is entirely intolerant of difference in the fields of power.* He takes all resistance and all alternatives as subversion and an attack on the dignity and sovereignty of the nation-state.

His goal is a unified *pueblo* of Ecuadorian brothers and sisters, freed from the hegemony of foreign military and other structural powers, and self-sufficient to the degree that this is possible in a globalized world. He stresses in many paradoxical ways collective powers of resistance, and seems to see his role as to enact transformative events. He seems to embrace, at times, cultural difference, multiculturality, and interculturality, provided these transformative dynamics are subsumed by and incorporated into the executive sector of the state apparatus. These positive goals lead him, at times, to be negatively disposed to the expressed needs of indigenous and Afro-Ecuadorian people, when they are conveyed by organizations of the people themselves. Nonetheless, he has worked hard to communicate publicly in the Quichua language and to represent what he takes to be their expressed interests when these interests do not conflict with those of his image of, and convictions about, the entire nation-state, its history, and its future.

Ethnography and Theory Construction

To complete this conclusion, we must curtail a strong urge to continue our analysis of the transformative dynamics of Ecuador in the twenty-first century. With some regret, we leave Ecuador at the current limen of its political trajectories and cultural transformations to return to a sticky and enduring issue in the analysis of culture. Consider again the quote by Karen Ho, who spends a considerable amount of time and space deconstructing that which Wall Street brokers and power wielders take to be a series of self-evident, indeed "true" abstractions: "What seems like an abstraction can actually be culturally decoded" (Ho 2009:34). The sticky issue is that "culture" itself is an abstraction subject to cultural decoding. And that is an issue with which we must live and a problematic to be addressed within the interface of ethnography and theory construction.

We have argued and demonstrated that in the decoding of culture we require the apparatus of the academy but we require equally the insights drawn from ethnography. From the academy we gain a disciplinary perspective often fraught with dissensus, polarization, mystification, and mythification. From those people with whom we undertake ethnography, who more often than not see things differently, speak in different languages, use initially unfamiliar symbols, and exist coevally in multiple modernities, we refresh our own paradigms and theoretical constructions, discarding some of the old, to develop some new insights. We also come to see larger issues, such as those of the nation-state, globalization, and history through new, refreshened perspectives. In the latter process, we seek to combine indigenous models of reality with anthropological modes of interpretation.

Ethnography and theory, taken together in a mutual, transformative dynamic, constitute what Bunzl (2004:439) calls "a history of the present" (see also Comaroff and Comaroff 2009:46). Ethnography as description and explication and theory as generalization and explanation, taken together as in these chapters, may be depicted in Homi Bhabha's terms as "the times and the spaces for the historical representation of the subjects of cultural difference in a postcolonial criticism" (Bhabha 2008[1994]:256).

As we have shown, historical and contemporary representations of cultural difference slide easily into racialized categorization, even, or perhaps particularly, among those sophisticated in the analysis of plural social systems. And with such categorization, racist generalizations may be made quite unconsciously. We again encounter power, as we have demonstrated in this book. The relatively powerless people in the Americas, from 1493 through the colonial, republican, and late modern eras, are more often than not those classed by the powerful as "black" and "indian." For this reason, we turn to people so classed, understanding their perspectives within their own milieus, through their languages, symbol systems, and insight generators, to come again and again to the Taussig (1987:135) proposition that "from the represented shall come that which overturns the representation." Or, for those who prefer such insights in a literary, poetic, and perhaps enigmatic phrase: "The truth of the referent is best exposed through the very ruses of representation" (Escobar 2007:3).

Maurice Godelier, long-time ethnographer of peoples of Papua New Guinea and renowned French theorist, puts this argument back within the discipline of anthropology, and gives us a way by which to close this book:

> [A]nthropology is more necessary than ever in the world in which we live. Neither molecular biology nor nanotechnology is going to teach us what it means to be Shia or Sunni or Pashtoun, or explain the history of Western colonial expansion. As anthropologists, we have to do fieldwork, remain conscious of the position we occupy, conduct systematic studies over a long term, with the co-operation and insight of those with whom we have come to live and work, and we have to subject our methods, analyses and conclusions to constant critical reflection. All of this makes anthropology an indispensable discipline for gaining a slightly better understanding of the globalized world in which we live and will continue to live. (Godelier 2010:10)

Notes

Introduction: To Remake the World

1. The contested dimension of this hallmark perspective of James Mooney locates the responsibility of the anthropologist to be directed to, and intellectually responsible to, the people who are the focus of ethnography (see also Boas 1940b[1887]; Stocking 1968:270–307). Before the 1890s, again during World War I, escalating during World War II and the Cold War, and currently in the U.S. wars in Iraq and Afghanistan–Pakistan and in the "War on Terror," a segment of anthropology has been and is "weaponized," as ethnography is turned against people studied by shifting the locus of professional responsibility to the imperialist, national-security state. For very recent examples with ample literature citations see González 2009, Network of Concerned Anthropologists 2009, and D. Price 2008.

Chapter 1: Colonial Mentality in Making the World

1. Irene Silverblatt 2004:5.
2. Marilyn Grace Miller 2004:14.
3. Today a benign concept of "hybridity" exists in many spheres of conceptualization. In biology and botany we have hybrid hogs and hybrid corn; the new hybrid automobiles of Toyota, Honda, and Ford, among others, offer the consumer willing to pay extra for a car the promise of much better mileage; and hybrid mutual funds offer investors balanced returns by mixing stocks and bonds. Cultural studies and cultural anthropology have substituted hybridity for assimilation, acculturation, syncretism, and even diaspora and creolization.

Contemporary definitions of hybridity stress, essentially, "anything of mixed origin." In this sense, all humans are hybrids. We all share the majority of our genes with our multiple ancestors. Distinction enters when we deal with racializations and the consequences of social and cultural constructs that apply and affirm the significance of racialized differences and contrasts. If one "race" is said by those in power to be superior to another, then mixture of the superior with the inferior is the hybridity about which I write in this essay.

In the racialized cultural and social constructions that stem from systems of domestic breeding, beginning in early European modernity (circa 1440–1520) and descending down to the twenty-first-century Americas, in some significant contexts, hybridity has referred to, and today all too often implies, a very special kind of mixing, one of civilized mixing with savage or barbarian; domestic mixing with wild. The hybrid offsprings in such situations are said by those in a dominating, hegemonic position to be inferior to the higher category but superior to the lower. It is in this sense that I separate hybridity from "mixing" (or "non-hybridized mixing") in this essay. What is suggested here is that what was explicit in early modernity as the fixities and fluidities of racialized representation is often implicit today in enduring hypostases of "race."

To complicate this discussion further, in some parts of Latin America the term *mestizo*, defined by some authors as "indigenous hybridity," is now used to denote fusions of indigenous cultures. For example, when one finds hierarchy associated with Arawakan language and culture among a Tupi-Guaraní–speaking people, the people are said to represent a "*mestizo* society" (Combès and Lowrey 2006). I think that this recent usage of *mestizo* and hybridity obfuscates the historical significance of the intellectual and ideological movement of racialized and nationalized *mestizaje* discussed in this book. In fact, by this definition, all peoples, everywhere, would be "*mestizo*."

4. In this essay I do not address relationships between actual people in actual places, past or present, who are, may be, or have been classed as *negro, zambo,* and *indio* in specific situations. The reader should not take my argument of fixity and fluidity to imply an "equality" between those classed as indigenous descended and African descended or their historical and contemporary mixtures. I wish to stress that relationships between historical and contemporary fixity and historical and contemporary fluidity are subject to empirical study in particular places and particular times. It is also beyond the scope of this chapter to explore the fascinating inner dimensions of inherent powers of real people in the fixed or fluid spaces of the colonial and modern regions of Latin America. Taussig (1987:171–187) suggests fruitful directions for such exploration when he writes of the Venezuelan folk painting called "Las Tres Potencias," the three powers (or potencies, often described as inner essences of spiritual force), usually depicted as El Negro Felipe, El Indio Guaicaipuro, and the very powerful spirit force of María Lionza. From experiences in the Cauca Valley of Colombia, he writes of the inner powers of "cunningly wrought colonial objet d'art" of mystical breeds (Taussig 1987:172) and goes on to say that these representations are not to be taken as "primitivism" but rather "third world modernism," defined as a neocolonial reworking of primitivism in the "dialectics of magic, healing, and race" (Taussig 1987:172; see also Taussig 1997; Weismantel 2001).

Chapter 2: Indigenous Constructions of "Blackness"

1. Christopher Columbus 1989[1492–1493]:134, 135.
2. Edmund Leach 1982:107.
3. See, e.g., Bateman 1990. The name "Seminole" derives from *cimarrón*; see Sturtevant 1971. Historians have pointed out that while black and indigenous relations in the Americas were sometimes antagonistic, there are numerous examples of cooperation in the areas of shamanism, ritual co-parenthood, and political subversion. However, instances of cooperation are much less likely to be found in the historical record. The more numerous colonial reports of conflict over cooperation should not be taken as representative of the real, lived historical relations between black and indigenous peoples. For example,

Stuart B. Schwartz and Frank Salomon (1999) cite the case of an indigenous leader named Francisco Chichima, who, in 1603, led black rebels to a space between the Andes and Amazonian regions, where he "tried to establish a 'land without whites'" (Schwartz and Salomon 1999:469). And while colonial officials feared such black–indigenous rebellions and the flight of self-liberated black people to indigenous communities, blacks were also suspected of offering refuge to indigenous people escaping the burden of colonial labor (Lane 2005:171). In one case in Nueva Granada, "a black slave was accused of hiding some indigenous workers from an *encomienda* labor draft" (Soulodre–La France 2005:139). In colonial Ecuador (Schwartz and Salomon 1999:463) and Colombia (Lane 2005:171), people of African descent and indigenous people were using Catholic sacraments to form ties of ritual co-parenthood. There are other historical examples of the intertwined histories and cultures of black and indigenous peoples. The foci of our essay are the contemporary representations of blackness in modern indigenous expressive cultures, but such expressions are the result of such intertwined histories.

4. We seek here to tease out dimensions of a dominant Euro-American racist paradigm as this emerges in various transformations from a few select indigenous cultures of Amazonia, the northwest coast, and the Andes of South America. We have no intention of cataloging such materials. The paradigm that emerges is *mutatis mutandis* comparable to others characteristic in North America (see, e.g., Blu 1980; Deagan and MacMahon 1995; Willis 1966). We are looking at broad analogical representations; we are not trying to make specific comparisons. Such mass comparisons might also be made between South American and North American contexts that conjoin ceremonial or festive representation of blackness and indigenous historicity.

For but one illustration, one could reflect on the Emberá concept of the black-Kampuniá imagery or the Yekuana and Salasaca soldier imagery or the libidinal black imagery of the Quito Runa and Salasaca Quichua vis-à-vis the Pueblo (Hopi, Zuñi, Tewa, and others) Chákwaina Kachina images. This major spirit being, portrayed in masked costume and figurines ("dolls"), represents a black *wuya* (Hopi), "chief" or "clan leader," a warrior-spirit image from the past that appears at an annual ceremonial period of fertility and healing. Various representations of this black figure from Pueblo history have been carried from community to community by leaders of different indigenous clans, with whom he, his mother's brother, his children, and other clan members are identified. According to Frederick J. Dockstader, the Chákwaina image "represents Estebán, the Negro [black, hispanicized, *ladino* explorer] or Moor guide, who led Fray Marcos de Niza to Cíbola in 1539 and was killed at Hawkiuh [a Zuñi community], for his arrogant behavior and molestation of Indian women. The appearance of this Kachina and the fact that Chákwaina is known in all the pueblos as a horrible ogre, support the legend" (Dockstader 1985:11; see also Washburn 1980; Wright 1977).

Given our methods, we would ask how the Kachina "Chákwaina" manifestations in costume and carving, and stories about "Estebán" (Estebánico, Estevánico), emerge in indigenous Pueblo discourse, mythology, ceremony, and festivity, and what analogies might be drawn with the Pueblo peoples' grasp of dominant Western paradigms and how their own contestations are configured (for more information on the expedition led by the guide Estebán, see, e.g., Núñez Cabeza de Vaca 1963[1542, 1555]).

5. Quichua and Incaic Quechua are both of the family Peripheral Quechua (Mannheim

1991) but, although related, Ecuadorian Amazonian Quichua probably does not derive from Incaic Quechua (chapter 7, this volume). Quechua languages are spoken by more than twelve million people in Colombia, Ecuador, Peru, Bolivia, Chile, and Argentina. It is the largest native language system in the Americas and extends from the Andes eastward into Amazonia and southward into the Southern Cone.

Chapter 3: *The Topology of* El Mestizaje

1. An early draft of this chapter was discussed at the conference "Mestizaje and Créolité" held at the University of Chicago in October 1999. I appreciate the invitation to the conference and cordialities extended by organizers Andrew Apter and Robin Derby during it. At this conference, the question was raised by a discussant of an early draft of this paper as to whether a North American scholar has sufficient sensitivity to the ideology (or in some cases cosmology) of *mestizaje*—especially in its Mexican revolutionary-egalitarian spirit as explicated by José Vasconcelos (e.g., 1989)—or whether we *gringos* are prone to succumb to the romance of "multiculturalism." I can only say that I had entered my forty-second year of research in and on Ecuador, which began with black people in Esmeraldas and continued (and continues) in different Andean and Amazonian regions. I cannot understand how one can watch developments of multiculturalism in Venezuela (e.g., Guss 2000), Colombia (e.g., Wade 1993, 1995), Ecuador, and Bolivia and claim that this phenomenon is a manifestation of North American romanticism. In presenting my Conferencia Magistral (Whitten 1999) in Quito in 1998, in which I directly addressed issues of "race" and racism, indigenous people and Afro-Ecuadorian people seemed to know exactly what I was talking about, while many other members of the audience clearly did not. The *mestizaje/multiculturalidad* polarity seems to me to endure and to emerge repeatedly in political and social arenas where conflict leads to change and transformation. The polarity is that of an elitist and historically hegemonic ideology (*mestizaje*; see, e.g., Roitman 2009; Stutzman 1981; Whitten 1974; Whitten, ed. 1981) versus a millennial ideology (*plurinacionalidad;* see, e.g., Handelsman 1999) propagated especially by indigenous people and people identifying with indigenous movements, including Afro-Ecuadorians. In millennial Ecuador, *multiculturalidad* and *plurinacionalidad* are interchangeable. My writings and those of Stutzman have been translated into Spanish and circulated widely in Ecuador, where they have been cited by Ecuadorians writing on the same subject. More often than not the person citing us agrees with our analyses.

I strongly believe that the devil is in the details and that the job of ethnography is to ferret these details out and construct meaningful generalizations. If canonical icons of universalism such as Vasconcelos (to whom I often turn to make sure I am accurate as to his position[s] vis-à-vis *la raza cósmica*) suffer deconstruction in the process, then perhaps we may learn to peer beyond the melting-pot assumptions of doctrinaire *mestizaje* to see just how those whose quotidian lives are the stuff of change and transformation perceive themselves and others. Ethnographic details present us with illuminating vulgarities, some of which I have salted into this essay to not only demonstrate my points but also to arouse some ire in those who cherish the dream—or hallucination—of the *indio* morphing into the *mestizo* and the *negro* into the *mulato*. The black voices and the indigenous voices are those by which I am guided in my quest for constructive understanding and that I put forth in this chapter on dimensions of symbolic inversion by focusing on facets of the topology of *mestizaje* in the Republic of Ecuador.

2. My use of symbol as a vehicle that conveys meaning comes especially from my readings of Clifford Geertz (1973, 1983, 1995). I often take his concepts, especially those designed for the understanding of "new nations," to comprehend social movements and their underpinnings in discourse systems and tropes. This would seem to be the same or a similar technique as that deployed by Eric R. Wolf (1999) when he discusses events, ideologies, rituals, myths, and semantics that "underwrite" social movements, social events, or cultural performances.

3. Most anthropologists (and other scholars) use the Spanish term *Otavaleños* to refer to native people of the Otavalo region. Some like to point out that "Otavalos" are the natives and anyone "from" the region can legitimately be called "Otavaleño." Many use *Otavalo* as an adjective to modify "indian." Lynn Meisch (e.g., 1997) usually deploys only the Spanish term *indígena* to refer to native people of the Otavalo region. I choose the Anglicized word *Otavalan* to refer to native Otavalo people. As noted in the text, Otavalans have no difficulty in their multivocalic definition of self and collective representation of selfhood; nouns include *gente, runacuna,* Otavalos, and *otavaleños.* When identity or representation as being from the Otavalo area is established, specific reference to community is made, in Quichua, by adding the suffix *manda,* as in Peguchemanda, "from Peguche."

4. In terms of the power of racialized tropes, it is significant that the editors of the special NACLA report on the social origins of race (see de la Cadena 2001; Whitten and Corr 2001) chose two photographs to grace its cover: on the left side is a woman of color with the banner over her head reading "*y tu abuela Aònde está,*" while the white woman on the right side is named by the banner "*la blanquita.*" Such is the nature of tropes and names in the arena of the topology of "*las razas.*"

Chapter 4: The Ecuadorian Indigenous Uprising of 1990

1. For a history of local-level indigenous uprisings beginning in the sixteenth century, see Albornoz 1976; Becker 2007, 2008; Garcés 1961; Newson 1995; Oberem 1971; and especially Santos-Granero 1993. Segundo Moreno Yanez (1976) wrote his doctoral dissertation on the subject of *sublevaciones indígenas* in Ecuador's history under the direction of the late Andeanist-Amazonianist ethnohistorian, archaeologist, and ethnographer Udo Oberem. Although many social movements by indigenous people (and by black people) have had repercussions throughout the nation (and, previously, colony), there has never been a nationwide uprising before. Indeed, the Levantamiento of 1990 was probably the most organized movement of people to make policy in a public arena in all of Ecuador's history. No political movement has been of this magnitude. In reworking his book for popular consumption after the Levantamiento, and in subsequent pronouncements, Moreno has changed from the focus on *sublevación* (uprising, rebellion, revolution)—the most neutral term available for an uprising—to *alzamiento,* which means, in all social contexts dealing with human beings, "people out of control." The concept of "inferior human" is part of the concept of *alzamiento,* for *blancos* cannot, by definition, be *alzados;* usually,

only *indios* and *negros* are so represented. Like his colleague Alfonso Calderón Cevallos, Dr. Moreno also worked with both the president of the republic and indigenous people to further develop the Janus-like system of vertical articulation that has led to increased misunderstanding and conflict across the ethnic antipodes of Ecuadorian modernization and developmentalism. Retrospective analyses of the Levantamiento of 1990 can be found in CONAIE 1989, 1991; see Chuji and Dávalos 1995 for an important document about how the two constitutions affected indigenous peoples and their ongoing social movements during the decade 1998–2008.

Chapter 6: Indigenous Ethnographers Portray Their World

1. Olga Fisch (personal communication 1979) and Fisch (1985). The influence of Olga Fisch has been discussed by a number of writers, such as Cuvi (1994), Hunt (1982), Miller (1983), Rodman (1982), and Scheinman (1981).

2. Based on a letter from two indigenous painters, Ribadeneira de Casares (1990) dates the first paintings to 1970, the year she says Julio Toaquiza began to paint. Fisch (1985:100, 117) does not give a specific date but mentions that when she was preparing her Renwick exhibition she included five paintings of *danzantes* by Julio Toaquiza. Napoleón (Napo) Albán, long-time employee of the renowned gift shop Folklore Olga Fisch, dates some of the earliest paintings by Julio to at least 1980, and probably to 1979 (Albán, personal communication 1999).

3. Expansion of cooperatives and their role in ensuing struggles to sell in El Ejido Park are detailed in Colloredo-Mansfeld 2009:141–164.

4. See Anonymous 1980a, 1980b, 1998, 1999; Colvin 1997, 2001; Colvin and Toaquiza 1994; Espinosa Cordero 1999; Muratorio 1999.

5. The catalogue of the first-mentioned exhibition, "Pintores de Tigua," is introduced by President Noboa's eloquent statement. The Guayasamín exhibition was organized around a series of large paintings by Alfonso Toaquiza, which illustrate his book, *El cóndor enamorado* (2002).

6. The huge statue of the Virgin of Quito is a modern rendition of the patroness of Quito and Ecuador, the Virgen de las Mercedes. The original winged sculpture, also known as La Inmaculada and the Virgen de Quito, was created by the eighteenth-century artist Bernardo de Legarda for the main altar of the colonial church San Francisco de Quito. Oettinger (1992:37) shows a painting by an unknown artist of the Virgin standing in the midst of patriotic banners and the national coat of arms. In the upper left corner, she rides on top of a four-engine Ecuadorian Air Force bomber en route to battle the Peruvians in the "War of 41."

7. I wish to remind the reader that native Quichua speakers may not speak or write perfect, grammatically correct Castilian Spanish. In a similar vein, their dating of important events in their paintings may be a fusion of different activities and therefore may not agree with reported dates such as the ouster of recent presidents. I have translated a number of their written messages to English but have not changed their dates.

8. Rodrigo Ugsha Cuyo no longer produces the paintings with which he financed his law school education. Now practicing law, he was an assistant in the analysis of the Constitutional Court of Ecuador, 2007–2009.

9. The Rodrigo Toaquiza Cuyo (born July 18, 1974) who painted the two versions of the coup of 2001, discussed earlier in this essay, was robbed and killed on June 9, 2009.

10. "Shamans' supermarket" is the description given to this event by Diego Quiroga and Tania Ledegerber de Quiroga.

11. An article published in *El Comercio* (June 17, 2002, p. C1) described efforts of Saraguros to rescue their traditional, alternative medical practices, with governmental help through the Provincial Department of Indigenous Health in Loja. The trained, certified medical team would include midwives, shamans, and specialists in natural, herbal medicines. The hope was to unify indigenous practices drawn from "a network of traditional medicine" with Western medical care. Two pages later (p. C3), this paper announced that six centers of natural medicine were closed in Salcedo (Cotopaxi Province) because the owners-curers lacked legal permission to work. Based on their findings of snakeskins, colored candles, and other questionable curative objects, the authorities suspected that these centers practiced witchcraft. Within weeks of the government's contradictory actions regarding alternative medical practice, physicians and public health workers throughout the nation went on indefinite strike because their salaries had not been paid for more than two months. About this time, ex-president León Febres Cordero returned to his doctors in Miami, a city favored by wealthy Ecuadorians for medical treatment, for an evaluation that led him to choose not to enter the 2002 presidential campaign.

Chapter 7: Indigenous Modernity

1. An Achuar version of this myth, which has different twists, turns, and implied meanings, is given by native Alejandro Taish (2004); see also Philippe Descola 1986, 1994. For Napo Runa versions of the lower Napo, see José Miguel Goldáraz 2004, 2005. More information is in N. Whitten and D. Whitten 2008.

2. To be sure I presented this fairly, I sent this section to Bruce Mannheim who, on July 22, 2008, replied: "I would add that one of the problems with the extant classifications of the Quechua family is that modern national boundaries were anachronistically used as nodes in the classifications, at least tacitly, creating chimerical subgroups like 'Ecuadorian Quichua,' 'Bolivian Quechua,' and the two Peruvian subgroups. This has much more to do with the institutional arrangements around the scholarship than with the histories of the languages themselves; so even descriptively, linguists have tended to think of (and describe) the lowland Quichua varieties as displaced highland Quichua—whence the disagreement you and I had with Rodolfo Cerrón at the workshop in Urbana two years ago. The issues are similar on the eastern slope of the Andes around the border with Bolivia."

3. Much of the information on myth and mythohistory comes from ceramic imagery and women's songs, fortified at times by male exegesis and tellers' narratives. For samples and illustrations of this imagery, see D. Whitten and N. Whitten 1988 and N. Whitten and D. Whitten 2008.

4. The original French version of *The Jealous Potter* is one of seven full-length books republished in one volume, *Oeuvres,* to celebrate Lévi-Strauss's importance to a new kind of ethnography and anthropology on the eve of his hundredth birthday. Reviewer Patrick Wilcken, writing for the *Times Literary Supplement* (2008), dubs this group of

publications "a mop-up operation." He goes on to say that "[i]n them he [Lévi-Strauss] tied up loose ends, pursued miscellaneous issues left over from the original *Mythologiques* quartet, while clarifying arguments and fielding criticisms." This reviewer, too, mentions only "Jívaro" mythology vis-à-vis pottery imagery and symbolism.

Conclusion: Ethnography and Theory in Cultural Life

1. Stoller 2009:156.

References

Acosta, Alberto, et al.
    2001   Nada solo para los indios. Quito: Abya-Yala.

Adorno, Rolena
    1986   Guaman Poma: Writing and Resistance in Colonial Peru. Austin: University of Texas Press.

Albornoz P., Oswaldo
    1976   Las luchas indígenas en el Ecuador. Guayaquil, Ecuador: Editorial Claridad.

Altschuler, Milton
    N.d.   River People of Ecuador: A Study of Cayapa Law, Politics, and Indian-Negro Adaptation. Developed from Altschuler's doctoral dissertation in the late 1960s. MS in the hands of author and N. Whitten.

Anderson, Benedict
    1991   [1983] Imagined Communities. 2nd edition. New York: Verso.

Andrews, George Reid
    2004   Afro–Latin America 1800–2000. New York: Oxford University Press.

Anonymous
    1980a   Arte y marginalidad, museo de artesanías. Quito: Banco Central del Ecuador and Dirección de Recursos Humanos y Empleo.
    1980b   Ecuador: Hands, Light and Color—Ecuadorian Popular Art. / Ecuador: Manos, luz y color—Arte popular ecuatoriano. Quito: Museo del Banco Central del Ecuador. Washington, DC: Interamerican Development Bank. Exhibition, March–September.
    1998   L'art naïf de Tigua: des peintres indigènes de L'Équatuer. Nice, France: Exhibition at Galerie Ecuador, April 24–August 29, 1998.
    1999   Pintores de Tigua en Bienal. Hoy, June 16, 5B.

Appadurai, Arjun, ed.
    2001   Globalization. Durham, NC: Duke University Press.

Appelbaum, Nancy P., Anne S. Macpherson, and Karin Alejandra Rosemblatt, eds.
    2003   Race and Nation in Modern Latin America. Chapel Hill: University of North Carolina Press.

Archivo General de Indias
    1666   Estado de la encomienda de Pelileo y agravios a sus indios. Seville AGI/S, Quito, 13, R.13, N38. November 15, 1666. http://pares.mcu.es.

Arens, William, and Ivan Karp, eds.
    1989   Creativity of Power. Washington, DC: Smithsonian Institution Press.
Arensberg, Conrad M., and Solon T. Kimball
    1940   Family and Community in Ireland. Cambridge, MA: Harvard University Press.
Arrom, José Juan
    1999   Introduction and Introductory Study. *In* An Account of the Antiquities of the Indians, by Fray Ramón Pané. Susan C. Griswold, trans. Pp. xi–xxix. Durham, NC: Duke University Press.
Arteaga P., José
    1992   Alfaro y los negros. *In* El negro en la historia: Raíces africanas en la nacionalidad ecuatoriana. P. Rafael Savoia, ed. Pp. 75–80. Quito: Centro Cultural Afroecuatoriano.
Babcock, Barbara
    1980   Reflexivity: Definition and Discriminations. Introduction to Semiotica 30(1/2):1–14.
    1987   Reflexivity. *In* Encyclopedia of Religion. Pp. 234–238. New York: Macmillan.
Babcock, Barbara, ed.
    1978   The Reversible World: Symbolic Inversion in Art and Society. Ithaca, NY: Cornell University Press.
Barrett, Samuel
    1925   The Cayapa Indians of Ecuador. Vols. 1 and 2. Indian Notes and Monographs, 40. New York: Museum of the American Indian, Heye Foundation.
Bateman, Rebecca
    1990   Africans and Indians: A Comparative Study of Black Carib and Black Seminole. Ethnohistory 37(1):1–24.
Becker, Marc
    2007   State Building and Ethnic Discourse in Ecuador's 1944–1945 Asamblea Constituyente 7. *In* Highland Indians and the State in Modern Ecuador. A. Kim Clark and Marc Becker, eds. Pp. 105–119. Pittsburgh: University of Pittsburgh Press.
    2008   Indians and Leftists in the Making of Ecuador's Modern Indigenous Movements. Durham, NC: Duke University Press.
Berlin, Ira
    1996   From Creole to African: Atlantic Creoles and the Origins of African-American Society in Mainland North America. William and Mary Quarterly, 3rd series (53):251–258.
Bhabha, Homi K.
    2008   [1994] The Location of Culture. With a new preface by the author. New York: Routledge.
Bielenberg, Aaron
    1996   Art from the Andean Heart Land. Américas 48(4):5.
    1997   Native Place: Art, Tourism and Community in the Ecuadorian Andes. Honors thesis, Department of Anthropology, Brown University, Providence, RI.

Biersack, Aletta
    1999   Local Knowledge, Local History: Geertz and Beyond. *In* Lynn Hunt, ed. Pp. 72–96. The New Cultural History. Berkeley: University of California Press.

Blanco, Adriana
    2010   Osvaldo Viteri: The Poetics of Mestizaje. Américas June:40–44.

Blomberg, Rolf, ed.
    1952   Ecuador: Andean Mosaic. Stockholm: Hugo Gebers Förlag.

Blu, Karen I.
    1980   The Lumbee Problem: The Making of an American Indian People. New York: Cambridge University Press.

Boas, Franz
    1940a   Race, Language and Culture. New York: Free Press.
    1940b   [1887] The Study of Geography. *In* Race, Language and Culture. Franz Boas. Pp. 639–647. New York: Free Press.

Boon, James
    1982   Other Tribes, Other Scribes: Symbolic Anthropology in the Comparative Study of Cultures, Histories, Religions, and Texts. Cambridge: Cambridge University Press.

Boorstin, Daniel J.
    1983   The Discoverers: A History of Man's Search to Know His World and Himself. New York: Random House.

Bourricaud, François
    1962   Changements à Puno. Paris: Institut de Hautes Études de l'Amérique Latine.

Braudel, Fernand
    1980   [1958] On History. Chicago: University of Chicago Press.

Bray, Tamara
    2008   Ecuador's Pre-Columbian Past. *In* The Ecuador Reader: History, Culture, Politics. Carlos de la Torre and Steve Striffler, eds. Pp. 15–26. Durham, NC: Duke University Press.

Brooks, George E.
    2003   Eurafricans in Western Africa: Commerce, Social Status, Gender and Religious Observance from the Sixteenth to the Eighteenth Century. Athens: Ohio University Press.

Brown, Michael F., and Eduardo Fernandez
    1991   War of Shadows: The Struggle for Utopia in the Peruvian Amazon. Berkeley: University of California Press.

Bunker, Stephen G.
    2006   The Snake with Golden Braids: Society, Nature, and Technology in Andean Irrigation. Lanham, MD: Lexington Books.

Bunzl, Matti
    2004   Boas, Foucault, and the "Native Anthropologist": Notes toward a Neo-Boasian Anthropology. American Anthropologist 106(3):435–442.

Burdick, John
    1992   The Myth of Racial Democracy. *In* The Black Americas: 1492–1992. Report on the Americas, NACLA (North American Congress of Latin America) 25(4):40–44, 48.

Butler, Barbara Y.
    2006   Holy Intoxication to Drunken Dissipation: Alcohol among Quichua Speakers in Otavalo, Ecuador. Albuquerque: University of New Mexico Press.

Cabello Balboa, Miguel
    1945   [ca. 1583] Obras, vol. 1. Quito: Editorial Ecuatoriana.

Cabodevilla, Miguel Ángel
    1994   Los huaorani en la historia de los pueblos del oriente. Coca, Ecuador: CICAME.

Cabodevilla, Miguel Ángel, Randy Smith, and Alex Rivas
    2004   Tiempos de guerra: Waorani contra Taromenane. Quito: Abya-Yala.

Calderón Cevallos, Alfonso
    1987   Reflexiones en las culturas orales. 4th edition. Quito: Abya-Yala.

Canby, Peter
    2004   Latin America's Longest War. The Nation, August 16/23, 31–38.

Carballo, Antonio Lago
    1989   Prólogo. *In* José Vasconcelos: Edición Justina Sarabia. Madrid: Ediciones Cultura Hispánica.

Carneiro da Cunha, Manuela
    2007   Foreword: Whose History and History for Whom? *In* Time and Memory in Indigenous Amazonia: Anthropological Perspectives. Carlos Fausto and Michael Heckenberger, eds. Pp. xi–xiii. Gainesville: University Press of Florida

Carrasco, Eulalia A.
    1983   El pueblo Chachi. Quito: Abya-Yala.

Carvajal, Gaspar de
    1934   [ca. 1541] The Discovery of the Amazon: According to the Account of Friar Carvajal and Other Documents. José Toribio Medina, comp. H. C. Heaton, ed. Special Publication 17. New York: American Geographical Society.

Chango, Alfonso
    1984   Yachaj Sami Yachachina. Quito: Abya-Yala.

Chango, María, and Agustín Jerez
    1995   Reis Pishta. *In* La fiesta religiosa indígena en el Ecuador. Luz del Alba Moya, ed. Pp. 115–30. Quito: Abya-Yala.

Chuji, Mónica, and Pablo Dávalos
    1995   Los derechos colectivos de las nacionalidades y pueblos del Ecuador: Evaluación de la década 1998–2008. Quito: CONAIE and Fundación Tucui Shimi.

Civrieux, Marc de
    1976   Los Caribes y la conquista de la Guayana Española. Montalbán 5:875–1021.
    1997   [1980] Watunna: An Orinoco Creation Cycle. David M. Guss, ed. and trans. Austin: University of Texas Press.

Colloredo-Mansfeld, Rudi
    1999   The Native Leisure Class: Consumption and Cultural Creativity in the Andes. Chicago: University of Chicago Press.

2003 Tigua Migrant Communities and the Possibilities for Autonomy among Urban *Indígenas*. *In* Millennial Ecuador: Critical Essays on Cultural Transformations and Social Dynamics. Norman E. Whitten Jr., ed. Pp. 275–295. Iowa City: University of Iowa Press.
2008 Globalization from Below and the Political Turn among Otavalo's Merchant Artisans. *In* The Ecuador Reader: History, Culture, Politics. Carlos de la Torre and Steve Striffler, eds. Pp. 377–384. Durham, NC: Duke University Press.
2009 Fighting Like a Community: Andean Civil Society in an Era of Indian Uprisings. Chicago: University of Chicago Press.

Columbus, Christopher
1989 [1492–1493] The Diario of Christopher Columbus's First Voyage to America, 1492–1493. Abstracted by Fray Bartolomé de las Casas. Transcribed and translated into English, with notes and a concordance of the Spanish by Oliver Dunn and James E. Kelley Jr. Norman: University of Oklahoma Press.

Colvin, Jean
1997 Les peintres de Tigua: L'art indigéne de l'Equateur. Paris: Exhibition at UNESCO Headquarters, December.
2001 Pintores del Tigua. Quito: Ediciones del Banco Central del Ecuador.
2004 Arte de Tigua: A Reflection of Indigenous Culture in Ecuador. Quito: Abya-Yala.

Colvin, Jean, and Alfredo Toaquiza
1994 Pintores de Tigua: Indigenous Artists of Ecuador. Washington, DC: Exhibition at The Organization of American States (OAS).

Comaroff, Jean
1985 Body of Power, Spirit of Resistance: The Culture and History of a South African People. Chicago: University of Chicago Press.

Comaroff, Jean, and John L. Comaroff, eds.
2001 Millennial Capitalism and the Culture of Neoliberalism. Durham, NC: Duke University Press.

Comaroff, John L., and Jean Comaroff
2009 Ethnicity, Inc. Chicago: University of Chicago Press.

Combès, Isabelle, and Kathleen Lowrey
2006 Slaves without Masters? Arawakan Dynasties among the Chiriguano (Bolivian Chaco, Sixteenth to Twentieth Centuries). Ethnohistory 53(4):689–714.

Combs-Schilling, M. E.
1989 Sacred Performances: Islam, Sexuality, and Sacrifice. New York: Columbia University Press.

CONAIE
1989, 1991 500 años de resistencia india: Las nacionalidades indígenas en el Ecuador. 2nd edition. Quito: Tincui/CONAIE and Abya-Yala.
2000 La dignidad de los pueblos: Levantamiento del 21 de Enero, 2000. Video. Quito: CONAIE.

Conzemius, Eduard
    1932   Ethnographical Survey of the Miskito and Sumu Indians of Honduras and Nicaragua. Bureau of American Ethnology Bulletin 106. Washington, DC: Smithsonian Institution.

Córdoba, Juan Tulio I.
    1983   Etnicidad y estructura social en el Chocó. Medellín, Colombia: Editorial Lealon.

Corkill, David, and David Cubitt
    1988   Ecuador: Fragile Democracy. London: Latin American Bureau.

Cornejo, Justino
    1974   Los que tenemos de Mandinga. Portoviejo, Ecuador: Editorial Gregorio de Portoviejo.

Corr, Rachel
    2010   Ritual and Remembrance in the Ecuadorian Andes. Tucson: University of Arizona Press.

Coulthard, G. R.
    1962   Race and Colour in Caribbean Literature. London: Oxford University Press.

Crapanzano, Vincent
    1992   Hermes' Dilemma and Hamlet's Desire: On the Epistemology of Interpretation. Cambridge, MA: Harvard University Press.

Crocker, Christopher
    1977   The Social Functions of Rhetorical Forms. In The Social Use of Metaphor: Essays on the Anthropology of Rhetoric. J. David Sapir and J. Christopher Crocker, eds. Pp. 33–66. Philadelphia: University of Pennsylvania Press.

Cuvi, Pablo
    1994   Crafts of Ecuador. Quito: Dinediciones.

Dávalos, Karen Mary
    2001   Exhibiting Mestizaje: Mexican (American) Museums in the Diaspora. Albuquerque: University of New Mexico Press.

Davis, Natalie Zemon
    N.d.   Braided Traditions. MS in preparation.

De la Cadena, Marisol
    2000   Indigenous Mestizos: The Politics of Race and Culture in Cuzco, Peru, 1919–1991. Durham, NC: Duke University Press.
    2001   Reconstructing Race: Racism, Culture and Mestizaje in Latin America. In The Social Origins of Race: Race and Racism in the Americas, Part I. NACLA (North American Congress of Latin America) 34(6):16–23, 45.

De la Torre, Carlos, and Steve Striffler
    2008   Conquest and Colonial Rule. In The Ecuador Reader: History, Culture, Politics. Carlos de la Torre and Steve Striffler, eds. Pp. 10–13. Durham, NC: Duke University Press.

De la Torre, Carlos, and Steve Striffler, eds.
    2008   The Ecuador Reader: History, Culture, Politics. Durham, NC: Duke University Press.

Deagan, Kathleen, and Darcie MacMahon
    1995   Fort Mose: Colonial America's Black Fortress of Freedom. Gainesville: University Press of Florida.
Dennis, Philip A.
    2004   The Miskitu People of Awastara. Austin: University of Texas Press.
Descola, Philippe
    1986   La nature domestíque: Techniques et symbolisme dans l'écologie des Achuar. Paris: Éditions de la Maison des Sciences de L'homme.
    1994   In the Society of Nature: A Native Ecology in Amazonia. New York: Cambridge University Press.
Dieterich, Heinz
    2000   La cuarta vía al poder: El 21 de enero desde una perspectiva latinoamericana. Quito: Abya-Yala.
Dilke, Christopher, ed. and trans.
    1978   Letter to a King: A Picture-History of the Inca Civilisation by Huamán Poma (don Felipe Huamán Poma de Ayala). London: George Allen and Unwin.
Dilthey, Wilhelm
    1996   Selected Works, vol. 4: Hermeneutics and the Study of History. Edited, with an Introduction, by Rudolf A. Makkreel and Frithjof Rodi. Princeton, NJ: Princeton University Press.
Dockstader, Frederick J.
    1985   The Kachina and the White Man: The Influences of White Culture on the Hopi Kachina Cult. Revised and enlarged edition. Albuquerque: University of New Mexico Press.
Dolgin, Janet L., David S. Kemnitzer, and David Schneider
    1977   Introduction: As People Express Their Lives. *In* Symbolic Anthropology: A Reader in the Study of Symbols and Meanings. Janet L. Dolgin, David S. Kemnitzer, and David Schneider, eds. Pp. 3–44. New York: Columbia University Press.
Donoso Pareja, Miguel
    1998   Ecuador: Identidad o esquizofrenia. Quito: Eskeletra Editorial.
Douglas, Mary
    1966   Purity and Danger: An Analysis of the Concepts of Pollution and Taboo. London: Routledge and Kegan Paul.
Eliade, Mircea, ed.
    1987   The Encyclopedia of Religion. New York: Macmillan.
England, Sarah
    2006   Afro Central Americans in New York City: Garifuna Tales of Transnational Movements in Racialized Space. Gainesville: University Press of Florida.
Escobar, Ticio
    2007   The Curse of Nemur: In Search of the Art, Myth, and Ritual of the Ishir. Pittsburgh: University of Pittsburgh Press.
Espinosa Apolo, Manuel
    1997   Los mestizos ecuatorianos y las señas de identidad cultural. Quito: Editorial Tramasocial.

Espinosa Cordero, Simón
    1999   Hoy, June 26, 9A.
Estupiñán Bass, Nelson
    1997   [1954] Bajo el cielo nublado. Quito: Coleción País Secreto, Sistema Nacional de Bibliotecas.
Fabian, Johannes
    2002   [1983] Time and the Other: How Anthropology Makes Its Object. New York: Columbia University Press.
Fausto, Carlos, and Michael Heckenberger
    2007   Introduction: Indigenous History and the History of the "Indians." *In* Time and Memory in Indigenous Amazonia: Anthropological Perspectives. Carlos Fausto and Michael Heckenberger, eds. Pp. 1–43. Gainesville: University Press of Florida.
Fausto, Carlos, and Michael Heckenberger, eds.
    2007   Time and Memory in Indigenous Amazonia: Anthropological Perspectives. Gainesville: University Press of Florida.
Fernandez, James W.
    1991   Beyond Metaphor: The Play of Tropes in Culture. Stanford: Stanford University Press.
Fine, Kathleen S.
    1991   Cotocollao: Ideología, historia, y acción en un barrio de Quito. Quito: Abya-Yala.
Fine-Dare, Kathleen S.
    2007   Más allá del folklore: La yumbada de Cotocollao como vitrina para los discursos de la identidad, de la intervención estatal, y del poder local en los Andes urbanos ecuatorianos. *In* Estudios Ecuatorianos: Un aporte a la discusón, tomo II. William F. Waters and Michael Hamerly, comps. Pp. 55–72. Quito: FLACSO.
Firth, Raymond T.
    1964   Foreword to Political Systems of Highland Burma, by Edmund Leach. Pp. v–viii. Boston: Beacon Press.
Fisch, Olga
    1985   El folclor que yo viví/The Folklore through My Eyes. Memorias de Olga Fisch/Memoirs of Olga Fisch. Cuenca, Ecuador: Centro Interamericano de Artesanías y Artes Populares.
Forbes, Jack D.
    1993   Africans and Native Americans: The Origins of Race and the Evolution of Red-Black Peoples. 2nd edition. Urbana: University of Illinois Press.
Freud, Sigmund
    1918   Totem and Taboo: Resemblances between the Psychic Lives of Savages and Neurotics. New York: Random House.
    1955   [1930] Civilization and Its Discontents. London: The Hogarth Press.
Friedemann, Nina S. de
    1974   Minería, descendencia y orfebría artesanal: Litoral, Pacífico (colombiano). Bogotá: Universidad Nacional, Facultad de Ciencias Humanas.

Friedemann, Nina S. de, and Jaime Arocha
    1995   Colombia. *In* No Longer Invisible: Afro–Latin Americans Today. Minority Rights Group, ed. Pp. 47–76. London: Minority Rights Publications.

Friedemann, Nina S. de, and Richard Cross
    1979   Ma Ngombe: Guerreros y ganaderos en Palenque. Bogotá: Carlos Valencia Editores.

Fuentes, Carlos
    1992   The Buried Mirror: Reflections on Spain and the New World. Boston: Houghton Mifflin.

Gabilondo, Joseba
    1997   [1979] Afterword to The Cosmic Race/La raza cósmica, by José Vasconcelos. Baltimore: Johns Hopkins University Press.

Garcés, Enrique
    1961   Daquilema, rex: Biografía de un dolor indio. Quito: Casa de la Cultura Ecuatoriana.

García Canclini, Néstor
    1995   Hybrid Cultures: Strategies for Entering and Leaving Modernity. Minneapolis: University of Minnesota Press.

Gates, Henry Louis, Jr.
    1988   The Signifying Monkey: A Theory of African-American Literary Criticism. New York: Oxford University Press.

Gay y Blasco, Paloma, and Huon Wardle
    2007   How to Read Ethnography. New York: Routledge.

Geertz, Clifford
    1967   The Cerebral Savage: On the Work of Claude Lévi-Strauss. Encounter 28(4):25–32.
    1973   The Interpretation of Cultures. New York: Basic Books.
    1983   Local Knowledge: Further Essays in Interpretive Anthropology. New York: Basic Books.
    1995   After the Fact: Two Countries, Four Decades, One Anthropologist. Cambridge, MA: Harvard University Press.
    2000   Available Light: Anthropological Reflections on Philosophical Topics. Princeton, NJ: Princeton University Press.
    2002   An Inconstant Profession: The Anthropological Life in Interesting Times. Annual Review of Anthropology 31:1–19.
    2005   Shifting Aims, Moving Targets: On the Anthropology of Religion. Journal of the Royal Anthropological Institute 11(1):1–15.

Gerth, H. H., and C. Wright Mills, eds. and trans.
    1958   [1946] From Max Weber: Essays in Sociology. New York: Oxford University Press.

Gillin, John
    1949   Mestizo America. *In* Most of the World. Ralph Linton, ed. Pp. 156–211. New York: Macmillan.

Gluckman, Max
    1954   Rituals of Rebellion in South-East Africa. Manchester, UK: University of Manchester Press.

1958 Analysis of a Social Situation in Modern Zululand. Rhodes-Livingstone Paper, 28. Manchester, UK: Manchester University Press.
1965 Politics, Law, and Ritual in Tribal Society. New York: New American Library.

Gluckman, Max, ed.
1962 Essays in the Ritual of Social Relations. Manchester, UK: Manchester University Press.

Gnerre, Maurizio
1973 Sources of Spanish Jivaro. Romance Philology 27(2):203–204.

Godelier, Maurice
2010 Community, Society, Culture: Three Keys to Understanding Today's Conflicted Identities. Journal of the Royal Anthropological Institute 16(1):1–11.

Goldáraz, José Miguel
2004 Kawsaykama (Hacia la vida sin fin), vol. 1: Mitos y tradiciones de los Naporuna. Ilustraciones de Marcelo Aguirre Belgrano. Quito: Ediciones CICAME.
2005 Kawsaykama (Hacia la vida sin fin), vol. 3: Napo mayumanta runakunapak sumak yuyarina yachaykuna. Ilustraciones de Miguel Varea. Quito: Ediciones CICAME.

Gonzalez, Nancie L.
1983 Foreword to Women and the Ancestors: Black Carib Kinship and Ritual, by Virginia Kerns. Pp. xi–xiv. Urbana: University of Illinois Press.
1988 Sojourners of the Caribbean: Ethnogenesis and Ethnohistory of the Garifuna. Urbana: University of Illinois Press.

González, Roberto J.
2009 American Counterinsurgency: Human Science and the Human Terrain. Chicago: Prickley Paradigm Press.

Gow, Peter
1993 Gringos and Wild Indians: Images of History in Western Amazonian Cultures. L'Homme 33:(126–128):327–347.

Graburn, Nelson H. H., ed.
1976 Ethnic and Tourist Arts: Cultural Expressions from the Fourth World. Berkeley: University of California Press.

Graeber, David
2004 Fragments of an Anarchist Anthropology. Chicago: Prickly Paradigm Press.

Grandin, Greg
2010 Muscling Latin America. The Nation. 290(5, February 8):9–13.

Greenberg, Joseph
1960 The General Classification of Central and South American Languages. *In* Selected Papers of the Fifth International Congress of Anthropological and Ethnological Sciences. Anthony F. C. Wallace, ed. Pp. 791–794. Philadelphia: University of Pennsylvania Press.

Greenblatt, Stephen
1989 Towards a Poetics of Culture. *In* The New Historicism. Harold Veeser, ed. Pp. 1–14. New York: Routledge.

1999 The Touch of the Real. *In* The Fate of "Culture": Geertz and Beyond. Sherry B. Ortner, ed. Pp. 14–29. Berkeley: University of California Press.

2006 Anthropology and Social Theory: Culture, Power, and the Acting Subject. Durham, NC: Duke University Press.

Guaman Poma de Ayala, Felipe
    1987 [1613] Primer nueva crónica i buen govierno. 3 vols. John V. Murra, Rolena Adorno, and Jorge L. Urioste, eds. Madrid: Crónicas de América.

Guevara, Dario
    1969–1970 La fiesta de Caporal y los Reyes Magos en Salasaca, Ecuador. Folklore Americano 16:94–133.

Guss, David M.
    1989 To Weave and Sing: Art, Symbol, and Narrative in the South American Rain Forest. Berkeley: University of California Press.
    1997 Preface for a New Millennium. *In* Watunna: An Orinoco Creation Cycle, by Marc de Civrieux. David M. Guss, ed. and trans. Pp. ix–xii. Austin: University of Texas Press.
    2000 The Festive State: Race, Ethnicity and Nationalism as Cultural Performance. Berkeley: University of California Press.

Guss, David M., and Lise Waxer
    1994 Afro-Venezuelans. *In* The Encyclopedia of World Cultures, vol. 7: South America. Pp. 24–29. Boston: G. K. Hall.

Hale, Charles
    1994 Resistance and Contradiction: Miskitu Indians and the Nicaraguan State, 1894–1987. Stanford, CA: Stanford University Press.

Hall, Gwendolyn Midlo
    2005 Slavery and American Ethnicities in the Americas: Restoring the Links. Chapel Hill: University of North Carolina Press.

Handelman, Don, and Galina Lindquist, eds.
    2004 Ritual in Its Own Right. New York: Berghahn Books.

Handelsman, Michael
    1999 Lo afro y la plurinacionalidad: El caso ecuatoriano visto desde su literatura. University of Mississippi Romance Monographs, 54. University, MS: Department of Modern Languages.

Harrison, Regina
    1996 Yaya Alfaro: Perspectivas indígenas. *In* La revolución alfarista: Ponencias del VII Congreso de la Asociación de Ecuatorianistas en Norteamerica Julio 17–21 de 1995. Guayaquil, Ecuador: Casa de la Cultura Ecuatoriana, Nucleo de Guayas.

Haslip-Viera, Gabriel, ed.
    2001 Taíno Revival: Critical Perspectives on Puerto Rican Identity and Cultural Politics. Princeton, NJ: Marcus Wiener.

Hebdige, D.
    1979 Subculture: The Meaning of Style. New York: Methuen.

Helms, Mary W.
    1977 Negro or Indian? The Changing Identity of a Frontier Population. *In* Old Roots in New Lands: Historical and Anthropological Perspectives on Black

Experiences in the Americas. Ann Pescatello, ed. Pp. 157–172. Westport, CT: Greenwood Press.

1988 Ulysses' Sail: An Ethnographic Odyssey of Power, Knowledge, and Geographical Distance. Princeton, NJ: Princeton University Press.

Hemming, John
1970 The Conquest of the Incas. New York: Harcourt.
2008 Tree of Rivers: The Story of the Amazon. New York: Thames and Hudson.

Hernández, José, Marco Aráuz, Byron Rodríguez V., and Leonel Bejarano
2000 21 de enero: La vorágine que acabó con Mahuad. Quito: El Comercio.

Herzfeld, Michael
1997 Cultural Intimacy: Social Poetics in the Nation-State. New York: Routledge.

Hill, Jonathan D.
1988 Introduction: Myth and History. *In* Rethinking History and Myth: Indigenous South American Perspectives on the Past. Jonathan D. Hill, ed. Pp. 1–17. Urbana: University of Illinois Press.
2009 Made-from-Bone: Trickster Myths, Music, and History from the Amazon. Urbana: University of Illinois Press.

Hill, Jonathan D., ed.
1996 History, Power, and Identity: Ethnogenesis in the Americas, 1492–1992. Iowa City: University of Iowa Press.

Hill, Jonathan D., and Fernando Santos-Granero, eds.
2002 Comparative Arawakan Histories: Rethinking Language Family and Culture Area in Amazonia. Urbana: University of Illinois Press.

Ho, Karen
2009 Liquidated: An Ethnography of Wall Street. Durham, NC: Duke University Press.

Hopkins, Dwight N.
2001 The Religion of Globalization. *In* Religions/Globalizations: Theories and Cases. Dwight N. Hopkins, Lois Ann Lorentzen, Eduardo Mendieta, and David Batstone, eds. Pp. 7–32. Durham, NC: Duke University Press.

Hopkins, Dwight N., Lois Ann Lorentzen, Eduardo Mendieta, and David Batstone, eds.
2001 Religions/Globalizations: Theories and Cases. Durham, NC: Duke University Press.

Hornborg, Alf
2005 Ethnogenesis, Regional Integration, and Ecology in Prehistoric Amazonia. Current Anthropology 46(4):589–620.

Hornborg, Alf, and Jonathan D. Hill, eds.
2011 Ethnicity in Ancient Amazonia: Reconstructing Past Identities from Archaeology, Linguistics, and Ethnohistory. Boulder: University Press of Colorado.

Horswell, Michael J.
2005 Decolonizing the Sodomite: Queer Tropes of Sexuality in Colonial Andean Culture. Austin: University of Texas Press.

Hristov, Jasmin
2009 Blood and Capital: The Paramilitarization of Colombia. Athens: Ohio University Press; Toronto: Between the Lines.

Hulme, Peter, and Neil L. Whitehead, eds.
    1992   Wild Majesty: Encounters with Caribs from Columbus to the Present Day. Oxford: Oxford University Press.

Hunt, Carla
    1982   Olga Fisch: Gran dama de las artes. Equinoccio 3(3):6–7.

Hunt, Lynn, ed.
    1989   The New Cultural History. Berkeley: University of California Press.

Hurtado, Osvaldo
    1980   [1977] Political Power in Ecuador. Nick D. Mills Jr., trans. Albuquerque: University of New Mexico Press.
    1997   [1977] El poder político en el Ecuador. Quito: Editorial Planeta-Letraviva.

Hyatt, Vera Lawrence, and Rex Nettleford, eds.
    1995   Race, Discourse, and the Origin of the Americas: A New World View. Washington, DC: Smithsonian Institution Press.

Isbell, Billie Jean
    2009   Finding Cholita. Urbana: University of Illinois Press.

Jaramillo Uribe, Jaime
    1963   Esclavos y señores en la sociedad colombiana del siglo XVIII. Anuario Colombiano de Historia Social y de la Cultura (Bogotá) 1(1):3–62.

Jijón y Chiluisa, Jacinto (parodic pseudonym)
    1997   Longos: Una crítica reflexiva e irreverente a lo que somos. Quito: Abya-Yala.

Jurado Noboa, Fernando
    1995   Historia social de Esmeraldas: Indios, negros, mulatos, españoles, y zambos del siglo XVI al XX. Quito: Editorial y Imprenta Delta.

Kane, Stephanie
    1994   The Phantom Gringo Boat: Shamanic Discourse and Development in Panama. Washington, DC: Smithsonian Press.

Karsten, Rafael
    1935   The Head-Hunters of Western Amazonas: The Life and Culture of the Jibaro Indians of Eastern Ecuador and Peru. Commentationes Humanarum Litterarum, vol. 7, no. 1. Helsinki: Societas Scientiarum Fennica.

Keesing, Roger H.
    1987   Anthropology as Interpretive Quest. Current Anthropology 28(2):161–176.
    1994   Theories of Culture Revisited. *In* Assessing Cultural Anthropology. Robert Borofsky, ed. Pp. 301–348. New York: McGraw Hill.

Kerns, Virginia
    1983   Women and the Ancestors: Black Carib Kinship and Ritual. Urbana: University of Illinois Press.

Kiddy, Elizabeth W.
    2005   Blacks of the Rosary: Memory and History in Minas Gerais, Brazil. University Park: Pennsylvania State University Press.

Kohn, Eduardo
    2008   Always Already Runa. Paper presented at the Annual Meeting of the American Anthropological Association, San Francisco, November 23.

Kozloff, Nikolas
    2005   A Real Racial Democracy? Hugo Chávez and the Politics of Race. Out of Bounds Magazine, October 14.

Lane, Kris
    2002   Quito 1599: City and Colony in Transition. Albuquerque: University of New Mexico Press.
    2005   Africans and Natives in the Mines of Spanish America. *In* Beyond Black and Red: African-Native Relations in Colonial Latin America. Matthew Restall, ed. Pp. 159–184. Albuquerque: University of New Mexico Press.

Lathrap, Donald W., Donald Collier, and Helen Chandra
    1975   Ancient Ecuador: Culture, Clay, and Creativity, 3000–300 B.C. Chicago: Field Museum of Natural History.

Leach, Edmund
    1964   [1954] Political Systems of Highland Burma. Boston: Beacon Press.
    1976   Culture and Communication: The Logic by Which Symbols Are Connected. New York: Cambridge University Press.
    1982   Social Anthropology. New York: Oxford University Press.

Leech, Garry
    2004   U.S./Colombia: Demobilizing the AUC? *In* Changing Identities: The Politics of Race and Globalization, Part I. NACLA (North American Congress of Latin America) 38(2):42–44.

Léry, Jean de
    1990   [1574] History of a Voyage to the Land of Brazil. Janet Whatley, trans. Berkeley: University of California Press.

Lévi-Strauss, Claude
    1963a   Structural Anthropology. New York: Basic Books.
    1963b   [1962] Totemism. Boston: Beacon Press.
    1966   [1962] The Savage Mind. Chicago: University of Chicago Press.
    1969   [1964] The Raw and the Cooked. Introduction to a Science of Mythology, 1. New York: Harper and Row.
    1981   [1971] The Naked Man. Introduction to a Science of Mythology, 4. New York: Harper and Row.
    1988   The Jealous Potter. Bénédicte Charier, trans. Chicago: University of Chicago Press.

Linke, Lilo
    1960   Ecuador: Country of Contrasts. 3rd edition. London: Oxford University Press.

Losonczy, Anne-Marie
    1997   Les saints et la forêt: Rituel, société et figures de l'échange avec les Indiens Emberá chez les Négro-Colombiens du Chocó. Paris: L'Harmattan.

Lucas, Kintto
    2000a   La rebelión de los indios. Quito: Abya-Yala.
    2000b   We Will Not Dance on Our Grandparents' Tombs: Indigenous Uprisings in Ecuador. London: Catholic Institute for International Relations (CIIR).

Luna, Eduardo Luis, and Pablo Amaringo
    1991   Ayahuasca Visions: The Religious Iconography of a Peruvian Shaman. Berkeley, CA: North Atlantic Books.

Macas, Luis
    1991   El Levantamiento Indígena visto por sus protagonistas. Quito: Instituto Científico de Culturas Indígenas, Amauta Runacunapac Yachai.

Malinowski, Bronislaw
    1922   Argonauts of the Western Pacific. New York: E. P. Dutton.
    1944   A Scientific Theory of Culture and Other Essays. New York: Routledge.

Mannheim, Bruce
    1991   The Language of the Inka since the European Invasion. Austin: University of Texas Press.

Marcos, Jorge G.
    1996   El origen de la agricultura. *In* Nueva historia del Ecuador, vol. 1. Enrique Ayla Mora, ed. Pp. 129–182. Quito: Corporación Editora Nacional.

Marcos, Jorge G., ed.
    1986   Arqueología de la costa ecuatoriana: Nuevos enfoques. Quito: Corporación Editora Nacional.

Martínez-Echazábal, Lourdes
    1998   Mestizaje and the Discourse of National/Cultural Identity in Latin America, 1845–1959. Latin American Perspectives 25(3):21–42.

Marx, Karl (with Friedrich Engels)
    1998   [1845] The German Ideology, Including Theses on Feuerbach and Introduction to the Critique of Political Economy. Amherst, NY: Prometheus Books.

Meisch, Lynn A.
    1992   We Will Not Dance on the Tomb of Our Grandparents: Five Hundred Years of Resistance in Ecuador. The Latin American Anthropology Review 4(2):55–74.
    1997   Traditional Communities, Transnational Lives: Coping with Globalization in Otavalo, Ecuador. Ph.D. dissertation, Department of Anthropology, Stanford University. Ann Arbor, MI: University Microfilms.

Mendoza, Carlos Poveda
    2001   ¿Quién derrocó a Mahuad? Quito: Ediecuatorial.

Merton, Robert K.
    1957   Patterns of Influence: Local and Cosmopolitan Influentials. *In* Social Theory and Social Structure, revised and enlarged edition. Pp. 387–420. Glencoe, IL: Free Press.

Miles, Ann
    2004   From Cuenca to Queens: An Anthropological Story of Transnational Migration. Austin: University of Texas Press.

Miller, Ivor
    2009   The Genesis of African and Indian Cooperation in Colonial North America: An Interview with Helen Hornbeck Tanner. Ethnohistory 56(2):285–302.

Miller, Marilyn Grace
    2004   Rise and Fall of the Cosmic Race: The Cult of Mestizaje in Latin America. Austin: University of Texas Press.

Miller, Tom
    1983   Folk Arts Thrive in a Quito Shop. New York Times, January 16, pp. 12, 16.

Mooney, James
    1896   The Ghost-Dance Religion and the Sioux Outbreak of 1890. Fourteenth Annual Report of the Bureau of Ethnology to the Secretary of the Smithsonian Institution, 1892–1893, pt. 2. Washington, DC: Government Printing Office.

Moore, Sally F., and Barbara G. Myerhoff, eds.
    1977   Secular Ritual. Amsterdam: Van Gorcum.

Moreno, Isidoro
    1983   Los cuadros de mestizaje. Madrid: José Porrua Editoriales.
    1997   La antigua hermanidad de los negros de Sevilla: Etnicidad, poder y sociedad en 600 años de historia. Sevilla: Universidad de Sevilla y la Consejería de Cultura de la Junta de Andalucía.
    1999   Festive Rituals, Religious Associations, and Ethnic Reaffirmation of Black Andalusians: Antecedents of the Black Confraternities and Cabildos in the Americas. *In* Representations of Blackness and the Performance of Identities. Jean Muteba Rahier, ed. Pp. 3–17. Westport, CT: Bergin and Garvey.

Moreno Yanez, Segundo
    1976   Sublevaciones indígenas en la audiencia de Quito desde comienzos del siglo XVIII hasta finales de la colonia. Bonn: Bonner Amerikanistische Studien/Estudios Americanistas de Bonn.

Mörner, Magnus
    1967   Race Mixture in the History of Latin America. Boston: Little, Brown.
    1985   The Andean Past: Land, Societies, and Conflicts. New York: Columbia University Press.

Muñoz, Arturo G.
    1996   Handling Hungry Spirits: Shamanic Rituals of the Emberá. Shaman's Drum, Fall, 36–48.

Muratorio, Blanca
    1999   Etnografía e historia visual de una etnicidad emergente: El caso de las pinturas de Tigua. Paper presented to the Seminario sobre Patrimonio Cultural, Quito.

Muratorio, Ricardo
    1981a   A Feast of Color: Corpus Christi Dance Costumes of Ecuador (from the Olga Fisch Collection). Washington, DC: Smithsonian Institution Press.
    1981b   Corpus Christi Dance Costumes of Ecuador. American Craft 41(1):8–13.
    1985   Danzantes de Corpus Christi (donación de Olga Fisch al Museo del Banco Central del Ecuador) (Spanish version of the 1981 catalog "A Feast of Color: Corpus Christi Dance Costumes of Ecuador," corrected and expanded).

Catalog by María Pilar Merlo de Cevallos. Quito: Museo del Banco Central del Ecuador.

Naranjo, Marcelo F.
- 1977 Zonas de refugio y adaptación étnica en el Oriente: Siglos XVI–XVII–XVIII. *In* Temas sobre la continuidad y adaptación cultural ecuatoriana. Marcelo F. Naranjo, José Pereira, and Norman E. Whitten Jr., eds. Pp. 99–153. Quito: Ediciones de la Universidad Católica.

Nash, June
- 1993 We Eat the Mines and the Mines Eat Us. New York: Columbia University Press.

Network of Concerned Anthropologists
- 2009 The Counter-Counterinsurgency Manual; Or, Notes on Demilitarizing American Society. Chicago: Prickly Paradigm Press.

Newson, Linda A.
- 1995 Life and Death in Early Colonial Ecuador. Norman: University of Oklahoma Press.

Nicholas del Techo
- 1897 Historia de la provincia del Paraguay de la compañía de Jesús, vol. 1. Madrid: A. de Uribe.

Ntarangwi, Mwenda
- 2009 East African Hip Hop: Youth Culture and Globalization. Urbana: University of Illinois Press.

Núñez Cabeza de Vaca, Alvar
- 1963 [1542, 1555] Castaways: The Narrative of Alvar Núñez Cabeza de Vaca. Enrique Pupo-Walker, ed., Frances M. López-Morillas, trans. Berkeley: University of California Press.

Nunley, John W.
- 1987 Moving with the Face of the Devil: Art and Politics in Urban West Africa. Urbana: University of Illinois Press.

Oberem, Udo
- 1971 Los Quijos: Historia de la transculturación de un grupo indígena en el oriente ecuatoriano (1538–1956). 2 vols. Madrid: Facultad de Filosofía y Letras de la Universidad de Madrid.
- 1988 El período incaico en el Ecuador. *In* Nueva historia del Ecuador, vol. 2. Enrique Ayla Mora, ed. Pp. 135–166. Quito: Corporación Editora Nacional.

O'Brien, Timothy, and Eric Dash
- 2004 The Midas Touch with Spin on It: Trump's Billionaire Persona Belies Troubles with His Empire. New York Times, September 8, pp. C1–C2.

Oettinger, Marion, Jr.
- 1992 The Folk Art of Latin America: Visiones del Pueblo. New York: Penguin Books.

Ohnuki-Tierney, Emiko, ed.
- 1990 Culture Through Time: Anthropological Approaches. Stanford, CA: Stanford University Press.

Ortiz, Adalberto
    1943   Juyungo: Historia de un negro, una isla y otros negros. Buenos Aires: Editorial Americalee.

Ortiz, Fernando
    1940   Contrapunto cubano del tobaco y azúcar. Havana: Jesús Montero.
    1947   Cuban Counterpoint: Tobacco and Sugar. Durham, NC: Duke University Press.
    1960   La antigua fiesta Afrocubana del día de reyes. La Habana: Ministerio de Relaciones Exteriores, Departamento de Asuntos Culturales.

Ortner, Sherry B., ed.
    1999   The Fate of "Culture:" Geertz and Beyond. Berkeley: University of California Press.
    2006   Anthropology and Social Theory: Culture, Power, and the Acting Subject. Durham, NC: Duke University Press.

Palencia-Roth, Michael
    1993   The Cannibal Law of 1503. *In* Early Images of the Américas. Jeremy M. Williams and Robert E. Lewis, eds. Pp. 21–64. Tucson: University of Arizona Press.

Pané, Fray Ramón
    1999   [ca. 1486–1488] An Account of the Antiquities of the Indians. A new edition with an introductory study, notes, and appendixes by José Juan Arrom. Susan C. Griswold, trans. Durham, NC: Duke University Press.

Parameshwar Gaonkar, Dilip, ed.
    2001   Alternative Modernities. Durham, NC: Duke University Press.

Parry, John H., and Robert G. Keith, eds.
    1984   Columbus' Letter to Santángel [1493]. *In* New Iberian World: A Documentary History of the Discovery and Settlement of Latin America to the Early Seventeenth Century, vol. 2: The Caribbean. Pp. 58–62. New York: Times Books.

Parsons, Talcott
    1937   The Structure of Social Action: A Study in Social Theory with Special Reference to a Group of Recent European Writers. Glencoe, IL: Free Press.

Parsons, Talcott, and Edward A. Shills
    1959   Toward a General Theory of Action. Cambridge, MA: Harvard University Press.

Pérez, Berta
    1997   Pantera Negra: An Ancestral Figure of the Aripaeños, Maroon Descendants in Southern Venezuela. History and Anthropology 10(2–3):219–240.
    1998   Pantera Negra: A Messianic Figure of Historical Resistance and Cultural Survival among Maroon Descendants in Southern Venezuela. *In* Blackness in Latin America and the Caribbean: Social Dynamics and Cultural Transformations, vol. 1. Norman E. Whitten Jr. and Arlene Torres, eds. Pp. 223–243. Bloomington: Indiana University Press.

Pérez Chiriboga, Isabel
    2002   Espíritus de vida y muerte: Los Miskitu hondureños en época de guerra. Tegucigalpa: Editorial Guaymuras.

Pérez-Torres, Rafael
    2006   Mestizaje: Critical Uses of Race in Chicano Culture. Minneapolis: University of Minnesota Press.

Phelan, John Leddy
    1967   The Kingdom of Quito in the Seventeenth Century: Bureaucratic Politics in the Spanish Empire. Madison: University of Wisconsin Press.

Pierre, François
    1983   [1889] Viaje de exploración al Oriente Ecuatoriano 1887–1888. Quito: Abya-Yala.

Pitt-Rivers, Julian
    1967   Race, Color, and Class in Central America and the Andes. Daedelus 96(2):542–559.
    1973   Race in Latin America: The Concept of "Raza." Archives Europeans de Sociologie 14(1):3–31.

Ponce, Javier
    2000   Y la madrugada los sorprendió en el poder. Quito: Planeta.

Porras Garcés, Pedro
    1987   Investigaciones arqueológicas de las faldas de Sangay. Quito: Impresión Artes Gráficas.

Price, David H.
    2008   Anthropological Intelligence: The Deployment and Neglect of American Anthropology in the Second World War. Durham, NC: Duke University Press.

Price, Richard
    1983   First-Time: The Historical Vision of an Afro-American People. Baltimore: Johns Hopkins University Press. 2nd edition, Chicago: University of Chicago Press, 2002.
    2008   Travels with Tooy: History, Memory, and the African American Imagination. Chicago: University of Chicago Press.

Price, Richard, ed.
    1979   [1973] Maroon Societies: Rebel Slave Communities in the Americas. 2nd edition with a new afterword. Baltimore: Johns Hopkins University Press.

Price, Richard, and Sally Price
    1993   Collective Fictions: Performance in Saramaka Folktales. *In* Imagery and Creativity: Ethnoaesthetics and Art Worlds in the Americas. Dorothea S. Whitten and Norman E. Whitten Jr., eds. Pp. 235–288. Tucson: University of Arizona Press.

Price-Mars, Jean
    1928   Ainse parla l'oncle. Paris: Imprimerie de Compliègne.

Proaño García, José, and Paola Colleoni
    2008   Taromenane Warani Nani: Pueblos indígenas en aislamiento voluntario—Tagaeri-Taromenane, en la amazonía ecuatoriana. Quito: Abya-Yala.

Quiroga, Diego
    1994   Saints, Virgins, and the Devil: Witchcraft, Magic, and Healing in the Northern Coast of Ecuador. Ph.D. dissertation, Department of Anthropology, University of Illinois at Urbana-Champaign. Ann Arbor, MI: University Microfilms.
    2003   The Devil and Development in Esmeraldas: Cosmology as a System of Critical Thought. *In* Millennial Ecuador: Critical Essays on Cultural Transformations and Social Dynamics. Norman E. Whitten Jr., ed. Pp. 154–183. Iowa City: University of Iowa Press.

Rahier, Jean Muteba
    1998   Blackness, the "Racial"/Spatial Order, Migrations, and Miss Ecuador 1995–1996. American Anthropologist 100(2):421–430.
    2003   Racist Stereotypes and the Embodiment of Blackness: Some Narratives of Female Sexuality in Quito. *In* Millennial Ecuador: Critical Essays on Cultural Transformations and Social Dynamics. Norman E. Whitten Jr., ed. Pp. 296–324. Iowa City: University of Iowa Press.

Rahier, Jean Muteba, ed.
    1999   Representations of Blackness and the Performance of Identities. Westport, CT: Bergin and Garvey.

Reeve, Mary-Elizabeth
    1985   Identity as Process: The Meaning of "Runapura" for Quichua Speakers of the Curaray River, Eastern Ecuador. Ph.D. dissertation, Department of Anthropology, University of Illinois at Urbana-Champaign. Ann Arbor, MI: University Microfilms.
    1988a   Los Quichuas del Curaray: El proceso de formación de la identidad. Quito: Abya-Yala.
    1988b   Cauchu Uras: Lowland Quichua Histories of the Amazon Rubber Boom. *In* Rethinking History and Myth: Indigenous South American Perspectives on the Past. Jonathan D. Hill, ed. Pp. 19–34. Urbana: University of Illinois Press.
    1993–1994   Narratives of Catastrophe: The Zaparoan Experience in Amazonian Ecuador. Bulletin de la Société Suisse des Américanistes 57–58:17–24.
    1994   Regional Interaction in the Western Amazon: The Early Colonial Encounter and the Jesuit Years: 1538–1767. Ethnohistory 41(1):106–138.
    2008   Extended Family Ties and Ethnicity within a Regional Social System in Amazonian Ecuador. Paper presented at the Annual Meeting of the American Anthropological Association, San Francisco, November 23.

Reichel-Dolmatoff, Gerardo
    1960   Notas etnográficas sobre los indios del Chocó. Revista Colombiana de Antropología 11:75–158.
    1976   Cosmology as Ecological Analysis: A View from the Rain Forest. Man (Journal of the Royal Anthropological Institute) 11(3):307–318.

Renner, S. S.
    1993   A History of Botanical Exploration in Amazonian Ecuador, 1739–1988.

Smithsonian Contributions to Botany, 82. Washington, DC: Smithsonian Institution Press.

Requena y Herrera, Francisco
    1991   [1784] Descripción del gobierno de Maynas. *In* Historia de Maynas: Un paraiso perdido en el Amazonas. María del Carmen Martín Rubio, comp. Madrid: Ediciones Atlas.

Restall, Matthew, ed.
    2005   Beyond Black and Red: African-Native Relations in Colonial Latin America. Albuquerque: University of New Mexico Press.

Ribadeneira de Casares, Mayra
    1990   Tigua: Arte primitivista ecuatoriano. Quito: Centro de Arte Exedra.

Richardson, James B., III
    1994   People of the Andes. Montreal: St. Remy Press.

Ricoeur, Paul
    1974   The Conflict of Interpretation. Evanston, IL: Northwestern University Press.

Rivera Cusicanqui, Silvia
    1991   Aymara Past, Aymara Future. *In* The First Nations, 1492–1992. NACLA (North American Congress of Latin America) 25(3):18–23.

Rodman, Selden
    1982   Artists in Tune with Their World. New York: Simon and Schuster.

Rodríguez Álvarez, Ángel
    2008   Mitología Taína o Eyeri—Ramón Pané y la relación sobre las antigüedades de los indios: El primer tratado etnográfico hecho en América. San Juan: Editorial Nuevo Mundo.

Roitman, Karem
    2009   Race, Ethnicity and Power in Ecuador: The Manipulation of Mestizaje. Boulder, CO: FirstForumPress.

Rosaldo, Renato
    1995   Foreword to Hybrid Cultures: Strategies for Entering and Leaving Modernity, by Néstor García Canclini. Pp. xi–xvii. Minneapolis: University of Minnesota Press.

Rout, Leslie B., Jr.
    1976   The African Experience in Spanish America: 1502 to the Present Day. New York: Cambridge University Press.

Rowe, John
    1946   Inca Culture at the Time of the Spanish Conquest. *In* Handbook of South American Indians, vol. 2: The Andean Civilizations. Julian H. Steward, ed. Pp. 183–330. Smithsonian Institution, Bureau of American Ethnology, Bulletin 143. Washington, DC: Smithsonian Institution, Bureau of American Ethnology.

Rueda Novoa, Rocío
    2001a   Las comunidades negras. *In* Enciclopedia del Ecuador. Pp. 284–306. Barcelona: Océano Grupo Editorial.

2001b   Zambaje y autonomía: Historia de la gente negra de la provincia de Esmeraldas Siglos XVI–XVIII. Esmeraldas and Quito: Municipalidad de Esmeraldas and Abya-Yala.

Russell-Wood, A. J. R.
1995   Before Columbus: Portugal's African Prelude to the Middle Passage and Contribution to Discourse on Race and Slavery. *In* Race, Discourse, and the Origin of the Americas: A New World View. Vera Lawrence Hyatt and Rex Nettleford, eds. Pp. 134–168. Washington, DC: Smithsonian Institution Press.

Sacoto, Antonio
1967   The Indian in the Ecuadorian Novel. New York: Las Américas Publishing.

Sahlins, Marshall
1976   The State of the Art in Social/Cultural Anthropology: Search for an Object. *In* Perspectives on Anthropology 1976. Anthony F. C. Wallace, J. Lawrence Angel, Richard Fox, Sally McLendon, Rachel Sady, and Robert Sharer, eds. Pp. 13–30. Special Publication 10. Washington, DC: American Anthropological Association.
1981   Historical Metaphors and Mythical Realities: Structure in the Early History of the Sandwich Islands Kingdom. Ann Arbor: University of Michigan Press.
1994   Goodbye to Tristes Tropes: Ethnography in the Context of Modern World History. *In* Assessing Cultural Anthropology. Robert Borofsky, ed. Pp. 377–395. New York: McGraw Hill.
1999   What Is Anthropological Enlightenment? Some Lessons of the Twentieth Century. Annual Review in Anthropology 28:i–xxiii.
2000   Culture in Practice: Selected Essays. New York: Zone Books.

Saignes, Thierry
1999   The Colonial Condition in the Quechua-Aymara Heartland (1570–1780). *In* The Cambridge History of the Native Peoples of the Americas, vol. 3: South America, Part 2. Frank Salomon and Stuart B. Schwartz, eds. Pp. 59–137. Cambridge: Cambridge University Press.

Salomon, Frank
1981   Killing the Yumbo: A Ritual Drama of Northern Quito. *In* Cultural Transformations and Ethnicity in Modern Ecuador. Norman E. Whitten Jr., ed. Pp. 162–208. Urbana: University of Illinois Press.
1983   Shamanism and Politics in Late Colonial Ecuador. American Ethnologist 10(3):413–428.
1986   Native Lords of Quito in the Age of the Incas: The Political Economy of North Andean Chiefdoms. New York: Cambridge University Press.
2008   Ancestors, Grave Robbers, and the Possible Antecedents of Cañari "Incaism." *In* The Ecuador Reader: History, Culture, Politics. Carlos de la Torre and Steve Striffler, eds. Pp. 27–39. Durham, NC: Duke University Press.

Santos-Granero, Fernando
1993   Ethnohistoria de la alta amazonía, siglos XV–XVIII. Quito: Abya-Yala.

Sapir, J. David
    1977   The Anatomy of Metaphor. *In* The Social Use of Metaphor: Essays on the Anthropology of Rhetoric. J. David Sapir and J. Christopher Crocker, eds. Pp. 3–32. Philadelphia: University of Pennsylvania Press.

Savoia, Padre Rafael
    1988   El negro Alonso de Illescas y sus descendientes (entre 1553–1867). El negro en la historia de Ecuador y del sur de Colombia. Actas del Primer Congreso de Historia del Negro en el Ecuador y Sur de Colombia, pp. 29–60. Quito: Centro Cultural Afro-Ecuatoriano.

Sawyer, Suzana
    2004   Crude Chronicles: Indigenous Politics, Multinational Oil, and Neoliberalism in Ecuador. Durham, NC: Duke University Press.

Scheinman, Pamela
    1981   Olga Fisch, Collector. American Craft 41(1):14–15, 75.

Scheller, Ulf
    1972   El mundo de los Salasacas. Guayaquil, Ecuador: Fundación Antropología Ecuatoriana.

Schwartz, Stuart B., and Hal Langfur
    2005   Tapanhuns, Negros da Terra, and Curibocas: Common Cause and Confrontation between Blacks and Natives in Colonial Brazil. *In* Beyond Black and Red: African-Native Relations in Colonial Latin America. Matthew Restall, ed. Pp. 81–114. Albuquerque: University of New Mexico Press.

Schwartz, Stuart B., and Frank Salomon
    1999   New Peoples and New Kinds of People: Adaptation, Readjustment, and Ethnogenesis in South American Indigenous Societies (Colonial Era). *In* The Cambridge History of the Native Peoples of the Americas, vol. 3: South America, Part 2. Frank Salomon and Stuart B. Schwartz, eds. Pp. 443–501. Cambridge: Cambridge University Press.

Scott, James C.
    2005   Afterword to Moral Economies, State Spaces, and Categorical Violence. American Anthropologist 107(3):395–402.

Selmeski, Brian
    2000   Imágenes impresiantes. Video. Quito: Fulbright Commission.

Serrano, Fernando
    1993   The Transformation of the Indian People of the Ecuadorian Amazon into Political Actors and Its Effects on the State's Modernization Policies. Master's thesis, Department of Anthropology, University of Florida.

Sewell, William H., Jr.
    1999   Geertz, Cultural Systems, and History: From Synchrony to Transformation. *In* The Fate of "Culture": Geertz and Beyond. Sherry B. Ortner, ed. Pp. 35–55. Berkeley: University of California Press.

Shaw, Rosalind
    2002   Memories of the Slave Trade: Ritual and the Historical Imagination in Sierra Leone. Chicago: University of Chicago Press.

Silverblatt, Irene
  2004 Modern Inquisitions: Peru and the Colonial Origins of the Civilized World. Durham, NC: Duke University Press.
Soulodre–La France, Renée
  2005 Whites and Mulattos, Our Enemies: Race Relations and Popular Political Culture in Nueva Granada. *In* Beyond Black and Red: African-Native Relations in Colonial Latin America. Matthew Restall, ed. Pp. 137–158. Albuquerque: University of New Mexico Press.
Spencer, Mark (photographs by Bradley E. Clift)
  2003 The Sacrifice of Gañansol. The Hartford Courant, December 7, pp. 1–32 (special section).
Staden, Hans
  2008 [1557] Hans Staden's True History: An Account of Cannibal Captivity in Brazil. Neil L. Whitehead and Michael Harbsmeier, eds. and trans. Durham, NC: Duke University Press.
Steigenga, Timothy J., and Edward J. Cleary, eds.
  2007 Conversion of a Continent: Contemporary Religious Change in Latin America. New Brunswick: Rutgers University Press.
Stirling, Matthew W.
  1938 Historical and Ethnographical Material on the Jivaro Indians. Bureau of American Ethnology Bulletin 117. Washington, DC: Smithsonian Institution.
Stocking, George W., Jr.
  1968 Race, Culture, and Evolution: Essays in the History of Anthropology. New York: Free Press.
  1992 The Ethnographer's Magic and Other Essays in the History of Anthropology. Madison: University of Wisconsin Press.
Stoller, Paul
  2009 The Power of the Between: An Anthropological Odyssey. Chicago: University of Chicago Press.
Sturtevant, William
  1971 Creek into Seminole: North American Indians. *In* Historical Perspective. Eleanor Leacock and Nancie Lurie, eds. Pp. 92–128. New York: Random House.
Stutzman, Ronald
  1981 Mestizaje: An All-Inclusive Ideology of Exclusion. *In* Cultural Transformations and Ethnicity in Modern Ecuador. Norman E. Whitten Jr., ed. Pp. 45–94. Urbana: University of Illinois Press.
Sullivan, Lawrence
  1988 Icanchu's Drum: An Orientation to Meaning in South American Religions. New York: Macmillan.
Taish Mayaprua, Alejandro
  2004 Nantu, Aujujai: Nantu nuya Ajujai najanarmauri/Nantu y Auju: de como la luna y el pájaro potoo fueron creador/Nantu and Auju: How the Moon

and the Potoo Bird Came to Be. Monterey, CA: Arutam Press, FINAE (Federación Interprovincial de Nacionalidades Achuar del Ecuador).

Taussig, Michael
- 1978 Destrucción y resistencia campesina: El caso del Litoral Pacífico. Bogotá: Punta de Lanza.
- 1980a Folk Healing and the Structure of Conquest in Southwest Colombia. Journal of Latin American Lore 6(2):217–78.
- 1980b The Devil and Commodity Fetishism in South America. Chapel Hill: University of North Carolina Press.
- 1987 Shamanism, Colonialism, and the Wild Man: A Study in Terror and Healing. Chicago: University of Chicago Press.
- 1993 Mimesis and Alterity: A Particular History of the Senses. New York: Routledge.
- 1997 The Magic of the State. New York: Routledge.
- 2004 My Cocaine Museum. Chicago: University of Chicago Press.

Taylor, Anne Christine
- 1999 The Western Margins of Amazonia from the Early Sixteenth to the Early Nineteenth Century. *In* The Cambridge History of the Native Peoples of the Americas, vol. 3: South America, Part 2. Frank Salomon and Stuart B. Schwartz, eds. Pp. 188–256. Cambridge: Cambridge University Press.

Thornton, John
- 1995 Perspectives on African Christianity. *In* Race, Discourse, and the Origin of the Americas: A New World View. Vera Lawrence Hyatt and Rex Nettleford, eds. Pp. 169–198. Washington, DC: Smithsonian Institution Press.
- 1998a [1992] Africa and Africans in the Making of the Atlantic World, 1400–1800. New York: Cambridge University Press.
- 1998b The Kongolese Saint Anthony: Dona Beatriz Kimpa Vita and the Antonian Movement, 1684–1706. New York: Cambridge University Press.

Tibanlombo Salazar, Juan
- 2008 FARC? en el Ecuador? Quito: Hoy, Edimprés S.A.

Toaquiza, Alfonso
- 2002 Kuntur Kuyashkamanta/El cóndor enamorado/The Condor Who Fell in Love. Quito: Imprenta Mariscal.

Tomoeda, Hiroyasu, and Luis Millones, eds.
- 1992 500 años de mestizaje en los Andes. Lima: Biblioteca Peruana de Psicoanális.

Torres, Arlene
- 1998 La gran familia Puertorriqueña "Ej prieta de beldá" (The Great Puerto Rican Family Is Really Really Black). *In* Blackness in Latin America and the Caribbean: Social Dynamics and Cultural Transformations, vol. 2. Arlene Torres and Norman E. Whitten Jr., eds. Pp. 285–306. Bloomington: Indiana University Press.

Torres, Arlene, and Norman E. Whitten Jr., eds.
- 1998 Blackness in Latin America and the Caribbean: Social Dynamics and Cultural Transformations, vol. 2. Bloomington: Indiana University Press.

Torres-Saillant, Silvio
 1998 The Tribulations of Blackness: Stages in Dominican Racial Identity. Latin American Perspectives 25(3):126–146.

Trouillot, Michel-Rolph
 1989 Haiti, State against Nation: The Origins and Legacy of Duvalierism. New York: Monthly Review Press.
 1995 Silencing the Past: Power and the Production of History. Boston: Beacon Press.
 2003 Global Transformations: Anthropology and the Modern World. New York: Palgrave Macmillan.

Turner, Terence
 1988 Commentary: Ethno-Ethnohistory: Myth and History in Native South American Representations of Contact with Western Society. *In* Rethinking History and Myth: Indigenous South American Perspectives on the Past. Jonathan D. Hill, ed. Pp. 235–281. Urbana: University of Illinois Press.

Turner, Victor
 1973 Symbols in African Ritual. Science 179:1100–1105.
 1974 Dramas, Fields, and Metaphors: Symbolic Action in Human Society. Ithaca, NY: Cornell University Press.
 1985 On the Edge of the Bush: Anthropology as Experience. Tucson: University of Arizona Press.

Umajinga, Baltazar
 1995 Zumbahua. *In* Identidades indias en el Ecuador contemporaneo. José Almeida Vinueza, ed. Pp. 247–271. Cayambe, Ecuador: Ediciones Abya-Yala.

Urban, Greg
 1991 A Discourse-Centered Approach to Culture: Native South American Myths and Rituals. Austin: University of Texas Press.

Uzendoski, Michael
 2004 The Horizontal Archipelago: The Quijos Upper Napo Regional System. Ethnohistory 51(2):318–357.
 2005 The Napo Runa of Amazonian Ecuador. Urbana: University of Illinois Press.

Vallejo, Raúl
 2004 Neocolonizados. El Comercio, June 19, p. A4.

Van Gennep, Arnold
 1960 [1909] The Rites of Passage. London: Routledge.

Vargas Guatatuca, Carlos Antonio
 2000 Nos faltó estrategia. *In* La cuatra vía al poder: El 21 de enero desde una perspectiva latinoamericana. Heinz Dieterich, comp. Pp. 42–48. Quito: Abya-Yala.

Varner, John Grier, and Jeanette Johnson Varner
 1983 Dogs of the Conquest. Norman: University of Oklahoma Press.

Vasco, Luis Guillermo
 1985 Jaibanás: Los verdaderos hombres. Bogotá: Banco Popular.

Vasconcelos, José
    1925   La raza cósmica—Misión de la raza iberoamericana—Notas de viaje a América del Sur. Barcelona: Agencia Mundial de Librería. Reprinted in José Vasconcelos: Edición Justina Sarabia. Madrid: Ediciones Cultura Hispánica, 1989.
    1937   Bolivarismo y Monroismo: Temas iberoamericanos. Santiago de Chile: Ediciones Ercilla.
    1989   Antología de pensamiento político, social y económico de América Latina. Madrid: Ediciones de Cultura Hispánica.
    1997   [1979] The Cosmic Race/La raza cósmica: A Bilingual Edition. Translated, with an introduction by Didier T. Jaen and an afterword by Joseba Gabilondo. Baltimore: Johns Hopkins University Press.

Veeser, Harold, ed.
    1989   The New Historicism. New York: Routledge.

Velásquez Runk, Julie
    2005   And the Creator Began to Carve Us Cocobolo: Culture, History, Forest Ecology and Conservation among Wounaan in Eastern Panama. Ph.D. dissertation, Department of Forestry and Environmental Studies and Anthropology, Yale University.

Vickers, William T.
    2003   The Modern Political Transformation of the Secoya. *In* Millennial Ecuador: Critical Essays on Cultural Transformations and Social Dynamics. Norman E. Whitten Jr., ed. Pp. 46–74. Iowa City: University of Iowa Press.

Viveiros de Castro, Eduardo
    1992   From the Enemy's Point of View: Humanity and Divinity in an Amazonian Society. Chicago: University of Chicago Press.

Vizcarrondo, Fortunato
    1942   ¿Y tu agüela, adonde ejtá? Poemas de Fortunato Vizcarrondo. Electronic document, http://poesiabreve.com/fortunatovizcarrondo.html, accessed April 9, 2007.

Wade, Peter
    1993   Blackness and Race Mixture: The Dynamics of Racial Identity in Colombia. Baltimore: Johns Hopkins University Press.
    1995   The Cultural Politics of Blackness in Colombia. American Ethnologist 22(2):342–358.
    1997   Race and Ethnicity in Latin America. London: Pluto Press.

Washburn, Dorothy K., ed.
    1980   Hopi Kachina: Spirit of Life. The California Academy of Sciences in Conjunction with the Exhibition "Hopi Kachina: Spirit of Life." Seattle: University of Washington Press.

Weber, Max
    1947   The Theory of Social and Economic Organization. A. M. Henderson and Talcott Parsons, trans. Glencoe, IL: Free Press; London: Collier Macmillan.

Weismantel, Mary J.
- 1985 Descriptive Notes: Tigua Paintings and Drums. Unpublished MS commissioned by the Sacha Runa Research Foundation, Urbana, Illinois.
- 1998 [1988] Food, Gender, and Poverty in the Ecuadorian Andes. Reprint. Prospect Heights, IL: Waveland Press.
- 2001 Cholas and Pishtacos: Stories of Race and Sex in the Andes. Chicago: University of Chicago Press.
- 2003 Mothers of the *Patria:* La Chola Cuencana and La Mama Negra. *In* Millennial Ecuador: Critical Essays on Cultural Transformations and Social Dynamics. Norman E. Whitten Jr., ed. Pp. 325–354. Iowa City: University of Iowa Press.

West, Robert Cooper
- 1952 Colonial Placer Mining in Colombia. Baton Rouge: Louisiana State University Press.
- 1957 The Pacific Lowlands of Colombia: A Negroid Area of the American Tropics. Baton Rouge: Louisiana State University Press.

Wey Gómez, Nicolás
- 2008 The Tropics of Empire: Why Columbus Sailed South to the Indies. Cambridge, MA: MIT Press.

Whitehead, Neil L.
- 1988 Lords of the Tiger Spirit: A History of the Caribs in Colonial Venezuela and Guyana, 1498–1820. Dordrecht-Holland: Foris Publications.
- 2002 Arawak Linguistic and Cultural Identity through Time: Contact, Colonialism, and Creolization. *In* Comparative Arawakan Histories: Rethinking Language Family and Culture Area in Amazonia. Jonathan D. Hill and Fernando Santos-Granero, eds. Pp. 51–73. Urbana: University of Illinois Press.
- 2003 Introduction. *In* Histories and Historicities in Amazonia. Neil L. Whitehead, ed. Pp. vii–xx. Lincoln: University of Nebraska Press.
- 2008 Introduction. *In* Hans Staden's True History: An Account of Cannibal Captivity in Brazil, by Hans Staden. Neil L. Whitehead and Michael Harbsmeier, eds. and trans. Pp. xv–civ. Durham, NC: Duke University Press.

Whitehead, Neil L., and Robin Wright, eds.
- 2004 In Darkness and Secrecy: The Anthropology of Assault Sorcery and Witchcraft in Amazonia. Durham, NC: Duke University Press.

Whitten, Dorothea Scott
- 2003 Connections: Creative Expressions of Canelos Quichua Women. *In* Crafting Gender. Eli Bartra, ed. Pp. 73–97. Durham, NC: Duke University Press.

Whitten, Dorothea Scott, and Norman E. Whitten Jr.
- 1988 From Myth to Creation: Art from Amazonian Ecuador. Urbana: University of Illinois Press.
- 1993 Introduction. *In* Imagery and Creativity: Ethnoaesthetics and Art Worlds in the Americas. Dorothea S. Whitten and Norman E. Whitten Jr., eds. Pp. 3–44. Tucson: University of Arizona Press.

1994 The Canelos Quichua. *In* Amazonian Worlds. Catalina Sosa and Noemi Paymal, eds. Pp. 100–110. Quito: Mariscal.

Whitten, Norman E., Jr.
1965 Class, Kinship, and Power in an Ecuadorian Town: The Negroes of San Lorenzo. Stanford, CA: Stanford University Press.
1974 Black Frontiersmen: Afro-Hispanic Culture of Ecuador and Colombia. Prospect Heights, IL: Waveland Press.
1976a Sacha Runa: Ethnicity and Adaptation of Ecuadorian Jungle Quichua. Urbana: University of Illinois Press.
1976b Ecuadorian Ethnocide and Indigenous Ethnogenesis: Amazonian Resurgence amidst Andean Colonization. Document No. 23. Copenhagen: International Work Group for Indigenous Affairs (IWGIA).
1978 Ecological Imagery and Cultural Adaptability: The Canelos Quichua of Eastern Ecuador. American Anthropologist 80(4):836–859.
1981 Afterword. *In* Cultural Transformations and Ethnicity in Modern Ecuador. Norman E. Whitten Jr., ed. Pp. 776–797. Urbana: University of Illinois Press.
1985 Sicuanga Runa: The Other Side of Development in Amazonian Ecuador. Urbana: University of Illinois Press.
1988 Historical and Mythic Evocations of Chthonic Power in South America. *In* Rethinking History and Myth: Indigenous South American Perspectives on the Past. Jonathan D. Hill, ed. Pp. 282–306. Urbana: University of Illinois Press.
1996a Ethnogenesis. *In* The Encyclopedia of Cultural Anthropology, vol. 2. Pp. 407–411. New York: Henry Holt and the Human Relations Area Files.
1996b The Ecuadorian Levantamiento Indígena of 1990 and the Epitomizing Symbol of 1992: Reflections on Nationalism, Ethnic-Bloc Formation, and Racialist Ideologies. *In* History, Power, and Identity: Ethnogenesis in the Americas, 1492–1992. Jonathan D. Hill, ed. Pp. 191–217. Iowa City: University of Iowa Press.
1999 Los paradigmas mentales de la conquista y el nacionalismo: La formación de los conceptos de las "razas" y las transformaciones del racismo. *In* Ecuador racista: Imágenes e identidades. Emma Cervone and Fredy Rivera, eds. Pp. 45–73. Quito: FLACSO.
2003a Introduction. *In* Millennial Ecuador: Critical Essays on Cultural Transformations and Social Dynamics. Norman E. Whitten Jr., ed. Pp. 1–45. Iowa City: University of Iowa Press.
2003b Epilogue. *In* Millennial Ecuador: Critical Essays on Cultural Transformations and Social Dynamics. Norman E. Whitten Jr., ed. Pp. 355–387. Iowa City: University of Iowa Press.
2004 *Review Article of* The Root of Roots, or How Afro-American Anthropology Got Its Start, by Richard Price and Sally Price. New West Indian Guide 78(3 and 4):308–310.
2005 Emerald Freedom: "With Pride in the Face of the Sun." Tipití: Journal of

the Society for the Anthropology of Lowland South America (SALSA) 3(1):1–28.

Whitten, Norman E., Jr., ed.
  1981 Cultural Transformations and Ethnicity in Modern Ecuador. Urbana: University of Illinois Press.
  2003 Millennial Ecuador: Critical Essays on Cultural Transformations and Social Dynamics. Iowa City: University of Iowa Press.

Whitten, Norman E., Jr., and Rachel Corr
  2001 Contesting the Images of Oppression: Indigenous Views of Blackness in the Americas. *In* The Social Origins of Race, Part 1. NACLA (North American Congress of Latin America) 34(6):24–28, 45–46.

Whitten, Norman E., Jr., and Nina S. de Friedemann
  1974 La cultura negra del litoral ecuatoriano y colombiano: Un model de adaptación étnica. Revista Colombiana de Antropología (Bogotá) 17:75–115.

Whitten, Norman E., Jr., and Diego Quiroga
  1998 "To Rescue National Dignity": Blackness as a Quality of Nationalist Creativity in Ecuador. *In* Blackness in Latin America and the Caribbean: Social Dynamics and Cultural Transformations, vol. 1. Norman E. Whitten Jr. and Arlene Torres, eds. Pp. 75–99. Bloomington: Indiana University Press.

Whitten, Norman E., Jr., and Arlene Torres
  1992 Blackness in the Americas. *In* The Black Americas: 1492–1992. Report on the Americas, NACLA (North American Congress of Latin America) 25(4):18–25.
  1998 To Forge the Future in the Fires of the Past. *In* Blackness in Latin America and the Caribbean: Social Dynamics and Cultural Transformations, vol. 1. Norman E. Whitten Jr. and Arlene Torres, eds. Pp. 3–33. Bloomington: Indiana University Press.

Whitten, Norman E., Jr., and Arlene Torres, eds.
  1998 Blackness in Latin America and the Caribbean: Social Dynamics and Cultural Transformations, vol. 1. Bloomington: Indiana University Press.

Whitten, Norman E., Jr., and Dorothea Scott Whitten
  2008 Puyo Runa: Imagery and Power in Modern Amazonia. Urbana: University of Illinois Press.

Whitten, Norman E., Jr., Dorothea S. Whitten, and Alfonso Chango
  1997 Return of the Yumbo: The Indigenous Caminata from Amazonia to Andean Quito. American Ethnologist 24(2):355–391.

Whitten, Norman E., Jr., Dorothea S. Whitten, and Diego Quiroga
  2001 Ecuador: Countries and Their Cultures. New York: Macmillan Reference USA.

Wibbelsman, Michelle
  2004 Rimarishpa Kaunsanchik: Dialogical Encounters, Festive Ritual Practice and the Making of the Otavalan Moral and Mythic Community. Ph.D. thesis, Department of Anthropology, University of Illinois at Urbana-Champaign. Ann Arbor, MI: University Microfilms.

- 2005 Otavaleños at the Crossroads: Physical and Metaphysical Coordinates of an Indigenous World. Journal of Latin American Anthropology 10(1):151–185.
- 2009 Ritual Encounters: Otavalan Modern and Mythic Community. Urbana: University of Illinois Press.

Wilcken, Patrick
- 2008 The Century of Claude Lévi-Strauss. The Times Literary Supplement. Timesonline. http://entertainment.timesonline.co.uk/tol/artsandentertainment/thetls/article5035934.ece, accessed October 29, 2008.

Williams, Brackette
- 1993 Stains on My Name and War in My Veins: Guyana and the Politics of Cultural Struggle. Durham, NC: Duke University Press.

Williams, Jerry M., and Robert D. Lewis, eds.
- 1993 Early Images of the Americas: Transfer and Invention. Tucson: University of Arizona Press.

Willis, William S., Jr.
- 1966 Divide and Rule: Red, White, and Black in the Southeast. *In* Red, White, and Black: Symposium on Indians in the Old South. Charles M. Hudson, ed. Pp. 99–115. Athens: University of Georgia Press (for the Southern Anthropological Society, Proceedings No. 5).

Wolf, Eric R.
- 1982 Europe and the People without History. Berkeley: University of California Press.
- 1999 Envisioning Power: Ideologies of Dominance and Crisis. Berkeley: University of California Press.

Worsley, Peter
- 1957 The Trumpet Shall Sound: A Study of "Cargo" Cults in Melanesia. London: Macgibbon and Kee.
- 1984 The Three Worlds: Culture and World Development. Chicago: University of Chicago Press.

Wright, Barton
- 1977 Hopi Kachinas: The Complete Guide to Collecting Kachina Dolls. Flagstaff, AZ: Northland Press.

Wright, Winthrop R.
- 1990 Café con Leche: Race, Class, and National Image in Venezuela. Austin: University of Texas Press.

Wynter, Sylvia
- 1995 1492: A New World View. *In* Race, Discourse, and the Origin of the Americas: A New World View. Vera Lawrence Hyatt and Rex Nettleford, eds. Pp. 5–57. Washington, DC: Smithsonian Institution Press.

Zuluaga R., Francisco U.
- 1988 Cimarronismo en el sur-occidente del antiguo virreinato de Santa Fe de Bogotá. *In* El negro en la historia de Ecuador y del sur de Colombia. P. Rafael Savoia, ed. Pp. 227–261. Actas del Primer Congreso de Historia del Negro en el Ecuador y Sur de Colombia. Quito: Centro Cultural Afro-Ecuatoriano.

Index

500 años de resistencia, 5, 34, 98, 111, 151
1492–1992, symbol of, 102, 103, 111, 113, 127

Achuar, 165, 169, 177, 178, 182; and claims of territorial rights, 100, 134–135; and interculturality, 170; language of, 168; and March for Land and Life, 171, 173. *See also* Jivaroans
African Americans, 27, 38. *See also* black people
African-descended people: ignored in Ecuador, 23, 32; intermixed with indigenous peoples, 29–30, 35–36, 39, 40
African-Portuguese mixing, 27–28
Africans, self-liberated, 14–15, 29
Afro-Americans, 45–47, 60–61, 63. *See also* black people
Afro-Ecuadorians, 16; and black pride, 41; and illegal logging, 135–136; and rejection of *mestizaje* ideology, 24; and view of 1492, 1
Afro-Hispanic peoples, 11, 15–16, 37, 40, 51, 172
agency, culture and, 102–105; indigenous, 94, 97, 108, 192
ALBA (Bolivarian Alliance for the Americas), 139, 140, 197
Alfaro Delgado, Eloy, 6, 137; black soldiers of, 55, 56–57; and mythic time of origin of blacks, 58; and times of destruction, 169
alternative modernity, 12, 37, 165, 181, 184; definition of, 38, 192
Altschuler, Milton, 54, 55
alzados/alzamiento, 5, 76, 98, 176–177, 207–208n1
Amazonas, 6–7, 51; Western, 168, 170, 183, 197
Amazonian Ecuador, 6–7, 9, 53, 58, 77, 85, 123, 126, 138, 166, 168, 198; and academic structuralism, 179, 182, 183; and Acuerdo de Sarayacu, 97, 100; and Andean relations, 129, 163, 165, 168, 176, 178; and emergent cultures, 38; and imagery of anaconda, 91, 172; and imagery of *mana tuparina ñambi*, 117, 133, 136; and images of black people, 55, 56, 58–59; and interculturality, 127; and language, 169–170; and March for Land and Life, 79, 93, 135, 148–149, 172, 176; and millenniality, 85; and national politics, 101, 177, 196; and natural resources exploitation, 118, 134, 136, 197; origin myth of, 166–167; and Puyo Runa, 193–194; and Spanish conquest/colonization, 11, 12–14, 177. *See also* Canelos Quichua
Ambato: and colonial trade route, 14; in indigenous movements, 77, 96, 97; and migration, 130; and national conference of shamans, 160
anaconda, 91; howler monkey (sounding), 116, 133; image of and March for Land and Life, 172; and kinship festival, 175; metaphor of, 181; and millennial symbolism, 92
Andean Ecuador, 163, 165, 168, 178; and emergent cultures, 38; and ethnogenesis, 19; hegemony of, 15, 16; and images of black people, 53–58, 59; in indigenous art, 145, 146, 147, 148, 154, 156, 158, 159; and interculturality, 20–21, 127; and language, 169–170; and March for Land and Life, 93, 171–172, 175; and national politics, 86, 122–123, 129, 196; and racism, 31–32, 68; and Yumbada, 79, 91, 176. *See also* Otavalo; Tigua

Anderson, Benedict, 81–82
Andoa, 165, 169, 170, 178, 182
anthropological theory, 2, 10, 20, 183. *See also* theory construction
anthropology, 5; and deconstruction of paradigm, 188; and historical moral sanctions, 46, 47; importance of, 202; and study of race, 60; weaponized, 203n1
Arco, 134, 135
arenas, social-political, 114, 133, 147; and formation of paradigms, 88, 99–102, 176, 193, 206n1, 207n1, 207n4
art, indigenous, 141–161
Asociación de Negros del Ecuador, La, 73
AUC (Autodefensas Unidas de Colombia), 123, 124–125
autodeterminación, 111; *étnica*, 106; *indígena*, 98, 99, 100; and nation-states, 106, 108
autogestión, 99, 100, 106, 108
Ayllu Jista (kinship festival), 172, 175–176

beginning times-places, 8; and Canelos Quichua cosmology, 166, 167; and creation of pottery, 173, 174, 175; and origin of blacks, 58; transformations in, 92
Bhabha, Homi, 201–202
blackness (*lo negro*), 11, 26, 72; and black pride, 41; concepts subsumed in study of, 48; as epitomizing symbol, 112; Guaman Poma's view of, 49; imagery of, 36; indigenous views of, 60, 61, 63; and racialization, 122; representation of in festivals, 47, 49, 57, 59; and shamanic blackness, 54; and slavery, 36; and the Watunna myth, 50, 54. *See also* black people; *négritud*; *negros*
black people: Andean Ecuadorian images of, 57–58; and assassination of Hurtado, 85–86; and *cimarronaje*, 52; and *cultura*, 103; and *la cultura negra*, 104–105; and interaction with indigenous people, 51, 56–57, 204–205n3; and protector/soldier image, 54, 55; Quito Runa imagery of, 53–55. *See also* blackness; *négritud*; *negros*
blancos, 23, 32, 62, 95; and elites, 24, 27, 70, 119, 200; indians self-identifying as, 69, 84; and tripartite racial system, 29, 36, 53, 59, 63, 95, 111
blanqueamiento, 80; and cosmic race, 31; and economic success, 70; and family, 84; and hegemony, 107–108; in Otavalo, 69; and perspective on social ladder, 32;
and socioculture structure, 95. *See also* whitening
Boas, Franz, 16, 194
Bolívar, Simón, 30–31, 33–34
Bolivarian revolutions, 30–31, 32–34
Bolivia, 33, 34, 36, 56, 95, 132, 169, 197
Borja Cevallos, Rodrigo, 121, 128, 129; and "500 years of oppression," 5; elitist rhetoric of, 101; and first Levantamiento Indígena, 96, 97, 100, 112
braided traditions, 60, 62, 183
Braudel, Fernand, 10, 179
Brazil, 17, 18, 19, 35, 125, 144, 170, 197
Bucaram Ortiz, Abdalá: and class politics, 85–86; and CODENPE, 78; and dollarization, 131; and multiculturalism, 119; ouster of, 81, 127
Bunzl, Matti, 19, 201
Bush, George W., 119

Calderón Cevallos, Alfonso, 100–101, 102
Canela, La, 13, 14, 168
Canelos, 12–14, 16, 168, 173, 177–178
Canelos Quichua, 93, 168–169, 170–171, 173; and black spirit power, 58–59; and conjuncture, 179–180; cosmology of, 166–167; and ethnogenesis, 182, 183; homelands of, 183; in military, 172–173
cannibalism, 18, 19, 39
capitalism: and blackness, 59; and emergent culture, 39; and indigenization of modernity, 172; and meaning of term *indios*, 178; and political stance of indigenous people, 12; and race, 46, 199; and settlement patterns, 58; as threat, 165
Caporales (festival), 55
Carnaval: in Bolivia, 56; Salasacan, 49, 55, 57
castas, 11, 15, 27–30, 71
Castro, Raúl, 139
caudillismo, 121, 128, 129, 137, 169, 196, 197
ceramics. *See* pottery
Chachi people, 54, 55, 58
Chango, Alfonso, 43, 92, 164
Chávez, Hugo, 33, 34, 139, 140, 197
Chevron-Texaco, 120, 134, 153
Chile, 139, 197
Chota-Mira Valley, 72
Christianity: and cannibalism, 18, 19; and conversion of Africans, 26, 46; and history of Canelos, 177–178; introduction of in Africa and Americas, 11–12, 13–14; and kinship festival, 175

chronotopes, 8–9, 12, 18, 184, 192–193, 194–195
Chuquín Amaguaña, Carmen, 43
cimarronaje, 15, 39, 52. *See also* liberation; self-liberation
cimarrones: conceptualization of, 58; and history of term, 51–52; and *la madre de agua*, 53; and *la pantera negra*, 51
clase dirigente, 73, 81, 128; and corruption, 87; and political ferment, 128, 130
clase política, 81, 86, 128, 129
class, 70–72, 79; and *levantamientos*, 76–77, 78; and *el mestizaje*, 79, 80; and race, 85, 95, 198–199, 200, 202; and social action, 81; as structure of domination, 110–111
Coast, the, 11, 38, 94, 134, 196; and 1990 Levantamiento Indígena, 96–97, 127; and interculturality, 127; and Manta military base, 123, 126; and racialization, 198
Coast Guard, U.S., 126, 131, 132, 133
CODENPE (Consejo de Desarrollo de los Pueblos y Nacionalidades de Ecuador), 78
COICE (Coordinadora de Movimientos Sociales), 126, 128
Colloredo-Mansfeld, Rudi, 68, 177
Colombia: drugs from, 124–126; and Ecuadorian border, 118, 123–124, 137; and illegal logging, 136; and military conflict, 85; and Operation Phoenix, 138–139
colonial history, 5–6, 20, 93–94, 96, 108, 110, 147, 199–200; and constructions of *lo negro* and *lo indio*, 45–64; and ethnogenesis, 177–178, 182; and ethnography of Guaman Poma, 18, 20–21; and mentality, 25–41; and postcolonial criticism, 202. *See also* European conquest; Spanish conquest and colonialism
colonialism, 20, 52, 62
Columbus, Christopher, 103, 104; and the Caribs, 39; and ethnography of indians, 17; and profitability, 27, 39, 45; and the term *indio*, 26–27, 46, 178, 199, 200
Columbus Day, 27, 30, 33, 34
Comaroff, Jean, 12, 19, 113, 193, 201
Comaroff, John, 12, 19, 193, 201
CONAIE (Confederación de Nacionalidades Indígenas del Ecuador), 96–97, 126, 128, 129; Amazonian leaders of, 177; and exclusion of indigenous people, 140; and the *golpe del 21*, 77, 128
CONFENAIE (Confederación de Nacionalidades Indígenas de la Amazonía Ecuatoriana), 100, 101, 126, 127, 140
conflict, articulations of, 101–102
Congreso de la Cultura Negra de las Américas, 104, 112
conjuncture: historical, 36, 198; indigenous-global, 165; and millennial Ecuador, 118, 133
conjuncture, structures of, 179–181, 182; and 1492, 12; and culture, 113; development of theory of, 190; and mythopoetics, 10; and race, 114
constitution, Ecuadorian, 6, 79; and Correa, 137–138, 139; and *interculturalidad*, 170–171; and racial fixity/fluidity, 36
contrapower, 21, 192. *See also* powers of resistance
Corpus Christi, 53, 79, 176
Correa Delgado, Rafael Vicente, 137; and 2009 indigenous uprising, 196; and Ciudad Alfaro, 6; and *ecuatorianidad*, 199, 200; and indigenous movement, 139–140; and narcissism, 197–198; and Operation Phoenix, 138–139; successes of, 196, 198
cosmogony, 7, 12, 93, 166, 173
cosmography, 18, 166, 194, 195
cosmology, Canelos Quichua, 166–167; and myth of creation of pottery, 173–174, 175; preconquest, 7–9
cosmovision, 2, 7, 20, 168, 173
Cotopaxi Province, 57, 72, 141, 143, 149, 151
counterhegemony, 68–70, 72–74, 79
cultural ecology, 179
culture, 191; and a-culturation, 182, 184; and agency, 102–105; anthropological study of, 5–6; of Canelos Quichua, 170–171; and *la cultura*, 103; as dynamic, 63; emergent, 37, 38; and ethnography, 16, 20, 201; and exaggeration, 106; and "improving the race," 72–73; and ineffability, 194; and interethnicity, 48, 61; and intimacy, 82; and paradigms, 102, 188; and race, 82, 199; racial, 105–109; and ritual and myth, 180; significative systems of, 47–48; and the term *el mestizaje*, 28; and the term *mestizo*, 204n3; and topography, 165–166, 167–168
Curaray, 175
cutu amarun, 116, 133, 137

Dagua, Delicia, 164
Dagua, Estela, 116, 164

democracy, in Ecuador, 117–118, 121, 123, 129, 137, 148
destruction, 152–154; times of, 167, 169, 171, 178
día de la raza, 27, 30, 33, 34
diaspora: African, 61, 63; Ecuadorian, 130–131
dignity, 73, 76
directionality, 167–168; in festivals, 175; and Levantamiento Indígena of 1990, 172; in myth, 174
discourse, racialist, 98–102, 105
diversity, 2, 30, 46, 59, 73, 78, 88, 121, 182; cultural, 27, 40, 61–62; and nationalities, 38, 127
dollarization, 131–132
domination: inversions of, 67, 121; Spanish and state, 11, 15, 20–21, 41, 54, 56, 63, 94, 98, 101–103, 105, 197; structures of, 109–112
Dorado, El, 13, 14, 168
drooling, 69, 74

economy, 80–81, 82, 95, 132. *See also* capitalism; political economy
Ecuador: geography of, 67; history of, 6–7, 10–16; and indigenous politics, 126–129, 140, 146–147; and modern political situation, 195–198; and *plurinacionalidad*, 206n1; political unrest in, 85–86; sociocultural structure of, 94–95. *See also* millennial Ecuador
ECUARUNARI (Ecuador Runacunapac Riccharimui), 126, 127, 128, 129
ecuatorianidad, 2, 67, 81, 199, 200; and diversity, 73, 78; and interculturality, 198; and *levantamiento* movements, 77; and *el mestizaje*, 70; and *multiculturalidad*, 78
El Dorado, Land of, 13, 14, 168
El Ejido Park: and artists, 141–142, 153; and March for Land and Life, 79, 172–174, 176
El Oriente, 56, 58, 94, 96, 116, 124, 127, 128, 135; in indigenous art, 153, 157, 158; and March for Land and Life, 152, 176; and petroleum resources, 56, 134; and shamanism, 159. *See also* Upper Amazonia
elite, Ecuadorian, 70–72, 103, 111. *See also blancos*
ELN (Ejército de Liberación Nacional), 124, 125
Emberá, 51–53, 54
environment, 85; destruction of, 152–154; and petroleum exploitation, 134–135

epistemic distortion, 77, 81, 176–177, 179–181, 182–184
Eschaton, 8–9; and Canelos Quichua festivals, 171, 176; and discourse of resistance, 113; and religious conversion, 12; Spanish invasion as, 11
Esmeraldas: and discourse of Esmeraldans, 72–73; history of, 14–16, 40; and illegal logging, 135–136; and localization of blackness, 55, 72
"Esmeraldas Ambassadors" (Sánchez Gallque painting, 1599), 15
Esmeraldas Province, 15, 38, 49, 54, 85, 98, 123, 156
esmeraldeños, 40, 49, 59, 61
ethnic bloc, 93–94, 99–100, 105–111, 126–127
ethnogenesis, 12, 37, 93–94; and Canelos Quichua, 169–170; duality of, 182–183; and ethnic-bloc formation, 106–107, 111; and Guaman Poma's work in the Andes, 19; and history of Canelos, 177–178; and indigenization of modernity, 171–173; and respect for diversity, 88; and structures of domination, 111
ethnography: and deconstruction of paradigm, 188; goals of, 194; and historical literature, 20, 21; and interpretation, 190–191; and landscape, 10; tasks of, 16–21, 193, 203n1; and theory construction, 1–5, 9–10, 187–202; and Whittens' work on race, 23–24
Euro-Africans, 14–15
European conquest, 11–12, 37, 51; and 1992 anniversary, 1, 98, 103; Columbus and, 46; and concept of *mestizaje*, 28; and fierce vs. tame indians, 39; and racial hybridity, 30; and racism, 95
evil: in cosmology and myth, 7–8, 50–51, 54, 61, 116; and hegemony, 113; and *mamelucos*, 35; and shamanic healing, 155–158

family, 82, 86; black, 49; Ecuadorian, 83–85, 122, 135, 144, 155, 157, 162
FARC (Revolutionary Armed Forces of Colombia), 85, 123–124, 125; and Operation Phoenix, 138–139
Febres Cordero, León, 119, 121, 129–130; and indigenous politics, 128
festivals: of Canelos Quichua, 171, 175–176; and first Levantamiento Indígena, 96; and March for Land and Life, 180
field, concept of, 82, 99, 100–102, 105, 190–195, 200

Freud, Sigmund, 197
Friedemann, Nina, 51, 107

Garífuna (Black Carib), 35, 38, 39, 40, 46
Geertz, Clifford, 164; and conjuncture of ethnography and history, 19; on cultural phenomena, 103, 104; and definition of culture, 191; and hermeneutics, 3–4; and ideologies, 94; and interculturality, 189; on interpretation, 190–191; on models of phenomena, 188; and the "said," 194; and significative systems of cultural phenomena, 47; and structures of signification, 4; and symbol, 207n2; and task of ethnography, 193
globalization, 12, 35, 40, 120, 165, 193, 201
Gluckman, Max, 88, 190
Gnerre, Maurizio, 183
Godelier, Maurice, 202
golpe del 21, 77, 81, 128
graffiti: Otavalan, 68, 81, 73–74; in Quito, 86–87
Greater Antilles, 12, 17, 18
Gualinga, Santa, 92
Guaman Poma de Ayala, Felipe, 18, 19; and Andean interculturality, 20–21; and blackness, 49
Guatemala, 29, 38, 39, 46, 126, 131, 147
Guss, David M., 7, 32–33, 50
Gutiérrez Borbúa, Lucio: and the *golpe del 21*, 77, 128; and indigenous politics, 128, 129, 196; and multiculturalism, 119; and *refundar el país*, 118; U.S. endorsement of, 121–122

Haiti, 52, 106, 107–109
hegemony, 1, 111; and 1492/1992, 98, 103, 113; and Ecuadorian elite, 70–72, 101; and European conquest, 46; and race, 36, 79, 80, 108; and Roman Catholic Church, 11–12; and symbolic inversion, 67, 88; of United States, 118, 121, 123–126, 131–132
hermeneutics, 3, 4, 5, 189; and indigenization of modernity, 181; and interpretation of ethnographic information, 191; and Stoller's "between," 195
hermetics, 3–4, 46, 70, 79, 84, 181, 191
Herzfeld, Michael, 82, 198
Hill, Jonathan D., 37, 91, 179
historicity: and constructions of blackness, 48, 57, 59–60; and ethnography, 193; and history of Canelos, 178
history: and alternative modernities, 38, 39–41; of Canelos, 177–178; and elitist models of race, 71; and ethnography, 19; and formation of racial images, 46, 48–49, 51–52, 56–58; and literary criticism, 20; of race in Ecuador, 25–30
history of the present, 19, 201
Ho, Karen, 194, 201
Honduras, 35, 38, 39, 46, 125, 197
Hurtado, Jaime, 85
Hurtado Larrea, Osvaldo, 32
hybridity: and elite imagery, 71; and interculturality, 118; and lightening/darkening, 31; and *mestizaje*, 182; modern confrontation of, 37; racial concepts of, 29, 203–204n3; and *zambos*, 30
hybridization, 27; and blending of civilization and savagery, 28, 204n3; and ethnic unities, 62; and family, 82
hypostasis, 25, 82, 95, 110, 111

Imbabura Province, 68, 72, 124, 147, 157
Inca: and cosmological orientation, 167–168; Guaman Poma's ethnography of, 18, 19; and invasion of Kingdom of Quito, 10–11; and modern racial identity, 31, 32, 75
Indi (the sun), 166, 167
indians: and Afro-American studies, 45–47, 60–61, 63; fierce vs. tame, 39, 178. *See also* indigenous people, Eucadorian; indigenous people, Latin American
indigenismo, 106, 108
indigenous, meaning of term, 199–200
indigenous people, Ecuadorian: alliance of against oil company, 134–135; and *cultura*, 103; and Esmeraldas, 15; and ethnic autonomy, 78; and ethnic space in Amazonia, 85; global cosmovision of, 7–9; and indigenization of modernity, 172, 180, 183–184; and interaction with black people, 51, 56–57, 204–205n3; and mythohistory, 10, 19, 20; and *las nacionalidades*, 104–105, 112; parliament and forum of, 120; and rejection of *mestizaje* ideology, 24; slavery of, 12; and social action, 76, 180; and symbols of unity, 112; and view of 1492, 1, 98. *See also* nationalities
indigenous people, Latin American, 28–30, 33–36, 38–39, 40, 48, 113
indigenous resistance, 168, 196. *See also* Levantamiento Indígena
indigenous rights, 135, 177
indios: and colonial hierarchy, 11, 103, 111; and Ecuadorian socioculture structure,

95; history of term, 11, 25, 26–27, 46, 60, 103, 199; meaning of term, 178, 200; and *mestizaje*, 83, 84, 86; and term *longo*, 69; and tripartite racial system, 29, 36, 53, 59, 63, 95, 111
interculturality (*interculturalidad*), 2, 4–6, 12, 34, 36–37, 118–119, 170, 183–184; of Canelos Quichua, 170; in contact period Caribbean, 20; and Ecuadorian constitution, 79; and *ecuatorianidad*, 198; and ethnography, 193; and Geertz's work, 189; and James Mooney, 16; and *levantamientos*, 78; and March for Land and Life, 172; and *mestizaje*, 34–35; and natural resources exploitation, 197; and *negreado*, 40; and *pachacutij*, 181; and racial fixity/fluidity, 36–37; in times of crisis, 127; and work of Guaman Poma, 20–21
interethnicity, 37, 48, 60–61, 63, 94, 98, 113–114, 191
intersubjectivity, 2, 4, 187, 190, 193
Inti Raymi, 53, 172
Iran, 197
Iza, Leonidas, 121, 128

jaguar, 8, 20, 153, 173, 175
Jatari Amauta political party, 128
Jealous Potter, The (Lévi-Strauss), 173, 209n4
Jilucu, 166, 172, 174, 175
Jivaroans, 167, 169, 173, 178, 180, 183, 210n4; Chirapa, 177, 178; language of, 165, 169
Junta de Salvación Nacional, 77
Juyungo, 54

Kane, Stephanie, 51, 52
Karp, Ivan, 191–192
Karsten, Rafael, 173
Kenney, Kristie, 120, 121, 126, 132, 133
Kingdom of Quito, 10, 11, 14
kinship, 101, 171. See also family
kinship festival, 171, 175–176, 177
knowledge, 170, 171, 180, 193–194

La Canela, Land of, 13, 14, 168
ladinos, 14, 29, 48, 206
land reapportionment, 36, 172, 177
landscape, 10, 18, 199
Lane, Kris, 15
languages, indigenous, 168, 169–170, 182, 183; language families of, 167, 205–206n5, 209n2
Latacunga, 57, 96

Latin America, 30–31, 32–34
Leach, Sir Edmund, 45, 47, 82, 109–110, 177–178
Legión Blanco, 128
Léry, Jean de, 18
levantamiento, 48, 98, 99; proposed, 128–129, 196
Levantamiento Indígena, 76–78; of 1990, 79, 98–99, 207n1; of 1994, 148; of 2000, 81, 87; of 2001, 149; Andean reinterpretation of, 171–172; and black movement, 41; in indigenous art, 148; indigenous demands of, 96–97, 100–101; and *interculturalidad*, 119, 127; and intercultural understanding, 5; and *las nacionalidades indígenas*, 104; and processes of liberation, 111–112; and symbol of 1492/1992, 102, 111, 113
Lévi-Strauss, Claude: on myth, 180; and myth of creation of pottery, 173, 174, 210n4; and structuralism, 179
Liberal Revolution, 55, 56
liberation: and black and indigenous self-liberation movements, 11, 15, 34, 36, 39, 48, 51–52, 58, 99, 101, 107; and Ecuadorian wars of independence, 16, 57; and ELN, 124; and indigenous self-determination, 108; processes of, 111–112; from slavery, 30; from structures of oppression, 1, 101, 110–112
libre (Emberá/Wounaan use), 51, 53
literary criticism, 19–20, 21
Local Knowledge (Geertz), 47, 189, 191
logging, 135–136
longo, 69, 72, 80, 84, 86

Macas, Luis, 78, 119. See also first color plate
Mahuad Witt, Jamil: and dollarization, 131; and the *golpe del 21*, 77; and multiculturalism, 119; ouster of, 81, 87, 127
Malinowski, Bronislaw, 17
Mama Negra (Black Mother) festival, 57
Manabí, 51, 55–56
mana tuparina ñambi, 117, 120, 126, 133, 136–137
mancha, la (stain [of race]), 24, 31
Mandinga, 31, 32, 75
manioc, 7, 140, 166, 167, 175, 180–181
Mannheim, Bruce, 169, 209n2
Manta military base (U.S.), 85, 123, 132; and Correa, 137; and Operation Phoenix, 138–139; and Plan Colombia, 125, 126
March for Land and Life, 5, 62, 65, 79, 85, 91,

93, 96–97, 127, 135, 145, 148–149, 151, 152, 171–174, 175–176, 177, 180
marronage. *See* liberation
Martí, José, 30
Marx, Karl, 181
Marxism, 190, 192
Maynas (mission and colonial province), 177
mestizaje (*el mestizaje*), 28–30; and *blanqueamiento*, 69–70; and class, 79; and Correa, 200; and diversity, 78, 88; and ethnic exclusion, 83, 86; history of, 11, 27–30; and hybridizing, 82; and *indigenismo*, 106; and interculturality, 34–35, 119; and Latin American ethnic polarities, 59; and multiculturalism, 86–88; as polarizing symbol, 31–32; and racial democracy, 32; and racism, 80; and *la raza cósmica*, 30; and social mobility, 84, 86, 99; triangles, 29, 30, 35; and validation of *lo negro*, 72–73
mestizos: and class, 71; history of, 28–29, 204n3; and modern self-identification, 74–76; and perspective on social ladder, 32; and status in Otavalo, 69
metaphor, 4, 102, 109, 133, 184; root, 181
Mexico, 30, 31
migration, 130–131
military, Ecuadorian: and Colombian border, 124, 125; coup of, 77, 127; and ethnicity during war with Peru, 172; and multiculturalism, 119; and oil dispute, 135; and Operation Phoenix, 138–139
millennial Ecuador, 85, 117–118, 133, 192; and indigenous political power, 119; and racialization, 122–123
millennialism (millenniarity), 6, 87–88, 184, 192
Miller, Marilyn Grace, 25, 30, 31, 34
Miskitu, 35, 38, 39–40, 46
Miss Universe contest, 120, 122, 133
modernity, indigenization of, 171–173, 180, 183–184
molecañas, 54, 56
Monroe, James, 30, 31
Montaño, Mae, 123
Mooney, James, 16–17, 203n1
Moon Man, 166, 173, 174, 175
Morales, Evo, 33, 139, 140, 197
moral sanctions, 45, 178: and anthropology, 46, 47; and power of names, 109–110; and racial terminology, 82, 83, 86

Morenada (Bolivian festival performance), 56
mulatos, 28, 29, 30, 71
multiculturalidad (multiculturalism), 78, 79, 206n1; and *mestizaje*, 80, 86–88; and racial fixity/fluidity, 36, 37
multiethnicity, 101
multinacionalidad (multinationality), 78, 79, 88, 101, 206n1
myth: and black people and blackness, 48, 50–51, 52–53, 54, 58, 59; and ceramic imagery, 209n3; of creation of pottery, 173–174, 175; and culture, 180; and evil, 7–8, 50–51, 54, 61, 116; origin, 166–167, 209n1
mythic time-space, 166, 167, 175. *See also* chronotopes
mythohistory, 10, 182, 209n3; and early ethnography, 19; and ethnogenesis, 182; and Western ethnographic/historical interpretation, 20
Mythologiques (Lévi-Strauss), 179, 180, 210n4
mythopoetics, 115, 163, 167, 180; and action within a political economy, 10; and indigenization of modernity, 180–181

Napo Runa, 167, 179, 181, 183
nationalism: of nation-state, 105–107; and racism, 80–82; and *las razas*, 84; and structures of domination, 109
nationalities, indigenous Ecuadorian, 38, 78–79, 104–105, 112, 127, 135, 155, 156, 165, 168–169, 170
nation-state, Ecuadorian: affected by indigenous people, 180; and ethnic-bloc formation, 110; and multinationality, 101, 102; and nationalism, 105–107, 108; sociocultural structure of, 94–95
natural resources, 135–136, 197; and water rights, 196. *See also* petroleum
negro, lo. *See* blackness
négritud (négritude), 98–99, 106, 107, 108, 111
negros: and colonial hierarchy, 11; and conquest of Americas, 103; and Ecuadorian socioculture structure, 95; and history of term, 11, 25, 26, 46, 60; meaning of term, 199; and *mestizaje*, 83, 84, 86; and tripartite racial system, 29, 36, 53, 59, 63, 95, 111
negro supai, 59
neoliberalism, 12, 119–120
Nicaragua, 35, 38, 39, 46, 197
Noboa Bejarano, Gustavo, 77–78, 131

North America, 30–31, 34–35, 38
numinous orientation, 7, 12
Nungüi, 167, 175

Occidental Petroleum, 134
ONHAE (Organización de la Nacionalidad Huaorani de la Amazonía Ecuatoriana), 136
OPIP (Organización de Pueblos Indígenas de Pastaza), 100, 101, 134, 135
Orellana, Francisco de, 13
Organization of American States, 120, 121
Oriente, El. *See* El Oriente
Otavalans (*Otavaleños*), 68, 69, 207n3
Otavalo, 23, 68–69, 87, 140, 141, 159, 207n3; in indigenous art, 150, 155, 156, 160

Pacari, Nina, 119
pachacutij, 88, 92, 118, 181, 184; and millenniarity, 192
Pachakutik social movement, 119, 128
Pacific Lowlands people, 38
paju, 116, 133; and millennial Ecuador, 117–118; in modern Ecuador, 137
Panama, 38, 48, 51–53, 125; and exile of Bucaram, 81, 86, 119
Pané, Ramón, 17, 18, 20
Pan-Indigenous Congress, 112, 140
pardo, 33, 34, 35
paro indígena, el, 77–78
Pastaza Province, 59, 96, 134–136, 152, 158; and call for indigenous rights, 79, 100–101, 177; interculturality in, 165, 172; Quichua dialect in, 117, 127
perspectivism, 20
Peru: Canelos Quichua territory in, 168, 183; immigration from, 130; and prehistoric trade, 7; and Quechua language, 169–170; and racial terms, 31, 95; and war with Ecuador, 77, 119, 124, 135, 172
Petroecuador, 120, 134
petroleum: and Chevron-Texaco lawsuit, 120, 134, 153; and image of black workers, 55, 56; and indigenous rights, 100; and millennial Ecuador, 118, 120, 134–136; and powers of resistance, 197
phenotypes: and fear of unified ethnicities, 62; and "improving the race," 72–73; and modern *mestizo* identity, 75; and racialist ideology, 107; and study of blackness, 48, 49
Pierre, François (Abbot), 13, 178
Pizarro, Gonzalo, 12–13, 14

Plan Colombia, 85, 118, 123–126
plurinacionalidad, 206n1
political economy: and cosmological schemes, 179, 181; and cultural directionality, 168; Ecuadorian, 196–197; and ethnic-bloc formation, 106–107; and mythopoetics, 10
politics, indigenous, 126–129, 146–147, 196. *See also* specific leaders
politics, national, 129–130, 195–198, 207n1. *See also* specific leaders
Poncho Plaza (Otavalo), 69
Potoo bird, 166, 172, 174, 175
pottery: and imagery during kinship festival, 175; myth of creation of, 173–174, 175; of Pastaza Province, 143; and shamanic knowledge of potters, 170, 171, 180
Powell, Colin L., 121–122, 126
power: and "the between," 195; and black Ecuadorians, 72–74; claimed by indigenous people in *levantamiento*, 100–101; contrastructural, 191–192, 198; and Ecuadorian socioculture structure, 70–72, 95; and ethnic blocs, 107; and indigenous Otavalans, 68–70; millennial statement of, 87; and racial terminology, 82–83; and structures of domination, 111; and symbolic inversion, 67; and transformation, 61, 62
powers of resistance, 192, 196, 197, 198, 200; and ethnic blocs, 107; and structures of domination, 110, 111. *See also* contrapower
Price, Richard and Sally, 51
Primordium, 8–9; and Canelos Quichua festival system, 171; and discourse of resistance, 113; and metaphor of anaconda, 181; and religious conversion, 12; and ritual performance of Yumbo, 176
Prince Henry the Navigator, 26, 46
problem (*el problema*), indian/black, 99, 100, 110, 114
pueblo, el, 78, 88
Puyo, 43, 114, 155, 168; and 2010 indigenous March, 140; early colonial history of, 13–14, 177–178; and indigenous people, 43–44; and March for Land and Life, 5, 65, 79, 91, 93, 127, 175; and millennial symbolism, 92–93; and Unión Base, 152

Quechua language, 169–170, 205–206n5
Quichua language: in Amazonia, 169–170; as epistemic distortion, 182, 183; political use of, 117; and racial terminology, 83–84

Quichua-speaking people, 100, 134–135. *See also* Runa
Quishpe Lozano, Salvador, 87, 192
Quito: and 1990 *levantamiento*, 76, 96; and 1992 Columbus Day March, 151; and 1997 Columbus Day March, 62; and 1999 *levantamiento*, 77; black population of, 72; founding of, 14; images of in indigenous art, 147, 150, 153–154; and March for Land and Life, 79, 93, 152, 173–174, 175; and racial terminology, 71; and racism in press, 121; and symbol of 1992, 98; and Yumbada, 54, 176. *See also* El Ejido Park
Quito Runa, 48, 53–55, 56, 60, 61

race: anthropological study of, 45–46, 60–61; and appearance, 28; and body odor, 122; and class, 198–199; and cultural whitening, 32; Ecuadorian terminology of, 23–24, 25, 27–30, 70–71, 72, 80–81, 82–85, 86, 109, 198; and endurance of reference points, 63; as *generación*, 26, 28; historical roots of, 59–60; in Latin America vs. North America, 30–31; in Otavalo, 69; and physical contamination, 68; and power, 202; and self-identification of Latin American leaders, 33; and settlement patterns, 58; and South American culture, 199; Spanish terminology of, 74–75, 76; and symbols of racial culture, 105–108; and Wounaan creation myth, 53
racial fixity, 26–27; and "Esmeraldas Ambassadors" painting, 40; in twenty-first century, 36, 37, 38
racial fluidity, 27–30, 85; and *la raza cósmica*, 30–31
racism: and *blanqueamiento*, 84; and "Entender el Racismo: El Caso de Ecuador" symposium, 74–76; and historical interpretation, 20; and the *mestizo*, 31–32; and national dignity, 73; and nationalism, 80–82; and the Otavalans, 68, 69; and Powell's visit to Ecuador, 121; terminology of, 95; and terminology of *levantamiento*, 98–99
Rahier, Jean Muteba, 44, 63, 115
raza, 28, 53, 55, 59, 62, 68, 75, 82–85. *See also* race
raza cósmica, la (cosmic race), 30–31, 35, 59, 206n1
Reflexiones en las culturas orales (Calderón), 100–101
reflexivity and culture, 2, 47, 61, 63, 70, 73, 171, 193

Reich, Otto, 119
Reichel-Dolmatoff, Gerardo, 53
reification, 35, 82, 85, 109–111
remaking the world, 1, 92, 112
Requena y Herrera, Francisco de, 177
Reyes, Raúl (Luis Edgar Devia Silva), 138
Rice, Condoleezza, 122
ritual: and battle, 96, 159, 177–178, 180; and cannibalism, 18; and chronotopes, 8–9; and culture, 40–48, 180; as drama, 165, 171, 190–192; enactment, 10, 38, 56–57; and history, 175–177; and structuralism, 180; and symbolic inversion, 67, 79, 87; and symbolic templates, 184
Roldós Aguilera, Jaime, 117, 119
Rosero, Padre Sebastián, 14
Royal Dutch Shell Oil, 134
Runa (fully human being), 54; concept of, 178; and ethnogenesis, 182; and metaphor of anaconda, 181; in origin myth, 167

Sahlins, Marshall, 184; and conjuncture, 190; and conjuncture of ethnography and history, 19; and essentialism, 183–184; and interpretation of power, 191; on practice and structure of conjuncture, 94; on structuralism and cultural ecology, 179; and structure of conjuncture, 10, 164, 165
Salasaca, 43, 96, 155, 158; and images of blackness in festivals, 55–58, 59; and Salasaca Quichua, 49, 60, 61
Salazar, Luzmila, 43
Sánchez Gallque, Andrés, 15
San Martín de Porres, 121, 122
Santángel, Luis de, 26
Santi, Virgilio, x, 164
Santi Gualinga, Marlon René, 177
Santi Simbaña, Clara, x, 164
Santi Simbaña, Marcelo, x, 163–164
Santo Domingo, church of, 76, 96, 97
Sarayacu, 14, 134; acuerdo of, 97, 101; and struggle with state, 177
savagery, 28, 71, 178, 204n3
Savoia, P. Rafael, 51
seeing (*ricuna*), 193–194
self-essentialization, 173
self-liberation, 11, 34, 36, 110, 112; in Emberá cosmology, 51–52; and study of blackness, 48. *See also cimarronaje*; liberation
Seminole, 46, 204n3
Sewell, William H., Jr., 19
shamans: and black people in Emberá myth, 52–53, 59; and healing, 154–161; hum of,

175; and *Ilex* trees, 167; in indigenous art, 143, 146, 154–161; and indigenous leadership, 152; and indigenous unity, 112; international conference of, 160; and March for Land and Life, 172; and *lo negro*, 54; and power of knowledge, 61; and seeing, 193, 194; and shamanic cleansing, 147, 150; and shamanic knowledge, 152, 154, 170, 171, 180; uprising led by, 13; and the Zambo/Yumbo, 62, 176

Sharupe (war leader of Jivaroan Chirapa), 178

Shiwiar: and claims of territorial rights, 100; and interculturality, 170; and March for Land and Life, 171, 173. *See also* Jivaroans

Shuar, 168, 177, 178; and 2009 indigenous uprising, 196; and claims of territorial rights, 100, 134–135; in Ecuadorian military, 172–173; pottery myth of, 173. *See also* Jivaroans

Sierra, 94, 96, 100, 129, 198. *See also* Andean Ecuador

signification, processes of, 1, 4–6, 10, 20–21, 67, 80, 86, 89, 110, 184, 189–190; and constructions of blackness, 59, 60; and culture, 104–105; and culture of *lo negro*, 47–48, 59; and ethnogenesis, 177; and resistance, 111–112

Silverblatt, Irene, 25, 28

simile, 109

slavery, 12; and blackness, 36; Guaman Poma's view of, 49; and race, 30, 45; and revolt against colonial rule, 30, 33–34; and Salasacan ritual image of *lo negro*, 57; and *zambaje*, 35

social action, 81, 87–88, 190; and indigenous Ecuadorians, 76, 180; and *mestizaje*, 67, 69

social inversion, 74, 76–78. *See also* symbolic inversion

sociedad, la, 70–72, 103, 111. *See also blancos*

song, 8, 91, 164, 209n3; of Jilucu, 174; and shamanic knowledge, 180; "¡Venceremos!," 139

Southern Command (U.S.), 85, 125. *See also* Manta military base

space-times, 8–9. *See also* chronotopes

Spanish conquest and colonialism, 10–11, 12–16, 49, 198, 200; and directional orientation, 167–168, 170; and image of blackness, 55, 56, 57, 58; and *nacionalidades*, 104

spirituality, 63, 110, 112

Squash Woman, 173, 174

Staden, Hans, 17–18, 19, 20

Stoller, Paul, 187, 195

strike, indigenous, 77–78, 81, 96–97. *See also levantamiento*

structuralism, 179–181, 182

Stutzman, Ronald, 11, 29, 80

Sullivan, Lawrence, 114, 171, 176, 181, 194; and cosmogonic polarities, 113; and ethnography and theory construction, 9; and mythic space-times, 8

symbolic inversion, 67, 87, 88; and Otavalan graffiti, 68–70, 73; and social praxis, 76–78

symbolism: of 1492/1992, 102, 113; of Canelos, 178; and ethnogenesis, 177, 182; of *indigenismo*, 106; in pottery, 91–92, 173; and structure of conjuncture, 182

Taíno, 17, 19–20, 27, 29, 51–52

Tapuy, Cristobal, 99

Taromenane (Taromenga) people, 136

Taussig, Michael, 86, 114; and Ecuador as Switzerland, 123; and interpretation of power, 191; and representation, 112, 202

Taylor, Anne Christine, 179, 182, 183

Texaco, 120, 134, 153

theory construction, 187–188; and culture, 194, 195; and ethnography, 1–5, 9–10, 201–202; and Geertz, 189; and interpretation, 190–191; and Sahlins, 190; and Turner, 190

Thevet, André, 18

Tigua, 141, 143, 144, 149, 151, 160

time. *See* beginning times-places; chronotopes; space-times

topography: cultural, 165; of Ecuador, 6, 184, 195; and localization of blackness, 61, 72; and metaphor for study of *mestizaje*, 67–68, 70, 72, 75–76, 79; political, 6, 167–168; sacred, 48

transculturation, 37–38

transformation: and cosmological schemes and political economy, 181; and globalization, 120–121; and indigenous people of Otavalo, 69; millennial, 2, 77, 88; and power, 61, 62; and symbol of 1992, 113

transformative dynamics, 2; and Correa, 200–201; and ethnography, 5, 201; and powers of resistance, 192; theoretical contribution of Geertz, 189

trekking, 164; and kinship festival, 175; and March for Land and Life, 172, 173; in origin myth, 167

tropes, 73–76, 86–88; racial, 32, 80–81, 82–

83, 189, 200, 207n2, 207n4; of resistance, 1, 4, 21, 92, 118, 123, 133, 137, 185
Trouillot, Michel-Rolph, 82, 182, 192
Trump, Donald, 120, 133
tucuna (tucurina), 176, 182
tupaj amarun, 92, 181
Tupi language and people, 17–18, 20, 171
Turner, Victor: and conjuncture of ethnography and history, 19; and cultural arenas, 99; and interpretation of power, 191; and processual structure, 190; and structural properties of symbols, 93; and structure, 192; and theory of powers of resistance, 192

UNASUR (Union of South American Nations), 139
United States: and Correa, 137; and Ecuador on global stage, 120; and hegemony in Ecuador, 118, 121, 123–126, 131–132; and interculturality, 34–35; and intervention in 2000 coup, 127–128; and Plan Colombia, 123, 125–126; and raid on FARC, 138–139
Upper Amazonia, 5, 16, 94, 166, 178; and March for Land and Life, 96–97; and national politics, 96, 101; and petroleum resources, 134. *See also* Canelos Quichua
Uribe Vélez, Álvaro, 124, 125, 138
Uzendoski, Michael, 184, 192; and culture, 20; and definition of culture, 191; and epistemic distortion of Napo Runa, 183; and *pachacutic*, 181

Vallejo, Raúl, 120, 126
Van Gennep, Charles, 190
Vargas, Apacha, 164
Vargas Canelos, Luis, 101
Vargas Dagua, Marta Jobita, 116
Vargas Guatatuca, Carlos Antonio: and 1990 Levantamiento Indígena, 127; and 2002 election, 128; and cabinet post, 129; and empowerment, 192; and the *golpe del 21*, 77
Vasconcelos, José, 30–31, 35, 59, 206n1
Venezuela, 30, 35, 36, 39, 84, 95, 107, 108, 125, 132; and racial democracy, 32–34; and Watunna myth, 48, 50–51, 54

Viveiros de Castro, Eduardo, 20
Vizcarrondo, Fortunato, 31

Wade, Peter, 36, 45–46
Waorani, 136, 168
Watunna, 7, 48, 58; and myth of origins of the races, 53; and myths of black people, 50, 54
Wayalumba Supai, 58, 59
Weber, Max, 189, 191
Weismantel, Mary, 99, 130
white. *See blancos*
Whitehead, Neil, 18, 179
whitening, 24, 30–31, 62, 70, 85, 107–108, 119; counter forces to, 32–34; cultural, 32; and *mestizaje*, 73; and racialist ideology, 107–108. *See also blanqueamiento*
Wibbelsman, Michelle, 65, 66, 73, 87
Wisuma, Bosco, 196
Wolf, Eric R., 191, 192, 207n2
worldview, 2, 7, 20, 168, 173
Worsley, Peter, 19, 191
Wounaan, 51–53, 54

yachaj, 43, 154, 157–158, 170, 193. *See also* shamans
Yachaj Sami Yachachina (Chango), 43
Yekuana, 7; and blacks as agents of Spanish oppression, 56; and meanings of blackness, 55; and Watunna myth, 50–51, 54
Yumbada, 53–54, 56, 79, 176
Yumbo, 54, 62, 91, 176

zambaje, 35–36, 40
zambo, 15, 29–30, 62; in colonial era, 35; and Emberá/Wounaan myth, 51, 52; and "Esmeraldas Ambassadors" painting, 40; history of, 27; and hybridization, 61–62; and Quito Runa Yumbada, 54; and savagery, 71
Zápara, 165, 169, 178, 182
Zaparoans, 13, 167, 169, 170, 177, 178; language of, 165, 169
Zelaya, Manuel, 139

NORMAN E. WHITTEN JR., a professor emeritus of anthropology at the University of Illinois at Urbana-Champaign, is the editor of the University of Illinois Press's series Interpretations of Culture in the New Millennium.

DOROTHEA SCOTT WHITTEN is a research associate at the Center for Latin American and Caribbean Studies and a Curator of the Spurlock Museum at the University of Illinois at Urbana-Champaign.

They have collaborated on many projects, including *Puyo Runa: Imagery and Power in Modern Amazonia*.

The University of Illinois Press
is a founding member of the
Association of American University Presses.

———————————————————

Composed in 10.5/13 Adobe Minion Pro
with Trade Gothic Bold No. 2 display
at the University of Illinois Press
Manufactured by Sheridan Books, Inc.

University of Illinois Press
1325 South Oak Street
Champaign, IL 61820-6903
www.press.uillinois.edu